Object-Oriented Software Design and Construction With C++

Dennis Kafura

Department of Computer Science
Virginia Tech

An Alan R. Apt Book

PRENTICE HALL, Upper Saddle River, New Jersey 07458

Library of Congress Cataloging-in-Publication Data

Kafura, Dennis
    Object-Oriented Software Design and Construction with C++
      p. cm.
    Includes bibliographical references and index.
    ISBN: 0-13-901349-0
CIP Data available

Publisher: **ALAN APT**
Editor: **LAURA STEELE**
Production editor: **EDWARD DEFELIPPIS**
Editor-in-chief: **MARCIA HORTON**
Managing editor: **BAYANI MENDOZA DE LEON**
Assistant Vice President of Production and Manufacturing: **DAVID W. RICCARDI**
Art director: **HEATHER SCOTT**
Cover designer: **MARJORY DRESSLER**
Copy editor: **MATTHEW D. SHINE**
Manufacturing buyer: **JULIA MEEHAN**
Editorial Assistant: **KATE KAIBNI**

©1998 by Prentice-Hall, Inc.
Simon & Schuster / A Viacom Company
Upper Saddle River, New Jersey 07458

Printed in the United States of America

10 9 8 7 6 5 4 3 2

ISBN: 0-13-901349-0

Prentice-Hall International (UK) Limited, *London*
Prentice-Hall of Australia Pty. Limited, *Sydney*
Prentice-Hall Canada Inc., *Toronto*
Prentice-Hall Hispanoamericana, S.A., *Mexico*
Prentice-Hall of India Private Limited, *New Delhi*
Prentice-Hall of Japan, Inc., *Tokyo*
Simon & Schuster Asia Pte. Ltd., *Singapore*
Editora Prentice-Hall do Brasil, Ltda., *Rio de Janeiro*

Audience

*T*his book is intended for undergraduate students. It is assumed that the reader has had a single preceding programming course. Students at Virginia Tech use this book in a first semester sophomore year course. In particular, only an understanding of basic data structures (e.g., linked lists, stacks) is needed, and that only in the second half of the course. A specific course on data structures in not required.

It is assumed that the basic syntax of "C" is known, or at least learned independently of this book. Only a basic familiarity with "C" is required; it is not necessary to be an expert in this language. A person competent in a statically typed procedural language other than "C" should be able to understand most of what is contained in these pages. Doing the programming exercises, of course, requires at least a minimal proficiency with "C."

The motivating examples and programming exercises do not assume familiarity with concepts or intuitions derived from experiences that would normally only occur during the junior or senior years of study. The problems are drawn from common graphical user interface (GUI) systems. Anyone who has used a GUI-based document preparation system, spreadsheet, drawing tool, or the like has the necessary context.

Intent

The most important intent of this book is to support a person's study of object-oriented programming in C++. While only the C++ language is described, the object-oriented concepts on which C++ is based are realized in numerous other object-oriented programming languages. The initial chapter describes the broad concepts of object-oriented programming without specific reference to C++ and gives pointers to other programming languages. The broader object-oriented context is also reflected by the use of terms from different languages and analysis methods. For example, the terms "member function," "method," "operation," and "action" are used interchageably. While distinctions can be drawn between these terms, the distinctions are not a real difference for beginning students of object-oriented programming.

An important secondary intent is that of raising the student's level of programming competence by emphasizing

reuse: The value of software reuse is conveyed by initial and pervasive reuse of software in the presentation, exercises, and projects. In fact, no exercise calls for the development of a program "from scratch." Almost all exercises use a provided set of classes and, later, an extensive class library.

tools: The tools and practices needed to develop systems are presented in addition to the language features. Knowing the language and writing the code is only half of what is required to build a real system. Developers must also cope with testing, debugging, project planning, and project management. While these are ideas that are often covered in a senior-level software engineering course, the foundations for that more advanced study are established here.

GUI library: Through the exercises and projects, students learn about an object-oriented library for building GUI-based systems. The library is intended to become part of the student's toolkit, being used in programming projects in subsequent courses. While a specific library is studied, the knowledge can be easily transferred to other similar class libraries.

event-driven systems: Exposure is given to event-driven systems. Beginning programming courses typically deal with problems where the program being written is totally in control at run-time. However, in event-driven systems the program is not in total control. Instead, the program reacts to external events. Seeing event-driven systems broadens the student's experience and perspective, and provides a source for intuitions useful in later courses on operating systems, computer architecture, networking, and similar courses that involve asynchronous events.

Pedagogy

http://www.prenhall.com/kafura

Web site

The web site that accompanies this text contains both interactive questions and Java applets. These additions enhance the quality of the conceptual material through

animation: This use of applets provides a visual representation that is often better able to communicate a concept than a static figure, a series of static figures, or simply a written description. This is particularly true for concepts that are inherently involved with change or action. The "picture" that a teacher has in their own head is better conveyed to a learner in this graphical and animated form.

interaction: Applets that have active elements (buttons, menus, etc.) allow the learner to gain experience with a concept in a way that allows the learner to have control of the experience. In particular, applets of this form are valuable in giving experience with constructive programming concepts without having to be concerned with the syntax and other non-essential issues.

feedback: Simple multiple-choice inline tests can allow the learner to gain a measure of their understanding and develop a sense of confidence. This method is more efficient and less loaded with psychological baggage than in-class quizzes or exams.

Beyond their ability to better convey certain concepts, the online questions and applets help to create an engaging learning environment.

The presentation is divided into small sections. Most sections are designed to match the content of a single 50-minute class meeting. The remaining have been done in two-class meetings. The individual sections are strong ordered due to the inherent dependency among the topics and because of the way example code is introduced, discussed, and used.

Mastery Exercises

Almost all sections are immediately followed by a set of exercises. Each exercise is designed to be completed in a short amount of time. In an ideal case, at least some of the exercises for a section should be done before proceeding to the next section. More realistically, students and instructors are encouraged to arrange deadlines that support the practice of completing as many as possible of the exercises in each set in a timely manner. The exercises are designed to instill mastery through practice. In this sense the exercises are primarily an aid to learning and not a tool for evaluation and grading. The exercises are important. Each exercise is focused on a single, new idea. A student who understands the concepts in a section pays little penalty in time to complete exercises for that section. A student who has some difficulty, has misunderstood the section, or who simply learns best by working with the concept in practice benefits from the task of working through all of the exercises.

Real World Examples

The examples and problems are designed to be engaging and to strengthen the relationship between the "objects" in the program and their "real world" counterparts. The examples and problems are based on components of a graphical user interface. For example, the first programming exercise involves the display of a window on the screen. Subsequent early exercises involve moving and resizing the window. In approximately three weeks the student is building simple systems that involve buttons, timed events, and text displays. Problems of this kind are more engaging of a student's interest than the more common objects like Date, String, Address, etc. In addition, the ability to see visually how the window moves on the screen in direct response to applying to MoveTo method in the class from which the window was created strengthens the notion that objects directly model their real-world counterpart.

Conceptual Presentation

The material presents a concept the "right way" the first time. For example, the class concept is not introduced by starting with a "C" struct and showing a sequence of "better" versions that finally culminates in the description of what a class is and how a class is really used. Instead, the class concept is presented as a cohesive structure that has a constructor, operations, and a destructor. There seems to be little point in showing several wrong ways to achieve some goal; show the "best practice" from the beginning so that the student can form the best initial model of the concept without backtracking or confusion.

Unique or Layered Organization

The material is organized in two related ways: by concept and by role. The conceptual organization as given in the first chapter is based on four concepts that underlie object-oriented programming languages: abstraction, separation, composition, and generalization. The first chapter allows all of these concepts to be understood at a very high level before proceeding with any of the detailed material in C++. However, it is also possible to interleave a study of the concepts with a study of how these concepts are realized in C++ and how they are put to use to build systems.

The second organization is that a definite progression of the various roles assumed by a programmer in writing software. The roles are

user of a single existing class: In this presentation the single class represents a graphical user interface window. Many important concepts can be presented naturally within this simple and intuitive context (e.g., overloaded methods, constructors, scope, static vs. dynamic objects). Note that from the first sentence the importance of classes and objects is stressed.

user of multiple existing classes: Composition is seen as a way to build systems by combining together interacting objects. At this point the student builds several small time-driven systems with button and text interactions.

implementor of a single class: It is only at this stage that the internal structure of a class is revealed. It is emphasized here that the role of an implementor involves more than coding, it also involves code management, debugging, and incremental testing and development.

implementor of multiple related classes: The first of two chapters about this role introduces inheritance as a mechanism for sharing implementation and/or interfaces among a set of related classes. The second chapter on this role presents templates as a mechanism for constructing parameterized (or generic) types.

This organization allows the language features to be presented in a rational and coherent manner. Each chapter focuses on what the student needs to learn in order to fulfill that role.

Acknowledgments

A number of people have contributed to the development of this book. Much of the work in writing the online test questions and answers was done by Mr. Michael Gussett. Several graduate teaching assistants contributed to the book through their interactions during the teaching of the class for which this book was targetted. These include Michael Gussett, Siva Challa, and Fernando Das-Neves. Two graduate students helped with the initial development of the applets: Sadanand Sahasrabudhe and Srinivas Gaddam. Eric Frias contributed many hours in helping to organize the software distributions for the classes.

Thanks!

Many individuals in the Prentice-Hall organization were also of great help and encouragement including Alan Apt, Laura Steel, Bruce Gregory, Ed DeFelippis, and Toni Holm.

Software

The examples, exercises, and projects are based on wxWindows, a multi-platform public domain class library for building graphical user interfaces developed by Julian Smart (http://web.ukonline.co.uk/julian.smart/wxwin/). Additional classes were developed to simplify the user interface components during the first half of the course. These simplifying classes are removed once inheritance has been presented.

Comments

Comments, helpful suggestions, and criticism are welcomed. Send email to kafura@cs.vt.edu or by postal mail at:

Department of Computer Science
Virginia Tech
Blacksburg, VA 24061

Dennis Kafura
Blacksburg, Virginia

This book is dedicated to

Mary and Craig

without whose patience, support, and encouragement this project and most other things of value in my life would not be possible.

CONTENTS

Introduction

1.1 Basic Concepts

Object-Oriented Strategies

*O*bject-oriented programming embodies in software structures a number of powerful design strategies that are based on practical and proven software engineering techniques. By incorporating support for these strategies in software structures, object-oriented programming enables the manageable construction of more complex software systems than was previously possible. The nature of these software structures has been shaped by decades of software engineering experience. The basic design strategies that are embodied in object-oriented programming, which are presented in Table 1–1, evolved as techniques for dealing with complex natural and man-made systems. These strategies are fundamental and pervasive; they are encountered in numerous design and problem-solving contexts and, in computer science, they are commonly found in the study of data structures, operating systems, and other programming language forms. What is stressed here is the relationship of these strategies to the design and construction of object-oriented software.

The design strategies in object-oriented programming languages are effective for constructing entities of the problem domain in software models. In fact, some have argued that software design is largely about constructing a software model of the "real world," where each "real" entity is represented in the program by a corresponding software component; the software component simulates the actions and conditions of its real-world counterpart. The programming-as-modeling philosophy is most evident in three-dimensional virtual environments, where the visual and auditory characteristics of the real world are simulated within the virtual world.

abstraction	Simplifying the description of a real-world entity to its essentials
separation	Treating "what" an entity does and "how" it does it independently of each other
composition	Building complex "whole" systems by assembling simpler "parts" in one of two basic ways: • association • aggregation
generalization	Identifying common elements among different entities in one of four ways: • hierarchy • genericity • polymorphism • patterns

Table 1–1   Design Strategies Embodied in Object-Oriented Programming

These strategies are widely supported by existing object-oriented languages though different languages may present them in different ways and some languages do not support all of the variations of each one. For example, some object-oriented languages may not support all of the types of generalization.

To master object-oriented programming one must understand the connections among the design strategies, the software structures supporting the strategies, and the software engineering goals that the strategies and structures are meant to achieve. Some of the principal connections are shown in Fig. 1–1. Understanding these connections enables the construction of useful and well-designed systems that solve important problems. The relationships depicted in Fig. 1–2 will be understood more deeply as the exploration of object-oriented programming unfolds.

At this point most of the terms given as design strategies, object-oriented software structures, and software engineering goals are undefined. While these terms will be explained, two observations can be made:

- the structures of objects and classes relate to three of the four design strategies and one of the most important software engineering goals, reusability

- the various forms of generalization relate to all of the software engineering goals, indicating the importance of understanding how to exploit these structures in creating quality software systems

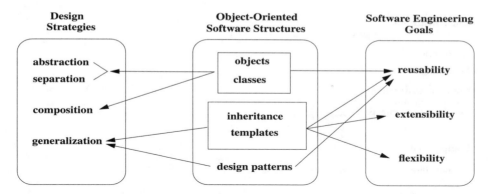

Figure 1–1   Connections among Strategies, Structures, and Goals

A Plan of Study

The study of a body of material often depends on the learning style of the individual and is often iterative in progression. Some people learn more efficiently by understanding the overall concepts first, before proceeding to more concrete details. Other people learn more efficiently by intermixing the abstract concepts and the concrete examples. Regardless of the preference for a breadth-first approach or a depth-first approach, there are necessarily some ideas that must be learned before others, because the ideas build on one another and are not independent. In either style, a single reading is usually not sufficient. Backtracking and revisiting earlier concepts often enriches understanding and allows the formation of deeper insights into the material.

The overall structure of the material presented here is shown in Fig. 1–2; the design strategies are shown at the left. It is possible to read about these design strategies top-to-bottom and obtain a broad overview of object-oriented concepts and ideas, while at any point it is also possible to follow one of the arrows to the right: following an arrow in this direction leads to a more concrete presentation of the concept and its eventual description in C++.

There are seven major milestones shown in the overall guide. Each milestone falls into one of three roles that are shown at the bottom of Fig. 1–2. Each milestone is associated with a major design concept and represents a significant step forward in the practical skill of developing object-oriented software systems. The milestones, however, are ordered. It is not possible to proceed to a later one (one lower and more to the right in Fig. 1–2) before all of the earlier ones (ones higher and to the left) have been completed.

The milestones form a progression of roles as shown along the bottom of Fig. 1–2. The simplest role is that of a programmer using a single class or several classes that has already been developed. Simple, but interesting systems will be constructed in this first role. Initially, a single class will be used to explore and

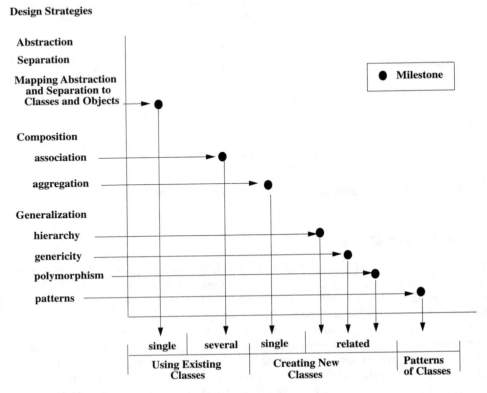

Figure 1–2   Object-Oriented Design Strategies

master basic issues of creating and manipulating objects. Several more classes are then added, allowing the construction of simple systems of interacting objects. Learning how to use existing classes to create and manipulate objects is the first step in learning about object-oriented programming. This first role is important not only because it establishes the foundation for the basic concepts of object-oriented programming, but also because this is the preferred role in developing real systems. As a user, you are able to benefit from the hard work already done by the designer and implementor of the existing classes. This opportunity to reuse existing classes is one of the major benefits of software reuse in general and object-oriented programming in particular. The second role is that of a developer creating one or more new classes. Initially, each class captures an independent abstraction. More difficult, but more powerful, is the development of collections of related classes using one of the forms of generalization. These first two roles will be extensively explored. The third role involves pattern—general organizations of classes and objects that have proven useful in solving commonly

Table 1–2 Organization of the Book

Chapter	Contents
1	overview of the design strategies
2	how abstraction and separation are related to the structure of a single class
3	creating relationships among different classes through association
4	using aggregation in defining a new class
5	tools for building and debugging a system
6	creating and exploiting relationships among related classes using inheritance and polymorphism
7	using templates to create parameterized, generic classes
8	how operator overloading gives new meaning to the built-in operators
9	design representations, strategies, and patterns

occurring design problems. This role will be explored, but only minimally. Mastery of the use of patterns requires considerable experience in building systems in one or more application domains.

Getting Started

While largely organized in terms of the design strategies and roles shown in Fig. 1–2, this book contains two additional topics. The first topic is the study of the tools needed to be a productive and efficient developer of object-oriented systems using C++. Tools for building and debugging a system are discussed together with the techniques for using the tool effectively and the concepts on which the tools are based. The second topic is operator overloading, an interesting language feature supported in C++ but not supported in some other object-oriented languages. Using operator overloading, the designer of a class may provide his or her own aplication-specific meaning for most of the built-in operators (+, -, *, /, =, ==, !=, <, >, etc.). Operator overloading is a useful means of providing an appealing, intuitive, and natural way to perform common operations on user-defined objects.

The overall organization of the book is summarized in Table 1-2. The remainder of this first chapter gives a high-level presentation of each of the design strategies. It will be useful to return to these high-level descriptions when studying later chapters that show how each of these strategies is realized in C++.

Lets get to it!

 Exercises

1. Search the World Wide Web to find references to different object-oriented languages. How many can you find? Can you recognize in their descriptions any of the basic strategies identified in this section?

2. Search the World Wide Web to find locations of other courses on object-oriented programming. What topics do these courses have in common? Save these links for reference during your study.

3. Look at the Free On-Line Dictionary of Computing:

   `http://wfn-shop.Princeton.EDU/foldoc/`

   Find definitions for the following terms:

   - abstraction
   - aggregation
   - encapsulation
   - hierarchy
   - genericity
   - polymorphism

4. Save this link for future reference.

5. Look at the C++ Virtual Library.

   `http://www.desy.de/ftp/pub/userwww/projects/C++.html`

   Browse this library for ten minutes and report on three interesting things that you find. Keep this link for reference.

1.2 Abstraction

Abstraction is a design technique that focuses on the essential aspects of an entity and ignores or conceals less important or nonessential aspects. Abstraction is an important tool for simplifying a complex situation to a level where analysis, experimentation, or understanding can take place. For example, in attempting to understand the mechanics of the solar system, early mathematicians and astronomers applied abstraction to a "planet," treating the planet as a body, all of whose mass is concentrated at a single point. Such an abstraction

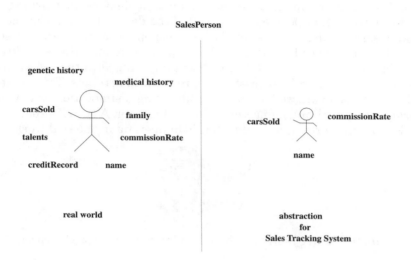

Figure 1–3   Abstraction of a SalesPerson

ignores a wealth of details about each planet—its actual diameter, its atmospheric content, its average temperature—which are not relevant to understanding and modeling the basic orbital mechanics of the solar system.

In software, abstraction is concerned with both the "attributes" and "behavior" of entities. Attributes are the properties or characteristics associated with an entity, while behavior refers to the set of actions that the entity can perform. In a software object, attributes are represented by data that is associated with the object. For a sales-tracking system, relevant attributes of a salesperson might be: name, number of vehicles sold, value of vehicles sold, list of customers, commission rate, total commissions. An action, or behavior, of the object corresponds to an operation or function associated with the object. Actions for a "salesperson" might include "sellCar," "reportIncome," and "increaseCommisionRate."

Abstraction is vital to creating tractable software objects because the real-world objects are far too complex to be captured in complete detail. Consider the simple salesperson object referred to above and illustrated in Fig. 1–3. A real salesperson has an identity, a family genealogy, a medical history, a genetic profile, a credit record, a set of talents, and many more unique attributes. Similarly there is a rich set of actions of which the salesperson is capable (sellCar, answerPhone, buyHouse, haveChild, getSick, increaseCreditLimit, payBills, etc.). Trying to capture even a small part of this enormous detail in a software object is pointless. It is important to capture only those aspects of a salesperson that are relevant to the development of a particular system (e.g., the sales-tracking system).

The objects in an object-oriented system are often intended to correspond directly to entities in the "real world." Objects, such as "salesperson" and "automobiles," that might occur in an automobile-dealership tracking system correspond to the actual people on the staff of the dealership and the actual cars owned and sold by the dealership. The correspondence between the software objects and the real-world entity that they represent is sometimes so direct that computer-based theft or fraud often involves tampering with the software objects that are trusted by others to correspond to real-world artifacts. This sense of correspondence is also expressed as the program being a simulation or model of the real world, changes in one being reflected in the other. A "good" program is one that models or simulates accurately what is happening in the real world.

The examples above motivate the following definition of abstraction:

Abstraction: A named, tangible representation of the attributes
and behavior relevant to modeling a given entity for some
particular purpose.

This definition also reflects the fact that for computer scientists and software engineers abstractions are not "abstract," ethereal concerns. Instead, abstraction is used to form concrete manifestations of the abstraction. At different stages in the software lifecycle the representation of an abstraction may take different forms. In the early design stages, hand-made drawings, diagrams, and lists may be used. Further in the design stage, a specific design notation may be used, often supported by design tools. Finally, in the implementation stage, the abstraction is represented in software, where it may be visible to the user and capable of conducting interactions with the user.

A single entity may have many valid abstractions. While the genetic profile of a salesperson is not relevant to a sales-tracking system, it may be relevant to a medical database system as shown in Fig. 1–4. Correspondingly, the medical-database system developer would not consider the number of vehicles sold to be a relevant aspect. The name of the abstraction is useful to distinguish among different abstractions for the same entity and among abstractions for different entities. A critical part of object-oriented design is deciding which attributes and behavior to include in a given abstraction.

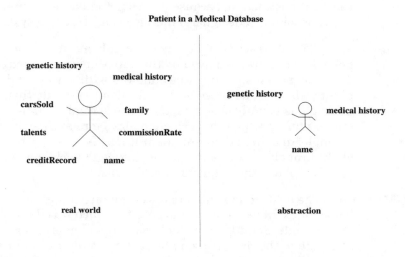

Figure 1–4 Abstraction of a Patient in a Medical Database

Properties of a Good Abstraction

While there may be many abstractions of the same entity, each abstraction should have certain properties that distinguish it as a "good" abstraction. A good abstraction is:

- **Well named**: The nature of an abstraction is conveyed by its name. An abstraction is well named if the meanings, intuitions, impressions, and expectations generated by a name accurately reflect the nature of the abstraction. Whether a name is meaningful depends on the community of people who will use the abstraction. In some cases the name might be a technical term in an application domain that perfectly communicates an abstraction to the group of people in that application area but may mean little to a non-technical group. In other cases, abstractions for widely known entities (e.g., "automobile" or "ZipCode") may have names recognizable by a general population.

- **Coherent**: The abstraction should contain a related set of attributes and behavior that makes sense from the viewpoint of the modeler. The attributes and behavior must be what is needed and expected in a given setting. For example, defining a SalesPerson abstraction that consists of the attributes "commisionRate," "family," and "talents" is not a coherent abstraction, because it does not make sense from the viewpoint of a designer building a sales-tracking system.

- **Accurate**:   The abstraction should contain only attributes or behavior that are displayed by the entity being modeled. The abstraction should not be endowed with powers and abilities far beyond those of the actual entity. While this principle is usually observed, there are special circumstances under which this principle may be relaxed. For example, in a virtual environment it may be possible to walk through the walls in a scene, although such behavior clearly violates the behavior of real walls.

- **Minimal**:   The abstraction should not contain attributes or behavior extraneous to the purpose for which it is defined. For example, adding a mailAddress or telephoneNumber attribute to the SalesPerson abstraction would be extraneous if these additional attributes were not required for the sales-tracking system.

- **Complete**:   The abstraction should contain all of the attributes and behavior necessary to manipulate the abstraction for its intended purpose. Assuming that the sales-tracking system needed to know the commisionRate for each SalesPerson, an abstraction not including this attribute would be incomplete.

These properties are clearly subjective and qualitative in nature, implying that the ability to form good abstractions requires good judgment as well as the benefit of practice and experience.

 Exercises

1. Define plausible abstractions for an "automobile" from the point of view of:
   a.   the manufacturer
   b.   the owner
   c.   the government vehicle licensing agency

2. Evaluate your "automobile" abstractions against the four properties of good abstractions.

3. Identify a common, real-world entity and at least three different points of view that would lead to different abstractions of that entity.

1.3 Separation

Separation is distinguishing between a goal or effect and the means or mechanism by which the goal or effect is achieved. This is often stated as separating *what* is to be done from *how* it is to be done. These and other pairs of terms reflecting the concept of separation are shown in Table 1–3.

Table 1–3 Terms Reflecting Separation.

what	how
goals	plans
policy	mechanism
product	process
interface specification requirement	implementation
ends	means

Separation is useful in simplifying a complex system because the goal or effect is often simpler to explain than the means needed to reach the goal or achieve the effect. For example, it is easier to state the goal of solving a maze puzzle ("Find a path from the entrance to the exit.") than it is to find the solution or to describe an algorithm for finding the solution.

Programmers are familiar with separation for it is present in all manuals and documentation. For example, a typical description of the command read(f, buffer, nbytes) is that the command transfers nbytes of data from file f to the specified buffer. The mechanism required to achieve this effect involves the disk hardware, software device drivers, the file system, the disk block management code, and run-time I/O library routines, none of which need to be mentioned in the description of the read command.

A well-established use of separation in software design is in distinguishing an interface from an implementation. The interface is viewed as the visible, external aspect of the software that must be understood to use the software; the implementation is viewed as the hidden, internal aspect of the software that is important only to the implementor. It is this form of separation that is taken as the definition:

Separation: in object-oriented programming, the independent specification of an interface and one or more implementations of that interface.

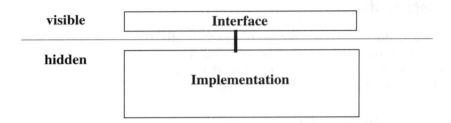

Figure 1–5   Separation of Interface from Implementation

An implementation **satisfies** an interface if the behavior specified by the interface is provided by the implementation.

The interface-implementation separation suggested by Fig. 1–5 appears at many different levels. Manual pages for libraries describe only the interface properties of individual operations without describing how any of the operations are implemented. A more complex layer of software (e.g., a windowing system or a networking environment) may be described by an application programmer's interface (API). The API defines what data structures and facilities are available for use by the application programmer without defining how the structure and facilities are implemented. A last example is a software standard, which is a commonly accepted definition of a service (e.g., the TCP/IP communication protocols standard) that defines the external behavior that a compliant system must exhibit but leaves the implementor free to implement that behavior in any way.

In addition to its simplifying advantages, separation provides flexibility to implementors because different implementations may satisfy the same interface. The several implementations may differ in time or space efficiency, purchase price, maintainability, documentation quality, reliability, or other non-functional characteristics. If separation is fully observed, one implementation for a given interface can be replaced by a different implementation of that interface without altering the overall operation of the larger system of which it is a part. The ability to associate different implementations with the same interface is shown in Fig. 1–6.

Two different interchangeable implementations of the same interface are said to be "plug compatible"; unplug the current implementation and plug in its replacement. Certainly many non-software products take advantage of such interchangeability: car tires, stereo speakers, and computer monitors are only a few examples.

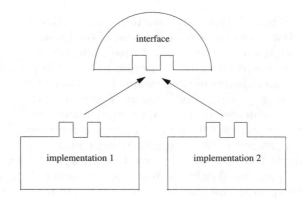

Figure 1–6   Interchangeability of Implementations

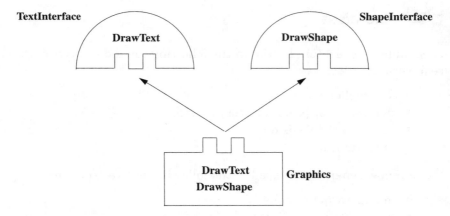

Figure 1–7   Interchangeability of Implementations

A single implementation can simultaneously satisfy several interfaces. In such a case, the implementation contains the union of all of the methods required by each of the interfaces (and possibly additional methods that are not used by any of the current interfaces). Fig. 1–7 shows a single implementation, named Graphics, that contains two methods, DrawText and DrawShape. Two interfaces are also shown: TextInterface that defines only a DrawText method, and ShapeInterface that defines only a DrawShape method. Clearly the Graphics implementation satisfies both of these interfaces.

As shown in Fig. 1–7, each interface provides a different view of the implementation: each view may expose only a subset of the implementation's full capabilities. Such a restricted view is useful in isolating those capabilities that are required in a given situation or by a specific part of the system. Isolating the most limited set of capabilities needed makes it possible to replace a more capable implementation (e.g., Graphics) that may contain present, but unneeded operations (e.g., DrawShape) by a smaller implementation that contains only those methods defined in the more limited interface. For example, suppose that a part of the system needed only the methods defined in the TextInterface. This need could be satisfied by the more general Graphics implementation or a more specific one that implemented only the TextInterface and not the ShapeInterface. Because it is more specific, the smaller implementation may be more efficient in execution time or may need less memory.

 Exercises

1. Explain how separation is used in the following commonly occurring, real-world entities:

   - a telephone
   - a package or postal delivery service
   - a stereo or television
   - a restaurant

2. Explain how separation is used in the following software entities:

   - an operating system
   - a web browser
   - a text editor
   - a compiler

3. Look at the documentation for your computer system and identify three instances of separation. For each instance, hypothesize several aspects of the implementation that are hidden by the separation.

1.4 Mapping Abstraction and Separation to Classes and Objects

Software development focuses on rendering abstractions in forms that allow them to be manipulated within a software system. An abstraction was described as a collection of attributes and a behavior. As shown in Fig. 1–8, the attributes

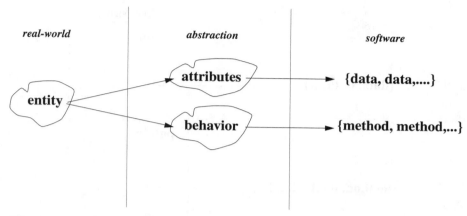

Figure 1–8 Mapping Abstractions to Software

of an abstraction are mapped to a set of data (variables, array, lists, complex data structures, etc.) and the behavior of an abstraction is mapped to a set of methods (also known as operations, functions, actions). The rendering of abstractions in software has always been the implicit goal of programming, though it may have been overshadowed by more mechanical considerations.

Object-oriented programming brings to the task of capturing abstractions in software more sophisticated structures, namely **classes** and **objects**, for representing abstractions. These new software structures permit abstractions to be represented more easily, directly, and explicitly.

Class

A class defines the specific structure of a given abstraction (what data and methods it has, how its methods are implemented). The class has a unique name conveying the meaning of the abstraction that it represents. The term *class* is used to suggest that it represents all the members of a given group (or class). For example, a Sales-Person class might represent all individuals in the group of "people selling cars at an automobile dealership." An object represents a specific member of this group.

Separation of interface from implementation is used to divide the class into two parts, commonly referred to as the **private** part and the **public** part. The data and methods are mapped to these two parts of the class as shown in Fig. 1–9. This separation of private data and code from the visible names of methods results from long years of software engineering experience showing that it is important to protect the data against unexpected, unwanted, and erroneous access from other parts of the software that is manipulating the object. The separation also serves to hide the algorithm used to perform a method.

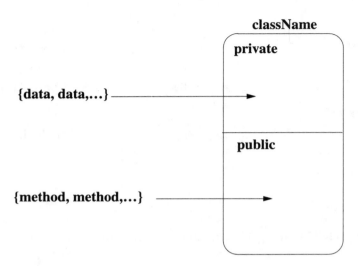

Figure 1–9   The General Structure of a Class

The relationship of a class to abstraction and separation are reflected in the following definition:

Class: A named software representation for an abstraction that sep-
arates the implementation of the representation from the
interface of the representation.

The obvious similarity in the definitions of the terms abstraction and class underscores how explicitly and directly a class is meant to model a real-world entity.

It is interesting to note that there are object-oriented languages that do not have classes but use other techniques to achieve a similar effect. Languages like C++, Java, and others that have a class concept are referred to as "class-based languages."

Object

While a class defines the structure of an entire collection of similar things (e.g., anyone who is a SalesPerson), an object represents a specific member of that class (e.g., the salesperson John Smith who has a commission rate of 15 percent, etc.). The class definition allows the common structure to be defined once and then reused when creating new objects that need the structure defined by the class. An object's properties are exactly those described by the class from which it was created.

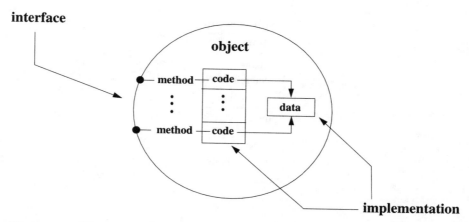

Figure 1–10 The General Structure of an Object

The key aspects of the object structure, as shown in Fig. 1–10, mirror the structure of the class from which it was created. As with a class, the two main parts of an object are its:

- implementation: the data and the implementation of the methods that are hidden inside of the object, and

- interface: the signature of all methods that are visible outside of the object

In Fig. 1–10, the methods that can be invoked from outside the object are shown as small dark circles on the object's boundary. The code that implements the methods is part of the object's implementation and is hidden inside the object. The term "encapsulation" is often used to describe the hiding of the object's implementation details; it is common to read that "an object encapsulates its data." Encapsulation is defined as:

Encapsulation: in object-oriented programming, the restriction of access to data within an object to only those methods defined by the object's class.

The notion of encapsulation is fundamental to an understanding of objects and object-oriented programming.

The term *instantiation* is used to describe the act of creating an object from a class and the object is called an *instance* of the class. Numerous instantiations can be made of a given class, each yielding a distinct object. This leads to definition of an object as:

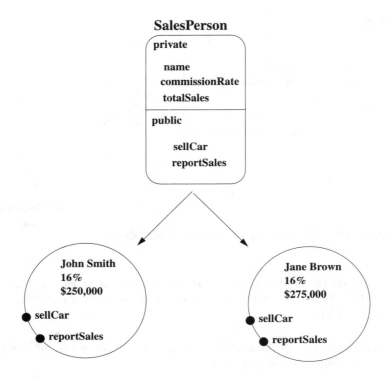

Figure 1–11   Multiple Instances of a Class

> **Object:**   a distinct instance of a given class that encapsulates its
> implementation details and is structurally identical to all
> other instances of that class.

This definition highlights the fact that all objects that are instances of a
given class are structurally identical: they have the same arrangement of data
and can respond to the same set of method invocations. However, as shown in
Fig. 1–11, each object may, and usually does, have different values for its data. In
the figure there are two instances of the SalesPerson class. Both objects encapsu-
late the same type of data (name, commissionRate, and totalSales). The two
objects currently have different values for the name and totalSales data but they
have the same value for the commissionRate data. Both objects have two methods that can be invoked: sellCar and reportSales.

The relationship between a class and the objects that can be created using
the class is often likened to that of a factory and the things produced by that factory. An automobile factory produces automobiles in the same way that an

Automobile class can be used to create Automobile objects. Likewise, an Automobile class can produce only Automobile objects just as an automobile factory can produce only automobiles, not vacuum cleaners or rocket ships.

Anthropomorphism

Classes and objects are often discussed by developers in lifelike, personal, anthropomorphic terms: a developer might say "The class should not be responsible for that," or "I expect the object to reply to inquiries about its current state." The developer may even assume the object's identity to better understand its role in a system's design. In this mode, a developer may ask, "What is expected of me?," "How will I be able to do that?," or "Why do you want to know that about me?" Questions such as these often lead a developer to a better intuitive understanding of an object and its relation to other objects.

A simple and popular design technique, which focuses on identifying for each object (or class of objects) its **responsibilities** and its **collaborators**, is intuitively related to the anthropomorphic view of objects. An object's (or class's) responsibilities are those properties or duties the object (or class) is obligated to maintain or perform. An object's (or class's) collaborators are those other objects (or classes) with which the given object (or class) must interact. The terms responsibilities and collaborators, of course, reflect the anthropomorphic view of objects.

The personification of objects reflects the correspondence that developers see between the real-world entity and its abstraction on the one hand, and the classes and objects that are their software counterparts on the other. This view also reflects the autonomy and encapsulation ascribed by designers to objects and classes.

 Exercises

1. Answer True or False to each of the following statements:

    a. Many objects can be created from the same class.

    b. A single object may belong to several classes.

    c. Two objects of the same class must have the same data and methods.

    d. Two objects of the same class must have the same values for their data.

    e. The data of a class is typically in the public part because it is a known attribute of the entity being modeled.

2. Define relevant attributes and behavior for each of the following entities:

    a. a telephone

    b. a calculator

    c. an automobile

    d. a patient in a hospital

    e. a vending machine

3. For each of the entities in question 2, show the general organization (the name, public part, and private part) of a class.

4. For each of the entities named in question 2, identify one or more attributes or parts that are encapsulated.

1.5 Composition

Composition deals with a single, complex system as an organization of numerous simpler systems and is often used to study and explain complex human organizations (the American government is divided into three major branches), complex biological systems (a human being consists of a respiratory system, a circulatory system, an immune system, a nervous system, a skeletal system, etc.), complex machines (an aircraft consists of a propulsion system, a control system, a navigation system, etc.), and complex programs (an operating system consists of a user interface, a file system, a network system, a memory management system, etc.). With composition it is important to understand the individual (simpler) systems and the relationships or collaborations among them.

As a constructive activity, composition refers to the assembly of interacting parts to form a whole. The part-whole relationship is a fundamental one in object-oriented programming as one of the major goals of object-oriented programming, software reuse, is accomplished, in part, by composing existing objects (the parts) in new and different ways to form new objects (the whole). Composition might be viewed as the "Lego" approach to software development because it uses standardized, specialized parts to construct a wide range of interesting artifacts.

Composition may be defined as:

Composition: an organized collection of components interacting to achieve a coherent, common behavior

The part-whole relationship is often expressed as a "has-a" relationship as for example, in the relationship between an automobile and the automobile's windshield: "the automobile has a windshield."

There are two forms of composition: **association** (or acquaintance) and **aggregation** (or containment). These two forms of composition are similar in that they are both part-whole constructions. What distinguishes aggregation from association is the visibility of the parts. In an aggregation, only the whole is visible and accessible. In association the interacting parts are externally visible and, in fact, may be shared by different compositions. A soda machine is an example of aggregation, as the machine is a whole composed of several internal parts (a cooling system, a coin acceptor, a change maker, a soda supply). These internal parts are not visible or accessible to the normal user of the soda machine. A computer workstation is an example of composition using association. The workstation consists of a keyboard, a mouse, a monitor, a modem, and a processor. Each of these interacting parts are visible to the user and can be directly manipulated by the user.

In some cases the more generic term composition will be used in favor of the more precise terms association or aggregation. This occurs when the statement applies to both forms, when the difference between the two forms is much less important than the general idea of forming a whole from parts, or when the precise form of composition may be inferred from context.

Both forms of composition are useful. Aggregation offers greater security because its structure is usually defined in advance and cannot be altered at run-time. The implementor of the aggregation is secure in the knowledge that the integrity of the aggregation and its proper functioning cannot be adversely affected by direct interference with its internal mechanisms. Association offers greater flexibility because the relationships among the visible parts can be redefined at run-time. An association can, therefore, be made to adapt to changing conditions in its execution environment by replacing one or more of its components. Interesting design decisions can revolve around which form of composition to use, balancing a need for security against a need for greater flexibility at run-time.

The two forms of composition are frequently used together and in combinations. The computer workstation was given as an example of an association among a mouse, keyboard, processor, modem, and monitor. However, as shown in Fig. 1–12, the processor of the computer workstation is itself an aggregation that consists of hidden parts including a CPU (processor chip), memory, and a disk. More detailed examination of the processor chip would show it to be an association of even smaller elements, some of which might be other associations or aggregations of parts.

Objects may also exhibit a complex structure formed by layers of associations and aggregations. The sections on associations and on aggregations will give examples of such structures.

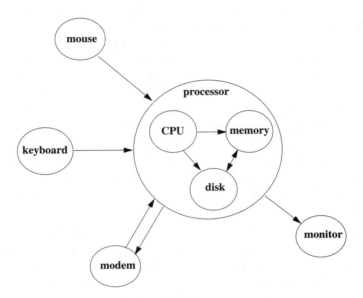

Figure 1–12   Association and Aggregation

 Exercises

1. Consider a merchandising company that accepts phone orders and relays the orders to a warehouse where the merchandise is packaged and shipped via a package-delivery service. Draw a diagram showing the associations and/or aggregations in this system.

2. Consider a home entertainment system with a satellite dish, a television, and a remote control. Draw a diagram showing the associations and/or aggregations in this system.

3. Consider an air traffic control system with radars, controllers, runways, and aircraft. Draw a diagram showing the associations and/or aggregations in this system.

Composition Using Association

Association is a part-whole organization in which the whole is exactly defined by the parts and the relationships among the parts. Each part of the composition maintains its identity, external visibility, and autonomy in the composition. The

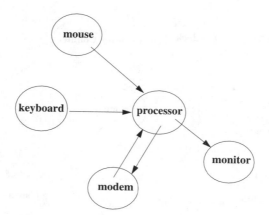

Figure 1-13   A Real-World Association

parts are often viewed as peers, collaborators, or acquaintances, such terms reflecting the primacy of the parts in the part-whole composition. In some sense, the whole is the sum of its parts. This leads to the following definition of association.

Association: a composition of independently constructed and externally visible parts.

A computer workstation, depicted in Fig. 1-13, is a typical example of a real-world association. Each of the parts shown in Fig. 1-13 is externally visible and can be manipulated in its own right. The notion of "computer workstation" refers to the particular assembly of these parts in a way that gives rise to the functionality expected of a computer workstation. The expectations of a computer workstation would not be met by an assembly of fewer parts (i.e., no monitor), extraneous parts (i.e., two keyboards), or the correct parts associated differently (i.e., the mouse connected to the modem).

An association among objects is created when an object contains references or pointers to other objects. An example of an association among objects is shown in Fig. 1-14. This association creates a simple one-second timer that is displayed in a graphical user-interface window and is controlled by Start and Stop buttons. The Clock object is responsible for determining the end of each one-second interval of time. At the end of each such interval the Clock object invokes an operation on the Counter object to increment its interval value. Incrementing its value causes the Counter object to send a string representation of its value to the TextBox object. The Frame object is responsible for maintaining the consistency between the TextBox string value and the characters displayed in the user interface. The Frame also displays two buttons with the labels Start and Stop through which the user is able to control when the timer is running.

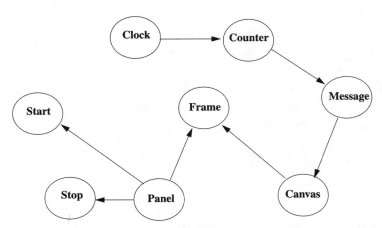

Figure 1-14   As Association of Objects

One advantage of an association form of composition is that the parts may be shared among different compositions. This is easily accomplished by having the same object be connected to (pointed to) from two objects, each of which is in a different composition. Using the computer workstation example already mentioned, it is possible to have a single printer shared by two different workstations. In the one-second timer example, it is possible to have multiple timers displayed in the same window through a shared Frame object. A shared Frame object is shown in Fig. 1-15. The dashed line indicates the logical partition between the two distinct one-second timers that are displayed in the same (shared) user-interface window (Frame).

A second advantage of an association is that the parts in an association can be dynamically changed simply by having a member in the composition connect to (point to) a different object. This change is dynamic in that it can be done at run-time. Again using the computer workstation example, it is possible to change the keyboard or mouse or to change the printer connected to the system. In the one second timer example, it is possible to replace the one second clock by a faster clock allowing more accurate timings to be made.

Composition Using Aggregation

Aggregation is a composition in which the whole subsumes and conceals its constituent parts as illustrated in Fig. 1-16. In contrast to an association, the parts of an aggregation are not visible externally, they do not have an identity as far as a user of the composition is concerned, and they do not possess autonomy to the same degree as parts of an association. The whole is the single visible entity. This suggests the following definition.

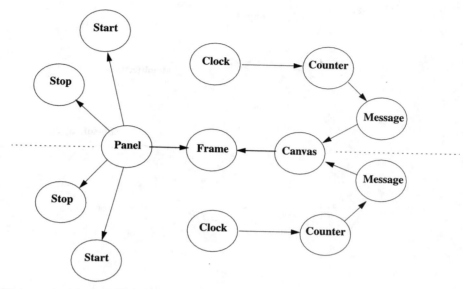

Figure 1–15 Shared Objects in an Association

Aggregation: a composition that encapsulates (hides) the parts of the composition.

Fig. 1–16 shows the general model of an object defined by aggregation. The outer objects contain inner (encapsulated) subobjects which themselves may have hidden internal objects (sub-subobjects).

Composition using aggregation occurs in many familiar natural and man-made systems. Table 1–4 shows how several familiar systems can be mapped to the structure in Fig. 1–16.

Table 1–4

Object	Subobject	Sub-Subobject
automobile	engine	pistons
computer	mother board	processor chip
molecules	atoms	quarks

An aggregation of objects is created when one object (the whole) contains in its encapsulated data one or more other objects (the parts). The simple one-second timer created above using association can also be implemented via

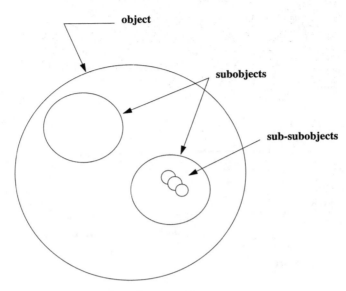

Figure 1–16   Structure of an Aggregation

aggregation as shown in Fig. 1–17. In this figure the basic objects that form the timer (Clock, Counter, TextBox, Frame, Start, and Stop) are contained within other objects (TimedCounter, Display and ControlButtons) that are, in turn, contained in the single encapsulating object, SimpleTimer. Notice that from the outside, only the SimpleTimer is visible; all other objects are concealed within the encapsulating boundary of the SimpleTimer object.

The first advantage of aggregation is that the outer object may be used without much, if any, concern for the operation, or even the existence, of the internal subobjects. When driving a car we are rarely concerned about the thousands of parts which are composed together to realize the car. The ability to ignore the finer structure of an object greatly simplifies the task of understanding how a system works or building a system that works in a particular way. The second advantage of aggregation is that internal parts may be changed without affecting the user's view of the external whole. The internal structure of the parts may be completely changed or only individual parts may be replaced. Improvement in efficiency, reliability, or cost may motivate the replacement of parts.

1.6 Generalization

Generalization identifies commonalities among a set of entities. The commonality may be of attributes, behavior, or both. For example, a statement such as "All

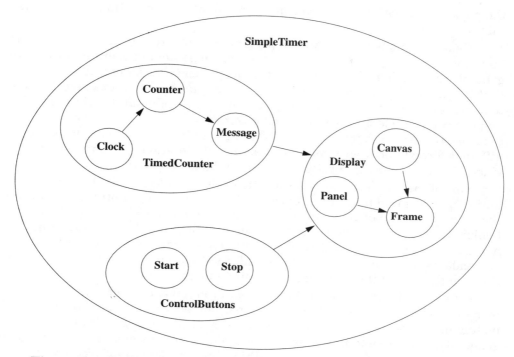

Figure 1–17   Composition via Aggregation

windows have a title" expresses a common attribute among all entities that are considered windows. Similarly, the statement "All windows can be resized" expresses a common behavior that all windows provide. Generalizations are usually easy to recognize as they contain words like all and every.

Generalization may thus be defined as:

Generalization: the identification, and possible organization, of
common properties of abstractions.

This definition shows that generalization is not abstraction, although the two are often confused. Abstraction aims at simplifying the description of an entity, while generalization looks for common properties among these abstractions.

Generalizations are clearly important and prevalent in many disciplines of study. In science and mathematics, for example, the statements of laws and theorems are often generalizations—they state some property that holds over a group of things: the more powerful the generalization, the more things to which the generalization applies. The search for the basic forms of matter represents the physicists' quest for a generalization that applies to everything in the physical universe.

Generalizations are equally important to software. Much of the effort in building software systems is to allow parts of the system to operate in the most general way possible. In some cases this might mean designing the system so that it can handle any *number* of things of the same kind. For example, the system might be expected to process any number of lines of input. In other cases the major design problem is how to handle things of *different* kinds or types. For example, the system might be expected to process input that comes from files of different formats or from local as well as remote locations. Generalization provides an approach to solving some of these problems in software.

One of the four forms of generalization is **hierarchy**, in which the commonalities are organized into a tree structure. At the root of any subtree are found all the attributes and behavior common to every descendant of that root. This particular kind of tree structure is referred to as a generalization/specialization hierarchy because the root provides more general properties shared by all its descendants while the descendants typically add specializing properties that distinguish them from their siblings and their siblings' descendants.

The second form of generalization is **genericity**, through which the commonality is expressed with the aid of a parameter. Various specializations are distinguished by what they provide for the parameter. For example, using genericity it is possible to represent the common properties of a stack through the generalization of a "stack of anything," where "anything" represents the parameter. Specialized forms of this generalization are "stack of integers" and "stack of characters."

The third form of generalization is **polymorphism**. Polymorphism captures commonality in algorithms. An algorithm may have a nested if-then-else (or "case statement") logic, which tests for the exact type of an object it is manipulating. The algorithm performs some operations on the object based on the exact type of the object. However, in many algorithms the operations to be performed are the same, only the type of the object on which they are performed varies. Polymorphism allows this nested logic (or case statement) to be collapsed to a single case in which the different object types are treated in a uniform manner. Through a mechanism called *dynamic binding*, the algorithm allows the object to determine which of its operations to perform in response to the algorithms invocation. Thus, the algorithm need not know the exact type of the object. The algorithm only needs to know that the object can respond to the invocation in some manner.

The fourth form of generalization is **patterns**. A pattern presents a general solution (the key components and relationships) to a commonly occurring design problem. The attributes and behavior of the individual components are only partially defined to allow the pattern to be interpreted and applied to a wide range of situations. For example, a "wheeled vehicle" pattern might be defined in terms of the components "wheel," "axle," "frame," "body," and "power source." The pattern would also show how these components would be arranged in relation to

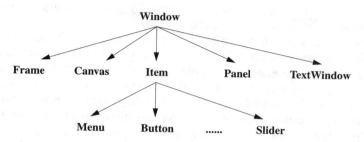

Figure 1–18 A Generalization/Specialization Hierarchy

each other (e.g., the axle must connect two wheels), and could be interpreted in many different ways to solve particular problems that differ in their requirements for speed, durability, payload, fuel source, available materials, and other factors. Example of the wheeled vehicle pattern are "automobile," "horse-drawn carriage," "ox cart," and "moon buggy".

Hierarchy

A hierarchical organization of components based on a relationship of generalization/specialization is an important device in object-oriented programming. While the power of such an organization can be fully appreciated only after more study, it is useful to at least hint at the role it will play. Fig. 1–18 shows how the components in a typical graphical user-interface system might be organized. The most general component, a Window, has attributes of location (the coordinates denoting where the window appears on the screen) and shape (the height and width), and a behavior that allows it to be repositioned and resized. Specialized kinds of windows are those that include a pull-down menu bar (Frame), support drawing graphical shapes (Canvas), are interactive (Items), maintain a prescribed layout of Items (Panel), and allow the scrollable display of simple text (TextWindow). Various kinds of interactive components are shown as specialized kinds of Items.

A generalization and its specializations are often said to be related by an "is-a" relationship, as in, referring to Fig. 1–18, "an Item is a Window." The "is-a" terminology reflects that the specialization has all of the attributes and behavior of the generalization.

The notion of hierarchy in object-oriented programming can be defined as follows:

Hierarchy: an organization of abstractions into a directed graph in which the arcs denote an "is-a" relation between a more generalized abstraction and the one or more specializations derived from it.

Most commonly, a tree structure hierarchy is used to organize the abstractions, although more general organizations are possible.

A generalization/specialization hierarchy serves at least four major purposes. First, it provides a form of knowledge representation. A higher, more generalized, level in the hierarchy encodes an understanding of the general attributes and behavior possessed by all of its specialized descendants. Thus, it is possible to make statements such as "all windows can be resized" and "all windows can be repositioned." Second, the names of the intermediate levels in the hierarchy provide a vocabulary that can be used among developers and between developers and domain experts (those knowledgeable about the application domain but not necessarily about computing). This vocabulary eliminates ambiguity in discussions because its terms identify specific, clearly defined concepts. Third, the hierarchy can be extended by adding new specializations at any level. These additions are easier to make because they occur within an existing framework that defines some, or perhaps many, of their attributes and behavior. For example, to add a new specialized Item, it is not necessary to redefine all of the attributes and behavior of a Window and an Item, as these are assumed to be part of the more generalized nature of the specialized Item being added. Fourth, new attributes and behavior can be added easily to the proper subset of specializations: any new attribute or behavior that might be needed for all Items can be added to Item. These additional attributes or behavior are then automatically part of all specialized Items but not of anything else.

Genericity

Genericity is a partial generalization that is variously referred to by the terms generic, template, parameterized class, or generic class. The generalization is "partial" because at least some of the properties captured by the generalization are expressed in terms of other properties that are not part of (are missing from) the generalization. For example, a generic BubbleSort class can capture very exactly the bubble sort sorting strategy. A basic step in the bubble sort strategy is the comparison such as if (A < B)..., where A and B are two elements being sorted. This strategy can be captured perfectly without identifying exactly what is meant by the "<" operator. In different uses the "<" operator may take on different interpretations. For example, in bubble sorting integers a numeric interpretation is applied; in bubble sorting character strings, a lexicographic interpretation is applied; in bubble sorting a user defined type, a user defined interpretation may be applied.

Genericity can be defined as follows:

Genericity: a named generalization expressed in terms of other unspecified abstractions that are denoted by parameters.

Pictorially, a generic class can be drawn as a class with a "hole" in it (Fig. 1–19). The hole, also referred to as the parameter of the generic class, represents the missing part of the generalization. Filling the hole completes the generalization. The

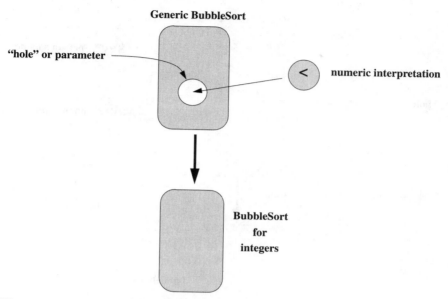

Figure 1–19 A Generic Class with One Parameter

completed generalization is then a fully formed class from which objects can be instantiated. It is not possible to create objects directly from the generic class because the generic class is incomplete.

Generic classes may have more than one hole or parameter. One common type of data organization in which this occurs is a generic LookupTable that maintains an association between a "value" and a "key" by which the value is identified. The fundamental operation of the LookupTable is to return a value given a key. Tables of this form could be used to maintain *(key, value)* associations such as *(name, phone number), (account number, balance)*, or *(name, account number)*. A generic class of this form is shown in Fig. 1–20.

The two parameters of this generic class represent the specific kind of key, in this case a person's name, and the specific kind of value, in this case a phone number. This combination of parameters yields a PhoneBook. Other combinations of keys and values would yield other useful forms of LookupTables.

Polymorphism

Polymorphism is a means of generalizing algorithms. The generality is achieved by allowing the algorithm to uniformly manipulate objects of different classes provided that the algorithm uses only common properties shared by the different classes. Any object known to possess the required common properties may be

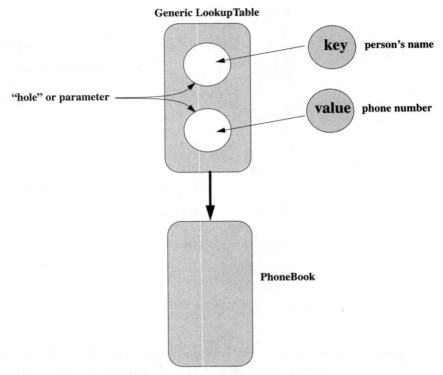

Figure 1–20   A Generic Class with Two Parameters

manipulated by the algorithm. Some object-oriented languages require that the compiler be able to verify at compile-time that an object possesses the required common properties. Other languages allow this verification to be deferred until run-time, risking a possible run-time error if, during execution, the object is discovered to be lacking one of the required common properties.

Polymorphism can be defined as follows:

Polymorphism: the ability to manipulate objects of distinct classes using only knowledge of their common properties without regard for their exact class.

The meaning of polymorphism is reflected in the root phrases from which the term is derived: *poly* denotes "many" or "several" while *morph* refers to "shape," "form," or "appearance." Thus, *polymorphism* refers to things of many shapes or many forms. In the object-oriented programming sense, the "shape, form, or appearance" is taken to mean the interface or properties of an object. The "poly" aspect implies that the interfaces or properties are different or varied across the objects being considered. The challenge is how to manipulate these various objects in a uniform manner.

People use polymorphism in many activities. One example is a store checkout clerk who determines the total amount of a customer's purchases. Each item being purchased has a bar-code label that the clerk scans by passing it over a bar-code reader. The bar-code reader reads the identifying information on the bar-code label, consults a database of merchandise, and reports the information to the cash register for totaling. The clerk follows a generalized algorithm which might be written as:

```
while ( more storeItems ) {
        pick up next storeItem;
        scan storeItem;
        put scanned storeItem in bag;
};
```

This algorithm does not take into account any of the many specific types of merchandise sold by the store; it only refers to a general "storeItem." The store-Item is only required to have a bar-code label so that the item can be scanned. Any item of merchandise having such a label can be handled by the clerk. Conversely, any item not possessing a bar-code label cannot be handled by the clerk. In this example, compile-time checking is equivalent to making sure that items have a bar-code label when they are put on the shelf (i.e., when the store is "programmed"). Run-time checking is equivalent to the clerk checking for the presence of a bar-code label and, if the item does not have such a label, calling a manager to report the problem. There are many similar everyday examples in which people act in a polymorphic manner: shelving books in a library, driving different kinds of cars, using different kinds of computers are a few of these.

Polymorphism enables open-ended software. New classes possessing the required common properties can be handled by a polymorphic algorithm: the algorithm need not be changed in any way to accommodate the additional classes. The same is true for the store clerk algorithm. The store clerk does not need any additional training (reprogramming) when new kinds of merchandise are added to the store's inventory.

A mechanism called **dynamic binding** is needed to implement polymorphism in object-oriented systems. In this context, the term *binding* refers to the association of an invocation made by the polymorphic algorithm with the code of a method implemented by the receiving object. Because the polymorphic algorithm is unaware of the exact class of the receiver, the binding must be done dynamically because the same invocation may be bound to different methods on different executions depending on what object is presented to the algorithm. Fig. 1–21 depicts the act of dynamic binding.

In this example, the polymorphic algorithm invokes a method F() that is one of the common properties shared among a set of classes. The algorithm is unaware of the exact type of the object to which the invocation is directed, it

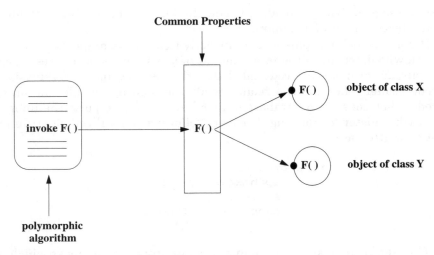

Figure 1-21   Dynamic Binding

is not known whether the object is of class X or class Y. The dynamic binding mechanism determines the type of the object and maps the invocation to the correct method in class X, if the object is of class X, or to the correct method in class Y, if the object is of class Y.

Patterns

A pattern is a generalization of a solution for a commonly occurring problem. A pattern is a generalization because the pattern does not give an immediately usable solution to a particular problem but instead gives the general form of a solution for any problem displaying particular characteristics. The user of the pattern must adapt the pattern to the case at hand and supply the missing details not given in the pattern. Experienced designers are believed to possess, perhaps even at an intuitive or subconscious level, a rich repertoire of patterns and the ability to recognize when a current problem can be solved by adapting a pattern used successfully as a solution for one or more previous problems. Lacking this reservoir of previous designs, novice designers are forced to solve each problem that is new to them as if it were a completely unsolved problem, often reinventing what previous generations of designers have already created.

Patterns are recognized on many levels of scale and in many disciplines. In computer science, a large-scale pattern is often presented as an *architecture* or a *model*. Examples of such large-scale patterns are the *client-server model, layered architecture,* and *micro-kernel architecture*. Small-scale patterns in computing are often called *plans* or *idioms* because they represent a common arrangement of programming language constructs. An example of a pattern at this scale is the

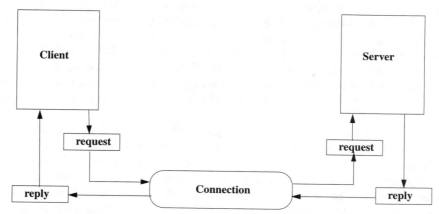

Figure 1–22   Client-Server Pattern

"counted loop with early exit" plan which might be used to scan an array of fixed length and terminate when the end of the array is reached or earlier if a given search criterion is satisfied. The plan specifies the initial conditions, the arrangement of the elements of the loop construct, and the termination conditions. The plan may be specified in a graphical or pseudo-code form so that it can be mapped by the user to different programming languages. Patterns are also common in other disciplines as pointed out by the authors of the book *Design Patterns*, who cite as part of their inspiration the role of patterns in the architecture of buildings and in literary forms.

A pattern can be defined as follows:

> **Pattern:**   a named generalization describing the elements and relationships of a solution for a commonly occurring design problem.

A pattern contains four essential parts: a name, a problem, a solution, and the consequences. The four parts of a pattern are illustrated by a simple client-server pattern. The name of the pattern is intended to convey briefly and succinctly the subject matter of the pattern. For this example the name *client-server* is appropriate. The problem portion of the pattern identifies the conditions under which the pattern is applicable (i.e., for what problem is this pattern a solution). The client-server problem is one of providing a service to multiple possible clients in a loosely coupled manner. The solution specifies the elements that comprise the solution, their individual responsibilities, and the manner in which they collaborate to achieve the solution. The elements of the client-server pattern could be given in pictorial form as shown in Fig. 1–22.

The client-server pattern involves five elements. The client would be given the responsibility of generating a request that is sent to the server which, in turn, performs its service and delivers a response in the form of a reply. The responsibility for conveying the requests and replies between the client and server is assigned to an intermediary known as the connection. The client and server each collaborate directly only with the connection (but only indirectly with each other). The collaboration between the elements is defined by the sequence of events beginning with the generation of a request by the client and its transmission to the server followed by the generation at the server of a reply and its transmission to the client.

Notice that the pattern does not specify the nature of the service provided, it could be a name service, a time service, a location service, a file service, a security service or any other. Also the pattern does not specify how the connection is to be implemented. The connection could be a memory buffer connecting two procedures within the same process, a memory buffer connecting two different processes on the same machine, or a network link between two processes on different machines. While these details vary, the pattern remains the same.

The pattern also specifies the positive and negative consequences of using the pattern. Some of the positive consequences are that the client and server may be implemented on different machines allowing each to take advantage of local specialized hardware or software resources, the client and server may be totally or largely unaware of and insensitive to the actual location of each other, and the server may be made available to many clients at the same time. Two negative consequences of the client-server pattern are that the client may be left hanging if its request or reply is lost or if the server crashes, and the client cannot demand or control the service from the server—it can only request such service.

A pattern for an object-oriented design is expressed in terms of classes and objects. The elements of the pattern are represented by classes. The relationships among the elements are defined by association, aggregation, and/or hierarchy. The responsibilities and collaborations are understood in terms of the behavior of each class and the interactions among the classes as defined by their associations.

A pattern is a distinct form of generalization; similar to genericity in that it is a partial generalization, but with details suppressed or omitted. However, genericity leads to at least partial code, while a pattern need not be expressed in code at all. A pattern may also use hierarchical relationships, but there is no aspect of a generalization/specialization relationship at the center of a pattern.

1.7 Object-Oriented Programming and Software Engineering

Object-oriented programming is an evolutionary development in software engineering. The foundations for many object-oriented languages were established by

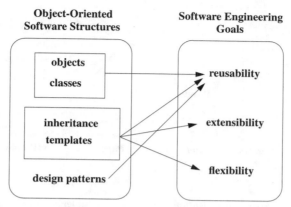

Figure 1–23 Software Engineering Goals

decades of software engineering experience that led to the invention of language features such as closed procedures, modules, and abstract data types. Also important was the widely recognized value of such software engineering techniques as information hiding, encapsulation, strict enforcement of interfaces, and layering.

Object-oriented programming addresses at least the three major software engineering goals shown in Fig. 1–23.

The language features that address these issues are those of objects, classes, inheritance, polymorphism, templates, and design patterns.

Reusability is an important issue in software engineering for at least two major reasons. First, reusability is one means to cope with the pressures of producing ever larger and more functional systems in an ever decreasing development cycle (time to market). Reusability allows developers to be more efficient because the same code can be developed once and used in many different applications. Second, reliability can be improved by reusing previously developed, and previously tested, components. The development of new code entails additional costs in time and money for testing, validation, and verification. Much of these expenses can be avoided by using "off-the-shelf" components.

Software reuse is certainly not a goal unique to object-oriented programming. But while libraries of procedures have proven this approach to be useful, in practice procedures are often too primitive a unit to promote extensive reuse. Objects and classes are more sophisticated mechanisms for achieving software reuse because they bind together more completely all the aspects of an entire abstraction. Therefore, the abstraction can more easily be transported across applications. Any of the forms of generalization also contribute to reuse: a class in an inheritance hierarchy can be reused directly when it serves as a generalized base class from which a new class is derived by specialization, templates can

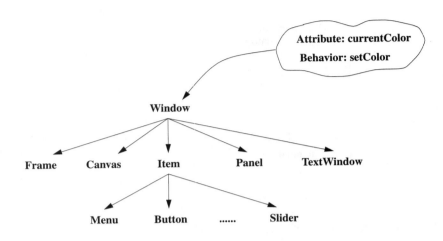

Figure 1–24   Adding New Attributes and Behavior

be reused by supplying different parameters for the template arguments, and design patterns allow design experience and success to be reused by many designers.

Extensibility in software is important because software systems are long lived and are subject to users' demands for new features and added capability. Object-oriented programming can help to satisfy this need through inheritance. Recall that inheritance is a generalization/specialization hierarchy. Referring to the Window hierarchy discussed earlier, extensibility is possible in two ways. The first way in which a generalization/specialization hierarchy supports extensibility is that any new attributes or behavior that is added to a more generalized concept (e.g., Window) will automatically become part of the attributes and behavior of its specializations (e.g., Frame, Item, Button). For example, as shown in Fig. 1–24, if the Window abstraction is enhanced to include a color with which the Window would be displayed on the screen, then the attribute "currentColor" and the behavior "setColor" might be added to Window. It would then be possible to manipulate not only the color of a Window but that of all its specializations as well.

The second way in which a generalization/specialization hierarchy supports extensibility is that the hierarchy itself can be extended. New additions can be made under any existing node. For example, as shown in Fig. 1–25, the TextWindow might be specialized to a HyperTextWindow by including additional attributes and additional behavior that distinguishes ordinary words from those words that are hyperlink and can be clicked-on to transfer to another place in the text.

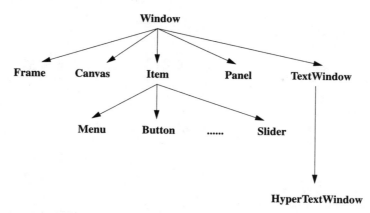

Figure 1–25   Adding New Specialized Classes

Flexibility in software systems means, in part, that additions, variations, or modification can be made without the need to modify numerous places in the system's code. Historically, many software systems were very brittle in that the addition of a small change could only be accommodated by making modifications in many, and often apparently unrelated, parts of the existing system. This brittle property stood in marked contrast to the prevailing notion that, unlike hardware systems, software systems were supposed to be extremely malleable and easily changed.

Object-oriented programming contributes to flexibility in two ways. First, the separation of an interface from its implementation allows the user of the interface to remain unaffected by changes in the implementation. Thus, a modification can be made to the implementation (e.g., to improve its efficiency or reliability) without requiring any changes in the code that uses the interface. Second, polymorphism allows variations and additions to be made to the set of classes over which the polymorphism applies. For example, referring to the Window hierarchy, consider adding a new kind of interaction Item, a RadioButton. Since Items can be placed in a Panel, it would seem necessary to modify the Panel to allow a Panel to manipulate the newly created RadioButton. However, the Panel can use polymorphism so that the Panel's algorithms only rely on the more general attributes and behavior of an object (i.e., that it is a kind of Item) and does not need to be aware of the exact "type" (i.e., RadioButton) of the object. Using this approach, the Panel can be designed to operate on Items. Any newly created Item, even one—like the RadioButton—that is created after the Panel is already written, automatically can be manipulated by a Panel without changing the code of the Panel.

Using Objects of a Single Class

2.1 Classes and Objects

*I*n C++, the keyword `class` is used to define a new class. It is an error in C++ to define two different classes with the same name or to define the same class twice. The following code defines a class named Frame that might represent the outer boundary of a window in a graphical user-interface system.

```
class Frame {        // represent a graphical user interface window
     /* the body of the class definition
        goes in here between the curly braces */
};
```

The body of the Frame class's definition will be seen shortly. The class definition ends with a semicolon.

Two different forms of comments are illustrated in the Frame class definition above. An adjacent pair of slash marks `//` introduces a comment that ends at the end of the current line. A multiline comment begins with the pair of characters `/*` and ends with the matching pair of characters `*/`.

An object-oriented program typically involves several, and perhaps many, different classes. Other classes related to a windowing system might be:

```
class Message {...};       // an unchanging line of text
class TextBox {...};       // editable lines of text
class Button  {...};       // a selector that can be "pushed"
```

These classes will be seen and used shortly.

The simplest way to create an object of a class is to declare a variable using the class's name. For example, using the Frame class defined above, a Frame object can be declared by:

```
Frame display(...);
```

This declares an object identified by the variable named `display`. The ellipsis (i.e., the . . .) is not part of C++ syntax, but is used to denote the values that are typically required to initialize the object being declared. The values that should be given here will be seen when the complete Frame class definition is presented.

As in C and many other languages, C++ requires that the definition of a class precede the use of that class in a declaration so that the C++ compiler can more easily check that the definition of a class and its use in declarations and other statements are consistent. This is part of the character of C++ as a statically-typed object-oriented language. The programmer must insure that the declaration-before-use rule is met by the organization of the program's text. It will be seen later how to achieve this organization in a straightforward way.

The declaration of an object illustrates the strong connection between the concept of a type and the concept of a class. Compare, for example, the following two declarations:

```
int counter;
Frame display(...);
```

The first declaration creates a variable whose type is `int` and which is named by the identifier `counter`. The type `int` determines what operations can be applied to the variable. For example, +, -, <, and = are some of the valid operations. The compiler will issue warnings or error messages if invalid operations are attempted. Similarly, the second declaration creates a variable (an object) whose type is Frame and which is named by the identifier `display`. As with all types, the compiler will check that the operations applied to `display` are appropriate. Since Frame is a programmer-defined type, the valid operations on objects are exactly those given in the definition of the Frame class.

Many objects can be created from the same class. For example, several Frame objects can be created as follows:

```
Frame display(...), viewer(...);
Frame editor(...);
```

These two declarations create three Frame objects. Notice that several objects can be created with one declaration, as is done with `display` and `viewer`. A comma must separate adjacent names in the same declaration. Also notice that, as in this example, the same class can be used in different declarations.

In C++, a class is a type. The declaration of a variable that names an object is syntactically the same as the declaration of a variable that names a predefined, or built-in, type such as `int`, `char`, or `float`. The rules of type checking apply to objects just as they do to predefined types. For example, one object may be assigned to another object only (at least for now) if they are of the same class. For example, it is permissible to assign the value of `viewer` (defined above) to display. However, if msg is an object of class Message, then msg cannot be assigned to viewer and viewer can not be assigned to msg—in each case the two variables are of different classes, and equivalently of different types.

 Exercises

1. Is it correct to have many classes with different names?

2. Is it correct have many objects of the same class?

3. Is it correct to define "class int {...};"?

4. Is it correct to declare "Frame Frame;"? That is, can an object and a class have the same name?

5. Is it correct to declare "Frame frame;"?

6. Is it correct to declare "Frame aFrame;"?

7. Write three declarations that create four Frame objects and two Message objects. Use the ellipsis notation to indicate where the initializing values would appear.

8. Write two declarations that create four Frame objects and two Message objects. Use the ellipsis notation to indicate where the initializing values would appear.

9. Name five other classes that might be part of a graphical user interface system. Present your answer in the form class ClassName {...}; where "ClassName" is the name of the class that you have chosen.

10. Give the declarations for the system described below in what you consider the best style.

    An application has two windows, one for receiving user commands and one for displaying status information. Each window has a message that identifies the window. The command window has two areas where editable text can be displayed, one area for a command and one for command options. The command window has two buttons, one used to execute the command and one to stop the command's execution. The status window has a second message that is used to display any error messages that result from a command's execution.

11. Compare your answer to the last question with someone who has a different style. Identify the ways in which the styles are different.

2.2 Structure of Classes and Objects

To use objects of an existing class it is necessary to understand something of their structure and operation, just as when learning to drive a car it is useful to understand something about the car's structure—where the driver sits and where the ignition key goes—and the car's operation—what the steering wheel does, what the accelerator pedal does, etc.

Public vs. Private Parts

For a programmer (re)using an existing class, the key element of the class's structure is its *public interface*. The class's public interface defines the behavior of all objects created from this class definition. The public interface contains a set of methods (also called procedures, member functions, or operations) that can be used to manipulate the objects created from this class. The only way to manipulate an object is by using the methods defined in the public interface of the class from which the object was created.

A class, and any object created from it, also contains a private (hidden, internal, encapsulated) implementation. The user of an object has no concern with how the object is implemented, just as the driver of a car need not have any concern with how the engine is constructed. The internal details of an object's implementation can be ignored by the user of the object.

In C++ the public and private portions of a class are denoted by keywords as shown in the following:

```
class Frame {
  private:
        // encapsulated implementation goes here
  public:
        // public interface goes here
};
```

The separation of the public interface from the private implementation is a major aspect of object-oriented programming. The public interface defines a contract between the object's implementor and the object's user. The contract specifies what service the implementor has agreed to provide and limits the ways in which the user is allowed to manipulate the object.

The separation of public interface from private implementation has several advantages:

- It promotes understanding and reuse by reducing the amount of information confronting the user of an object
- It increases implementation flexibility by allowing the implementor to change the implementation (say to a more efficient one) so that in future programs the object looks and acts the same to the object's user, who is unaware that a different implementation is involved,

- It eases the difficult task of debugging by providing a boundary that can be used to isolate the source of an error
- It improves the overall design of the system by allowing it to be presented and understood as a collection of public interfaces

These benefits will be understood more deeply as the ideas of object-oriented programming are developed and as experience is gained in working with and building object-oriented systems.

Methods in the Public Interface

The public interface may (and usually does) contain three different kinds of methods:

- Constructors: methods that define how the object is initialized. There commonly are several constructors, allowing the object to be initialized in different ways. A constructor is invoked implicitly when an object is created. An object cannot be created without a constructor being invoked.
- A destructor: there is only one such method in each class that is invoked implicitly when an object is destroyed.
- Behavioral methods: these define how the object behaves or can be manipulated during its lifetime. These methods are often subdivided into:
  - accessor/interrogator methods that return information about the state of the object but do not change the state of the object, and
  - manipulator/mutator methods that (potentially) change the state of the object.

If no constructor or destructor is defined, a default one is provided. The default constructor and default destructor do nothing.

Note that constructors and destructors are invoked implicitly. That is, they are invoked automatically as a result of the execution of some statement. For example, a constructor is invoked implicitly when a declared object is created; the constructor is invoked as a result of the declaration statement. Constructors and destructors are never invoked explicitly by the programmer's code.

An Abstraction for a GUI Window

The Frame class is the first of several abstractions of a graphical user-interface (GUI) window. A GUI window has numerous capabilities as shown in Fig. 2–1. A real-world GUI window has operations that can be performed on it to affect its placement and size, is capable of displaying a wide range of information-bearing elements (graphical, iconic, textual), and affords a means of interacting with the user through control elements (buttons, menus, etc.). To avoid confronting all of

Graphical User-Interface Window

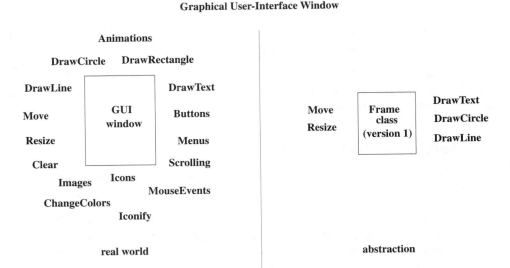

Figure 2–1   Abstraction of a GUI Window

these powerful capabilities in the first class being studied, a series of simpler abstractions will be shown. Fig. 2–1 shows the first of these simpler abstractions.

Consistent with the ideas of mapping an abstraction to a class, the first version of the Frame class is defined as shown in Code Sample 2-1.

In Code Sample 2-1, the constructor method has the same name as the name of the class (Frame). This constructor requires five arguments: the name to be associated with the Frame; the initial (x,y) coordinates of the Frame's upper left corner, given by the pair (initXCoord, initYCoord); and the Frame's initial dimensions (width and height). The last method, named ~Frame, is the destructor; placed here are any actions that the must be taken when the Frame object is destroyed. The IsNamed method is an accessor method that allows the program to determine if the name of the Frame matches the method's input argument. All other methods are manipulator methods. The two methods Resize and MoveTo provide operations to relocate the Frame on the screen and to change its size. The DrawLine and DrawCircle methods allow simple graphical shapes to be drawn in the Frame. The method DrawText allows text to be written into the Frame. The upper left-hand corner of the area where the text is written within the Frame is specified by the (atX, atY) coordinates. The Clear method erases all text and graphics from the Frame. A real Frame class would have more methods, but these suffice for a number of interesting examples.

Code Sample 2-1 *The Frame Class*

```
class Frame {                        // Version 1
  private:
          // encapsulated data  goes here
  public:
        Frame        (char *name, int initXCoord, int initYCoord,
                                 int initWidth,  int initHeight);
    void Resize      (int newHeight, int newWidth  );
    void MoveTo      (int newXCoord, int newYCoord );
    int  IsNamed     (char *name);
    void Clear       ();
    void DrawText    (char *text, int atX, int atY);
    void DrawLine    (int fromX, int fromY, int toX, int toY);
    void DrawCircle  (int centerX, int centerY, int radius);
        ~Frame       ();
};
```

Notice in Code Sample 2-1 that no executable code is given for any of the methods. This is in keeping with the desire to hide all of the implementation details of an object—the user of the class cares only about what operations are defined, not how these operations are implemented. The creator of the class must, of course, write the code for these methods and provide the other private data as well. We will see later how this is done.

 Exercises

1. Illustrate the difference between the public interface and the private implementation in the following ordinary objects:

   - a personal computer
   - a telephone
   - a radio

   For each ordinary object identify several operations in its public interface and name one or more things that are probably in its private implementation.

2. For one of the ordinary objects in the last question show how the public vs. private separation results in the advantages cited above (i.e, reuse, flexibility, debugging, design).

3. Write a class definition (without the private section) for a "stack of integers" class.

4. Write a class definition (without the private section) for a "file of characters" class.

5. Write a variation of the Frame class (version 1) that moves the Frame by a relative amount (i.e., up or down a given number of units and left or right a given number of units).

6. Write a variation of the Frame class (version 1) that changes the size of the Frame by a fractional amount (e.g., makes it 50 percent bigger or 50 percent smaller).

7. Write a variation of the Frame class (version 1) that allows rectangles and triangles to be drawn in the Frame.

2.3 Creating and Operating on an Object

Applying Operations

The operations defined in the public interface of a class may be applied to any object of that class. Continuing with the example of the Frame class, a Frame object can be created and manipulated as follows:

```
Frame display("Test Window", 10,20, 100, 200);

display.MoveTo(50, 50);
display.Resize(200,200);
display.DrawText("Really Neat!", 50,50);
```

Here, a Frame object named `display` is declared. The Frame constructor method is called implicitly using the arguments provided in the declaration. These constructor arguments create a Frame whose upper left-hand corner is at location (10,20) and whose height and width are 100 and 200, respectively.

Once the display object has been constructed, it may be operated upon. In this example, the display object is first moved to location (50,50) using the MoveTo method and then the Frame is changed to a 200 x 200 square shape using the Resize method. Finally the text "Really Neat!" is written in the Frame at the location (50,50) relative to the upper left-hand corner of the Frame.

Notice that the "." (dot) operator is used to invoke one of the methods of an object. Thus, `display.MoveTo(...)` means to invoke the `MoveTo` method on the object `display`. People programming in object-oriented languages often use phrasing like "ask the display object to move itself" to refer to operations being taken on objects, reflecting the point of view that an object is an entity that is capable of performing certain actions (e.g., a Frame object knows how to move itself to a new location).

A Simple Programming Environment

Programming with graphical user-interface objects—like objects of the Frame class and others that will be introduced later—involves a programming environment that is qualitatively different from that typically seen in introductory programming courses. The difference in the programming environment is due to the fact that graphical user-interface systems are *event-driven* or *reactive* systems, meaning that the system is driven by the occurrence of external events (mouse clicks, clock alarms) to which the system must react. The typical life cycle of an event-driven or reactive system proceeds as follows:

1. receive notification that an event has occurred
2. use information about the current state of the system to decide how to react to the event
3. react to the event by updating the display and changing the system's state information
4. return and await the next notification.

The program does not read its inputs or control when such inputs occur, it simply reacts to their occurrence. Some simple examples are given below, using objects of the Frame class as an example.

The events in a graphical user-interface system come from two different sources: the user and the hardware clock. In a typical workstation environment the user generates events by moving the mouse, pressing and releasing mouse buttons, or by pressing keys on the keyboard. With other peripheral devices the user might generate events by movements of a joystick, track-ball, or virtual reality devices (gloves, head-mounted displays, etc.). Only mouse events are dealt with in the first, simple programming environment. The hardware clock generates timing events that are needed to create animated components of a user interface. A very simple example of this is blinking text that draws the user's attention to an important part of the interface. For the program to make the text blink, the program must have some idea of the passage of time. A stream or sequence of timer events provides the program with that.

A simple programming environment that is similar to those found in many object-oriented windowing systems (it is very close, in fact, to the basic model

Code Sample 2-2   *Simple Programming Environment*

```
// This is the file Program.cc

#include "Program.h"

// include any necessary header files here (e.g., "Frame.h")

// define here any global objects or variables


void OnStart(void) {}

void OnMouseEvent(char *frameName, int x, int y, int buttonState) {}

void OnTimerEvent(void) {}

void OnPaint(void) {}
```

used in the Java Abstract Windowing Toolkit) will be used. However, the initial programming environment is not object-oriented itself. As more is learned about object-oriented programming, portions of the environment will be captured in a better object-oriented manner. Eventually, the entire graphical user-interface program will be represented as an application object.

It will be noted that the simple environment lacks a main program. Object-oriented languages, including C++, do have a main program that defines their initial point of execution and, in many programs, the main program is written by the application developer. However, in a graphical user interface application (and in other applications where a complex run-time library is being used), the main program is more often written by the implementor of the run-time library that provides many of the low-level support functions.

The simple programming environment has four procedures contained in a single file named Program.cc that is shown in Code Sample 2-2. The region outside of the procedures is a global scope in which program-wide objects (such as long-lasting Frame objects) can be declared. This global scope can also be used to define variables that denote the current state of the application. The global objects and global variables can be manipulated inside each of the four procedures. Note that this file's name, Program.cc, is purely arbitrary and has no general significance in C++ or in graphical user-interface programming.

The OnStart function is called exactly once. It can be used to initialize any global object and data as well as create the initial display that the user sees. The OnPaint method is called whenever the system suspects that the user's display may have been damaged and should be redrawn. Common actions that trigger this function being called are a window being moved, resized, or exposed to view after being partially, or completely, obscured by an overlapping window. Whenever, within the display area of a Frame object, the user clicks a mouse button or moves the mouse, the OnMouseEvent function is called. This function has input parameters giving the name of the Frame object in which the event occurred, the x and y coordinates of the mouse's current location, and the condition of the mouse buttons. The OnTimerEvent function is called whenever a clock alarm occurs. The role of each of the four functions in the simple programming environment is briefly summarized in Table 2–1.

Table 2–1 Summary of Functions in Simple Programming Environment

OnStart	initialize global objects, global variables, and the user display
OnPaint	redraw the user display when needed
OnTimerEvent	react to a clock alarm
OnMouse Event	react to mouse clicks and/or mouse movement

For two reasons, global variables are used in the simple programming environment despite the fact that this seems to contradict the usual (and usually strong and correct) advice to avoid the use of global data. First, the global variables are a temporary expedient—as more is learned about object-oriented programming much, if not all, of the global data will disappear. For the moment, the global data will be tolerated so that experimenting with basic object-oriented ideas can begin. Second, global *objects* are somewhat less objectionable than global *data*. At least the object defines an interface that protects its encapsulated data from obvious misuse. Global data has no such protections. Furthermore, in building an association of objects it is not always possible to remove all global data. The objects that form the association sometimes must be defined as global data. By analogy, if an automobile is viewed as an association, it is not possible to conceal some of its constituent parts, such as the steering wheel, the brakes, and the turn signals.

A program is written in the simple programming environment by providing code for some, or all, of the four functions defined in the simple programming environment and creating an executable program that uses your definitions of these functions. Providing the code for the four functions is done by editing the file Program.cc. This file must then be compiled and linked with the appropriate run-time libraries. This mechanical step is automated by a "make" file that is provided. After editing Program.cc, simply type the command "make," with no arguments. The make program will create an executable file named "Program." For simplicity, the names Program.cc and Program cannot be changed.

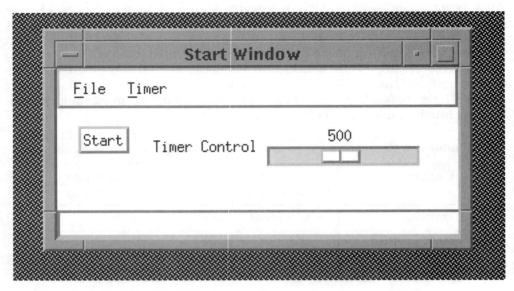

Figure 2–2   The Start Window

When executed, programs developed in the simple programming environment first display a Start window that provides controls for initiating the program, terminating the program, and controlling a simple timer. The Start window is shown in Fig. 2–2. When depressed, the Start button will cause the OnStart function to be called, after which the Start button will disappear. At any time, the entire program can be terminated by selection of the Quit item in the File menu. The Timer menu contains two items for turning on and off a timer (a source of clock alarms). The occurrence of a clock alarm will cause the OnTimerEvent function to be called. The interval of this timer (the duration between alarms) is controlled by the slider bar labelled "Timer Control." The slider and the timer are calibrated in milliseconds. The initial slider setting is at 500 milliseconds (one half of one second). The range of timer settings is between 50 milliseconds (one twentieth of one second) and 1000 milliseconds (one second). When the timer is running, its interval can only be changed by stopping the clock, changing the slider position, and then restarting the timer. Changing the slider while the clock is running will not change the timer interval.

Sample Programs

Three simple programs are presented that illustrate the simple programming environment. The first program is a simple "Hello World" program, the second

Code Sample 2-3 *Hello World Program*

```
#include "Frame.h"

Frame window("Hello World Program", 200, 200, 400, 400);

void OnStart(void) {
  window.Clear();
  window.DrawText("Hello World!", 20, 20);
}

void OnMouseEvent(char *frameName, int x, int y, int buttonState){}

void OnTimerEvent(void){}

void OnPaint(void){
  window.Clear();
  window.DrawText("Hello World!", 20, 20);
}
```

modifies the "Hello World" program to include the handling of mouse button clicks, and the third adds to the second program the use of timer events.

The Hello World program is shown in Code Sample 2-3. This program includes "Frame.h" because it uses the Frame class definition to declare a Frame object named *window* located at position (200,200) on the display and is 400 pixels wide and 400 pixels tall. This window will have a title of "Hello World Program" when it appears on the display. Both the OnStart and the OnPaint functions clear the window object and write the string "Hello World" near the upper left-hand corner of the window.

Code Sample 2-4 shows how to handle mouse events. In this version of the Hello World program, the string "Hello World!" is written wherever in the window the user clicks the left mouse button. The OnMouseEvent function is called whenever the mouse is moved or a mouse button is clicked. In this program, the OnMouseEvent function checks to see if the state of the mouse buttons indicates that the left mouse button is "down" (i.e., depressed). If the button is down (signalling that the user clicked the mouse button), the window is cleared and the string "Hello World!" is written at the coordinates of the mouse event. The "buttonState" parameter to the OnMouseEvent function is treated as a bit map. The code

```
if( buttonState & leftButtonDown)...
```

simply tests if the bit corresponding to the left button being down is set. If the bit is set, then the mouse button is down. The item "leftButtonDown" is a value defined in an enumeration given in the file Program.h. Other values are right-

Code Sample 2-4   *Hello World Program with Mouse Events*

```
#include "Program.h"
#include "Frame.h"



Frame window("Hello World Program", 200, 200, 400, 400);
int lastx;
int lasty;


void OnStart(void) {
  window.Clear();
  window.DrawText("Hello World!", 20,20);
  lastx = 20;
  lasty = 20;
}

void OnMouseEvent(char *frameName, int x, int y, int buttonState){
  if (buttonState & leftButtonDown) {
    window.Clear();
    window.DrawText("Hello World!",x,y);
    lastx = x;
    lasty = y;
  }
}

void OnTimerEvent(void){}

void OnPaint(void){
    window.Clear();
    window.DrawText("Hello World!", lastx, lasty);
}
```

ButtonDown, middleButtonDown, and isDragging. Also important in this program is the use of state information represented by the variables *lastx* and *lasty* that record the position of the last place where the "Hello World!" string was written. It is necessary to keep track of this state information so that the OnPaint function will know where in the window the string should be placed when the window needs to be redrawn. Notice that *lastx* and *lasty* are initialized in the OnStart function and updated in the OnMouseEvent function whenever a mouse click is recognized.

Code Sample 2-5 illustrates how timer events (clock alarms) are handled. In this program the "Hello World!" string is turned into blinking text by

Code Sample 2-5 *Hello World Program with Mouse and Timer Events*

```
#include "Program.h"
#include "Frame.h"


Frame window("Hello World Program", 200, 200, 400, 400);
int lastx;
int lasty;
int visible;


void OnStart(void) {
  window.Clear();
  window.DrawText("Hello World!", 20, 20);
  lastx = 20;
  lasty = 20;
  visible = 1;
}

void OnMouseEvent(char *frameName, int x, int y, int buttonState){
  if (buttonState & leftButtonDown) {
    window.Clear();
    if (visible)  window.DrawText("Hello World!",x,y);
    lastx = x;
    lasty = y;
  }
}

void OnTimerEvent(void){
  window.Clear();
  if (visible) visible = 0;
  else { visible = 1;
        window.DrawText("Hello World!", lastx, lasty);
      }
}

void OnPaint(void){
    window.Clear();
    if (visible) window.DrawText("Hello World!", lastx, lasty);
}
```

alternately clearing and writing the string on successive timer events. The rate of blinking is controlled by the timer interval. Remember that the timer events will not occur until the timer is turned on using the Timer menu in the Start window. Also remember that the slider bar in the Start window controls the interval between timer events.

Code Sample 2-5 uses additional state information, given by the variable *visible,* to record whether the string is or is not visible at the current time. In addition to the OnTimerEvent, the OnMouseEvent and OnPaint functions use this state information to decide whether or not to write the string of text in the window.

The following exercises contain a number of interesting small programs that can be written using the Frame class and the simple programming environment.

 Exercises

1. Write a declaration that creates a Frame object at location (20,30) with a width of 150 and a height of 175.

2. Write a segment of code to move the Frame you created in the step above to location (50,50) and change its size to a width of 100 and a height of 200.

3. Write a program that displays your full name approximately centered in a Frame that is itself approximately centered on the screen. Note that you may have to do some experimentation with the sizes and locations.

4. Write a program that draws a circle of radius 20 in each corner of a Frame of size 400 x 400.

5. Analog Clock: Write a program that draws a picture of an analog clock in a Frame. A circle can be used for the clock face and a single lines can be used to draw one hand on the clock. Place the hand pointing straight up.

6. Two-Handed Analog Clock: Modify the Analog Clock program so that it has both a shorter (hours) hand and a longer (minutes) hand. Place the hands so that the time on the clock reads three o'clock.

7. Analog Clock with Numbers: Modify the Analog Clock program so that the numbers 1 through 12 appear around the outside of the clock face.

8. Animated Analog Clock: Modify one of the Analog Clock programs so that the hand(s) move. On each timer event move the hand(s) to the next position.

9. Corner Tour: Write a program that places a circle in the upper left corner of a Frame. The program should then move this circle to the upper right, lower right, and lower left corners before returning the circle to

its original position. Repeat this cycle ten times. At each position, display in the window a line of text appropriate for the current position of the window, such as "Upper Left," Upper Right," "Lower Right," "Lower Left."

10. Border Walk: Write a program that moves a circle in small steps around the outside border of the screen starting from an initial location in the upper left hand corner of the screen. Can you make the motion appear smooth?

2.4 Overloaded Operations

In some situations, frequently with constructors, a class may provide alternative ways to perform the same operation. These alternatives are defined as methods with the same name but with different argument lists. The revised Frame class with overload constructors and overloaded methods is shown in Code Sample 2-6.

The first constructor requires five arguments—one for the name, two for the placement and two for the size. The second constructor specifies only the name and the placement arguments. When this constructor is used, the two arguments determine where the Frame is placed on the screen, but the object selects, by an algorithm or by a simple default, the size of the Frame. In the third constructor, the user provides the name for the Frame but the constructor itself determines, by an algorithm or by simple defaults, both the placement and size of the Frame. Finally the last constructor, with no arguments, allows the object to select its own name, its own placement and its own shape.

Examples of using the overloaded constructors are:

```
Frame exact   ("First Window",  50, 50, 100, 200);
                              // uses first   constructor
Frame here    ("Second Window", 50, 50);
                              // uses second constructor
Frame simple ("Third Window");  // uses third   constructor
Frame any;                      // uses fourth  constructor
```

Overloaded constructors are useful in cases where common default values or easily computed values are the common case. Thus, the user of the object is spared the burden of specifying information that is typical or that is not important. A set of overload constructors gives the user of the class more flexibility in the amount of control needed over the construction of the object.

The Resize method shows how overloading is used for non-constructor methods. The version with two integer parameters resizes the window to the specified width and height. The second version of Resize changes the window's dimensions by a given factor; factors larger than 1.0 cause the window to expand

Code Sample 2-6   *Frame Class—Version 2*

```
class Frame {                       // Version 2
 private:
         // encapsulated implementation goes here
 public:

        Frame    (char *name, int initXCoord, int initYCoord,
                              int initWidth,  int initHeight);

        Frame    (char *name, int initXCoord, int initYCoord);
        Frame    (char *name);
        Frame    ();

    void Resize  ( int newHeight, int newWidth  );
    void Resize  ( float factor );

    void Clear();              // clear entire frame
    void Clear(int x, int y, int w, int h);
                              // clear rectangular area

    void TextSize(char* text, int& w, int& h);
                              // convenience method

        ...      // other methods the same as in version 1
};
```

in both width and height while factors less than 1.0 cause the window to shrink in width and height.

The Resize method is used in the following ways:

```
exact.Resize(100, 100);      // change to a 100 X 100 square
exact.Resize(1.5);           // enlarge by 50%
exact.Resize(0.5);           // shrink to 50%  current size
```

The Clear method is also overloaded. The version of this method with no arguments clears the entire frame. The version of the Clear method with four arguments allows a rectangular area within the frame to be cleared without erasing anything outside of this rectangle. To make this overloaded Clear method usable for erasing text, a helpful method, named TextSize, is added to the Frame class that determines the width and height of the rectangular area occupied by a text string. For example, to find the rectangular dimensions of the text "Hello World," the TextSize method would be used as follows:

```
int w, h;      // variables to hold the result
exact.TextSize("Hello World", w, h);
```

Notice that the two integer arguments are output parameters; they are declared as references to integers (int&).

A more complete use of the overloaded Clear method is shown below. This segment of code erases from a Frame object one text string (the "Hello World" string), leaving a second text string visible (the string "This is Great!").

```
Frame window("Clear Test", 100,100, 200,200);

window.DrawText("Hello World", 20, 20);
window.DrawText("This is Great!", 50,50);

int w, h;
window.TextSize("Hello World", w, h);
window.Clear(20, 20, w, h);              // erase "Hello World"
```

 Exercises

1. Construct a window using the constructor with no arguments and see what name the constructor chooses for the window. Create two such windows and compare their names.

2. Simple Button: Write a program that displays within a frame your first name toward the top and, near the middle, a circle around the text "Push Here". When the user clicks anywhere inside the circle, erase just your first name and replace it with your last name. Clicking again within the circle should cause your last name to be erased and your first name to be displayed. Subsequent clicks within the circle should alternate in this way showing either your first or last name.

3. Shrinking Window 1: Write a program that places a window of size 500 x 500 near the center of the screen. Leaving its position fixed, resize the window nineteen times, each time making it smaller by an additional twenty five units. Use the version of Resize that takes two integer arguments.

4. Shrinking Window 2: Write a program that places a window of size 500 x 500 near the center of the screen. Leaving its position fixed, resize the window nineteen times, each time making it smaller by 10 percent of its current size. Use the version of Resize that takes a single float argument.

5. Heart Beat 1: Write a program that first shrinks and then expands a window back to its original size using the approach in the Shrinking Window 1 problem.

6. Heart Beat 2: Write a program that first shrinks and then expands a window back to its original size using the approach in the Shrinking Window 2 problem.

2.5 Default Arguments

Default arguments are formal parameters that are assigned a value (the default value) to use when the caller does not supply an actual parameter value. Of course, actual parameter values, when given, override the default values.

The syntax and utility of default arguments is illustrated by the following example based on the Frame class.

```
class Frame {
private:
    . . .
public:
    . . .          void Resize (int width = 100, int height = 150);
    . . .    };
```

In this example, the width and height arguments are both given default values. To see the effect of these default values consider the following use of the Resize method:

```
Frame window (100, 100, 300, 400);

    . . .

window.Resize(200, 250);          // case 1
window.Resize(200);               // case 2
window.Resize();                  // case 3
```

In the first case the window is resized to be 200 x 250: since both parameters are given the default values are ignored. In the second case, the Frame object is resized to be 200 x 150: the default value of 150 is used for the absent second (height) argument while the supplied 200 is used for the first (width) argument. In the third case, the window is resized to be 100 x 200 since both default values are used.

Default values can also be used with constructors. For example, the Frame class could be redefined as follows:

```
class Frame {
private:
    ...
public:
    Frame( char *name, int initXcoord = 50, int initYcoord = 50,
                   int initWidth = 100, int initHeight = 100 );
    ...
};
```

This single constructor can be used in any of the following ways:

```
Frame display1("Fully Specified", 200, 200, 300, 350);
Frame display2("No Height",        200, 200, 300);
Frame display3("Position Only",    200, 200);
Frame display4("No YCoordinate", 200)
Frame display5("Name Only");
```

The Frame display1 is given a name and will be located at position (200,200) with a shape of 300 x 350. The Frame display2 is like display1 except that it has a default height of 100 as specified by the default value for initHeight. The Frame display3 is given a name and will be located at position (200,200) and it will have a shape of 100 x 100 as determined by the default values for initWidth and initHeight. The Frame display4 is similar to display3 except that it has a different name and will be located at (200,50), the y coordinate of 50 being determined by the default value for the parameter initYcoord. Finally, display5 will have the name indicated and the default values will determine its position—(50,50)—and it shape—100 x 100.

Notice that as with overloaded methods, the use of default parameters give the caller of a method added flexibility in how to invoke the method. The caller need only specify those parameters that are essential and allow the default values to apply for all other parameters. Callers who need more exact control of the methods arguments can override the default values by providing their own values.

Default values can be used when:

- A default value represents a commonly occurring value
- A "safe" value guaranteeing that a sensible computation will result
- An "unreasonable" (e.g., out of range) value that causes the method to use some algorithm to compensate for the missing argument value

Examples of common or safe default values are an integer "counter" whose default initial value is zero or a text value whose initial value is blank or null. A variation of the Frame class, in which the default values for the x coordinate, the y coordinate, the height, and the width are -1, illustrate the case of default values that are clearly unreasonable. The Frame constructor when confronted with (some of) these default values uses an internal algorithm to determine what values to use for each defaulted argument. The algorithm may, for example, attempt to minimize the overlap of this window with other windows on the screen.

The rule for specifying default values is that an argument without a default value can not occur after (to the right of) an argument with a default value. The following example illustrates why this rule is needed:

```
class Cube {
public:
     ...
     Resize( int height = 10, int width = 20, int depth);
     ...
};
```

Notice that this violates the rule for default arguments because the argument depth has no default and occurs after width which has a default value. Consider the following code that uses the Resize method:

```
Cube cube;
...
cube.Resize(30, 50);
```

This invocation of Resize could reasonably mean any one of three things:

```
cube.Resize(10, 30, 50);          // uses height default
cube.Resize(30, 20, 50);          // uses width default
cube.Resize(30, 50);              // ERROR - no depth argument
```

This ambiguity is avoided for the benefit of both the compiler and the programmer by the rule given above.

 ## Exercises

1. For the Frame class, write a single constructor with default values that could replace its four overloaded constructors.

2. Can the overloaded Resize method in the Frame class be combined into a single method using default values? Explain.

3. Write a definition for the MoveTo method in the Frame class using default values. Explain and justify the default values you selected.

4. Write a definition for the Resize(int,int) method in the Frame class using default values. Explain and justify the default values you selected.

5. Write a definition for the Resize(float) method in the Frame class using default values. Explain and justify the default values you selected.

6. Is is possible to have both of the following methods in the same class:
   `Resize(int height = 100, int width = 100);`, and
   `Resize();`?

2.6 Basic Input/Output

Stream Operators

Operator overloading is the basis for input and output (I/O) in C++. Overloading is useful for I/O because the same operation (input or output) is being performed, but on different types. This is exactly the situation that operator overloading is meant to address. In C++, there is an overloaded operator that is programmed to handle I/O for each built-in type. Thus, the same operator is used for all types. At compile time the type of the data being input or output determines which of the overloaded operations will be used.

The operator that is overloaded to handle I/O is not an operator with a name like "input" or "output," but is a symbolic operator. The symbolic operator << is used to represent output and the symbolic operator >> is used to represent input. It will be seen later that most of the C++ operators (e.g., +, -, *, /, <, >, =, ==) can be overloaded.

In C++, I/O is based on a stream model. In a stream model the input data is viewed as a continuous stream of data that flows from a source into the sequence of variables presented to the input stream. The type of the variables determines how the input stream is interpreted to provide values for the variables. On output, the values of variables flow into a (logically) continuous stream to the destination. The source (for input) and the destination (for output) may be the user or a file.

Interactive stream I/O is provided by two classes:

```
class istream {...};          // stream input
class ostream {...};          // stream output
```

These classes use elements of the C++ language that have not been covered yet. The study of the C++ I/O classes is taken up later. For now, a minimal understanding of how to use these classes is sufficient.

The standard C++ I/O library includes two predefined variables:

```
istream cin;          // interactive input
ostream cout;          // interactive output
```

These variables are declared in the file "stream.h" that can be included in a program using the include directive:

```
#include <stream.h>
```

Any single built-in type can be output by the << operator as shown in the following example:

```
cout << 10;          // output an integer
cout << 1.234;          // output a float
```

```
cout << 'x';                   // output a character
cout << "Hello World."   // output a string
cout << '\n';                  // output a "newline" character
```

Because output is viewed as a stream, the five statements above can be reduced to the following single line:

```
cout <<  10  << 1.234 << 'x' << "Hello World." << '\n';
```

The values are entered into the output stream in a left-to-right order. For readability, blanks are often inserted into the output stream as in this example:

```
cout << 10 << "   " << 20 << '\n';
```

which inserts two blanks between the 10 and the 20. The newline character ('\n') can be used to end a line of output. As an alternative to the newline character, the standard I/O library defines a symbol "endl" (for "end line") that will also end the current line of output. The above example can thus be rewritten as:

```
cout << 10 << "   " << 20 << endl;
```

using the endl symbol.

Notice that there is no relationship between the number of lines of code that produce output and the number of lines of text that appear in the output. For example, the following three code fragments each output the same two lines of text:

```
(1)   cout << 10;
      cout << endl;
      cout << 20 << endl;

(2)   cout << 10 << endl << 20 << endl;

(3)   cout 10 << endl << 20;
      cout << endl;
```

The values of variables can be output using the stream operators as shown in the following example:

```
int x, y;                 // two integers
char c;                   // a character
char *s = "Hello";        // a string
float z = 1.415;          // a floating point value

x = 100; y = 200;

cout << x << "   " << y << endl << s << z << endl;
```

This produces the output string:

```
100   200
Hello   1.415
```

The output will appear as two lines because the `endl` symbol appeared twice in the output stream.

Interactive input uses the predefined variable "`cin`" and the `>>` operator in a similar manner. For example, the statements

```
int x;

cin >> x;
```

cause an integer value to be read from the standard input and assigned as the value of the variable x. When reading, "whitespace" characters, such as blanks and tabs, are ignored.

A dialogue with the user usually consists of a prompt-response sequence. The program prompts the user to enter data and then reads that data. For example, a program that wants to read two integer values that represent the hour and minute might look like:

```
int hour, minute;

cout << "Enter hour (integer) and minute (integer): " << endl;

cin >> hour >> minute;
```

Input from and output to disk files use a similar strategy. Two additional classes are defined in the standard C++ library:

```
class ifstream {
  private:
    . . .
  public:
    ifstream(char* filename);
                        // name of file to use for input
    . . .
};

class ofstream {
  private:
    . . .
  public:
    ofstream(char* filename);
                        // name of file to use for output
    . . .
};
```

The following example shows how data in files is manipulated using the stream I/O operators:

```
ifstream is("file.dat");
ofstream os("out.dat");
   int x, y;
is >> x >> y;              // reads two integers from file.dat
os << "The sum is:  "; // output heading to out.dat
os << (x + y) << '\n'; // output sum and end line
```

Stream Output to a Window

A variation of the Frame class, named TextFrame, allows stream output to a window. This class presents a very simplified version of the stream I/O model; it is restricted so that only output is possible and that only for the most basic built-in types (int, long, float, double, char, and char*).

A partial definition of the TextFrame class is in Code Sample 2-7. The constructors for a TextFrame are similar to those for a Frame object, as are the MoveTo and Resize methods. Keep in mind that the TextFrame class is not part of the standard C++ library—like the Frame class, it is only part of the materials used here for learning about C++.

The TextFrame class can be used as shown in the code below. This code creates two Frame objects and a TextFrame object. The code outputs to the Text-Frame the name of the Frame object in which each mouse event occurs.

```
Frame window1("Window1", 100,100, 200, 200);
Frame window2("Window2", 400,400, 200, 200);
TextFrame out("Display", 400, 20, 200, 200);

OnStart() {
 window1.DrawText("Click in this window", 20,20);
 window2.DrawText("Click in this window", 20,20);
  out << "Name of window clicked in will appear below" << '\n';
}


OnPaint() {
   window1.DrawText("Click in this window", 20,20);
   window2.DrawText("Click in this window", 20,20);
   out << "Name of window clicked in will appear below" << '\n';
}

  OnMouseEvent(char* frameName, int x, int y, int buttonState) {
   out << name ;
   out << '\';
}

OnTimerEvent() {}
```

Code Sample 2-7 *The TextFrame Class*

```
class TextFrame {
 private:
                 // encapsulated, hidden data
 public:

   TextFrame(char *name, int x, int y, int w, int h);
   TextFrame(char* name, int x, int y);
   TextFrame(char* name);
   TextFrame();

   ~TextFrame();

   void      MoveTo( Location newLocation);
                             // change position
   void      Resize( Shape newShape);
                             // change shape
   void      Resize( float factor);
                             //
   int       IsNamed(char* n);
                             // is this your name?

   ...

};
```

The TextFrame class is useful for displaying textual information to a user and is also convenient for displaying status information during development, testing, and debugging.

String Streams

The stream I/O facilities may be used to transfer formatted data to a character array, or to read formatted data from a character array. Although the stream I/O operators are used, the stream operators in this case only cause the transfer of information between the character array and other variables in memory. The string stream operations do not involve an input or output device or file.

Stream processing using a character array is useful when formatted data (e.g., several integer values) are being passed to an interface that accepts only a single string (a char*) parameter. This occurs, for example, in the Frame class's DrawText method. To display one or more integer values in a Frame using Draw-Text, the integer data must first be converted to a single string. Using the stream output operators on a string stream, the integer data is written into the string stream. The string stream places the data in a character array. The stream output operations maintain an end-of-string character ('\0') after the last character added to the character array. Thus, the character array can then be handled as a normal character array or string. It is also possible to use the stream input operators to read formatted data from a character array.

String stream processing involves two classes that are defined in the standard C++ library:

```
class istrstream {...};
class ostrstream {...};
```

The constructor for a string stream object requires a pointer to the beginning of the character array (or memory buffer) and an integer argument giving the length of the array (or buffer). Once constructed, the stream output operator (<<) can be applied to an ostrstream object and the stream input operator (>>) can be applied to an istrstream object. An example of using string stream processing is shown in the example below, which writes to a character array a simple arithmetic expression to add two integer values. The simple expression is formatted using the output string stream object named "expression" and parsed using an input string stream object named parser.

```
char text[100];

ostrstream expression(text, 100);    // create string stream

expression << 10 << " + " << 20 << endl;

...

istrstream parser(text, 100);

int value1, value2;

char operator;

parser >> value1           // value1   = 10
       >> operator         // operator = '+'
       >> value2;          // value2   = 20
```

Notice that the two string streams are constructed using the "text" character array. It is into this character array that "expression" places its formatted data and from which "parser" reads characters to produce the formatted data requested of it.

Other Methods on Streams

In addition to the stream I/O operators, stream objects also provide methods that may be invoked using the dot operator (.). These methods provide ways to query the status of the stream and to perform operations that are not readily described by an operator notation.

Examples of operators that query the state of the stream are those that test whether the end of an input stream has been reached or whether the last operation performed on a stream has succeeded or failed. These two methods are used in the following code fragment:

```
if (cin.eof()) ...      // at end of standard input stream
if (cin.fail()) ...     // last input operation failed
```

An operation may fail, for example, if the stream was unable to parse the contents of an input stream adequately to produce a value of the required type. For example, if an integer is to be read next from the input stream and the next text in the input stream is "abcd," that cannot be read as an integer value.

Reading an entire string or an entire line of input is also done through methods that use the dot operator, because this operation does not fit the stream operator model (i.e., there is no data type that corresponds to a line of input in C++). The method for reading a string or line of input is named "get" and it has three parameters:

 Exercises

1. a character array into which the data is read
2. the maximum number of characters to be placed in the character array from the input stream (not to exceed one less than the length of the character array)
3. a character which, if encountered in the stream, will terminate the reading

Several details about the get method that help to understand its operation are these:

- An end-of-string character ('\0') is placed in the character array after the last character read from the input stream. This allows the character buffer to be used wherever a null terminated string is needed. Because the end-of-string character takes one space in the character array, the maximum number of characters that can be read from the input stream is one less than the length of the character array.

- The get method will stop reading characters from the stream when either the maximum length is reached or when the special terminating character is encountered, whichever comes first

- The special terminating character is not removed from the stream nor is it placed in the character array.

An example of using the get method to read a line of input is shown in the following example:

```
char line[100];

. . .

cin.get(line, 100, '\n');
```

Notice that the dot operator has been used to apply the get method to the standard input stream object.

 Exercises

1. Write a program that creates a Frame object with all default values. The program should then read location and shape information and a character string from a file named "window.dat." The Frame object should then be moved and resized using the location and shape information read from the file and the character string read from the file written into the Frame object.

2. Mouse Tracker: Write a program that displays in a Frame the current mouse coordinates. The coordinates should be written in the form (x,y)—including the parentheses and comma—at the current mouse location. A string stream must be used to format the string to be written in the Frame.

3. Simplest Timer: Write a program to output to a TextFrame the current value of an integer variable that is incremented and output on each timer event. The TextFrame should initially display a zero.

4. Mouse Reporter: Write a program to output to a TextFrame a line each time the left mouse button is clicked in a Frame object. The line of output should be of the form (x,y)—including the parentheses and comma—where x and y are the coordinates of the mouse event.

5. Mouse Reporter 2: Write a program that extends the Mouse Reporter program by having two Frame objects and the line of output in the TextFrame is of the form name:(x,y) where name is the name of the Frame in which the mouse click occurred and x and y are the coordinates of the mouse event.

6. File Viewer: Write a program that reads a disk file named "viewer.dat" a line at a time and writes each line to a TextFrame.

7. File Scanner: Revise the FileViewer program so that a single line of text from the file is read and written to the TextFrame on each timer event.

2.7 Arrays of Objects

An array of objects, all of whose elements are of the same class, can be declared, just as an array of any built-in type can. Each element of the array is an object of that class. Being able to declare arrays of objects in this way underscores the fact that a class is similar to a type.

Declaring Arrays of Objects

The simplest way to create an array of Frame objects is with the following declaration:

```
Frame windowList[5];       // an array of 5  Frame objects
```

An important aspect of declaring arrays of objects in this way is that all of the objects in the array must be constructed in the same way. It is not possible with this declaration to give each different object in the array a different set of constructor values. Furthermore, since no constructor arguments are given, the class must contain a constructor that has no arguments. Arrays of this form are useful when all of the objects should be constructed in a uniform way or when the "real" constructor information will not be know until sometime during the computation. In the latter case, the array can be declared and the individual objects manipulated when the information is discovered. For example, the user may be asked to supply the name of a file which contains the desired locations and shapes for each of the windowList objects. This information can be read and each array element then moved and resized accordingly.

In other cases, it is desired that each of the objects in an array be specifically and individually constructed at the time the array is declared. This can be done as follows:

```
Frame windowList[5] = {Frame("Window 0",    0, 100, 100, 100),
                       Frame("Window 1",   25, 100, 100, 100),
                       Frame("Window 2",   50, 100, 100, 100),
                       Frame("Window 3",   75, 100, 100, 100),
                       Frame("Window 4",  100, 100, 100, 100)
                      };
```

Each object in the array is constructed using explicitly specified values for each constructor argument. This allows the programmer complete control over the initialization of the objects in the array.

It is not necessary to specify all of the constructor arguments if there are overloaded constructors, as there are for the Frame class. An object in an array can be constructed using any of the constructors. For example, if it was only desired to specify the name and initial location, but not the shape, for each object in the array, then the following declaration would suffice:

```
Frame windowList[5] = {Frame("Window 0",    0, 100),
                       Frame("Window 1",   25, 100),
                       Frame("Window 2",   50, 100),
                       Frame("Window 3",   75, 100),
                       Frame("Window 4",  100, 100)
                      };
```

In this case the overload constructor will determine the shape of each object. It is also possible to use different constructors for each object as shown here:

```
Frame windowList[5] = {Frame("Window 0",    0, 100, 100, 100),
                       Frame("Window 1",   25, 100),
                       Frame("Window 2"),
                       Frame(),
                       Frame("Window 4",  100, 100, 100, 100)
                      };
```

In this version, the first and last objects in the array are constructed by explicitly providing each constructor argument. The constructor for the object named "Window 1" specifies only the location. The constructor for the object named "Window2" specifies only the name. The constructor for the object at subscript position 3 specifies no constructor arguments, allowing all defaults, including the name, to apply.

Manipulating Objects in an Array

An object in an array can be manipulated by a combination of the subscripting operator [ ]—to select which object of the array is to be manipulated—and the dot operator—to apply the operation to the selected object. For example,

```
windowList[3].MoveTo(100, 50);
```

moves the object with subscript 3 to a new position. (Remember that the subscripts begin with 0.)

One of the advantages of working with arrays of objects is that it is easy to program the same operation over all of the objects. For example, a single loop can shrink all of the windows by 10 percent as follows:

```
for (int i = 0; i++; i<5)
    windowList[i].resize(0.9);
```

More complex operations involving the elements in the array are also possible. For example the following loop positions the windows along a diagonal from upper left to lower right, and makes them all of the size:

```
for (int i = 0; i++; i<5) {
    windowList[i].MoveTo(10*i+1, 10*i+1);
    windowList[i].Resize(50, 50);
}
```

 Exercises

1. Do you think it is possible to have a two-dimensional array of objects? Write a small test program to verify your theory.

2. Frame Wave: Write a program that has ten windows. The windows are the same shape and are aligned horizontally with the vertical edges of adjacent windows touching. From left to right, each window has one of the numbers from 1 to 10 written in it. Each "wave" begins with the leftmost window moving up vertically and then back to its original position. This same action is repeated for each window from left to right. Repeat this for a few waves. In this version declare the array so that the constructor with no arguments is used.

3. Modify the "Frame Wave" program so that each object in the array is constructed by giving values for each constructor argument.

4. Modify either version of the "Frame Wave" program so that a new wave begins when the previous wave has reached the middle of the line of windows.

5. Moving Ball: Write a program that has ten windows, all of the same size and arranged in a horizontal or vertical line. The first (leftmost or topmost) window has a circle drawn in it. The circle should move from the current window to the adjacent window. When it reaches the last

(rightmost or bottommost) window, it reappears in the first window. Repeat this process indefinitely.

6. Tic-tac-toe: Write a program with ten windows. Nine windows (the game windows) are arranged in a three by three grid pattern and the tenth window (the restart window) is placed off to one side. Initially all the game windows are empty. When a left mouse click occurs in an empty game window, either an "O" or an "X" will appear beginning with an "O" and alternating thereafter. Make the "O" with a circle and the "X" out of two lines. Clicking in a game window that is not empty has no effect. Clicking in the tenth window causes all of the game windows to become empty.

7. Leap Frog: Write a program that has five windows, all of the same size and with the same y-coordinate. The first window is placed near the left edge of the screen. The second window is placed somewhat to the right of the first window and overlapping the first window; the third window is similarly placed to the right of and overlapping the second window; and so on. On successive iterations the leftmost window is moved so it is somewhat to the right and overlapping the rightmost window. The window just moved is now the new rightmost window. Continue this movement for some number of iterations.

2.8 Scope

The scope of a variable or object refers to that portion of the program where the variable or object is visible (i.e., where it can be manipulated). The objects used in the previous sections have a scope that is identical to the scope of the variable that names the object. The effect of scope on objects is discussed in this section. A different way of creating objects that are affected differently by scope is discussed in Section 2.9.

Scope may be global or local. An object with global scope is declared as a global variable, and can be accessed from anywhere in the program. Global objects are constructed immediately before the program begins execution and are destructed after the program has terminated normally. Objects with local scope are constructed at the site of their declaration and are destructed when control reaches the end of the program unit (function, method, block) that contains the declaration.

Global and local scopes are illustrated in the following example in which the globalWindow object has global scope; it can be accessed from within the function, from within the for loop, and from within the then clause. The functionWindow object has a local scope that is the body of function. Similarly the `loopWindow` object has a scope limited to the for loop and the `ifWindow` object has a local scope limited to the then clause of the if construct.

```
Frame globalWindow;              // global scope

void function() {
    Frame functionWindow;
                                 // start of functionWindow scope
    ...
    for( int i=0; i<10; i++) {
        Frame loopWindow;   // start of loopWindow scope
        ...
            if (i < 5) {
                Frame ifWindow;
                             // start of ifWindow scope
                ...
            }                // end of ifWindow scope
    }                        // end of loopWindow scope
}                            // end of functionWindow scope
```

While objects with global scope exist throughout the execution of the entire program, objects with local scope do not. For example, the functionWindow object is constructed when control enters the function and is destructed when control leaves the function via a return or by encountering the end of the function. Similarly, the loopWindow object is constructed and destructed on each iteration of the loop and the ifWindow is constructed when the then clause is entered and destructed when the end of the then clause is reached.

 Exercises

1. Assume that a program calls function() in the above example two times. How many objects are constructed/destructed throughout the entire execution of the program?

2. Name three other program units that create a distinct scope. For each of the three program units, write a short example similar to the example above showing an object local to that scope.

3. What is a major problem with using global variables? Does this problem also apply to global objects? Explain why or why not.

4. Write a program similar to the function in the example in this section. Execute the program and observe the creation and destruction of the windows as the scopes are entered and exited. Add some detail to the original code so that the windows from different scopes are far apart

on the screen while those in the same scope are near, but not on top of, each other.

2.9 Dynamic Objects

Dynamic objects have lifetimes unbounded by the existence of the scope in which they were created. Thus, objects can be constructed in a function that continue to exist after the function returns; or objects can be created in an if-then construct that exists after the if-then construct has been executed. Dynamic object give the programmer greater flexibility in managing objects. However, the programmer also assumes greater responsibility for insuring that dynamic objects are managed properly. Two problems that can occur with dynamic objects are destructing the object too soon and failing to destruct the objects at all.

A dynamic object is created using a "new" operator that returns a pointer to the newly constructed object and is destructed by a "delete" operator. A pointer variable is used to hold the pointer to the object that is returned by the new operator. The delete operator takes a pointer variable as an operand and destructs the object pointed to by that variable. The following example illustrates how dynamic objects can be created and deleted.

```
Frame *window, *view;        // declaration of pointer variables

window = new Frame("First", 10, 20, 50, 50);
                             // create a new Frame object
view    = new Frame("Second",70, 20, 50, 50);
                             // create a new Frame object

Frame *edit = new Frame ("Editor", 50, 75, 100, 100);
                             // combine declaration of pointer
                             // variable and object construction

Frame *default = new Frame; // use default constructor values
delete window;              // destruct window Frame
delete view;                // destruct view   Frame
delete edit;                // destruct edit   Frame
```

In this example, window and view are declared as variables that point to Frame objects. It is important to realize that this declaration **does not** create two frames; it merely creates two variables that will point to Frame objects that are created sometime in the future. The two Frame objects are then created and the variables "window" and "view" are set pointing to these objects. The declaration of the pointer variable and the construction of the object to which it points can be combined in a single statement as shown with the edit and default. Finally, the three Frame objects are deleted.

Notice the syntax of creating dynamic objects. The name of the class appears immediately after the keyword "new." The constructor arguments, if any, are given in parentheses after the name of the class. When there are no constructor arguments, the parenthesis are omitted as shown in the creation of the default object.

An operation is applied to a dynamic object using the -> operator. This "arrow" operator is two adjacent characters, a minus sign and a greater than symbol. An example of operating on a dynamic object is the following:

```
Frame* display = new Frame ("A Display", 10, 20, 100, 200);
display->MoveTo(50, 50);
display->Resize(200, 200);
```

In this example the display object is moved and resized using the arrow operator to apply the corresponding methods.

Two types of serious errors can occur if dynamic objects are not used properly. These errors are serious in two senses. First, the errors can cause the program to abort or exhibit unpredictable behavior. Second, in real programs, the causes of these errors are among the hardest to find.

The first type of error that can occur with dynamic objects is deleting a dynamic object too soon. The example below shows a situation where a Frame object is pointed to by two different variables, display and view. The shared object is destructed by the "delete display;" statement. The error then occurs when, using the view variable, an attempt is made to operate on the now destructed object.

```
Frame *display = new Frame ("Shared", 10, 20, 100, 100);
Frame *view;

view = display;              // both point to same Frame object

display->MoveTo(50, 50);     // OK - moves shared Frame object
view->Resize(200, 200);      // OK - resizes shared Frame object

delete display;              // delete shared object

view->MoveTo(20, 20);        // ERROR - object already deleted!
```

The best outcome of using already-deleted objects is that the program aborts. In this case, the debugging can usually begin at or very close to the actual point of the error. However, and much worse, the program may continue to execute. The run-time system may not be able to detect that the object is deleted and will proceed to alter the memory previously occupied by the object. The effects of this are unpredictable. Often, some other part of the program will discover that an object has mysteriously been damaged. Finding the source of this problem in a large program is extremely difficult.

The second type of error that can occur with dynamic objects is not deleting a dynamic object that is no longer accessible. This type of error is referred to as a "memory leak" because the pool of available memory appears to be leaking away. In a long-running program (air-traffic control, electronic funds transfer, etc.), sufficient memory can be leaked away so that the program aborts. Severe memory leaks can cause hundreds of megabytes of memory to be leaked.

An example of a memory leak is shown in the example below.

```
Frame *display;

    for (int i=0; i<100; i++) {
       display = new Frame ("Memory Leak", 50, 50, 100, 100);
       // display used but not deleted
    }
```

In this example, 100 Frame objects are created but none of them are deleted though all but the last of these Frame objects are inaccessible because the pointer to them has been overwritten. However, the memory to hold these objects is still allocated. To the run-time system, the program is still using the memory, but the program has lost any means of finding the objects. Thus, the memory is allocated but inaccessible—it has leaked away.

The errors in the two examples immediately above are easily identified because so little code is involved in each example. But imagine a program with tens of classes, hundreds of methods, and thousands of objects, where numerous objects are shared between various parts of the system. In these cases—the really important ones—it is extremely difficult to locate what causes these types of errors.

 Exercises

1. Simple Dialog: Write a program that displays a Frame containing the text "Click Here for Help". When the user clicks the left mouse button in this Frame, a new Frame is dynamically created that contains two lines of text: "Yes Master. You Rang?" and "Click to Dismiss." When the user clicks the left mouse button in the dynamically created Frame, the Frame should be deleted. Analyze your program to determine if there is the potential for a memory leak. You do not have to fix this problem; simply identify it.

2. Rewrite the Corner Tour program using only one dynamic Frame object.

3. Rewrite the Corner Tour program so that a new dynamic Frame object is created at each corner and the object in the previous corner is deleted.

4. Rewrite the Border Walk program using only one dynamic Frame object.

5. Rewrite the Border Walk program so that a new dynamic Frame object is created at each step.

6. Write a program that deliberately accesses a deleted Frame object. How did the program behave?

7. Write a program that leaks Frame objects. How long did the program run before aborting? How did it abort?

8. What is the main difference between the declarations "`Frame display;`" and "`Frame *display;`"?

9. What is the main difference between the declarations "`Frame display[10];`" and "`Frame *display[10];`"?

Using Objects of Different Classes

3.1 Using Objects for Communication

*A*n object-oriented system is an organized group of interacting objects forming associations and aggregations. Each object in the system performs a specialized role and communicates with other objects as needed to perform its role as an individual and as a collaborating member of a larger assembly. The interacting objects may be of different classes or of the same class. When the interacting objects are of different classes, the definition of one class must refer to objects of another class. When the objects are in the same class, the definition of the class must refer to itself in some way.

Objects that interact with one another often use other objects to communicate information among themselves. The object used for the communication is generated by a *sender* object and is made available to a *receiver* object. The communication may be unidirectional (from sender to receiver) or bidirectional (information supplied by the sender is modified by the receiver and returned to the sender). The communication may also be structured so that is short-lived (relevant only during the immediate method invocation) or more prolonged (a shared object is used to allow interaction over an interval of time longer than the immediate method invocation).

There are three ways in which objects can be used to communicate information:

- **by name:** one of the objects is in a scope where its name is visible to the other object. An example of this is an object that is in a global scope and can be manipulated by any other object.

- **by parameter passing:** a method of one class takes an object as one or more of its parameters. In this case the caller plays the role of the sender while the object containing the method being invoked plays the role of the receiver.

- **by return value:** the value returned by a method in one class may be an object. In this case the object whose method is returning the object plays the role of the sender and the object accepting the returned result plays the role of the receiver.

It is primarily the last two techniques, parameter passing and return value, that will be examined in more detail.

A method that receives an object as a parameter or returns an object as its result specifies how that parameter object can be manipulated by the method and how the return result can be manipulated. The specification defines the answer to four important questions about the parameter or result object:

- Is the object copied before being sent or returned?
- Can the receiver of the object modify the object?
- Are any changes made by the receiver visible to the sender of the object?
- What syntax(. or ->) is used to access the object?

Table 3–1 summarizes the various techniques that are used and what answers each provides to these questions.

Table 3–1 Characteristics of Communicated Objects

Technique	Copied	Changeable	Visible	Syntax
by copy	yes	yes	no	.
by reference	no	yes	yes	.
by pointer	no	yes	yes	->
by const reference	no	no	no	.
by const pointer	no	no	no	->

Passing an object by copy (also known as "by value") has this name because a copy of the object is made and the copy is passed to the receiver. Passing an object by copy is appropriate when the sender wants to be sure that any actions taken by the receiver do not change the object from the sender's perspective. This is a safe form of passing information that is meant to be consumed by the receiver. In effect, a unidirectional form of communication is provided via the by copy semantics.

Passing an object by copy is not appropriate in three situations. First, if the passed object is to be shared between the sender and the receiver, passing the object by copy results in the sender and the receiver operating on different copies of an object, not a single, shared object. An example of sharing will be seen below. Second, if the sender wants the receiver to modify the passed object, then the object itself, and not a copy of it, must be passed. Third, very large objects (e.g., a 1-megabyte bitmapped image object) are typically not passed by copy to avoid the overhead in memory usage and copying time. However, these cases must be carefully handled to guard against unintended modifications made by the called code.

Passing objects by reference or by pointer communicates the *identity* of the object being passed instead of a copy of the object. Passing an object by reference or by pointer avoids the cost of copying the object and allows the sender and receiver to share the same object. In the simple form, passing objects by reference or by pointer also allows the sender to observe any changes that the receiver might make in the shared object. Oftentimes, observing these changes is how the communication between the sender and the receiver is achieved. In other cases it is desired that the object be protected against change by the receiver.

The *const reference* and *const pointer* forms of passing an object provide a way to avoid copying the object (as with the simpler by reference and by pointer) without allowing the receiver to change the passed object. The "const" attribute is short for "constant," meaning that the receiver is limited to using only those methods of the const object that are known by the compiler not to change the object. Thus, the receiver can use accessor methods to query or interrogate the object but cannot use mutator methods that change the state of the objects. Methods that are declared as not changing the state of an object are called const methods.

3.2 Communicating Objects by Copy

An object being used for communication can be passed by copy as an input parameter to a method of a receiving object or the object can be the returned result of a method. Both of these cases will be illustrated by refining the interface of the Frame class into a more object-oriented form.

Objects as Input Parameters

The examples that follow make use of two new classes. In the original definition of the Frame class the location and shape of the frame were described by four integer values. Both of these concepts, however, can be captured in classes shown in Code Samples 3-1 and 3-2.

The methods Xcoord, Ycoord in the Location class and Height and Width in the Shape class are often called "accessor" or "query" methods because they

Code Sample 3-1 *The Location Class*

```
class Location {   // Version 1
    private:
        // encapsulated implementation goes here
    public:
        Location(int x, int y); // specific location
        Location(); // default location
    int Xcoord(); // return x-axis coordinate
    int Ycoord(); // return y-axis coordinate
    };
```

Code Sample 3-2 *The Shape Class*

```
class Shape {                                // Version 1
    private:
        // encapsulated implementation goes here
    public:
        Shape(int width, int height);   // specific shape
        Shape();                        // default shape
    int Height();                       // return height
    int Width();                        // return width
    };
```

allow, albeit indirectly, information about the state of the object to accessed or queried.

Objects of these new classes can be declared as follows:

```
Location nearTop(20, 20), nearCenter(500, 500);
Shape    smallSquare(50, 50);
Shape    largeSquare(500, 500);
```

These two classes have two immediate advantages (five more will be seen shortly). First, they capture the concept of location and shape. This is largely what object-oriented programming is about—building classes that capture the concepts of some application. A good class need not be one that has an important-looking interface: the Location and Shape classes are modest ones that cleanly capture a simple, but useful, concept. Second, the declarations above show that named objects can convey useful information to the reader about the intention of the programmer. The name "largeSquare" is more suggestive about the intention to have a window that is large and square than are the two integers 500 and 500 used in a parameter list with two other integers and one or more other values.

The Frame class can now be redefined to use the definitions of Shape and Location as shown in Code Sample 3-3.

Code Sample 3-3 *Frame Class (Version 3)*

```
class Frame {                              // Version 3
    private:
          // encapsulated implementation goes here
    public:
          Frame(char* name, Location p, Shape s);
                              // exact description
          Frame(char* name, Shape s, Location p);
                              // exact description
          Frame(char* name, Location p);
                              // default shape
          Frame(char* name, Shape s);
                              // default location
          Frame(char* name );
                              // name only
          Frame();
                              // all defaults;
    void MoveTo(Location newLocation); // move the window
    void Resize(Shape    newShape);    // change shape
    void Resize(float factor);         // grow/shrink by factor

          ...                          // other methods
};
```

The third advantage of defining the Shape and Location classes is seen in the first two overload constructors. Since Shape and Position are distinguished classes, it is possible to define constructors that take them in either order. This cannot be done when the shape and location information is represented by four integer values. The fourth advantage is seen in the overloaded constructor "Frame(Shape s);" which did not (and could not) exist in the earlier version (version 2) of the Frame class. When the location and shape information is represented as four integers, what does a constructor with only two integers mean? Depending on how the four arguments are ordered it means either that the shape is missing or the location is missing, but it cannot mean both! However, both overloadings are possible by introducing different classes that distinguish the two integers that are the shape from the two integers that are the location.

Frame objects can be created as follows:

```
Frame  smallTop    ("Square Near Top", nearTop,   smallSquare);
Frame  largeCenter ("Big at Middle", nearCenter, largeSquare);
Frame  someWhere   ("Big Somewhere", largeSquare);
Frame  someSize    ("At Middle", nearCenter);
Frame  anyKind     ("Name Only - Rest Defaults");
```

Code Sample 3-4   *Frame Class (Version 3) Continued*

```
class Frame {                                  // Version 3 (continued)
    private:
            ...
    public:
            ...                                // other methods

        void DrawText(char *text, Location loc);
        void DrawLine(Location end1, Location end2);
        void DrawCircle(Location center, int radius);
        void Clear();
        void Clear(Location corner, Shape rectangle);

        ...

};
```

These declarations of Frame objects illustrate the last three advantages of the Shape and Location classes.

The fifth advantage is that the declarations are much more readable with the Shape and Location classes than without. Sixth, the Shape and Location objects (e.g., largeSquare and nearCenter) can be reused, avoiding the additional programming effort of remembering the exact coordinates of the near-to-the-center point. Seventh, by changing the declaration of the Shape and Location objects (e.g., nearTop) the declarations of the Frames will then be adjusted accordingly. It is not necessary to go through the code looking for all the declaration of Frame objects and changing their integer parameters.

The Location and Shape classes have uses beyond those for which they were immediately conceived. Since the Location class captures a reasonably abstract notion—a point in a two-dimensional coordinate system—it may be useful anywhere such a coordinate system appears. For example, just as the Location class helps to record where on the screen a window should be placed it can also be used by other interface items to record where within a window an item should be placed.

The text and graphical items that can be displayed within a Frame also use the concepts of location and shape. For example, the DrawText method specifies that a given text string should be displayed at a given location. Also, the Draw-Line method specifies the endpoints (two locations) of a line segment. These and similar methods of the Frame class can also benefit from the Location and Shape classes as shown in Code Sample 3-4.

Notice that the Clear method uses both the Location and the Shape classes, as this method needs to specify both the placement and dimensions of a rectangular area within the Frame. This illustrates the point made above: The Location and Shape classes are useful wherever a two-dimensional coordinate system is used to specify placement or where rectangular dimensions are required, whether this is information about a Frame on a screen or an item displayed within that Frame.

Returning Objects by Copy: Frame Example (*continued*)

Objects can also be returned as the result of a method's execution. Returning an object, rather than a single primitive type, allows the method to communicate a complex entity as its result. Two examples are given to illustrate how objects are returned by copy. One example uses the Frame class and one example uses two new classes.

The TextSize method in the Frame class should be redefined to return an object as its result. The TextSize method computes the dimensions of the rectangular area occupied by a given text string. This computation depends on the font used by the Frame, the length of the string, and the characters in the string (some characters, like w and m, are wider than other characters, like i and t). The earlier Frame class declared this method as:

```
class Frame {                                // Version 1
    ...
 public:
    ...
    void TextSize (char *msg, int& width, int& height);
    ...
};
```

where the dimensions were returned as two distinct integer values. However, this definition has two problems:

- The method does not clearly capture the responsibility of the TextSize method to return the dimensions of a rectangular area as well as if a Shape object were used to convey this information, and
- The TextSize parameters do not match closely the parameters of other related methods (e.g., the Clear method) in the Frame class.

The following example code that displays and then erases a text string illustrates how the TextSize method does not match the parameters of the Clear method:

```
Frame      display;
int width, height;
char *msg = "Hello World!";
Location msgLocation(50,50);
...
display.DrawText(msg, msgLocation);
```

```
...
display.TextSize(msg, width, height);
Shape msgShape(width, height);
display.Clear(msgLocation, msgShape);
```

Notice that the code writer must explicitly create the msgShape object. This must be done so that the two integer values modified by the TextSize method can be put into the form (a Shape object) that is required by the Clear method.

The TextSize method can be redefined to return a Shape object as follows:

```
class Frame {                        // Version 3 (continued)
...
public:
    ...
    Shape TextSize(char *msg);
    ...
};
```

Notice that this definition more clearly expresses the responsibility of the TextSize method: to compute and return an object (of the Shape class) that describes the dimensions of a rectangular area on the screen.

With this definition of the TextSize method, the earlier example of displaying and then erasing a text string can be written more succinctly as follows:

```
Frame     display;
char *msg = "Hello World!";
Location msgLocation(50,50);
...
display.DrawText(msg, msgLocation);
...
Shape msgShape = display.TextSize(msg);
display.Clear(msgLocation, msgShape);
```

Notice that the returned result of the TextSize class now matches the parameters required by the Clear method. Also notice that the declaration of the msgShape object can be given at the point in the code where the msgShape object is first used. Alternatively, the declaration could be given earlier as in:

```
Shape msgShape;
...
msgShape = display.TextSize(msg);
...
```

Some programmers prefer to place the declaration at the point of first use, particularly if this is the only use of the object, because it helps to improve the readability of the code. Others prefer to place all declarations together at the beginning, particularly if the object is used several times in different places in the code, because this makes it easier to find the declaration of any object by simply looking in this one place. In some cases it is simply a matter of taste or style.

Code Sample 3-5   *The Frame Class (Version 3)*

```
class Frame {            // Version 3
   private:
                         // encapsulated implementation goes here
   public:
         Frame(char* name, Location p, Shape s);
                         // exact description
         Frame(char* name, Shape s, Location p);
                         // exact description
         Frame(char* name, Location p);
                         // default shape
         Frame(char* name, Shape s);
                         // default location
         Frame(char* name );
                         // name only
         Frame();      // all defaults;
   int   IsNamed(char* aName);
                         // is this your name?
   void  MoveTo(Location newLocation);
                         // move the window
   void  Resize(Shape    newShape);
                         // change shape
   void  Resize(float factor);
                         // grow/shrink by factor
   void  DrawText(char *text, Location loc);
                         // display text string
   Shape TextSize(char *msg);
                         // get shape of string
   void  DrawLine(Location p1, Location p2);
                         // draw line segment
   void  DrawCircle(Location center,
                    int radius);
                         // draw circle
   void  Clear();    // erase entire Frame contents
   void  Clear(Location corner,
               Shape rectangle);
                         // erase rectangular area
      ~Frame();
};
```

Revised Frame Class

All of the methods in the Frame class that can take advantage of passing information by copy have been redefined. The individual changes are collected
together in Code Sample 3-5. It should be clear that by using the Location and

Code Sample 3-6 *The File Class*

```
class File {
private:
                            // encapsulated implementation goes here
public:

     File(char* fileName);  // represents file with given name
     File();                // unknown, as yet, file
char* Name();               // reply name of file
int   Exists();            // does file Exist?
void  View();              // scrollable view window
void  Edit(char* editor);  // edit file using "editor"
void  Delete();            // delete from file system (gone!)
     ~File();               // free name
};
```

Shape classes the readability and utility of the Frame class has been significantly improved.

Returning Objects by Copy: File Dialogue Example

The second example of methods returning objects as their results involves a class that represents a disk file, the File class, and three classes that embody different dialog methods for soliciting a file name from a user: FileQuery, FileChooser, and FileNavigator.

The File class captures the notion of a named, viewable body of text stored in the file system. The definition of the class is shown in Code Sample 3-6.

The constructor allows the file to be given a name and the Name method allows that name to be queried. Because a file object may be created and not bound to a name, and to guard against a user entering the name of a non-existent file, the Exists method returns a value indicating whether the file exists in the file system.

The View method opens a window on the screen within which the file is viewable. The user is able to scroll horizontally and vertically through the file, but the file can only be viewed, not changed. The file can be edited using the Edit method that takes as its parameter the name of the editor to be used to perform the editing. The file can be removed from the file system using the Delete method. After the Delete method has executed, the File object still exists, but the file itself does not.

The FileQuery class initiates a dialog with the user. The user is prompted to enter the name of a file. The FileQuery object returns a File object that

Code Sample 3-7 *The File Query Class*

```
class FileQuery {
private:
                             // encapsulated implementation goes here
public:

        FileQuery( char* path, char* filter );
                         // prompt with path and filter
        FileQuery( char* path );
                         // prompt with path default filter
        FileQuery( );   // use all defaults
   File AskUser();       // get file from user via dialogue
   ~FileQuery();
};
```

represents the file named by the user. The FileQuery class is defined in Code Sample 3-7.

The constructors of the FileQuery allow a directory path (e.g., "/home/user") and a pattern for the expected file name. The pattern uses the traditional Unix wild-card symbols. For example, the filter *.*ps* would describe any file with a *.ps* suffix. If not given, the path defaults to the current working directory and the filter defaults to any file (i.e., *).

The FileQuery is very permissive. The path and filter information is provided as hints to the user, but they are not enforced. The user is free to enter any file name. Alternative, more restrictive, and safer methods for soliciting a file name from the user will be explored shortly.

The principle member function of the FileQuery class is the AskUser method. This method returns a File that is associated with the name entered by the user in the dialogue initiated by the AskUser method.

An example of using the File and FileQuery class is the following:

```
FileQuery query("/home/kafura", "*.ps");
File file = query.AskUser();
file.View();
```

In this example, the FileQuery object conducts the interaction with the user and returns a File object that is then presented to the user for viewing.

Objects of a given class may be returned from more than one other class. The FileQuery class defined above is only one way in which a File object may be produced as a result of a dialog with the user. The weakness of the technique used by the FileQuery class is that it relies heavily on the user's memory to recall the name of the file and the user's ability to enter without errors that name.

Code Sample 3-8   *The FileChooser and FileNavigator Classes*

```
class FileChooser {
  private:
                            // encapsulated implementation goes here
  public:

        FileChooser(char* path, char* filter);
                        // search at path with filter
        FileChooser(char* path);
                        // search at path, no filter
        FileChooser();  // search at CWD, no filter
    File AskUser();     // get file via dialogue
        ~FileChooser(); // clean up
  };

class FileNavigator {
  private:
                            // encapsulated implementation goes here
  public:
        FileNavigator(char* path, char* filter);
                        // start at path using filter
        FileNavigator(char* path);
                        // start at path, no filter
        FileNavigator();
                        // start at CWD, no filter
    File AskUser();     // get file via dialogue
        ~FileNavigator();
                        // clean up
  };
```

Two other classes for producing File objects use choosing and navigating techniques. Choosing means that the user is presented a list of files among which exactly one is chosen. Navigating means that the user is able to traverse the file tree in search of the desired file. The two classes below for choosing and navigating use a path name for the directory and a filter.

The FileChooser and FileNavigator classes are defined as shown in Code Sample 3-8.

An important aspect of object-oriented programming is seen in the public interfaces of the three classes FileQuery, FileChooser, and FileNavigator: except for the difference in their names, they all use the same interface. The constructor arguments are the same as in the AskUser method. Each class provides the same functionality to the program, though each achieves its functionality in a distinct way. However, the similarity of these classes does not allow them to be used transparently by the program. Due to the type checking, it is not possible, using the C++ language that we have seen so far, to interchange one with the other without rewriting the source code. We will see later that there are effective ways to organize and manipulate classes that have such similarity.

 Exercises

1. Give at least two other good names that could be used for the Shape class.

2. Give at least two other good names that could be used for the Location class.

3. Give the declarations of at least four Location objects that are on the top and left-hand side of the display.

4. Give the declarations of at least four Shape objects that are thin rectangles that are short or long in length.

5. Give the declarations for at least four Frame objects that use different combinations of the Location and Shape objects defined in the last two questions.

6. Draw a picture of a screen showing how the Frame object declared in question 5 would appear on the screen. Label each Frame in the picture with the name of the object that it represents.

7. Write a program that creates a 200 × 200-size window near the middle of the screen with your complete name displayed near the middle of that window.

8. Write a program that creates a 200 × 200-size window near the middle of the screen with your first name centered at the top of the window and your last name centered at the bottom of the window.

9. Expanding/Contracting Line: Write a program to display a horizontal line of length 200 near the middle of the screen which contracts and expands as follows: Initially, each timer event causes the line to become shorter on both of its ends; the line should appear to be contracting toward its midpoint. The contracting continues until the length of the line is 0 (zero). Each timer event should then cause the line to become longer on each end; it should appear to be expanding outward from its midpoint. Continue this contracting and expanding indefinitely. Experiment with the amount by which the line contracts and expands—pick an amount that "looks right" to you.

10. File Viewer 1: Write a program using the FileQuery class that views a file whose name is selected by the user. Initially the user should see a

window displayed on the screen with the message "Click Here to View a File". When the user clicks in the screen using the left mouse button, a FileQuery object is used to obtain a File which is then made viewable.

11. File Viewer 2: Write a program using the FileChooser class that views a file whose name is selected by the user. Initially the user should see a window displayed on the screen with the message "Click Here to View a File". When the user clicks in the screen using the left mouse button, a FileChooser object is used to obtain a File, which is then made viewable.

12. File Viewer 3: Write a program using the FileNavigator class that views a file whose name is selected by the user. Initially the user should see a window displayed on the screen with the message "Click Here to View a File". When the user clicks in the screen using the left mouse button, a FileNavigator object is used to obtain a File, which is then made viewable.

13. Write a program using the FileChooser class that edits a file whose name is selected by the user.

14. Write a program using the FileNavigator class that edits a file whose name is selected by the user.

15. Write a program using the FileNavigator class that deletes a file whose name is selected by the user.

3.3 Anonymous Objects

In some cases an object is needed only temporarily. Explicitly introducing a variable to name this temporary object can be avoided by creating an *anonymous object*, which is an object in every sense except that it has no name. Consider the following example:

```
Location initialLocation(100, 100),
         displayLocation(200,200);

Shape    initialShape(150, 200),
         displayShape(300, 200);

Frame window  (initialLocation, initialShape);
Frame display (displayLocation, displayShape);

  . . .

Location newLocation(300,300);
```

```
Location newShape    (150,150);

window.MoveTo(newLocation);
display.Resize(newShape);
```

Assume that all of the Location and Shape objects have no other uses than the ones shown in the example.

Using explicitly declared and named objects that are used only once has several disadvantages. First, the programmer has to write a separate declaration and invent a meaningful name for an object that plays a very minor, perhaps trivial role. This effort may not be seen as worthwhile. Second, the object may continue to exist for some time after it has been used even though it is not needed. In the above example, the scope of "initialLocation" and "window" are the same. However, the window object may be needed far longer than the Location object, though both objects will continue to exist. It is a more efficient use of memory to be able to delete the Location object as soon as its useful lifetime has ended. Third, the reader of the code is not given a clear indication that objects such as "initialLocation" and "displayLocation" are, in fact, used in such a localized way. Only by reading all of the code in this scope can it be determined whether those objects are used only once or again later.

Anonymous objects are a more efficient and clearer way to create and use an object that is needed only to be used in a single, localized place. An anonymous object is constructed directly in the place where it is needed.

The example above can be re-written using anonymous objects as follows:

```
Frame window  ( Location(100,100), Shape(150, 200) );
Frame display ( Location(200,200), Shape(300, 200) );
  ...
window.MoveTo( Location(300,300) );
display.Resize( Shape(150,150) );
```

In the construction of the window object, two anonymous objects are created: one anonymous Location object and one anonymous Shape object. The display object is also created using two anonymous objects. Finally, the MoveTo and Resize operations use anonymous objects as well. It is important to realize that the example with named objects and the one with anonymous objects each have exactly the same observable effects.

Anonymous objects are also useful in providing the default value for a parameter that is an object of a class rather than a built-in type. For example, the MoveTo method in the Frame class takes a Location object as its parameter. If a default value was desired for this parameter, it could be specified as follows:

```
class Frame {
 private:
  ...
 public:
  ...
```

```
      void MoveTo (Location loc = Location(10,10));
   ...
 };
```

This definition of the MoveTo method specifies that if the MoveTo method is invoked with no arguments, then the default Location of (10,10) will be used.

Moreover, anonymous objects are used in assigning a new value or updating the value of an object. Suppose that a Frame object named "window", has been created using a Location object, named "current." The Frame is to be shifted by a relative amount (five pixels in each direction) on the screen. What is needed is a way to update the Location object. However, the Location class does not define any mutator methods that allow Location objects to be updated—they can only be constructed and examined. Three different ways of using anonymous objects are shown in the following code examples.

```
// First example

  Location current(100,100);
Frame window  (current);
  ...
window.MoveTo(Location(current.XCoord()+5, current.YCoord()+5) );
```

This first example shows that an anonymous object can be constructed from an existing object. In this case the current Location object is queried using the accessor methods defined in the Location class and the results are used to define the constructor arguments for a new, anonymous Location object.

```
// Second example

Location current(100,100);
Frame window  (current);
  ...
current = Location(105,105);
window.MoveTo( current );
```

In the second example, an anonymous object is created with the new coordinates and is assigned to the object named current. Object assignment is a simple, byte-level copy operation: each object resides in a block of memory. The default assignment operation overwrites the bytes in the block of memory holding the object on the left-hand side of the assignment (current) with the bytes copied from the right-hand side of the assignment. In this sense, default object assignment is exactly similar to the assignment "x = 10" that overwrites the memory holding the value of the variable x with the bit pattern that represents the value 10.

```
// Third example

Location current(100,100);
```

```
Frame window  (current);
    ...
current = Location(current.XCoord()+5, current.YCoord()+5);
window.MoveTo( current );
```

The third example uses an assignment among objects that mirrors the familiar assignment of ordinary variables such as "x = x + 1" where the value of the existing variable is used to compute a value that is then assigned as the new value of the variable. In the same way, the value of the object current is queried, using the accessor methods defined by the Location class, and a value is computed (the anonymous Location object) that is then assigned as the new value of the current object. This example differs from the second example in that it is not necessary to know the absolute coordinates of the new Location—the new value of the Location object is computed relative to the existing value of the object.

Notice that anonymous objects remove the three problems noted above. First, no separate declaration is needed for the anonymous objects. They are simply created at the site of use without the need for an identifier name. Second, the object is constructed only when it is needed and destructed as soon as its immediate use is over. This reduces to a minimum the lifetime of the anonymous object and reduces its resource usage. Third, it is clear to the reader that the anonymous object is not used elsewhere—such other usage being impossible since there is no way to refer to the object.

 ## Exercises

1. Using only anonymous objects, write a declaration for a Frame object that is located at the coordinates (50,50) and has a width of 200 and a height of 300.

2. Using only an anonymous object, write the line of code to move a Frame identified by the variable name "window" to the coordinates (100,100).

3. Using only an anonymous object, write the line of code to resize a Frame identified by the variable name "window" so that it has a width of 200 and a height of 300.

4. Suppose that a Frame object identified by the variable name "window" is currently located at the coordinates given by the Location object identified by the variable name "position." Using an anonymous object, write a single line of code that moves the Frame object 10 pixels to the right and 50 pixels down.

5. Suppose that a Frame object identified by the variable name "window" currently has the dimensions given by the Shape object identified by

the variable name "size." Using an anonymous object, write a single line of code that changes the dimensions of the Frame object to be 50 pixels wider and 50 pixels shorter.

3.4 Communicating Objects by Reference and by Pointer

Three major structures are built using objects communicated by reference or by pointer:

- **result parameters:** to allow the sender to see the changes made to the object by the execution of the receiver's method,
- **managers:** to allow an object of one class to create, distribute, or otherwise manage objects of another class, and
- **associations:** to establish connections among objects that allow the objects to interact beyond the duration of a single method invocation.

All of these uses will be explored in this section. Additional features of associations are presented in the next two sections.

The difference between communicating objects by reference or by pointer is largely syntactic, as they each accomplish the important goal of passing original, not copied, objects. In C++, the ampersand symbol (&) is used to denote communicating an object by reference and the asterisk symbol (*) is used to denote communicating an object by pointer. Remember, though, that these two symbols have several meanings in C++ depending on the context in which they are used, so to indicate communicating objects by reference or by pointer, the symbols "&" and "*" must appear after a class name in a parameter list or in a return type.

Result Parameters

Passing an object as a parameter by reference or by pointer allows the sender to see changes made to the object by the receiver. In some cases the object is used purely in an output form, that is, the object's initial value is not used by the receiver. In other cases the receiver uses the object in an input-output form, that is, the receiver uses the initial value of the parameter object and the receiver possibly changes the object in some way. This latter use will be illustrated below.

A simple information-retrieval example illustrates how objects are passed by reference and by pointer. In this example, a simple text file will be searched for the first line containing a given search string. Various applications can be built on this model, among them:

Code Sample 3-9 *The Query Class*

```
class Query {
 private:
                              // encapsulated implementation
 public:

   Query (char* searchText);
   Query();
   void    SetSearch(char* searchText);
   char*   GetSearch();
   void    AskUser();
   void    SetResult(char* resultText);
   char*   GetResult();
   ~Query();
};
```

- Searching a library catalog file for a given author's name
- Searching a bookmark file for a URL of a given organization
- Searching a phone-book file for the phone number of a given person

Many other examples follow the same basic organization.

The simple information-retrieval example extends the File class by adding a method to search a file object for a given search string.

An information retrieval query is represented by the class shown in Code Sample 3-9.

The Query class contains two text strings, a search string, and a result string, each of which has an associated pair of accessor and mutator methods to set and get the string's value. The two "get" methods return a null pointer if their respective strings are undefined. The AskUser method initiates a dialogue that allows the user to provide a search string. This design anticipates that the sender defines the search string (via the constructor, the SetSearch method, or the AskUser method), that the receiver doing the search defines the result string (via the SetResult method), and that the sender retrieves the result string (via the GetResult method).

The File class is extended by adding a method to search a File object for a given query, modifying the Query object if the search is successful. The additions to the File class are:

```
class File {
 private:

 public:
     ...
    void SearchFor (Query& q);              // by reference
```

```
        void SearchFor (Query* q);                  // by pointer
            ...
    };
```

The specification "Query&" denotes passing a Query object by reference. The specification "Query*" denotes passing a Query object by pointer. In neither case is the Query object copied.

The Query class and the extended File class can be used as shown below. This code also illustrates the syntactic differences between by reference and by pointer objects.

```
    Query query1("object"), query2("oriented");
    Query *query3;
    Query *query4;

    query3 = new Query("programming");
    query3 = new Query("C++");
    File bookList("booklist");
    booklist.SearchFor( query1);             // by reference
    booklist.SearchFor(&query2);             // by pointer
    booklist.SearchFor( query3);             // by pointer
    booklist.SearchFor(*query4);             // by reference

    char* result1 = query1.GetResult();
    char* result2 = query2.GetResult();
    char* result3 = query3->GetResult();
    char* result4 = query4->GetResult();
```

In this example, query1 and query2 are names for objects, while query3 and query4 are pointers to objects. The first use of the SearchFor method, using query1, is by reference because query1 is an object. Passing the query1 object matches with the by reference overloading of the SearchFor method. The second use of the SearchFor method, using query2, is by pointer because the parameter, "&query2" is a pointer. The "&" operator in this context is the "address of" operator. Thus, what is passed is the "address of query2" (i.e., a pointer to the query2 object) which matches the by pointer overloading of the SearchFor method. The third use of the SearchFor method, using query3, is also by pointer because query3 is, by its declaration, a pointer to a Query object. The fourth use of the SearchFor method, using query4, is by reference. While query4 is a pointer to a Query object, the actual parameter is "*query4." The "*" operator is the dereference operator yielding the object that is being pointed to. Thus, the actual parameter is an object. When the actual parameter is an object, it will match with the by reference overloading of the SearchFor method.

Table 3–2 summarizes the syntactic aspects of passing arguments by reference and by pointer. The first line of the table indicates that, moving left to right,

- The receiver declares the formal parameter, named "y" by the receiver, to be a reference to an object of class T
- The sender declares the actual parameter, named "x" by the sender, as an object of the class T
- The sender would invoke the receiver's method using the name of the object, "x"
- The sender accesses the methods of the actual parameter using the "dot" notation
- The receiver accesses the methods of the formal parameter using the "dot" notation.

The first row corresponds to the first use of the SearchFor method using the query1 object in the example code above. The subsequent rows in the table correspond to query2, query3, and query4, respectively.

Table 3–2 By Reference and By Pointer: Matching the Sender and Receiver

Receiver's Declaration	Sender's Declaration	Actual Parameter	Sender Access	Receiver Access
T & y	T x	x	x.f()	y.f()
T* y	T x	&x	x.f()	y->f()
T* y	T *x	x	x->f()	y->f()
T & y	T *x	*x	x->f()	y.f()

Managers

Manager objects commonly return objects by reference or by pointer. In some cases the manager object is responsible for creating and distributing objects of another class. In this role, managers are also called "factory" objects. In other cases the manager object is responsible for maintaining a set of managed objects, organizing them according to some attribute (e.g, alphabetically by a string attribute), or finding a managed object with a certain attribute value (e.g., a given name). In this role, managers are also called "collections." Manager objects are able to simplify a system by concealing the design decisions surrounding the construction, duplication, indexing, storage, and distribution of the managed objects. Other parts of the system are able to use the managed objects with less concern for the low-level management details. To fulfill its role as a manager, pointers and references are essential because

Code Sample 3-10   *Extended File Class*

```
class File {
 private:

 public:
    ...
    fstream&    GetStream();
                    // return stream for this file
    TextWindow* View();
                    // return pointer to window for this file
    ...
};
```

maintaining a collection of copies of the managed objects is usually pointless; it is the original objects that are to be managed.

Two examples are given to illustrate the use of pointers and references in defining managers. The first example extends the File class so that a file object can return a file stream object for the underlying disk file or a text window in which the file can be viewed. In this example, the File object acts as a factory that produces a particular kind of file stream or text window object. The second example, illustrating the concept of a collection, defines a Frame manager that maintains a set of Frame objects. The Frame manager is similar in concept to the "window manager" found on most systems.

File Class Example

The File class is extended to illustrate returning objects by reference and by pointer. One extension of the File class is a new method GetStream() that returns a reference to a file stream object (an object in the class fstream), through which the disk file represented by the File object can be manipulated. The second extension to the File class is a change in the View() method that will make it return a pointer to a TextWindow object. The TextWindow pointed to is the window in which the File object is currently displayed. Returning a pointer to this window allows the program to manipulate the window (i.e., to move it or resize it). The two extensions to the File class are shown in Code Sample 3-10.

The design of the GetStream method allows the File class to make available the full functionality of the stream I/O model without duplicating all of the stream I/O methods in its own interface. For example, the following code uses the extended File class to output to a file selected interactively by the user:

```
FileNavigator nav;
File aFile = nav.AskUser();
```

```
fstream& fileStream = file.GetStream();
fileStream << "add new data to file" << endl;
```

The GetStream method also enables more complicated uses, such as enabling different parts of a system to obtain a reference to the same stream object. This allows different parts of the system to share access to the same underlying disk file. One other advantage of the GetStream method is that the code using the File object need not be aware of the File's name or how the name of the file was obtained.

The redefinition of the View method allows the window containing the contents of the disk file to be manipulated under program control. An example of this usage is shown in the following code:

```
FileNavigator nav;
File aFile = nav.AskUser();

TextWindow* tw = aFile.View();    // present file for viewing,
                                  // return pointer to viewing
                                  // window
tw->MoveTo(Location(10,10));      // move viewing window
tw->Resize(Shape(200,500));       // resize viewing window
```

As illustrated in this code, the View method creates a TextWindow and returns a pointer to this TextWindow. The text contents of the file are viewable in this window. The viewing window is then moved and resized by the program.

Frame Manager Example

A simple FrameManager class will be designed to illustrate how objects can be returned by pointer. The FrameManager is responsible for maintaining a collection of Frame objects and returning that Frame object in the collection with a given name. Recall that the construction of a Frame object allows the object to be given a name. It is this name that is used by the FrameManager to identify a given Frame object among all those currently in the FrameManger's collection. Not considered are small details such as how the Manager behaves if there are two Frame objects with the same name.

The definition of the FrameManager is shown in Code Sample 3-11. The constructor of the FrameManager allows the maximum number of Frames that the manger will have at any one time to be specified. The default value limits the FrameManager to hold at most ten Frame objects at any one time. The Add and Remove methods are both overloaded to allow the argument to be given by either a pointer or a reference to a Frame object. Also, the Remove method has an additional overloading that allows the Frame object to be identified by its name. The FindByName methods returns a pointer to the Frame object whose name matches the input argument of the method; if no such Frame object can be found by the FrameManager, the method returns a null pointer.

Code Sample 3-11   *FrameManager Class*

```
class FrameManager {
private:
public:
        FrameManager(int maxFrames = 10);
  void    Add(Frame& frame);
  void    Add(Frame* frame);
  Frame&  FindByName(char* frameName);
  void    Remove(char* frameName);
  void    Remove(Frame& frame);
  void    Remove(Frame* frame);
        ~FrameManager();
};
```

An example of using the FrameManager is shown in the skeleton code below. In this code, an application has several windows open simultaneously. Whenever a mouse event occurs in one of these windows, the OnMouseEvent function is called and the name of the Frame is passed as the first argument. Within the OnMouseEvent function, it is usually necessary to operate on the Frame object in which the mouse event occurred. The FrameManager provides an easy way to discover the needed Frame object given its name.

```
Frame *dialogWindow;
Frame* drawingWindow;
// .. declare pointers to other windows

FrameManager windowManager(5);

void OnStart()
  { dialogWindow = new Frame("Dialogue",...);
    drawingWindow = new Frame"Drawing",...);
    //... instantiate other windows
    windowManager.Add(dialogueWindow);
    windowManager.Add(drawingWindow);
    //... add other windows to Manager
  }
void OnMouseEvent (char* frameName, int x, int y, int buttonState)
  {  Frame* frame = windowManager.FindByName(frameName));
     if (frame != (Frame*)0          // check for null return value
       {       // process mouse event in frame using frame->
       }
       else { // handle case of frame not known to FrameManager
           }
  }
```

Code Sample 3-12 *The Message Class*

```
class Message {
  private:
                  //encapsulated implementation
  public:

      Message (char *textString, Location whereAt);
      Message (Location whereAt);
void  DisplayIn (Frame&amp;   whichFrame);
void  MoveTo (Location newLocation);
void  setText(char* newText);
char* getText();
void  Clear();
void  Draw ();
      ~Message ();
};
```

As illustrated in the above code, the FrameManager plays a useful role in simplifying the coding of the OnMouseEvent function—a single, simple call to the FrameManager returns the requested frame if it is known by the Frame-Manager.

Associations

A simple association will be created using a newly defined class, the Message class, and the existing Frame class. The Message class is an abstraction of a displayable text string. A Message object knows what text should be written to a Frame and where within the Frame the text should appear. In addition, a Message object will be responsible for erasing its text from the Frame and for updating the Frame when the Message is changed. The definition of the Message class is given in Code Sample 3-12.

Notice that the DisplayIn method passes the parameter object whichFrame by reference; the & symbol following the class name "Frame" indicates the passing by reference.

To make the idea of an association concrete, a portion of the Message class's implementation is examined. The private data of the Message class contains two pointers, one for the text string that the Message object displays and one for the Frame object in which the string will be displayed. The Message also contains a Location object indicating where the text string is to appear within the Frame. The private data of the Message class is declared as:

```
class Message {
  private:
                                      //encapsulated implementation

    char     *msgText;        // display this text string
    Frame    *msgFrame;       // in this Frame
  Location msgLocation;       // at this Location in the Frame

  public:
        . . .
};
```

Avoiding some syntactic details, the code for the DisplayIn method is:

```
DisplayIn (Frame& whichFrame) {
   msgFrame = &whichFrame;
}
```

This method simply takes the address of the whichFrame object and records that address as the value of the Frame pointer msgFrame. To see the effect of this method, consider the following declarations and code:

```
// declaration

   Frame window("Message Test", Location(100,100), Shape(200,200));
   Message greeting("Hello World!", Location(20,20));

// code

      greeting.DisplayIn(window);
```

This code will create an association between the greeting object and the window object that can be pictured as shown in Fig. 3–1. This association is created because the greeting object retains a lasting pointer to the window object. This pointer will remain valid until it is changed by the greeting object (i.e., the DisplayIn method is called to have the Message point to a different Frame object) or the greeting object itself is destroyed.

Associations must be managed carefully to avoid the problems of dangling pointers and memory leaks. The example above with the greeting object and the window object can be used to illustrate these two pitfalls. If the window object is deleted, then the greeting object has a dangling pointer because the greeting object still points to the memory space previously occupied by the now destructed window object. A memory leak occurs when the greeting object is deleted but not the window object. In this case, there may be no way to refer to the window object. Such objects continue to occupy memory but are inaccessible. In long-running programs, memory leaks can cause total system failures.

The association between the Message object and the Frame object is used by the Clear method in the Message class. The code for this method is:

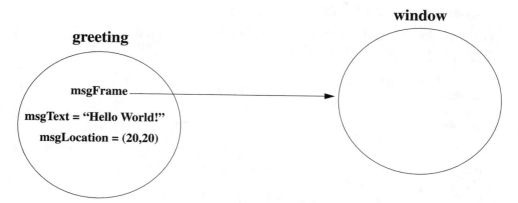

Figure 3–1 A Simple Association

```
Clear() {                         // in Message Class

    Shape msgShape = msgFrame->TextSize(msgText);
    msgFrame->Clear(msgLocation, msgShape);


}
```

This code uses the private data members msgFrame and msgText to obtain from the Frame object the shape of the text displayed by the Message object. The Clear method of the Frame class is then used to erase the rectangular area containing the Message object's text. Note that msgText, msgFrame, and msg-Location are private data members that are part of the Message object. These data members are visible to the methods of the Message object and the data members exist as long as the object itself exists (though the value of these data members may change). The Shape object msgShape, however, is a local object of the Clear method; this object exists only during the execution of the Clear method itself.

Also notice that both the Message class and the Frame class have a Clear() method. There is no confusion about which Clear method is intended in a given invocation because the class of the object to which the method is applied determines which method is executed. For example, the invocation

```
greeting.Clear();
```

invokes the Clear method in the Message class because greeting is an object of the Message class. Similarly, the invocation

```
window.Clear();
```

Code Sample 3-13 *Hello World Using the Message Class*

```
Frame window("Message Test", Location(100,100), Shape(200,200));
Message greeting("Hello World!", Location(20,20));

void OnStart()
{ window.Clear();
  greeting.DisplayIn(window);
  greeting.Draw();
};

void OnMouseEvent(char *frameName, int x, int y, int buttonState)
{ if(buttonState & leftIsDown)
    greeting.MoveTo(Location(x,y));
}

void OnPaint() {
 greeting.Draw();
}
```

invokes the Clear method in the Frame class because window is an object of the Frame class.

A simple association between a Message object and a Frame object is shown in the Hello World example in Code Sample 3-13. In this version, the text "Hello World" can be dragged by the cursor. The Blinking Text example shown in the next section elaborates on the idea of an association.

This version of the Hello World problem is considerably simpler than the one that would result without the Message class. The Message class contains the machinery necessary for a Message object to manage itself more completely. Thus, to move the text on the screen it is only necessary to tell the Message object to move itself—it is not necessary to keep track of this information outside of the Message object.

 Exercises

1. Alternating Text: Write a program that implements a simple association using the Message and Frame classes so that "Hello" and "World!" blink alternately. That is, at any one time, only one of the words is visible.

2. Use the Query class to implement a small information retrieval system that: (1) uses a FileNavigator to get file to search from the user,

(2) gets the search string from the user, and (3) displays in a window the query, the file name, and the result of the query.

3. Revise either of the two Shrinking Window programs created in the Exercises for Section 2.4 (see page 57) so that the window contains two Message objects that display the current height and width of the window. The window should also contain a Message with your full name.

4. Revise the Border Walk program created in the Exercises for Section 2.3 (see page 48) so that the window contains two Messages that display the current location of the window. The window should also contain a Message with your full name.

5. Write a Falling Text program in which a text string moves from the top of the display to the bottom of the display. On reaching the bottom of the display, the text string should reappear at the top of the display.

3.5 A Simple Association

An association is one of the most basic structures in object-oriented systems. An association is a set of independent, interacting, collaborating objects. The objects are independent in that they must be constructed individually; each object has an identity and visibility apart from its role in the association. The objects interact in that the entire purpose of the association is to allow the objects to know about or be connected to each other. In an association an object can use the methods of any other object to which it is connected. Mechanically, passing objects by pointer or by reference is used to create the connections among objects. Finally, the objects are collaborating because they are configured so that they form a system that behaves in some coherent, coordinated manner.

Building systems by association promotes software reuse. If the objects forming the association can be created from existing classes, then the system can be constructed with little additional programming, as the objects are simply instantiated and hooked together to build the system. This method of building systems is often referred to as the plug-and-play technique because the builder simply plugs the objects together and plays with (experiments, validates, evaluates) the system. A well-designed class is one that has the potential to be (re)used in many different associations. Even when developing a class for a specific system, designers of classes often try to anticipate as wide a variety of situations where the class being designed may be useful.

The structure of an association is determined by how the responsibilities of the system are partitioned among the objects forming the association. By changing the mapping of responsibilities to objects, different structures can be derived for systems that achieve the same overall behavior. Creating a design in object-oriented   programming   often   means   determining   the   assignment   of

Code Sample 3-14 *PrimitiveMessage class*

```
class PrimitiveMessage
{
  private:
  public:
          PrimitiveMessage(char *text);
    void  SetText(char* newText);
    char* GetText();
          ~PrimitiveMessage();
};
```

responsibilities to individual objects or classes. Similarly, understanding the behavior of a given class often amounts to understanding what responsibilities that class assumes. Changing the responsibilities of a class can affect the class's implementation, the class's interface, and the ways in which objects of the class interact with other collaborating objects.

A simple example involving two classes will be used to illustrate a system created by association and the effects that altering responsibilities in this system has on the system's structure. While the "system" is trivially small, the concept that is being illustrated is not. The same concept is found, though in different degrees, in larger systems.

The example deals with a very small system—blinking text. The blinking-text problem is simply to display a string of characters that appear to blink. Web pages frequently have such blinking elements, whether text or graphics, to draw attention to themselves. The blinking effect is achieved by alternately displaying and erasing the string of characters from the screen. The time between these two actions determines whether the string blinks rapidly or slowly.

Three variations of this simple system are presented and discussed. In successive variations of the simple system, the class that represents the blinking-text abstraction is given successively more responsibility. The effect of this on the interface of the class and the other elements of the system is observed.

Step 1: Minimal Responsibility

A first solution to this problem, seen in Code Sample 3-14, assigns extremely little responsibility to the PrimitiveMessage class. This class is an abstraction of the blinking text, capturing only the text aspect of the blinking text. The PrimitiveMessage class is only responsible for remembering the text. The text of the PrimitiveMessage must be given on construction and can be retrieved, via Get-Text, or altered, via SetText.

The complete code necessary to display a blinking "Hello World!" text string is shown in Code Sample 3-15. There is clearly some repetition in this code that

Code Sample 3-15 *Blinking Text Using PrimitiveMessage Class*

```
Frame window("Blinking Text", Location(100,100), Shape(200,200));
PrimitiveMessage greeting("Hello World!");
Location greetingLocation(20, 50);
int onoff;              // is text visible: yes=1, no=0

void OnStart()
{ window.Clear();
  window.DrawText(greeting.GetText(), greetingLocation);
  onoff = 1;
}

void OnTimerEvent()
{ if (onoff == 1) // text is visible
  { Shape greetingShape = window.TextShape(greeting.GetText());
    window.Clear(greetingLocation, greetingShape);
    onoff = 0;
  }
  else             // text is not visible
  { window.DrawText(greeting.GetText(), greetingLocation);
    onoff = 1;
  }
}

void OnPaint()
{ if (onoff == 1) // text is visible
    window.DrawText(greeting.GetText(), greetingLocation);
}
```

comes from keeping track of the information about each of the two strings; it arises from the lack of responsibility assumed by the PrimitiveMessage class. The responsibilities of each party are analyzed below.

There are three participants in the Blinking Text system shown in Code Sample 3-15: the PrimitiveMessage objects, the Frame object, and the simple programming environment functions (OnStart, OnTimerEvent, OnPaint). The responsibilities of these three participants is shown in Table 3–3. In examining these responsibilities it might be concluded that the simple programming environment functions are bearing too much of the responsibilities of the system, whereas the PrimitiveMessage objects are bearing too little. It certainly makes sense to argue that the PrimitiveMessage object might reasonably be charged with keeping track of more of the information specifically related to its text and performing more of the actions specifically related to the management of its text.

Table 3–3

Participant	Responsibility
PrimitiveMessage objects	text to display
Frame object	draw/erase given text at given location
simple programming environment functions	when to draw/erase text location/shape of text state of text (visible) Frame in which to display text

Step 2: More Responsibility

The responsibilities of the class that represents the blinking-text abstraction are increased so that the information and processing directly associated with the text are made part of the class. The class would then be responsible for maintaining the Location and Shape information for the text string and for clearing and drawing the text itself, all responsibilities that are closely connected with the text. One implication of this change is that the class must have access to a Frame object in order to (1) be able to draw and clear itself from this Frame object, and (2) to determine the Shape of the text, as this must be obtained from a Frame object using the Frame class's TextShape method. The revised set of responsibilities are shown in Table 3–4.

Table 3–4

Participant	Responsibility
Message object	text to display location/shape of text Frame in which to display text
Frame object	draw/erase given text at given location
simple programming environment functions	when to draw/erase text state of text (visible)

Adding these responsibilities changes the interface of the class to that of the Message class developed earlier and shown in Code Sample 3-16. The DisplayIn method in the Message class interface allows an association with a

Code Sample 3-16 *The Message Class*

```
class Message {
  private:
                  //encapsulated implementation
  public:

      Message (char *textString, Location whereAt);
      Message (Location whereAt);
void  DisplayIn (Frame&  whichFrame);
void  MoveTo (Location newLocation);
void  SetText(char* newText);
char* GetText();
void  Clear();
void  Draw ();
      ~Message ();
};
```

Frame class object. It is in this Frame object that the Message object will display itself and from which the Message object can discover the Shape of its current text. Because the Message class assumes responsibility for managing its Location, a method to change this Location is also part of the Message class interface.

Notice that the DisplayIn method passes the parameter object whichFrame by reference; the & symbol following the class name "Frame" indicates the passing by reference.

The complete system for the blinking-text problem using the Message class is shown in Code Sample 3-17. Because of the changes in responsibilities, the Message class assumes more of the responsibilities for its own self-management. As a result, the code for the OnTimerEvent() and OnPaint() methods are simplified.

This version of the Blinking Text system is considerably simpler than the one that would result without the Message class. The Message class contains the machinery necessary for a Message object to manage itself more completely. Thus, to erase the text from the screen it is necessary only to tell the Message object to Clear itself—it is not necessary to manipulate the Frame object directly.

Step 3: Complete Responsibility

A more ambitious design might invest even more responsibility in the blinking-text abstraction. Notice that in the Message class design, the simple programming environment functions were responsible for remembering the state of the text (i.e., whether the text was visible of not). If this responsibility were shifted to the blinking text class itself, then the interface of the revised class, now named the BlinkingMessage class, would be as shown in Code Sample 3-18.

Code Sample 3-17   *The Blinking Text Using the Message Class*

```
Frame window("Message Test", Location(100,100), Shape(200,200));
Message greeting("Hello World",  Location(20, 50));
int onoff;

void OnStart()
{ window.Clear()
  greeting.DisplayIn(window);
  greeting.Draw();
  onoff = 1;
};

void OnTimerEvent()
{ if onoff){greeting.Clear(); onoff = 0; }
  else      {greeting.Draw();  onoff = 1; }
}

void OnPaint()
{ if (onoff) greeting.Draw();
}
```

Code Sample 3-18   *BlinkingMessage Class*

```
class BlinkingMessage {
  private:
                    //encapsulated implementation
  public:

      BlinkingMessage (char *textString, Location whereAt);
      BlinkingMessage (Location whereAt);
void  DisplayIn (Frame&   whichFrame);
void  MoveTo (Location newLocation);
void  SetText(char* newText);
char* GetText();
void  Blink();
void  Redraw();
    ~BlinkingMessage();
};
```

Notice that in the BlinkingMessage class the Draw() and Clear() methods have been replaced by a single method, Blink(). This replacement is in keeping with the notion that the objects of this class, not the users of those objects, are responsible for determining if the text is to be drawn or cleared. Also notice that

Code Sample 3-19 *Blinking Text Problem Using BlinkingMessage Class*

```
Frame window("Message Test", Location(100,100), Shape(200,200));
BlinkingMessage greeting("Hello World", Location(20,50));

void OnStart()
{ window.Clear()
  greeting.DisplayIn(window);
  greeting.Blink();
};

void OnTimerEvent()
{ greeting.Blink();
}

void OnPaint()
{ greeting.Redraw();
}
```

a Redraw() method has been added to account for the need to be able to redisplay the BlinkingText without knowing whether or not the text is visible. The need for the Redraw() method can been seen in the OnPaint() method shown in Code Sample 3-19.

The third, and final, version of the Blinking Text system is shown in Code Sample 3-19 using the BlinkingMessage class. Because the BlinkingMessage class assumed the responsibility for keeping track of its own state, the "onoff" variable is no longer needed.

Comparing the Three Alternatives

The classes developed for the three versions of the blinking-text problem illustrate the difficulty of evaluating the trade-off between the functionality of these classes and their reusability. The examples would seem to show that the BlinkingMessage class is the best because it allows the blinking-text problem to be solved in the most natural manner. However, a disadvantage of the BlinkingMessage class is that it is appropriate only when the text is fixed and blinking. If the text is varying or need not blink, then the functionality provided by the BlinkingMessage class is inappropriate. In other words, the BlinkingMessage class has sacrificed some degree of generality for an additional degree of ease in solving a particular problem. From this point of view, the BlinkingMessage class is an over-specialization. Overly specialized classes tend to work well when they are an exact match for the problem at hand but are not likely to be (re)used in problems that are close to, but not exactly, the one for which it was designed. From this point of view, the Message class strikes a better balance because it has an interface that can be used in more varied problems, though it may not be an ideal match to any one of them. In other words, the Message class has improved its reusability by limiting its specialization. This is not to say that the Message class is always to be preferred to the BlinkingMessage class—if one is solving a problem that contains repeated uses of the abstraction of blinking text then the BlinkingMessage class should clearly be used. Finally, although the PrimitiveMessage class appears to be to the weakest of the three alternatives, in situations where a line of text needs to be stored without any need for displaying it in a window, then both the BlinkingText and the Message class are disadvantageous because they contain unneeded functionality. In these cases, the PrimitiveMessage class may be preferable. The point of this evaluation is that many factors complicate the design process and the "best" design is often very difficult to determine.

These three classes, PrimitiveMessage, Message, and BlinkingMessage, suggest that a concept more powerful than association is needed. Why should a designer be forced to choose only one of these three possibilities? Why is it not possible to make the entire spectrum of possible choices available? This would be particularly desirable because, in some sense, the Message class is a specialization of the PrimitiveMessage class and the BlinkingMessage class is a specialization of the Message class. These questions can be answered by using the concept of hierarchy to develop a related set of classes.

Associations with Simple Counters and Timers

Several new classes will be introduced to illustrate building systems by association. These classes are a simple incrementing or decrementing counter, several kinds of buttons, and a simple timer. Though these classes are simple, they can be configured to form a number of interesting systems. The classes are also very specialized because only a part of the C++ language is being used to define them. Techniques that will be learned later can be used to extend the generality of these classes.

Simple systems of three or four objects will be built that count discrete events, either individual user interface actions or ticks of a timer. The existing Message and Frame classes will be used. In addition two new classes, Counter and Timer, will be defined and composed together in an association to form a small system. More complex examples are considered later.

The class Counter models a simple integer counter that can count upward or downward depending on how it is constructed. The Counter displays its current value in a Message, and if the Message object is itself displayed in a Frame object, the value of the Counter object will appear on the display. The Reset method allows the Counter object to be returned to its original state. The Counter class definition is shown in Code Sample 3-20.

In the first constructor, the Counter counts upwards by one if "start" is less than "stop," and it counts downward by one otherwise. The second constructor defines a counter that counts upward by one without bound. The current value of the Counter is displayed in the Message object specified in the ConnectTo

Code Sample 3-20 *The Counter Class*

```
class Counter {

  private:
                        // encapsulated implementation goes here
    public:
      Counter (int start, int end);
                        // count up/down from start to end
      Counter();        // count upwards from zero
    void Next();        // increment/decrement by 1
    void Reset();       // reset to original state
    void Reset(int nowThis);
                        // reset to specified value
    void ConnectTo(Message& msg);
                        // show current value here
      ~Counter();       // destructor
};
```

method. The current value of the Counter is incremented or decremented by the Next method. Whenever the value of the Counter is changed by the Next method, the Message object, if any, to which the Counter object is connect is updated accordingly using the Message object's ChangeMessage method. The Reset method causes the Counter object to be restored to its initial state.

A simple system that counts left-mouse-click events is shown in the code below. This system uses a Counter to record the number of left-mouse-click events, a TextBox object to display the Counter object's current value, and a Frame object to make this display visible to the user.

```
Frame window("Counter", Location(100,100), Shape (200,200));
TextBox countDisplay("", Location(10,10));
Counter clickCount;

void OnStart() {
  countDisplay.DisplayIn(window);
  clickCount.ConnectTo(countDisplay);
}

void OnPaint() {
  countDisplay.Draw();
}
```

Code Sample 3-21 *The Clock Class*

```
class Clock {
  private:
          // encapsulated implementation goes here
  public:
        Clock (int interval);
            // milliseconds between "ticks"
    void ConnectTo(Counter &amp; count);
            // change count on each "tick"
    void Start();                        // (re)start Clock
    void Stop();                         // halt Clock
  };
```

```
void OnTimerEvent() {}

void OnMouseEvent() {(char *frameName, int x, int y, int buttonState) {
   if (buttonState & leftButtonDown) {
      clickCount.Next();
   }
}
```

There are two significant things to observe in this example:

- The OnStart function plugs the parts of the system together. The Message object is associated with the Frame object and the Counter object is associated with the Message object.

- The OnMouseEvent has little processing to do: it simply informs the Counter object to performs its Next method whenever a left mouse click is detected.

When the Next event in the Counter object is called, a series of actions is triggered among the parts of the system so that the Counter object's internal count is incremented, its corresponding Message representation is changed, and the Message object changes what is being displayed in the Frame object visible to the user.

The Clock class is an abstraction of the system's interval timer. The Clock class increments a Counter at fixed intervals of time. The resolution of the Clock (i.e., the timer's interval) is set on construction. The Clock can be started and stopped. The definition of the Clock class is shown in Code Sample 3-21.

The constructor specifies the interval of time, in milliseconds, between successive clock "ticks." On each tick of the clock, the Clock calls the Next method in the Counter to which the Clock is connected. The connection between the Clock and a Counter is established by the ConnectTo method. The Start and Stop methods can be used to control the Clock.

An example of how a Clock and a Counter can be used to build a simple timer system is the following:

```
Frame    window ("Timer", Location(100,100), Shape(200,200));
Message  label("Seconds:", Location(10,10));
Message  display("", Location(100,10));
Counter  seconds;
Clock    timer(1000);

void OnStart() {
timer.ConnectTo(seconds);
second.ConnectTo(display);
display.DisplayIn(window);
timer.Start();
}

void OnPaint() {
  display.Draw();
}

void OnTimerEvent() {}

voidOnMouseEvent() {char *frameName, int x, int y, intbuttonState) {}
```

This examples creates a one-second Clock connected to a Counter that counts upward from 0 (zero). The value of the Counter is presented in a Message labeled "Seconds" that is visible in the window Frame.

Exercises

1. Using the Counter, Message, and Frame classes write, a program that counts left-mouse-button clicks and resets its count when a right-mouse-button click occurs.

2. Using the Counter, Message, and Frame classes write a program that has two counters, one that displays a count of left-mouse-button clicks and one that displays the number of right-mouse-button clicks. Use Message objects to label the counts that appear on the display.

3. Using the Counter, Message, and Frame classes write a program that implements a simple timer. Use the OnTimerEvent function to update the Counter object.

4. Using the Counter, Message, and Frame classes write a program that implements a simple timer. Use the OnTimerEvent function to update the Counter object. Use a left-mouse-button click to control whether the OnTimerEvent updates the Counter object. The first left-mouse-button click starts the timing (subsequent OnTimerEvent function calls update the Counter object by using the Counter object's Next method). The second left-mouse-button click stops the timing. Thereafter, alternate left-mouse-button clicks start and stop the timing.

5. Using the Clock, Counter, Message, and Frame classes write a program that displays elapsed time in two granularities using two Messages. One Message displays the value of a Counter that is incremented each second. The second message displays the value of a Counter object that is incremented each one-tenth of a second. Use two other Messages to identify the two changing values as "1 Second" and "1/10 Second." Use two different Clock objects.

3.6 More Complex Associations

Realistic object-oriented systems involve associations among numerous objects from a variety of classes. Commercial software systems might use many tens of classes and hundreds or thousands of objects. The examples involved here do not approach that scale. However, several additional classes will be introduced that use the same techniques and illustrate how such complex and realistic systems are structured.

A more realistic version of the Frame class employing association will be devised. Association is necessary because the interface of the Frame class would become unbearably complex if all of the rich functionality of a window were captured directly and exclusively in this one interface. For example, only two shapes are currently drawable (a line and a circle). But many more shapes are commonly available, including ovals, rectangles, splines, and polygons, in addition to a variety of properties that can be defined for each shape, such as its color, line thickness, line pattern, fill pattern. Clearly, attempting to control all of these details through the Frame interface alone would create an extremely long and complex interface. Furthermore, the Frame class also needs to be extended to include a wide range of interactive elements through which the user can manipulate the user interface. These interactive elements include buttons, editable text, sliders, check boxes, scrollable lists, radio buttons, and others. Even the

Code Sample 3-22   *The Frame Class (Version 4)*

```
class Frame {                                    // Version 4
   private:
         // encapsulated implementation goes here
   public:
         Frame(char* name, Location p, Shape s);
                                          // exact description
         Frame(char* name, Shape s, Location p);
                                          // exact description
         Frame(char* name, Location p);
                                          // default shape
         Frame(char* name, Shape s);
                                          // default location
         Frame(char* name );              // name only
         Frame();                         // all defaults;
   int   IsNamed(char* aName);            // is this your name?
   void  MoveTo(Location newLocation);    // move the window
   void  Resize(Shape    newShape);       // change shape
   void  Resize(float factor);            // grow/shrink by factor
         ~Frame();
};
```

addition to the Frame class of one or two methods for each of these interactive elements is clearly a step toward a large, unruly interface.

The responsibilities for the graphical and interactive elements of a window will be partitioned among three associated classes:

- **Frame:** a rectangular area on the display screen that may be moved and resized.
- **Canvas:** an area within a Frame for drawing text and graphics and responding to mouse movements
- **Panel:** an area within a Frame that contains interactive elements.

The Frame class is simplified so that it retains only those responsibilities not assigned to the Canvas and Panel classes. The Canvas class assumes the responsibilities for all drawing functions. Mouse events with a Canvas area are now associated with the Canvas and not the Frame. The Panel class assumes all responsibilities for managing interactive elements.

The definition for the revised Frame class and the new Canvas are shown in Code Sample 3-22 and Code Sample 3-23. The Panel class will be presented next.

Notice that all of the methods related to drawing (e.g., DrawText, Draw-Line) have been removed from the Frame class, as the drawing methods are to be

Code Sample 3-23   *The Canvas Class*

```
class Canvas {
    private:
          // encapsulated implementation goes here
    public:
          Canvas(Frame& fr, char* nm, Location loc, Shape sh);
    int   IsNamed(char* aName);    // is this your name?
    void  DrawText(char *text, Location loc);
                                   // display text string
    Shape TextSize(char *msg);     // get shape of string
    void  DrawLine(Location p1, Location p2);
                                   // draw line segment
    void  DrawCircle(Location center,
                     int radius); // draw circle
    void  Clear();
                                   // erase entire Frame contents
    void  Clear(Location corner,
                Shape rectangle); // erase rectangular area
          ~Frame();
    };
```

placed in the newly defined Canvas class. The methods that remain in the Frame class are those that specifically pertain to the definition and management of the Frame itself. In this way, the Frame class presents an abstraction of a bordered area on the user's display that can, under program control, be changed in position and shape. The contents of the Frame are defined by what other classes (like the Canvas and Panel classes) add to the Frame.

Notice that the methods for drawing text and graphical shapes have been moved to the Canvas class. Also notice that a Canvas object can only be constructed by associating it with a single Frame. Thus, it is not possible to have a Canvas object that is in two different Frames, nor is it possible to create a Canvas object that is not associated with a Frame.

The association between a Canvas object and a Frame object is established by the Canvas's constructor. By contrast, other examples have shown that the association between two objects can be created by a method other than a constructor (e.g., the ConnectTo methods in the Counter and Clock classes). The constructor can be used to establish a static association (one that is created when the Canvas object is created and one which does not change during the lifetime of the Canvas object). In other cases, the associations may be more dynamic. For example, a given Message object can be displayed in different Frames at different points in time during the Message object's lifetime. Dynamic associations are more naturally expressed as non-constructor methods so that these methods can be called during the lifetime of the object to change the association.

Code Sample 3-24 *The Panel Class*

```
class Panel {
 private:
        // hidden data
 public:
   Panel(Frame& fr, char *nm, Location loc, Shape sh);
   char* getName();
   void Add(Button& button);
   void Add(TextBox& tbox);
   ~Panel();
};
```

Three additional classes defining interactive control elements are introduced. By using objects of these new classes, a more interactive user interface can be created. These three classes are:

- **Panel**: mentioned earlier, it is an area within a Frame that contains interactive elements, like Button and TextBox objects.
- **Button**: captures the abstraction of a simple, pushable, named button that the user can "push" by clicking within the boundary of the button's displayed image. The button is displayed as a rectangle containing the button's name.
- **TextBox:** provides a mechanism for the user to edit a passage of text that may be read subsequently by the program.

Together, these three classes provide basic controls for the user to enter data and trigger actions to be taken by the program.

The definition of the Panel class is given in Code Sample 3-24. As in the Canvas class, the constructor for a Panel object takes a Frame object as a parameter. The location and shape of the Panel in the Frame with which it is associated is also required by the constructor. The overloaded Add method allows any number of Buttons and TextBoxes to appear in the Panel.

The Button class is defined in Code Sample 3-25. The Button class constructor requires that the name of the Button object be defined. This name is used in two ways. First, the name will appear on the user's display as the label on the Button's graphical representation. Thus, a Button object named "Start" will appear as a bordered rectangular box on the screen surrounding the word Start. Second, when the user "pushes" the Button (i.e., the user clicks within the bordered rectangular box corresponding to the Button) the function OnPush(char*) is called, where the name of the Button is passed as the argument. The OnPush(char*) function is a new function that is being added to the simple programming environment. Thus, it is possible for the programmer to determine which of several Buttons the user has pressed by using the argument to the OnPush function and the Button object's IsNamed method.

Code Sample 3-25 *The Button Class*

```
class Button {
 private:
                  // hidden implementation
 public:
   Button(char* name, Location loc, Shape sh);
   int IsNamed(char* name);
 ~Button();
 };
```

Code Sample 3-26 *The TextBox Class*

```
class TextBox {
private:
                  // hidden implementation
public:
       TextBox( Location p, Shape s, char* label);
       TextBox( Location p, Shape s);
       TextBox( char* label);
       TextBox();
      ~TextBox();
  char* GetText();
  void  SetText(char* val);
};
```

The TextBox class, given in Code Sample 3-26, allows the user to edit and/
or enter data. Each TextBox appears to the user as a bordered rectangular area
in which a typing cursor will appear when the mouse cursor is moved within the
TextBox area. When this cursor is visible, the user may edit, erase, or add to any
text that is visible in the TextBox. The TextBox will scroll long lines of text so
that only a portion of the text may be visible at any one time. The current value
of the TextBox may be set or queried by the program using the TextBox's methods SetText and GetText.

The TextBox is optionally constructed with a label which will appear to the
left of the TextBox on the screen. The Shape of the TextBox must be wide enough
to accommodate both the label and the length of the string that the user is
expected to enter.

A small system that uses all of the new classes is shown in Code Sample 3-27.
This system presents the user with a TextBox in which the user can enter a string
and, when a button labelled Copy is pressed, the current contents of the TextBox are
read by the program and written to a Canvas area. Notice that the Button and the
TextBox are contained within (associated with) a Panel and that both the Panel and
the Canvas are contained within (associated with) a Frame object. Also notice that

Code Sample 3-27 *An Example System*

```
Frame    window ("TestWindow", Location(100,100), Shape(500, 300));
Canvas canvas (window, "DrawAreas", Location(1, 1), Shape(100, 100));
Panel panel (window, "Controls", Location(150, 10), Shape(300, 100));
Button   button ("Copy", Location(5, 5), Shape(50,30));
TextBox tbox    (Location(5,50), Shape(150,30), "Enter:");
char     *text;

void OnStart()           // called once when "Start" button pushed
{  canvas.Clear();
   panel.Add(button);
   panel.Add(tbox);
   text = (char*)0;
}

void OnPush(char *buttonLabel)
{  if (button.IsNamed(buttonLabel))
   {   canvas.Clear();
       canvas.DrawText(tbox.GetText(), Location(20, 20));
       text = copystring(buttonLabel);
   }
}

void OnPaint()
{  canvas.DrawText(text, Location(20,20));
}
```

the OnPush method uses the IsNamed method of the Button class to test the identity of the Button object that was pushed.

The Clock class can be extended to improve the Clock class's usability. The programmer may want to make use of several different Clocks (e.g., to time different events, to have different time intervals) and the programmer needs the flexibility of defining what actions should take place whenever a Clock causes a timer event. To allow for this flexibility, the Clock class is extended as shown in Code Sample 3-28. Each Clock object is constructed with a name that may be used to uniquely identify the Clock. The Clock's interval may be given on construction or, whenever the Clock is stopped, by the SetInterval method. The Clock can be controlled by its Start and Stop methods. Finally, similar to a Button object, a Clock object has an IsNamed method that tests the name of the object against the character string passed as an argument. Notice that, as in the earlier definition, the Clock may be connected to a Counter object. At the end of each time interval, a Clock object will either call the Next() method of a Counter

Code Sample 3-28 *Revised Clock Class*

```
class Clock {
private:
                // hidden implementation
public:
  Clock (char* name, int interval=1000);
  void SetInterval(int newInterval);
  void Start();
  void Stop();
  int  IsNamed(char* name);
  void ConnectTo(Counter& count);
  ~Clock();
};
```

Code Sample 3-29 *The Modified Message Class*

```
class Message {
private:
                //encapsulated implementation
public:

    ...
    void  DisplayIn (Canvas&   whichCanvas);
    ...
};
```

object to which it is connected or, if it is not connected to a Counter object, it will call the OnTimerEvent() function as described below.

An extension of simple programming environment allows the programmer to define what action to take when a given Clock generates a timer event. The OnTimerEvent function is redefined to take a character string argument that is the name of the Clock which generated the timer event.

Due to the changes in the Frame class, the Message class must also be slightly modified. A Message object is no longer displayed directly in a Frame; instead it is displayed in a Canvas. This small change is shown in Code Sample 3-29.

The use of a Clock object, an object of the modified Message class, and the modified OnTimerEvent function is shown in Code Sample 3–30. This program is a revised version of the Blinking Text Hello World program. In this program a Clock object is used to control the blinking of the text contained in a Message object. The Clock's interval is defined in the constructor to be 500 milliseconds. The Clock is started in the OnStart method and its timer events are responded to by the OnTimerEvent method that tests the name passed as argument against the name of the Clock object.

Code Sample 3–30 *An Example Using Clocks*

```
Frame   window  ("Message Test", Location(100,100), Shape(200,200));
Canvas canvas (window, "Message Area", Location(10,10), Shape(180,180));
Message greeting ("Hello World!", Location(20,20));
Clock   timer     ("timer", 500);
int      onoff;

void OnStart()
{  greeting.DisplayIn(canvas);
   greeting.Draw();
   onoff = 1;
   timer.Start();
};

void OnTimerEvent(char* clockName)
{
   if( timer.IsNamed(clockName) )
   {   if (onoff) { greeting.Clear(); onoff = 0; }
       else        { greeting.Draw();  onoff = 1; }
   }
}

void OnPaint()
{ if (onoff) greeting.Draw();
}
```

 Exercises

1. Using the Counter, Message, and Frame classes, write a program that implements a simple timer. Use the OnTimerEvent function to update the Counter object. Use a left mouse button click to control whether the OnTimerEvent updates the Counter object. The first left mouse button click "starts" the timing (subsequent OnTimerEvent function calls update the Counter object by using the Counter object's Next method). The second left mouse button click "stops" the timing. Thereafter, alternate left mouse button clicks start and stop the timing.

2. Button Timer. Using the Clock, Counter, Message, Button, and Frame classes write a program that implements a one button, simple timer. Use a Clock object to trigger the call to the OnTimerEvent function that will update the Counter object. Use a Button object, labelled "Control", to control whether the OnTimerEvent updates the Counter

object. Pushing the Button for the first time "starts" the timing (subsequent OnTimerEvent function calls update the Counter object by using the Counter object's Next method). Pushing the Button a second time "stops" the timing. Thereafter, pushing the Button alternately starts and stops the timing.

3. Construct a system that displays three Messages, with each Message displaying the value of a different Counter. The Counter in "Tens" should be incremented once for every ten times the counter in "Units" is incremented; similarly for "Hundreds" and "Tens." Use three other Messages to identify the three changing values as "Units," "Tens," and "Hundreds."

4. Construct a system that has a one-second Clock displayed on the screen that can be both started and stopped by the user clicking appropriately labeled buttons.

5. Construct a system that has two Clocks, one operating on a one-second interval and one on a 0.1-second interval. Each Clock is connected to a different counter and each can be controlled by start and stop buttons. Both counters appear on the screen with appropriate labels.

6. Construct a system that has a one second Clock displayed on the screen that can be started, stopped, and reset. To reset the Clock, the user must first stop the Clock, enter a new time in the TextBox, press the reset button, and then press the start button.

3.7 Self-Referencing Class Definitions

The definition of a class may refer to itself. One situation in which this occurs is when a class's operation has an object as a parameter where that object is of that same class as the one containing the operation. Examples of where this occurs are the following:

- A Location object is to decide if it has the same screen coordinates as another Location object
- A Shape object is to decide if it has the same height and width as another Shape object
- A File object is to copy itself to or from another File

In each case the operation needs as its parameter an object in the same class as the one containing the operation.

A second situation in which a class may refer to itself occurs when a class's method returns an instance of that class as a result. Some examples of methods that return objects in their own class are the following:

Code Sample 3–31 *Extended File Class*

```
class File {                                      // Version 2
  private:
                      // encapsulated implementation goes here
  public:

      File(char* fileName);
                            // represents file with given name
         File();          // unknown, as yet, file
  char* Name();           // reply name of file
  int   Exists();         // does file Exist?
  void  View();           // scrollable view window
  void  Edit(char* editor);  // edit file using "editor"
  void  Delete();         // delete file
  void  CopyTo(File& other);
                          // copy me to other
  void  CopyFrom(File& other);
                          // copy other to me
      ~File();            // free name
};
```

- A Shape object returns a new Shape object whose dimensions are some percentage less or more than the size of the original Shape object
- A Location object returns a new Location object that is horizontally or vertically offset from the original Location object
- A File object returns a new File object that represents a temporary copy of itself

The File class is extended to add a method that will perform the copying operations described above. The extended definition is shown in Code Sample 3–31.

In this revised version of the File class, the CopyTo and CopyFrom methods take as their input arguments references to other File objects, which the called object copies itself to or from. This class can be used in the following way:

```
FileNavigator nav;
File sourceFile = nav.AskUser();
File targetFile = nav.AskUser();

sourceFile.CopyTo(targetFile);
sourceFile.View();
targetFile.View();
```

In this example, the user is asked to select two existing files. The file first selected is copied to the second file. The two viewing windows that are created can be used to visually confirm that the files are identical.

Code Sample 3–32 *Revised Location Class*

```
class Location {                          // Version 2
   private:
       // encapsulated implementation goes here
   public:
             Location(int x, int y); // specific location
             Location();             // default location
   int       Xcoord();               // return x-axis coordinate
   int       Ycoord();               // return y-axis coordinate
   Location Xmove(int amount);       // move right/left
   Location Ymove(int amount);       // move up/down
   };
```

Code Sample 3–33 *Revised Shape Class*

```
class Shape {                             // Version 2
   private:
       // encapsulated implementation goes here
   public:
           Shape(int width, int height);// specific shape
           Shape();                      // default shape
   int     Height();                     // return height
   int     Width();                      // return width
   Shape Resize(float factor);           // return adjusted shape
   };
```

As noted in the examples above, it is also useful for an operation of a class to return an object of that same class. This is illustrated by the revisions to the Location and Shape classes shown in Code Samples 3–32 and 3–33.

Using these revisions to the Shape and Location class we can operate on a window as follows:

```
Frame window(nearTop, largeSquare);

Shape      currentShape    = window.WhatShape();
Location currentLocation = window.WhereAt();
Shape      newShape        = currentShape.Resize(0.9);
Location newLocation       = currentLocation.Xmove(50);

window.MoveTo( newLocation );
window.Resize( newShape   );
```

In this example, a window is made smaller by ten percent and moved to a location that is fifty units to the right of its starting location.

Exercises

1. Redefine the Location class to include a method SameAs that decides if the called Location object has the same screen coordinates as another Location object.

2. Redefine the Shape class to include a method SameAs that decides if the call Shape object has the same height and width as another Shape object.

3. Redefine the Location class to include another useful method that has a Location object as its parameter. Explain briefly what your new method does.

4. Redefine the Shape class to include another useful method that has a Shape object as its parameter. Explain briefly what your new method does.

Implementing a New Class

4.1 Introduction

*U*nderstanding how to implement a new class or modify an existing class is a basic skill in object-oriented programming. While it is always preferable to reuse intact an existing class that is suited to the needs of the system being built, it is often the case that a suitable class does not exist or the existing classes do not fully provide the attributes and behavior that are required. In these cases is it necessary to design and implement a new class or alter the design and implementation of an existing class.

Implementing a new class is a challenging activity because it involves the interaction of several very different types of knowledge and abilities, among which are:

- **aggregation:** This is the conceptual foundation of a class. A good class cannot be designed without a good understanding of how to recognize aggregations, identify the parts of the aggregation, and define the relationships among these parts.

- **language features:** This is the programming foundation of a class. To implement a class it is necessary to have a thorough understanding of the syntax and meaning of the parts of the language that bear on the structure and operation of an object. For example, understanding how to construct fully and destruct safely objects with complex internal structures is necessary.

- **style:** Like many creative activities, programming involves an element of style, which in this context refers to the arrangement, naming, and presentation of the code for a class. Beyond purely aesthetic considerations, good programming style materially improves the readability of code.

- **tools:** Almost any system involves not a single new class but many new classes that must not only be designed and implemented but also tested, debugged, recompiled, and managed. Performing these tasks efficiently involves proficiency in the use of tools. Basic tools for debugging and (re)building a system are studied in this chapter.

- **design:** The design of a system—the assignment of responsibilities and the organization of collaborations—largely determines the performance and software engineering properties (e.g., maintainability) of the system. A good design results from the combination of insight, understanding, inspiration, experience, and hard work. Two basic aspects of design are how to recognize abstractions that should be represented as classes and how to represent the design of a system in a succinct, diagrammatic form.

Because all of these areas of knowledge and skills are interwoven, they cannot be separated perfectly for study individually. Any approach to learning these topics must focus on some of them and defer others, not because the deferred topics are less important but only because some place must be chosen as the starting point.

This chapter is primarily concerned with the issues of aggregation and language features. The use of tools and the ideas about design are covered in Chapters 5 and 9, respectively.

4.2 Implementing a New Class Using Aggregation

The Concept of Aggregation

The term aggregation describes a structure in which one component, the whole, contains the other components, the parts. In object-oriented programming terms, the contained components are *subobjects* that are encapsulated within an enclosing object. The enclosing (outer, whole) object uses the functionality provided by the subobjects to implement its own behavior. While the Location class seen in Section 3.2 contained only built-in types (two ints), it is more common to find classes that use other classes, in addition to built-in types, to define their private data. Numerous examples of such classes will be seen in this chapter.

Aggregation is related to, but distinct from, association. The difference between aggregation and composition is illustrated in Figs. 4–1 through 4–4, which show the objects making up a timer system developed earlier. As shown in Fig. 4–1, creating the timer system by association involves creating the Clock,

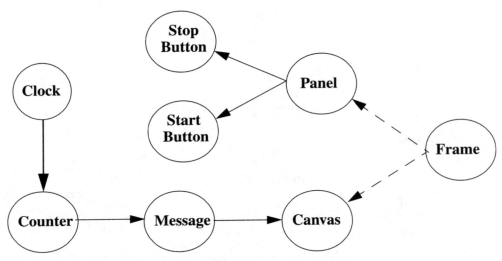

Figure 4-1   Using Association to Build a StopWatch

Counter, Message, Panel, Canvas, and Button objects individually, and using their methods to build up the desired structure of connections among them.

In Fig. 4–1, the solid-line arrows show objects connected by pointers. The Counter object, for example, maintains a pointer to the Message object to which it communicates its current value. The dotted-line arrows in the figure represent the relationship between a Frame object and the user-interface components that are displayed in that Frame.

Fig. 4–2 shows how the same system would appear when aggregation is used. With aggregation, the basic machinery of the timer system is encapsulated inside another object whose class, StopWatch, will be developed throughout this section. The public interface of the StopWatch class provides methods that allow the timer system to be manipulated as a whole.

A given class, for example the Clock class, may be used in several different aggregations. For example, a different timer system might not need user-control buttons. Such a system, a SimpleTimer, could be built using aggregation as shown in Fig. 4–3.

Another timer system might be used only for the measurement of time relevant to the program and would not be displayed to the user. This timer system, an InternalTimer, could be organized as shown in Fig. 4–4.

Similarly, there might be a variety of systems that aggregate other combinations of these and other classes.

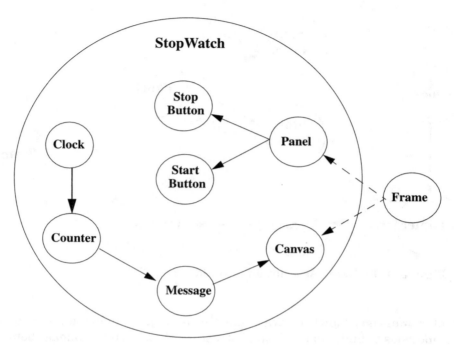

Figure 4–2   Using Aggregation to Build a StopWatch

Advantages of Aggregation

Aggregation confers several advantages most of which flow from the use of encapsulation and they are important to recognize and reiterate:

simplicity: The aggregating class or object allows the entire assembly encapsulated subobjects to be referred to as a single unit. This makes it easier to construct and manage multiple, independent instances of the system of subobjects. Image, for example, the difference in building a system that has three independent timer systems. Using composition, the code would directly manipulate fifteen different objects (three Clock objects, three Counter objects, three Textbox objects, and six Button objects) in addition to one Frame object. Using aggregation, the code would directly manipulate only three objects (three StopWatch objects) in addition to one Frame object.

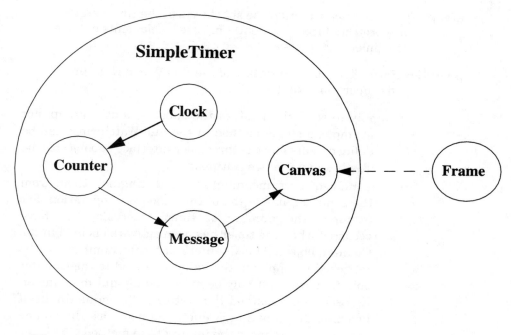

Figure 4–3 SimpleTimer Aggregation

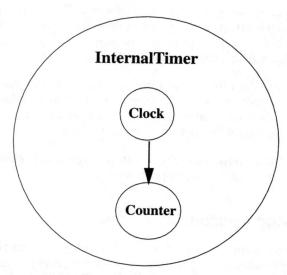

Figure 4–4 InternalTimer Aggregation

safety: Through encapsulation the subobjects of the timer system are protected from accidental misuse by elements outside the timer system itself.

specialization: The public interface of the StopWatch class provides operations that:

- apply to several (or all) of the subobjects as a group. For example, a single method in the StopWatch class can be defined to display the three user interface subobjects (the Textbox and the two Buttons).
- are named more meaningfully to distinguish them from the generic name of the of the subobject's operation. For example, the number of timer intervals that have occurred when the timer has been activated is held in the Counter object. The Counter's internal number can be retrieved by applying the Value() method to the Counter object. However, it may be more meaningful to define an ElapsedTime() method that returns this value (by itself invoking the Counter::Value() method), as this name more directly conveys the intent of the method.

structure: The existence of the encapsulating boundary captures the designer's intent that the components of the timer system are meant to function as a unit. Their organization and relationships are expressed directly in the StopWatch class, which can be studied and understood as a separate entity apart from any specific application.

substitution: An alternative implementation of the object defined by aggregation can be substituted without affecting other parts of the system as long as the public interface of the aggregating object remain unchanged.

It is clear from these advantages that developing skill in defining and implementing aggregations is an important goal.

Types of Aggregation

Two types of aggregation are described: *static aggregation* and *dynamic aggregation*. In static aggregation, the lifetimes of the subobjects are identical to the lifetimes of the containing object. The subobjects are explicitly declared in the class of the containing object, they are constructed when the containing object is constructed, and they are destructed when the containing object is destructed. In dynamic aggregation, at least some of the objects known only to the containing object are created dynamically, via the new operator, at run-time.

An intuitive example that illustrates the difference between static and dynamic aggregations is the contrast between an automobile, which has a fixed number of tires, and a tire store, where tires arrive from the factory and are sold to customers. For the automobile, the number of tires is known in advance. However, for the tire store, the type of its contents (i.e., automobile tires) is known, but the number of tires at any one time is variable and cannot be determined in advance.

Static aggregations are usually simpler, safer, and more efficient for a system to manage and thus should be used whenever possible. However, dynamic aggregations are needed for those equally important cases where the type, but not the number, of subobjects is known at design time. Both forms of aggregation are useful, and a good designer must be able to distinguish between them and use whichever is appropriate for the problem at hand.

Defining a New Class

Aggregation, whether static or dynamic, inherently involves defining a new class. An object of the new class is the outer (encapsulating, whole) component of the aggregation. The subobjects (the parts) are declared in the private data of the new class. To create high-quality aggregations it is necessary to be proficient in defining and implementing new classes.

A good class definition and implementation must have a number of desirable properties. Because a class captures an abstraction, the class must have all of the properties of a good abstraction. But as an executable representation a class must also have three major properties beyond those of an abstraction:

correctness: An object of the class must maintain its state properly and respond to invocations of its methods with the expected results. The most stringent level of correctness is a formal proof, though such proofs are usually reserved for safety-critical components due to the high cost of proving correctness of software. More common are less-stringent levels achieved through testing. No amount of testing establishes the formal correctness of a class. However, useful and measurable degrees of reliability and dependability can be achieved through rigorous testing.

safety: When used in obvious ways, an object of a class should not produce unexpected or harmful consequences. In particular, the class should behave safely when passed as a parameter or when objects are assigned to one another. In C++, special constructors for copying and special actions for assignment can be given.

efficiency: The object should make efficient use of processor and memory resources. While the most important means for ensuring efficiency reside in the overall system design and the choice of critical data structures and algorithms, the class implementor can improve the efficiency of the implementation in several ways such as declaring some elements to be constant and by using in-line methods.

Given the desired properties of abstractions and those of a class, it is clear that good object-oriented design is a creative and challenging activity.

The implementor of classes must be a proficient user of basic tools. In addition to the obvious need for a compiler is the need for proficiency in using a symbolic debugger during development and testing. Any system beyond the most trivial ones also requires the use of tools to (re)build the executable system from its source code when some part of that code has changed. For trivial systems all of the code can be recompiled every time any part of it is changed. But with modest and large systems, this brute-force approach is impractical because the time to recompile and relink the system is excessive. However, it is not practical for the implementor to remember all of the ways in which parts of the system must be rebuilt when some parts have changed. Thus, tools must be used to make the (re)building process efficient and accurate.

4.3 Defining the Implementation

General Concepts

Implementing a class consists of defining:

- data—the encapsulated (hidden, private) variables that record the current state of the object, and
- code—the member functions (operations, methods) that perform actions using the data and their own input parameters.

The data is often referred to as the "state" variables or the "instance" variables of the class. The term state reflects the point of view that an object moves from one state to another in time as directed by the execution of its methods. For example, when the MoveTo method is applied to a Frame object, the object is moved from a state in which it is at one location to a state in which it is at a different location. The term instance denotes the fact that each object is an instance of the class; each instance of a given class being distinct from all other instances and possessing its own private data.

The encapsulated data in a class is accessible to the member functions of that class. Such access is allowed, of course, because the member functions and

Code Sample 4–1   *Interface of the Location Class*

```
class Location {
   private:

      int  currentX, currentY;

   public:

         Location(int x, int y);
         Location();
      int Xcoord();
      int Ycoord();
         ~Location();
   };
```

Code Sample 4–2   *Implementation of the Location Class*

```
   Location::Location(int x, int y)
      { currentX = x; currentY = y; }

   Location::Location ()
      { currentX = -1; currentY = -1; }

int Location::Xcoord()
      { return currentX; }

int Location::Ycoord()
      { return currentY; }

   Location::~Location() {}
```

the data are parts of the same implementation: to be written, the writer of the code must know the details of the data. The data is, however, completely inaccessible to all non-member functions.

A Simple Example

The Location class illustrates the syntax and placement of the data and the code for a class. The interface and the implementation for the Location class are shown separately in Code Samples 4–1 and 4–2. Together, these two samples contain the complete code for the Location class.

Notice that the data is placed in the private portion of the class definition. It is natural to wonder why, if the data is hidden, it is textually visible in the class definition: Why not make the data hidden both conceptually and visually? In fact, the placement of the data in the class definition is a compromise in the design of the overall system software that simplifies the job of the compiler and linker at the expense of exposing to view (but not to access) the variables declared in the private section of the class definition.

The general syntax of the implementation of a member function is:

```
ReturnType  ClassName::memberFunctionName ( ArgumentList )
      { Statements }
```

where

ReturnType: is the type of the value returned by the member function (e.g., int),

ClassName: is the name of the class of which this function is a member (e.g., Location),

memberFunctionName: is the name of the member function (e.g., Xcoord),

ArgumentList: is a list of the argument for this member function (e.g., x and y for the first constructor); the list is empty if there are not arguments.

Statements: the code that defines what the member function does when it is invoked.

The ClassName must be repeated on each member function. This is necessary because, with overloaded member functions, it is possible for different classes to have member functions with the same name and arguments; only their class names distinguish these different member functions. Notice also that the complete argument list must be given even though it may already have been given earlier in the class definition.

A More Complicated Example

The Counter class provides another example of how a class is implemented. The interface of the Counter class is shown in Code Sample 4–3. The private data of the Counter class consists of several integers that define the state of the Counter.

The code for the Counter class is shown in Code Sample 4–4. The Counter constructor allows the Counter to be initialized by a starting value that by default is zero. The starting value is both the value of the Counter

Code Sample 4–3 *Private Data of the Counter Class*

```
class Counter
{
  private:
    int initial;
    int value;
    Message* message;

  public:
    Counter(int start = 0);
    void ConnectTo(Message& msg);
    void Next();
    void Reset();
   ~Counter();
};
```

Code Sample 4–4 *Implementation of the Counter Class*

```
Counter::Counter (int start)
{ initial = start;
  value   = start;
  message = (Message*)0;
}

void Counter::ConnectTo(Message& msg)
{ message =&msg; }

void Counter::Next()
{ value = value + 1;
  char asString[10];
  ostrstream convert(asString, 10);
  convert << value << '\0';
  if (message) message->SetText(asString);
}

void Counter::Reset()
{ value = initial; }

Counter::~Counter() {}
```

immediately after construction and also the initial value to which the Counter's value will be set by a Reset() operation. The Next() method increases the value of the Counter by one. In the constructor, the Message pointer is set to null. Notice that the syntax for assigning a null pointer in this case is:

```
message = (Message*)0
```

which type casts the value of zero, normally an int type, to be of type "pointer to Message."

Also notice that the Next() method uses the string stream to convert the integer value to a string.

Encapsulation Reconsidered

To gain a deeper understanding of the concept of encapsulation, consider an extended Counter class that allows two Counter objects to be compared. It is typical that two Counter objects need to be compared to determine if they represent the same value; that is, whether the encapsulated integer data values of the two objects are equal. With the existing Counter class interface the comparison cannot be made because there is no method that returns the Counter's value. While such an accessor method could be added to the public interface of the Counter class, it is often undesirable to expose the internal components of a class to examination from outside of the class.

The comparison method, named Equal, can be defined and implemented as shown in Code Sample 4–5, but note that only the relevant portions of the Counter class are shown. The parameter ("other") of the Equal method is passed by reference to avoid copying the Counter object to which the called object is being compared.

Because encapsulation is a class property, and not an object property, this implementation of the Equal method does not violate the encapsulation property. On the surface, the encapsulation appears to be violated because the value of the "other" object is accessed directly and not via a public accessor method. Specifically, the expression "other.value" directly accesses the supposedly encapsulated data of the "other" object. However, encapsulation must be understood from a class perspective: the private data defined within a class can only be accessed by methods (member functions) of that class. Since the Equal method is a member function of the Counter class it may access any of the private data members of that class in any Counter object to which it has access. This does not violate the notion of encapsulation because the benefit of encapsulation derives from the limitation on which methods, not which objects, can access the private data of a class. To underscore this idea, suppose that the name or type of the internal value in the Counter were changed. The only code that would have to be altered to accommodate this change is code in the Counter class itself. Also notice that because a method of a class can access the data of all objects of a class, the needed to introduce possibly unwanted accessor methods is avoided.

Code Sample 4–5 *Adding the Equal Method to the Counter Class*

```
class Counter{
   private:
      ...
      int  value;
      ...

   public:

         ...
      int Equal(Counter& other);   // test for equal values
         ...
};

// implementation follows

   int Counter::Equal(Counter& other)
   { if (value == other.value)
         return 1;   // equal
      else return 0;   // not equal
   }
```

 ## Exercises

1. Show how to define and implement an Equal method in the Location class that determines if the x and y coordinates of two Location objects are the same. Implement this method using the accessor methods Xcoord and Ycoord of the Location class.

2. Show how to define and implement an Equal method in the Location class that determines if the x and y coordinates of two Location objects are the same. Implement this method *without* using the accessor methods Xcoord and Ycoord of the Location class.

3. Show how to define and implement a LessThan method in the Counter class that determines if the value of one Counter object is strictly less than the value of another Counter object.

4. Without looking at the software distribution, show how to implement the Shape class.

5. Define and implement an extension to the Location class that adds a method MoveBy(int dx, int dy) that changes the coordinates of the

Location object to which it is applied by the amount given by the two parameters. For example, if a Location object has the coordinates (100,100), applying the operation MoveBy(20, -10) changes the coordinates of the object to be (120, 90).

6. Design, implement, and test a class to represent simple fractions. For example, the class might be used as follows:

```
Fraction half(1,2);
Fraction quarter(1,4);
Fraction sum = half.plus(quarter);
```

Add other interesting and useful methods to the class.

4.4 Organizing the Code

The code that defines, implements, and uses classes is organized as a collection of files. For very small programs it is possible to put all of the code in a single file. Clearly, though, this is a poor practice for anything but the most trivial systems. The organization that is described below works for all cases and is the pattern universally used in practice.

Separating the Interface Definition and the Implementation

The definitions of classes are placed in header files while code files contain the code that implements or uses the classes. By convention, the header files are named with a ".h" suffix. The conventional suffix for code files varies with the compiler or system; typical code file suffixes are ".C", ".cc", or ".cpp". The base part of a file's name is, of course, chosen to reflect the nature of its contents. Which code file suffix is used is not important—what is important is using the same suffix consistently.

Each header file contains one class definition or several highly related class definitions. For example, the header file named "Frame.h" contains only the Frame class. In a windowing system there might also be separate header files giving the class definitions for buttons, sliders, pens, and other elements typically found in graphical user-interface systems. In many cases there are groups of class definitions that are closely related and are grouped together in one header file. Such grouping occurs in one of two cases. First, the definition of a window class may involve the use of other classes, in which case these other classes may also be defined in the same header file. Second, the designer of a set of classes may believe that most often a user will want an entire set of class definitions; putting them in one header file makes it easier for the user since the user need only examine on header file to find all of the related classes. For example, a graphics system might provide classes for rectangles, circles, colors, and rulers. A single header file, perhaps named "Graphics.h", could be used to hold all of these definitions. In organizing the header files, it is important to be sure that only highly related class definitions are put in the same file.

The code implementing a class is placed in its own code file; for example, the code implementing the Frame class might be placed in the file "Frame.cc". Even if several classes are defined in the same header file, their implementations are typically placed in separate code files.

Definition before Use

Because C++ is a statically typed language, the C++ compiler must see the definition of a class before any uses are made of that class. Three important cases in which this rule must be satisfied are:

- Compiling the implementation of a class: In translating each of the methods in a code file, the compiler must check that the signature of the method being compiled matches that of the signature of the method given in the header file. The compiler will detect errors if the method names do not match or if the number and/or types of arguments of a method do not match. In this case the compiler must see the header file of the class before it can successfully compile the code for that class's implementation.

- Compiling the code of one class whose interface refers to another class: In several earlier examples it was seen that an object of one class (the argument class) is passed as a parameter in a method being invoked on a different class (the called class). In this case, the C++ compiler, when asked to compile the called class, must check that the argument class actually exists. In this case the compiler must see the definition of the argument class before it sees the definition of the interface of the called class.

- Compiling the code of one class whose implementation refers to another class: It is common that methods in one class (the sender) invoke the methods of another class (the receiver). In this case the C++ compiler must check that the signature of the method invocation in the sender matches a method defined in the class of the receiver object. The compiler will detect an error and issue an error message if a match cannot be found. In this case the compiler must see the header file of the receiver class before it is able to compile the implementation of the sender class.

Examples of these three cases are shown in Code Samples 4–6, 4–7, and 4–8.

The Preprocessor

To insure that the source code is presented to the compiler in a define-before-use order, the source code is first scanned by a simple preprocessor. The preprocessor (often named "cpp" for the C/C++ Preprocessor Program) looks for simple commands or directives in the files that it is scanning. A directive begins with a pound sign (#) in the first column and the rest of the line contains information about the directive. These directives are, strictly speaking, not part of the C++ language, and are understood only by the preprocessor. The preprocessor may scan many files, but it always produces exactly one output file. Each line of input that is not a directive is either copied unchanged to the output file or simply ignored and not copied to the output file. The preprocessor may also modify lines before they are output, but how or why this is done is not of concern here.

One of the most basic directives of the preprocessor allows new files to be included in the set of files being scanned. This directive has the syntax *#include filename*. When multiple files are included, the preprocessor scans the files with the aid of a stack data structure. For example suppose that the preprocessor is told to scan file A and that:

- File A contains some text, A1, then includes files B and C, then contains some text, A2
- File B contains some text, B1, then includes file D, then contains some text, B2
- File C contains some text, C1, then includes file D
- File D includes file E and then contains some text D1
- File E contains only text E1

In this case, the preprocessor would produce as its single output file the text in this order:

```
A1, B1, E1, D1, B2, C1, E1, D1, A2
```

Notice that the processing order is stack-like. After scanning the text A1, the scanning of file A is suspended ("pushed on the stack"), while the scanning of the included files B and C is undertaken. Only after finishing the scanning of these included files is the scanning of file A resumed ("popped from the stack"). Also notice that files D and E appear twice in the output stream because file D was included twice, once from file B and once from file C.

Including Header Files

The preprocessor #include directive is used to insure that the compiler is presented with the source text in a define-before-use order. The examples in Code Samples 4–6, 4–7, and 4–8 show how this directive should be used in header files and in the code files.

Code Sample 4–6 *Use of #include Directive in the Location Class*

Interface (in file Location.h)	Implementation (in file Location.cpp)

```
class Location {                   #include "Location.h"
  private:
    int currentX, currentY;        Location::Location( int x, int y )
                                      { currentX = x; currentY = y; }
  public:
                                   Location::Location ()
                                      { currentX = -1; currentY = -1; }
    Location(int x, int y);
    Location();                    int Location::Xcoord()
    int Xcoord();                     { return currentX; }
    int Ycoord();
};                                 int Location::Ycoord()
                                      { return currentY; }
```

The Location class illustrates the first case in which a header file must be included. The interface and implementation of the Location class are shown again in Code Sample 4–6. Notice that the code file begins with an include directive.

The Message class is an example of the second case where include directives are needed. As shown in Code Sample 4–7, the Message class interface refers to the Location and Frame classes because a Location object and Frame pointer appear as part of the private data of the class, and because the Message class methods take a Location object or a Frame reference as a parameter as well.

Notice that the code file (Message.cpp) includes the header file (Message.h) and that the header file of the Message class includes the header files of both the Location and Frame classes. It is not necessary for the code file to include the Location and Frame class header files because those have already been included by the Message class header file.

An example of the third case of using the include directive involves the FileChooser class that is shown in Code Sample 4–8. Notice that the interface of the FileChooser class uses only the single built-in type "char*" so there is no need to include any other files. The interface of the FileChooser does not depend on the interface of any other class. However, the implementation of the FileChooser does use two other classes, the Directory class and the Selector class. Objects of these two classes are used in the FileChooser's AskUser method. When compiling the code for the FileChooser class the compiler will need to verify that the Directory class defines methods named First() and Next() and that the Selector class defines methods named Add and AskUser. To satisfy the

Code Sample 4–7 *Use of #include Directive in the MessageClass*

Interface (in file Message.h)

```
#include "Frame.h"
#include "Location.h"

class Message {
  private:
      char*    messageText;
      Frame*   frame;
      Location location;

  public:

      Message (char *textString,
               Location whereAt);
      Message (Location whereAt);
void  DisplayIn (Frame& aFrame);
void  MoveTo (Location newLocation);
void  setText(char* newText);
char* getText();
void  Clear();
void  Draw ();
      ~Message ();
};
```

Implementation (in file Message.cpp)

```
#include "Message.h"

Message::Message(char *textString,...)
   { ... }

Message::Message(Location whereAt)
   { ... }

void Message::DisplayIn(Frame& aFrame)
   { ... }

void Message::MoveTo(Location newLocation)
   { ... }

// rest of the Message class implementation
```

Code Sample 4–8 *Use of #include Directive in the FileChooser Class*

Interface (in file Choose.h)	Implementation (in file Choose.cpp)
<pre>class FileChooser {

private:
  char* thePath;
  char* theFilter;

public:

 FileChooser(char* path,
            char* filter);
 FileChooser(char* path);
 FileChooser();
 File AskUser();
 ~FileChooser();
};</pre> | <pre>#include "Choose.h"
#include "Directry.h"
#include "Selector.h"

// other code not shown

File FileChooser::AskUser()
{ Directory directory(thePath,
                      theFilter);
  Selector selector(thePath);
  char* nextName;
  char* fileChosen;

  nextName = directory.First();
  while (nextName) {
    selector.Add(nextName);
    nextName = directory.Next();
  }

  fileChosen = selector.AskUser();
  return File(fileChosen);

}</pre> |

compiler's requirement, the implementation file, Choose.cpp, includes both Directry.h and Selector.h. It is important to note that the header file does not need to include either of these two files because the interface does not depend on the Directory and Selector classes, only the implementation depends on these two classes.

Avoiding Duplicate Definitions

Care must be taken to avoid presenting the compiler with multiple definitions of the same class, even if these definitions are exactly the same. If the compiler sees two (even identical) definitions of the same class, it will issue an error message referring in some way to "multiple definitions" for the class. This situation can occur easily in practice when the preprocessor includes a header file twice in its output file. An example that follows will illustrate how easily it can happen. Additional preprocessor directives prevent this situation.

Code Sample 4–9

File	Contents
BlinkingText.cpp	```#include "Frame.h" #include "Message.h" Frame window(...); Message greeting(...); ...```

Frame.h	```#include "Location.h"
	
	class Frame
	{...
	  void MoveTo(Location loc);
	  ...
	}```

Message.h	```#include "Location.h"
	
	class Message
	{...
	  void MoveTo(Location loc);
	  ...
	}```

The BlinkingText program will be used to illustrate the problem of presenting the compiler with multiple definitions. The significant pieces of the files are
shown in Code Sample 4–9. Notice that the use of the #include directives in each
file is correct: for example, the BlinkingText.cpp file must include both the
Frame.h and the Message.h header files because objects of both of these classes
are declared. Also, the Location.h header file must be included by both the
Frame.h file and the Message.h file because a Location object is a parameter to
one or more of the methods in these files.

The problem of multiple definitions arises when the preprocessor scans the
BlinkingText.cpp file; in this case the preprocessed output presented to the compiler will contain the following class definitions:

```
Location, Frame, Location, Message
```

The Location class appears twice because it is included by both the Frame.h
file and the Message.h file.

Use of preprocessor variables will prevent duplicate class definitions. These
variables help the preprocessor understand when an included file should be

Code Sample 4–10 *Location.h File with Preprocessor Directives*

```
#ifndef _LOCATION_H
#define _LOCATION_H
class Location
{
    ... // class definition
};

#endif
```

written to the preprocessor's output file or when the included file has already been written to the output file and should not be written again. A preprocessor variable is denoted by any string of characters, and for our purposes here, a preprocessor variable is either undefined (not currently known to the preprocessor) or defined (currently known to the preprocessor). Preprocessor variables that are defined may also have values attached to them, but how and why this is done is not relevant here. The preprocessor variables have nothing to do with the variables that are in the C++ code itself; they are simply names that are used during the preprocessing.

A preprocessor variable is defined by the preprocessor directive *#define variablename*. Any variable that has not been defined is undefined. Whether a variable is defined or not can be tested by another preprocessor directive, *#ifndef variablename*, which is true if the variable name is not defined and false otherwise, and a directive, *#endif*, that delimits the extent of the *#ifndef*. The preprocessor reacts to this directive in the following ways:

- if the *#ifndef* is true, then continue placing the lines of the file being scanned in the output file
- if the *#ifndef* is false, then skip all lines of the file being scanned until an *#endif* is found

These three preprocessor directives (*#define*, *#ifndef*, and *#endif*) are used in a standard pattern to avoid the duplication of class definitions as shown for the Location.h file in Code Sample 4–10. Notice that the preprocessor variable has the rather strange name "_LOCATION_H". In standard practice the name of the preprocessor variable is some variation of the file name. This standard practice makes it easy to uniquely define each preprocessor variable, since there is only one file with a given name.

This usage causes the preprocessor to act in the following way:

- The first time the file is included the preprocessor variable (_LOCATION_H) will not be defined. As a result, all of the lines of the file except other preprocessor commands are processed and sent to the output file. Thus, the definition of the Location class will be written to the output file. One of the preprocessor commands encountered during this processing is the #define command that defines the preprocessor variable. In this case the #endif directive has no effect and is not copied to the output file.

- The second time (and all subsequent times) the file is included the preprocessor variable (_LOCATION_H) will be defined. As a result, the preprocessor will ignore (not copy to the output file) all lines of the file until an #endif directive is encountered. Thus, the definition of the Location class is not duplicated in the output of the preprocessor.

After a little practice it becomes automatic to include these preprocessor directives in all header files.

 Exercises

1. For the compiler that you are using, find out how to run the preprocessor and save the output produced by it. There are usually options, settings, or flags that allow this to be done. Run the preprocessor using one of the sample programs or a program that you wrote for an earlier exercise. Notice what has been included and in what order. Can you explain what you see in this output?

2. Temporarily remove the #ifndef, #define, and #endif directives from the Location.h file and try to compile a program that would cause this header file to be included more than once. What is the error message that you get? Replace the three directives and recompile the program to be sure that you have replaced them correctly.

3. Suppose that the preprocessor is told to scan file A and that:

   - File A includes file B, then contains some text, A1, then includes file C, then contains some text, A2
   - File B includes file D, then contains some text, B1
   - File C contains some text, C1, then include file E, then contains some text, C2
   - File D contains only text, D1
   - File E contains only text E1

In what order would the text appear in the preprocessor output file?

Code Sample 4–11 *Interface of the Rectangle Class*

```
class Rectangle
{
  private:
          Location upperLeft;
          Location upperRight;
          Location lowerLeft;
          Location lowerRight;
          Shape    area;

  public:
          Rectangle (Location corner, Shape shape);
          void MoveUp    (int deltaY);
          void MoveDown (int deltaY);
          void MoveLeft (int deltaX);
          void MoveRight (int deltaX);
          void Draw(Canvas& canvas);
          void Clear(Canvas& canvas);
          ~Rectangle();
};
```

4.5 Simple Static Aggregation

The concept of a *static aggregation* is illustrated by a class that captures the abstraction of a rectangle. The Rectangle class will be responsible for maintaining the position of the rectangle and drawing itself in a specified canvas. The position of a Rectangle object within a Canvas will be defined by a Location object that gives the coordinates of the upper left-hand corner of the Rectangle. The height and width of the rectangle are defined by a Shape object that is passed as an argument to the Rectangle's constructor. The interface of the Rectangle class is shown in Code Sample 4–11.

The Rectangle class maintains its state information to expedite its operations. The implementation of the Rectangle class is given in Code Sample 4–12. Drawing a rectangle on a canvas is accomplished by four separate DrawLine operations. Each DrawLine operation requires two Location object parameters that specify the endpoints of the line. To expedite the drawing of the rectangle, each of the four Location objects specifies the coordinates of one of the corners of the rectangle. The Rectangle class is also provided with public methods to change its position relative to its current location (the MoveUp, MoveDown, MoveLeft, and MoveRight methods), to draw itself on a canvas (the Draw method), and to erase itself from a canvas (the Clear method). Since the Canvas's

Code Sample 4–12 *Rectangle Class Implementation*

```
Rectangle::Rectangle(Location corner, Shape shape)
{ upperLeft  = corner;
  area = shape;
  upperRight = Location(upperLeft.Xcoord() + area.Width(),
                        upperLeft.Ycoord());
  lowerLeft  = Location(upperLeft.Xcoord() ,
                        upperLeft.Ycoord() + area.Height());
  lowerRight = Location(upperLeft.Xcoord() + area.Width(),
                        upperLeft.Ycoord() + area.Height());
}

void Rectangle::MoveUp(int deltaY)
{ upperLeft  = Location(upperLeft.Xcoord(),
                        upperLeft.Ycoord() + deltaY);
  upperRight = Location(upperLeft.Xcoord() + area.Width(),
                        upperLeft.Ycoord());
  lowerLeft  = Location(upperLeft.Xcoord() ,
                        upperLeft.Ycoord() + area.Height());
  lowerRight = Location(upperLeft.Xcoord() + area.Width(),
                        upperLeft.Ycoord() + area.Height())
}

// ... MoveDown, MoveLeft, MoveRight similar to MoveUp

void Rectangle::Draw(Canvas& canvas)
{ canvas.DrawLine(upperLeft,  upperRight);
  canvas.DrawLine(upperRight, lowerRight);
  canvas.DrawLine(lowerRight, lowerLeft);
  canvas.DrawLine(lowerLeft,  upperLeft);
}

void Rectangle::Clear(Canvas& canvas)
{ canvas.Clear(upperLeft, area)
}

Rectangle::~Rectangle() {}
```

Clear method requires a Shape parameter, the Rectangle maintains the Shape information as part of its state information as well.

The Rectangle class is an example of a static aggregation because the four Location objects and the Shape object aggregated in each Rectangle object are fixed, named, and defined at the time that the class is written. As in all static aggregations, the lifetime of the aggregated objects is identical to that of the aggregating object. Thus, the lifetime of the upperLeft Location object (and the other three Location objects and the Shape object as well) is exactly the same as the lifetime of the Rectangle object of which it is a part: the Location subobjects and the Shape subobject are constructed when the Rectangle object of which they are a part is constructed and the Location and Shape subobjects are destructed when that Rectangle object is destructed. The static aggregation properties of the Rectangle class can be seen explicitly in the constructor and destructor of the class.

The Rectangle constructor initializes the four encapsulated Location objects and the encapsulated Shape object using the constructor's parameters. The initialization used here actually involves two steps for each subobject: construction and initialization. Before the body of the Rectangle constructor is entered, each of the five subobjects is constructed using their default constructors (recall that the Location class and the Shape class have default constructors). In the body of the Rectangle constructor, the subobjects are given new values through assignment. This means of constructing and initializing the subobjects will work in many cases but:

- it is not possible in those cases where the subobject does not have a default constructor,
- it is inefficient for large objects to construct them using the default constructor, which does one initialization, and then immediately replace these values by assignment.

A different technique for constructing the subobjects is shown in the Stop-Watch example in Section 4.6.

Somewhat surprisingly, the Rectangle destructor is defined but has no code when it would seem that some actions should be taken to cause the destruction of the contained subobjects. The subobjects are destructed automatically, they do not have to be explicitly programmed to do so. The automatic destruction of the subobjects is done because:

- it is clear from the structure of a static aggregation that the subobjects must be destructed when the containing object is destructed, so there is no reason for the compiler and run-time system not to arrange for this to be done automatically, and
- it relieves the programmer of the task of programming the explicit destruction of the subobjects.

It must be emphasized that the automatic destruction occurs only for subobjects (objects created via a declaration)—not for any objects that were created dynamically (objects created via a new operation). Another way to state this rule is that subobjects accessed by name are automatically destructed while subobjects accessed via pointers are not automatically destructed. The role of the

Code Sample 4–13 *Trivialized Classes for Experimentation*

Location class

```
class Location
{
  private:
        int X, Y;

  public:
        Location(int x, int y);
        Location();
        ~Location();
};

Location::Location(int x, int y)
{ X = x;
  Y = y;
  cout << "Location ("
       << X << "," << Y
       << ") constructor" << endl;

}

Location::Location()
{X = 0;
  Y = 0;
  cout << "Location default"
       << " constructor" << endl;
}

Location::~Location()
{cout << "Location ("
       << X << "," << Y
       << ") destructor" << endl;
}
```

destructor in the case of dynamically allocated objects is seen in dynamic aggregations.

Construction/Destruction Sequence

To understand better the construction and destruction processes, two trivialized versions of the Location and Rectangle classes are defined here. The code of these two classes is shown in Code Sample 4–13. Neither class has any methods except for their constructors and destructors, all of which generate a line of output when they are executed. The structures of the trivialized classes are similar

Code Sample 4–13 *Trivialized Classes for Experimentation (cont.)*

Rectangle class

```
class Rectangle
{
  private:
        Location loc1;
        Location loc2;
        Location loc3;
        Location loc4;

  public:
        Rectangle(Location& loc);
        ~Rectangle();
};

Rectangle::Rectangle(Location& loc)
{cout << "Rectangle constructor"
        << endl;
 loc1 = loc;
 loc2 = loc;
 loc3 = loc;
 loc4 = loc;
}


Rectangle::~Rectangle()
{ cout << "Rectangle destructor"
        << endl;
}
```

to the original Location and Rectangle classes: the trivialized Location has two integer values as its private data and the Rectangle class has four trivialized Location subobjects.

The sequence of construction and destruction actions can be followed by using the trivialized Location and Rectangle classes in a small test program and observing the output of the program. The test program and its output are shown in Code Sample 4–14.

The important things to notice from the output of the test program about the construction and destruction actions are:

- Each constructor action is matched by a corresponding destructor action. The Location constructors were called five times and the Location destructor was called five times. The Rectangle class's constructor and destructor

Code Sample 4–14 *Example of Construction / Destruction Sequence*

Test Program	Output of Test Program
| ```c++
void main()
{
  cout << " Begin Test"
      << endl;

  Location location(10,10);
  Rectangle rect(location);

  cout << " End Test" << endl;

}
``` | ```
Begin Test
Location (10,10) constructor
Location default constructor
Location default constructor
Location default constructor
Location default constructor
Rectangle constructor
 End Test
Rectangle destructor
Location (10,10) destructor
Location (10,10) destructor
Location (10,10) destructor
Location (10,10) destructor
Location (10,10) destructor
``` |

were each called once. This demonstrates that all objects have been reclaimed; there are no memory leaks.

- The destructors are invoked implicitly; there are no explicit statements that invoke them. When the end of the main program is reached, the Rectangle and Location objects declared in the main program go out of scope and are automatically destructed.

- The destructors for the four Location subobjects have been executed. This demonstrates that the destruction of the subobjects is performed when their containing object (in this case the Rectangle object) is destructed.

- The subobjects are constructed *before* their containing object is constructed. In the output it can be seen that the output from the Location subobjects' constructors comes before the output from the Rectangle's constructor. This sequence is deliberate; it allows the constructor for the containing object to invoke the methods of its subobjects (e.g., to query their state or connect them in an association). To allow the constructor of the containing object to operate on its subobjects, it is necessary that the subobjects be fully constructed in advance of the execution of the containing object's constructor.

- the subobjects are destructed *after* their containing object is destructed. In the output it can be seen that the output from the Location subobjects' destructor comes after the output from the Rectangle's destructor. This sequence is deliberate; it allows the destructor of the containing object to invoke methods of its subobjects (e.g., to adjust the state of the subobjects prior to their destruction. In the StopWatch example it will be seen that the Clock subobject must be stopped prior to the subobject of the Stop-Watch being destructed. This avoids the possibility of the Clock subobject ticking during the destruction process). To allow the destructor of the containing object to operate on its subobjects, it is necessary that the subobjects be destructed only after the execution of the containing object's destructor has completed.

This example illustrates the main ideas about the sequence of subobject construction and subobject destruction. The exercises below help to discover a few other details.

 Exercises

1. Demonstrate your understanding of a static aggregation by defining, implementing, and testing a Circle class that has a Location subobject defining the center of the circle and an integer value defining the radius of the Circle. Your Circle object should be able to draw itself on a Canvas.

2. Demonstrate your understanding of a static aggregation by defining, implementing, and testing a Triangle class that has three Location subobjects defining the vertices of the triangle. Your Triangle object should be able to draw itself on a Canvas.

3. In the output from the test program it is not possible to tell if the Location object in the main program is destructed before or after the Location subobjects. Rewrite the test program so that the order can be determined.

4. Rewrite the constructor for the trivialized Rectangle class so that the Location object is passed by copy and not by reference. Rerun the test program with this change. Explain any differences that you see between the output of the test program using the original Rectangle class and the test program using the modified Rectangle class.

5. Modify the main test program to include a global Rectangle object (i.e., one declared outside of the main program). Rerun the test program with this change. Explain any differences that you see between the output of the original test program and the output of the test program with the global variable.

6. Modify the trivialized Location class to remove the default constructor (the one with no arguments). Recompile the test program using this modified Location class. Explain any error messages that result.

7. Modify the trivialized Rectangle class so that its private data includes a pointer to a Location object. In the constructor of the Rectangle class initialize this pointer to a Location object that has been dynamically allocated using the new operator. Rerun the test program using this modified trivialized Rectangle class. Examine the output of the test program and determine how many Location objects were constructed and how many Location objects were destructed. Explain your observations.

4.6 More Complex Static Aggregation

In this section, StopWatch class is implemented to illustrate a more complex aggregation, one in which the aggregation subobjects are more functional and in which the problems of properly constructing the aggregation are more challenging. Before considering the issue of how to construct this more elaborate aggregation, a general design issue is described, involving the degree to which the internal subobjects of the aggregation are implicitly revealed through the aggregation's public interface. This is termed *the problem of indirect control*.

The Problem of Indirect Control

When using aggregation, an important design issue is the degree of indirect control over the encapsulated objects that is reflected in the public interface of the aggregating class, indirect control being the ability of the object's user to affect the detailed organization or operation of the subobjects through the public interface of the aggregating class. In the StopWatch example the following indirect control questions arise:

- At what Locations in a window are the two Buttons and the Textbox displayed?
- What is the relative placement of the Buttons and the Textbox in a window? Buttons beside? Buttons below? Buttons above?
- What is the timer interval? Is it fixed? user selectable? set by the program?
- How many digits can appear in the Textbox?
- What are the names of the Buttons as they appear in a window?
- Does the StopWatch object always start at time zero or can it be given an initial value?
- Can the Clock object be started/stopped by the program? only the user? both?

As can be seen, these questions touch on all of the encapsulated subobjects in the StopWatch class.

Ideally, no indirect control over the encapsulated objects should be allowed, but this may not always be reasonable or possible. Beware, though, that providing excessive indirect control over the encapsulated objects begins to weaken the advantages of aggregation. In the extreme case, the aggregating class relinquishes complete control of its subobjects, becoming little more than a weak wrapper to hold the subobjects together as a group. The designer of a good class must strike a balance between providing sufficient indirect control of the encapsulated objects so as to be usable in different applications, yet not so much as to lose the benefits of aggregation.

The designer of an aggregating class has several options for dealing with the issue of subobject control. First, several similar classes can be designed, each providing a different degree of control. At the expense of creating and naming several classes, this approach allows a spectrum of choices for programmers who may have varying needs for control over the subobjects. Second, the interface of the aggregating class may use default arguments so that control reverts to the aggregating class itself if these arguments are not specified. While this approach also promises a spectrum of choices, the argument lists become more complicated and more difficult to design. Due to the ordering of the default arguments, a user of the aggregating class may find it necessary to assume more control than is desired. Third, one or more auxiliary classes can be defined for specifying the control information. An instance of this auxiliary class is provided as an argument to the aggregating class. This argument may also have a default value, or the auxiliary class may have a default constructor so that users may assume no indirect control. In the case of the StopWatch class, the arrangement of the user interface components can be collected into a StopWatchLayout class, which would contain all of the placement and labeling information for a StopWatch. The default StopWatchLayout constructor would provide standard (default) values for this information. The constructor for the StopWatch class would have a StopWatchLayout argument whose default value is a StopWatchLayout object constructed by the default constructor of the StopWatchLayout class.

Implementing the StopWatch Class

The definition of the StopWatch class is given in Code Sample 4–15. The public interface provides methods to start and stop the StopWatch from the program level, to identify a Frame in which the StopWatch can display its user interface components (TextBox and Buttons), and to query the StopWatch for its current elapsed time.

Notice that this design makes a number of decisions about the control issues raised earlier. This is not to suggest that these are the right decisions, they are only reasonable and illustrative ones.

The methods of the StopWatch class can be implemented as shown in Code Sample 4–16.

Code Sample 4–15 *StopWatch Class Interface*

```
class StopWatch
{
  private:
    Button   startButton;
    Button   stopButton;
    Clock    clock;
    Counter  clockCount;
    Message  clockDisplay;
    Panel    buttonPanel;
    Canvas   canvas;

  public:
    StopWatch(Frame& frame, Location where,
                            int interval = 1000);
    void ButtonPushed(char* buttonName);
    void Tick();
    int ElapsedTime();
    ~StopWatch();
};
```

Code Sample 4–16 *StopWatch Class Implementation*

```
void StopWatch::ButtonPushed(char* buttonName)
{ if (startButton.IsNamed(buttonName))
     clock.Start();
  else
  if (stopButton.IsNamed(buttonName))
     clock.Stop();
}

void StopWatch::Tick()
{ clockCount.Next();
}

int StopWatch::ElapsedTime()
{ return clockCount.Value();
}

StopWatch::~StopWatch() {}
```

Code Sample 4–16 illustrate how the methods of the StopWatch class achieve their effect by manipulating the internal subobjects. For example, for the

StopWatch to start or stop itself in response to one of its buttons being pressed, the ButtonPushed method simply calls the Start() or Stop() method of the Clock subobject. Similarly, the elapsed time of the StopWatch is found simply by querying the value of the Counter subobject.

The constructor for the StopWatch class was not included in Code Sample 4–16, but will be shown in the next section, where the concept of constructing subobjects is considered separately.

Constructing Subobjects

The constructor of an aggregating class must insure that its subobjects are properly initialized. It is expected, for example, that when a StopWatch object is constructed, all of its subobjects are also properly constructed and ready for use.

The constructor for a subobject may be related to the constructor of the aggregating class in one of three ways:

- independent: The subobject constructor is fixed and independent of the arguments of the aggregating class.
- direct: The subobject constructor depends directly on one or more arguments of the aggregating class's constructor.
- indirect: The subobject constructor depends on one or more values computed from the aggregating class's constructor arguments.

These relationships are shown pictorially in Fig. 4–6.

In the independent case, the subobject has a fixed constructor that does not depend in any way on the construction of the aggregating class. For example, in the StopWatch design, the Counter subobject is always initialized to zero regardless of any other properties of the StopWatch object being constructed. Also the Start button, the Stop button, and the Message are constructed without reference to the StopWatch constructor values.

The direct case is illustrated by the Clock subobject in the StopWatch class. Here, the Clock object's constructor argument, the timer interval, is taken exactly from the StopWatch constructor argument. No change is made in this value.

The indirect case is illustrated by the construction of the Canvas and Panel. The StopWatch constructor has a single Location argument relative to which these two user interface objects are positioned. Assume that the user interface subobjects are positioned as shown in Fig. 4–5.

Using Fig. 4–5, the locations of the user-interface subobjects would be determined as shown in Table 4–1. The computation of the subobject locations involves invoking methods (Xcoord and Ycoord) of the StopWatch constructor argument (where), performing simple addition, and constructing a new (anonymous) Location object.

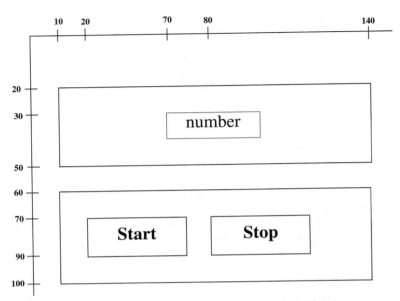

Figure 4–5   Layout of the StopWatch User-Interface Subobjects

Table 4–1 Location and Shape of User Interface Subobjects

Message:	Location(60,10) in Canvas (shape determined by number of digits)
StartButton:	Location(10,10) in Panel Shape(50,20)
StopButton:	Location(70,10) in Panel Shape(50,20)
Canvas:	Location(where.Xcoord() + 10, where.Ycoord() + 20) in Frame Shape(130, 30)
Panel:	Location(where.Xcoord() + 10, where.Ycoord() + 60) in Frame Shape(130, 40)

In C++, the subobject constructors are placed as shown in this general form:

```
ClassName::ClassName( <argument list> ) :
      <subobject constructor list> { <body of constructor> }
```

where <subobject constructor list> is a comma-separated list of constructors for subobjects. This list may contain only constructors for subobjects.

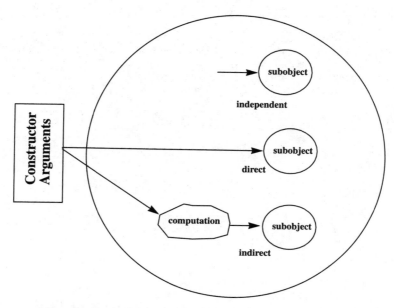

Figure 4–6   Subobject Construction

Using the layout decisions made above and the C++ syntax just introduced, the constructor for the StopWatch class can now be written as shown in Code Sample 4–17.

 Exercises

1. Add a label (a Message subobject) to the StopWatch class such that the label appears above the existing Message displaying the numeric value of the StopWatch. Add appropriate constructor arguments to the StopWatch constructor to give a character string for the label.

2. Implement and test the SimpleTimer class described in Section 4.2.

3. Implement and test the InternalTimer class described above.

4. Modify the StopWatch class so that it gives more control over the layout of the user interface subobjects by using default argument values on the StopWatch constructor.

5. Implement and test the StopWatchLayout class described above.

6. Implement and test a modified version of the StopWatch class that allows the layout to be customized by the user without changing the code. This customization should be achieved by reading the layout information from a file when a StopWatch object is constructed.

Code Sample 4–17 *StopWatch Class Constructor*

```
Location StartButtonLocation = Location(10,10);
Shape    StartButtonShape    = Shape(50,20);

Location StopButtonLocation  = Location(70,10);
Shape    StopButtonShape     = Shape(50,20);

Location ButtonPanelLocation = Location(10,60);
Shape    ButtonPanelShape    = Shape(130,40);

Location CanvasLocation      = Location(10,20);
Shape    CanvasShape         = Shape(130,30);

Location ClockDisplayLocation= Location(60,10);

StopWatch::StopWatch(Frame& frame, Location where,
                                   int interval)
: // subobject constructor list
  counter(0),
  clock("StopWatchClock", interval),
  buttonPanel( frame,   "ButtonPanel",
             Location(where.Xcoord() +
                        ButtonPanelLocation.Xcoord(),
                      where.Ycoord() +
                        ButtonPanelLocation.Ycoord()),
             ButtonPanelShape),

  startButton("Start",
             StartButtonLocation,
             StartButtonShape),

  stopButton ("Stop",
             StopButtonLocation,
             StopButtonShape),

  canvas     ( frame,   "StopWatchCanvas",
             Location(where.Xcoord() +
                        CanvasLocation.Xcoord(),
                      where.Ycoord() +
                        CanvasLocation.Ycoord()),
             CanvasShape),

  clockDisplay( "0", ClockDisplayLocation)
{ // constructor body
  buttonPanel.Add(stopButton);
  buttonPanel.Add(startButton);
  canvas.Clear();
  clockCount.ConnectTo(clockDisplay);
  clockDisplay.DisplayIn(canvas);
  clock.Start();
}
```

4.7 Dynamic Aggregation

The distinguishing feature of a dynamic aggregation is that at least some of the objects encapsulated within such an aggregation are dynamically created (via the new operator) at run-time. Dynamic aggregations are needed when the *type* of the encapsulated subobjects is know when the class is defined but the *number* of such objects is not. At run-time the dynamic aggregation must allocate and manage new subobjects.

The subobjects in a dynamic aggregation are not automatically destructed when the object is destructed because the subobjects are dynamically allocated. The responsibility for properly destructing the subobjects, thus preventing memory leaks, lies with the programmer. Failure to manage the dynamic subobjects properly is a common source of errors; usually these errors that are difficult to identify due to the dynamic nature of the subobjects.

An abstraction that must be represented as a dynamic aggregation is a closed polygon-like shape that has an arbitrary number of sides. To illustrate the mechanics of a dynamic aggregation, a class for a polygon-like shape will be defined and implemented. This class will allow the vertices of the shape to be defined dynamically at run-time. The class must maintain a list of vertices whose length is not know in advance. When required to draw itself on a canvas, the class is responsible for drawing lines between each successive pair of points, treating the last vertex and the first vertex as adjacent. Thus, if there are n vertices, n lines will be drawn: the first line is drawn from vertex 0 to vertex 1, the second line from vertex 1 to vertex 2, and so on, with the last line being drawn from the vertex n-1 to vertex 0.

The interface of the PolyShape class is shown in Code Sample 4–18.

A PolyShape object is constructed with the Location, the x and y coordinates, of its first vertex. These coordinates are used to initialize the current location of the PolyShape, represented by the state variables currentX and currentY. The other parts of the constructor will be explained later. The Up, Down, Left, and Right methods change the *current location* by the amount of the method's parameter. The name of the method suggests which coordinate of the *current location* is affected and in what manner. For example, if the *current location* is (100, 100) then the method Up(10) changes the Y coordinate so that the *current location* becomes (100, 90), a location "up" in the sense that it is closer to the top of the canvas area. Similarly, the call Right(20) would change the *current location* (100, 100) to become (120, 100), a location 20 pixels toward the right edge of the canvas. The implementation of these methods is shown in Code Sample 4–19. The Mark() method adds the *current location* to the linked list of Locations maintained by the PolyShape object. The Draw method draws the PolyShape on the canvas. The implementation of the Mark() and Draw() methods is discussed further below.

Code Sample 4–18 *PolyShape Class Interface*

```
class PolyShape
{
private:
        LocationNode *head;
        LocationNode *tail;
        int currentX, currentY;
        int length;
public:

        PolyShape(int x, int y);
        void Up    (int n);
        void Down  (int n);
        void Left  (int n);
        void Right (int n);
        void Mark();
        void Draw(Canvas& canvas);
        ~PolyShape();
};
```

Code Sample 4–19 *Basic Methods of the PolyShape Class*

```
PolyShape::PolyShape (int x, int y)
{ currentX = x; currentY = y;
  Location *start = new Location(x,y);
  head = tail = new LocationNode(start);
  length = 1; }

void PolyShape::Up(int n)
{ currentY = currentY - n; }

void PolyShape::Down(int n)
{ currentY = currentY + n; }

void PolyShape::Left(int n)
{ currentX = currentX - n; }

void PolyShape::Right(int n)
{ currentX = currentX + n; }
```

A significant issue for the designer of the PolyShape class is how to maintain the ordered list giving the Locations of its vertices. Because the number of vertices is unknown (at least unknown at design-time and compile-time), some form of dynamic aggregation is used.

The first solution to implementing the PolyShape data structure uses a linked-list technique. The Location class provides a convenient means to maintain an (x, y) coordinate pair but it does not provide a capability for Location objects to be members of a list. While the Location class could be changed to add the necessary data and methods to provide a linked-list capability, this approach is not followed. Three reasons argue against modifying the Location class in this way:

- There is nothing inherent in the abstraction of a Location to suggest that it is a member of a list of Locations. Thus, modifying the Location class would weaken the abstraction on which the class is based.

- The additional methods and data are costs incurred by all Location objects regardless of whether they are needed. Thus, modifying the Location class lessens the efficiency of Location objects in many situations. In the worst case, applications that do not use a list of Locations receive no benefit from the list mechanisms added to the Location class.

- This approach may not always be possible. In some situations, the objects to put on a list are instances of classes that cannot be changed. This occurs when the class is a library class provided by a vendor and the source code is not available to be changed.

Instead of modifying the Location class to add linked-list features, another approach that allows lists of Location objects, but does not modify the Location class, will be used.

The linked-list technique used in the PolyShape class depends on an auxiliary class, the LocationNode class. The LocationNode class provides the ability to form a linked list of Location objects. The relationship between a PolyShape object, the LocationNode objects, and the Location objects is shown in Fig. 4–7. As illustrated, each LocationNode object contains a pointer (contents) that identifies the Location object with which the LocationNode is paired. The LocationNode also contains a pointer (next) that identifies the next LocationNode (if any) in the list of LocationNodes. The two pointers in each LocationNode provide the abilities to form a list, by using the next pointer, and to represent a Location object, by using the contents pointer.

As illustrated in Fig. 4–7 and shown in the PolyShape class definition, a PolyShape object maintains two pointers, head and tail, that indicate the first and last elements in the linked list of LocationNodes.

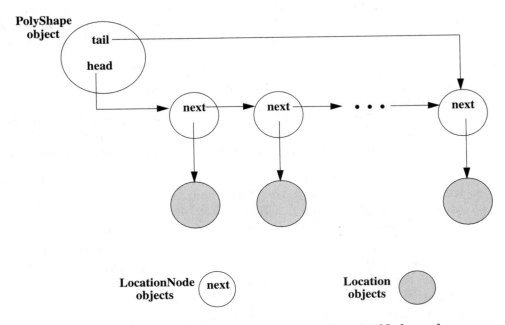

Figure 4–7   Relationships among PolyShape, LocationNode, and
Location Objects

The code for the LocationNode class is given in Code Sample 4–20. Notice
that no changes are needed in the Location class in order to implement the LocationNode class. Thus, the three problems noted earlier are avoided by the design
of the LocationNode class.

Notice that the destructor in the LocationNode class deletes the Location
object to which the LocationNode points with its contents pointer. Also notice
that no action is taken regarding the next pointer in the LocationNode.

The Mark and Draw methods of the PolyShape class operate on the linked
list of LocationNodes as shown in Code Sample 4–21. The Mark method creates
a new Location object using the current location of the PolyShape and creates a
new LocationNode object whose contents points to the Location object just created, then adds the just-created LocationNode to the tail of the linked list of
LocationNodes.

The Draw method uses the DrawLine method of the Canvas class to draw a
sequence of lines. Each line is drawn between a pair of consecutive Location
objects extracted from the linked list of LocationNodes. The code for the Mark
and Draw methods is shown in Code Sample 4–21.

Code Sample 4–20 *LocationNode Class*

```
class LocationNode
{private:
   LocationNode *next;
   Location *location;
 public:
    LocationNode(Location *loc);
        LocationNode* Next();
        void Next(LocationNode* nxt);
        Location& Contents();
   ~LocationNode();
};

LocationNode::LocationNode(Location *loc)
{ location = loc;
  next = (LocationNode*)0; }

LocationNode* LocationNode::Next()
{ return next; }

void LocationNode::Next(LocationNode* nxt)
{ next = nxt; }

Location& LocationNode::Contents()
{ return *location; }

LocationNode::~LocationNode()
{ delete location; }
```

The destructor in a dynamic aggregation plays a key role in ensuring the proper reclamation of the subobjects dynamically created during the lifetime of the containing (aggregating) object. The destructor for a PolyShape object must destruct all of the dynamically created LocationNode and Location objects that are part of the linked list of the PolyShape object. The destructor for the Poly-Shape class is shown in Code Sample 4–22.

The PolyShape destructor performs a list traversal, destructing each LocationNode in sequence. Recall that, when destructed, a LocationNode object will destruct the Location object to which it points. Thus, the PolyShape directly destructs all LocationNode objects and indirectly causes the destruction of all Location objects.

Code Sample 4–21 *Code for the Mark and Draw Methods*

```
void PolyShape::Mark()
{ Location *newPoint    = new Location(currentX, currentY);
  LocationNode *newNode = new LocationNode(newPoint);
  tail->Next(newNode);
  tail = newNode;
  length = length + 1;
}

void PolyShape::Draw(Canvas& canvas)
{ if (length == 1) return;
  LocationNode *node, *next;
  node = head;
  for(int i=0; i<length-1; i++)
  { next = node->Next();
    canvas.DrawLine(node->Contents(),
                    next->Contents());
    node = next;
  }
  canvas.DrawLine(head->Contents(),
                  tail->Contents());
}
```

Code Sample 4–22 *PolyShape Class Destructor*

```
PolyShape::~PolyShape()
{ LocationNode *next = head;
  while (next)
  { LocationNode *node = next->Next();
    delete next;
    next = node;
  }
}
```

 Exercises

1. Change the destructors of the LocationNode and the PolyShape
   classes to what is shown below. Explain why this code correctly
   destructs all LocationNode and Location objects in the PolyShape.

```
LocationNode::~LocationNode()
{ delete contents;
  delete next;
}

PolyShape::~PolyShape()
{ delete head;
}
```

2. Use the linked list technique developed in this section to define and implement a linked list of Message objects without changing the Message class. A partial specification of the MessageList class interface is given below. The MessageList::Draw method should invoke the Message::Draw method in each Message object on its list. Similarly for the MessageList::Clear method. The MessageList destructor should not destruct the Message objects but should destruct all dynamic structures created by the MessageList class.

```
class MessageList
{...
  public:
    MessageList();
    void Add(Message& msg);
    void Draw();
    void Clear();
    ~MessageList();
};
```

4.8 Controlling Change

Variables, methods, and parameters may be declared such that their ability to cause change or be changed is restricted. A variable may be limited so that it has a constant, unchanging value, a method limited so that it does not change the object on which it is operating, and a parameter limited so that it cannot be changed by the method to which it is passed.

Limiting variables, methods, and parameters in this way is useful for three reasons. First, the additional declaration provides a more specific statement of the intention of the programmer. Often these intentions cannot be expressed and are, perhaps inadvertently, violated, causing unintended behavior and system errors. With the additional declaration, the compiler is able to detect and prevent unintended usage. Second, when errors do occur, the additional declarations help to reduce the area of the system that must be examined. If data has been improperly changed, the direct cause cannot be in those areas declared not to cause or allow such changes. Third, the additional information often helps the compiler to better optimize the executable code. For example, if the compiler knows that a variable cannot change, it need never generate code that would save and restore its value.

In C++ the keyword *const* is used as a modifier on declarations of methods, variables, and parameters to indicate a limitation on its ability to cause change or be changed. The keyword appears in different positions in a declaration depending on whether it is applied to a method, a variable, or a parameter. Also, the use of const with pointers is a little more difficult to understand, as will be seen below.

The enforcement of const properties is done by the compiler. Thus, for example, a compile-time error will result if an assignment is attempted to a constant variable or object. An error will also be detected at compile-time if a constant method that attempts to change some part of the object's data is written.

Constant Variables and Objects

The simplest use of the const attribute is with variables and objects, in which case its purpose is to specify that the variable or object cannot be changed. This allows variables and objects to have a value that is guaranteed to remain unaltered during the execution of the program. Examples of values that should be declared const include mathematical constants (e.g., the value of pi), system limits (e.g., array bounds), program conventions (e.g., a code or value for a flag), program information (e.g., a version number), and fixed application information (e.g., the default location of a standard dialog window); code for these constants looks like this:

```
const double Pi = 2.141598;            // mathematical constant
const int MAX_ARRAY_LENGTH = 100;  // system limit
const int YesAnswer = 0;               // program convention
const int  NoAnswer = 1;               // program convention
const int VersionNumber = 1;           // program information
const int ReleaseNumber = 5;           // program information
const Location dialogLocation (200,200);
                                       // application information
```

Notice that both built-in types (int, double, etc.) as well as objects of user-defined classes (e.g., Shape) may be declared constant. Also notice that variables declared const must be given an initial value when they are declared, as there is no other way to provide a value for the variable—since it is const it cannot be altered after it is declared.

As discussed, assignments to constant variables or objects are detected as errors by the compiler. For example, using the above declarations, the statements:

```
Pi = 2.5;
NoAnswer = 2;
dialogLocation = Location(100,100);
```

would all be detected as compile-time errors.

Constant Methods

The keyword const, when used as a modifier on the declarations of a method, indicates that the method does not change the object to which the method is applied. A modified version of the Location class (Code Sample 4–23) shows how the const modifier is used on methods. For the purposes of this example, two other methods that change the values of the coordinates maintained by the Location, setX() and setY(), are added.

In Code Sample 4–23 the const modifier is used to declare that the two methods Xcoord() and Ycoord() do not change the Location object on which they operate. These two methods are typical of const methods: they return information about the object without changing the object itself. Methods of this kind simply query the object without altering it. The two methods setX() and setY() cannot, however, be declared const because they do change the object to which they are applied.

Note in the above example that the const modifier must appear both where the method appears in the class definition and again in the implementation part where the method's implementation is given.

Constant methods may be applied to a constant object. Because the constant method does not change the object, the use of a constant method does not violate the object's constant property. For example:

```
const Location dialogLocation (200,200);
                                    // application information

    . . .

int dialogX = dialogLocation.Xcoord();          // OK
int dialogY = dialogLocation.Ycoord();          // OK

dialogLocation.setX(300);                       // ERROR
```

In this example, the constant methods Xcoord() and Ycoord() may be applied to the constant object dialogLocation. However, non-constant methods, like setX(), cannot be applied to a constant object because they may change the object thus violating the constant property of the object.

Code Sample 4–23 *Constant Methods in the Location Class*

```
class Location {                                // Extension 1
 private:

   int  currentX, currentY;

 public:

        Location(int x, int y);        // specific location
        Location();                    // default location
   int  Xcoord() const;               // return x-axis coordinate
   int  Ycoord() const;               // return y-axis coordinate
   void setX(int newx);               // change x coordinate
   void setY(int newy);               // change y coordinate
 };

  // the implementation follows

  Location::Location( int x, int y ) { currentX = x;
                                       currentY = y; }

  Location::Location () { currentX = -1; currentY = -1; }

int Location::Xcoord() const { return currentX; }

int Location::Ycoord() const { return currentY; }

void Location::setX(int newx) { currentX = newX; }

void Location::setY(int newy) { currentY = newY; }
```

An object that is not constant may be the subject of constant and non-constant methods. For example:

```
    Location loc(300,300);             // not a constant object

    ...

    int x = loc.Xcoord();              // OK
    loc.setX(x+20);                    // OK - can change object
```

In this example, the object "loc" is not a constant object. Thus, any valid method may be applied to this object, const and non-const methods alike.

Constant Parameters

The const modifier is often used in conjunction parameters that are passed by reference to achieve the safety of passing by-copy while at the same time achieving the efficiency of by-reference. Recall that by-reference is more efficient because it does not create a copy of the object being passed, which efficiency is particularly important when the object is large (e.g., a megabyte-sized jpeg image).

A different extended version of the Location class is shown in Code Sample 4–24 to illustrate how const is used with a by-reference parameter. This extended definition adds a new method that tests whether the coordinates defined by a Location object are the same as the coordinates of a Location object that is passed as a parameter. The parameter object is passed by-reference to avoid any cost associated with passing the object by copy, and the parameter is declared const because it is not necessary to modify the parameter object to determine whether the two Locations are the same.

Notice again that the const modifier for the parameter appears in both the class definition and the implementation where the code for the method is given.

Notice also that the isSameAs() method is itself declared to be a const method because it does not change the object to which it is applied. Thus, it is possible to apply this method to constant Location objects as in the following example:

```
const Location dialogLocation (200,200);
                                // application information

...

Location someWhere();
                                // manipulate someWhere...
if (dialogLocation.isSameAs(someWhere)) {...}
```

Notice that the parameter object named someWhere need not be a constant object. The reference that the isSameAs method works with, however, is modified by const so that the isSameAs method may not change the parameter even if, as in this case, the parameter is not itself a constant object. In other words, for the purposes of this method invocation, the parameter is treated as if it was a constant object, whether it really is or not.

Using const with Pointers

The const modifier can be used in conjunction with a pointer in one of three ways, depending on whether the modifier applies to: the object being pointed to (lp1 in Fig. 4–8), the pointer to the object (lp2 in Fig. 4–8), or both the pointer and the object being pointed to (lp3 in Fig. 4–8). The placement of the const modifier varies in each case, and in the third case it appears twice. The three different uses of

Code Sample 4–24   *Constant Parameters in the Location Class*

```
class Location {                         // Extension 2
  private:

    int  currentX, currentY;

  public:

      Location(int x, int y);       // specific location
      Location();                   // default location
    int Xcoord() const;             // return x-axis coordinate
    int Ycoord() const;             // return y-axis coordinate
    int isSameAs(const Location& other) const;
                                    // are two locations the same
  };

  // the implementation follows

  Location::Location( int x, int y ) { currentX = x;
                                       currentY = y; }

  Location::Location () { currentX = -1; currentY = -1; }

int Location::Xcoord() const { return currentX; }

int Location::Ycoord() const { return currentY; }

int Location::isSameAs(const Location& other) const
{
    if ((currentX == other.Xcoord()) &&
        (currentY == other.Ycoord()) )
        return 1;
    else return 0;
}
```

const with pointers is shown graphically in Fig. 4–8, then its code is given and explained.

In the code, the declaration for lp1 specifies that the object being pointed to is constant, that is the object "loc" may not be changed when it is accessed via the lp1 pointer. In the example code, the use of lp1 to apply the Xcoord() method is legal but the use of lp1 to apply the setX() method would be illegal. Also, since lp1 itself is not constant, it can be made to point to another Location object (e.g., other). However, using lp1 it would not be possible to modify the other object.

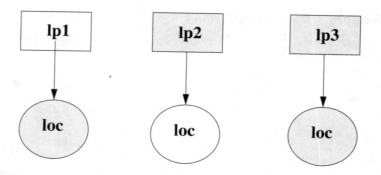

The shaded parts are "const"

Figure 4–8 Uses of const with Pointers

The declaration of lp2 specifies that the pointer, but not the object, is constant. Thus, it is legal to apply methods that modify the object being pointed to by lp2. However, it is not legal to assign a new value to lp2 itself. The const in this case indicates that the pointer value is constant and cannot be changed to point to another object.

The declaration of lp3 specifies that both the pointer and the object are constant. Thus, const methods, like Xcoord(), can be applied to the object. However, the object cannot be changed by using mutator methods like setX() and the pointer itself cannot be changed to point to another object.

```
Location loc(100,100);
Location other(50,50);

const Location *lp1          = &loc;   // object constant
Location const *lp2          = &loc;   // pointer constant
const Location * const lp3 = &loc;     // both constant

lp1->Xcoord();                         // OK
lp1->setX(10);                         // ERROR
lp1 = &other;                          // OK

lp2->Xcoord();                         // OK
lp2->setX(10);                         // OK
lp2 = &other;                          // ERROR

lp3->Xcoord();                         // OK
lp3->setX(10);                         // ERROR
lp3 = &other;                          // ERROR
```

Code Sample 4–25 *Constant Pointers in the Location Class*

```
class Location {                              // Extension 3
  private:

    int   currentX, currentY;

  public:

      Location(int x, int y); // specific location
      Location();             // default location
    int Xcoord() const;       // return x-axis coordinate
    int Ycoord() const;       // return y-axis coordinate
    int isInList(const Location * const list) const;
                              // check if this object is in list
  };

  // the implementation follows

    Location::Location( int x, int y ) { currentX = x;
                                         currentY = y; }

    Location::Location () { currentX = -1; currentY = -1; }

int Location::Xcoord() const { return currentX; }

int Location::Ycoord() const { return currentY; }

int Location::isInList(const Location * const list,  int
length) const
{
  for( int i = 0; i<length; i++)
    if( (currentX == list[i].Xcoord()) &&
        (currentY == list[i].Ycoord()) )
      return 1;
  return 0;
}
```

A final variation of the Location class is presented in Code Sample 4–25 and illustrates the use of const and pointers for parameters. In this example, the isInList() method is added, which determines if the coordinates of the object also appear in an array of Location objects passed as a parameter. The declaration of the parameter in the isInList method specifies that both the pointer and the array being pointed to cannot be changed by the execution of the method. Also, the isInList method itself is declared to be const, meaning that it cannot change the data of the object performing the method (i.e., the object searching the list for its coordinates).

To complete the above example, here is the code that uses the isInList method.

```
Location finder(100,100);

Location list[10];
int length = 10;

//...give values to objects in array list

if (finder.isInList(list, 10))
    { finder's coordinates are in the list }
else { finder's coordinates are not in the list )
```

In this code, the array of Location objects is passed as a pointer consistent with the C language form of passing arrays.

 Exercises

1. Write the declaration of a constant Location object that specifies the center position on a 800 x 600 display.

2. Rewrite the declaration of the Shape class to include the use of const.

3. Examine the interface of the Frame class and identify all of the parameters and methods that could be declared as constant parameters or constant methods.

4. Examine the interface of the TextBox class and identify all of the parameters and methods that could be declared as constant parameters or constant methods.

4.9 Copy Constructors

Through a special constructor called a copy constructor a class can define how its instances are copied. A copy constructor uses an existing object's attributes (data, state, instance variables) to initialize the new object being created.

A copy constructor is a constructor that has a certain, fixed signature. Like other constructors, the copy constructor cannot be called explicitly, but only implicitly when the C++ language dictates that a copy of an object is required.

Code Sample 4–26   *StatusLine Class Interface*

```
Class StatusLine {

  private:
    Message statusMessage;

  public:

    StatusLine(Message msg);
    void SetStatus(Message newMsg);


};
```

If a class does not define a copy constructor, a default copy constructor is used that performs a byte-by-byte copy from the existing object to the new object. In many simple cases the default copy constructor is adequate. However, as the examples below will show, the default copy constructor is often inadequate. In addition, many consider it good style to always define a copy constructor even if it has the same effect as the default copy constructor.

The first of two circumstances under which a copy constructor is implicitly used is when a new object is declared and initialized using an existing object. This circumstance is illustrated in the following code:

```
Frame  window1("First", Location(100, 100), Shape (200,300));
Frame  window2("Second", Location(100, 100), Shape (200,300));
Message originalMsg("Hello World");

Message copiedMsg( originalMsg );   // copy constructor used
                                    // to initialize new object
```

In this example, the declaration of the Message object copiedMsg uses the copy constructor defined for the Message class. The initial values for the data members of the object copiedMsg are initialized based on the data members in the object originalMsg. The second circumstance where a copy constructor is implicitly used is when an object is passed as a parameter by-copy. This circumstance is illustrated in the case of the StatusLine class defined in Code Sample 4–26. When either the StatusLine constructor or its SetStatus method is used, a copy of the Message parameter is made because both of these parameters are passed by-copy.

The default copy constructor is not sufficient to allow Message class objects to be copied safely in the circumstances described above. Recall that the implementation of the Message class uses a character string (a char*) to hold a pointer that defines the text to be displayed on the screen. To avoid a memory leak, the

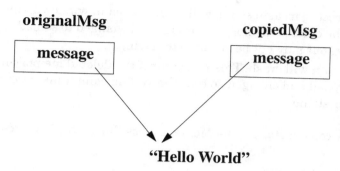

Figure 4–9 Shared Data

destructor for the Message class appropriately deletes this character string when the Message object is deleted. The relevant portion of the Message class is:

```
class Message {
private:
  char*     message;
  ...
public:
  ...
  ~Message();                                    // delete message

};
Message::~Message(){ delete message; }
```

When a copy of a Message object is made using the default copy constructor, the pointer (message), but not the string to which it points, is copied. This default copying results in the situation shown in Fig. 4–9.

Both objects point to the same place in memory. As long as both objects exist, there is no problem. However, if either of the objects is deleted, the character string will be deallocated by that object's destructor, leaving the other object pointing to a place in memory that has an undefined content.

The errors that can result from this situation are as follows. In the case above, the first call on the Display method will create a copy of the originalMsg object. This copy will be destructed at the end of the Display method. Thus, both the originalMsg object and the copiedMsg object are pointing to memory with undefined content. When the second call on Display is made one of three things can happen:

1. The correct string ("Hello World") is displayed in window2; this will occur if the deleted memory is not immediately recycled or, even if recycled, is not immediately changed. The memory may remain the same for some indeterminate period.

2. An incorrect (garbage) string will be displayed in window2; this will occur if the deleted memory is recycled and changed to something that looks like, but may not be, a character string.

3. The program will crash. This will occur if the deleted memory has been recycled and changed so that the system cannot interpret it as a character string.

The copy constructor for the Message class illustrates how a copy constructor is defined:

```
class Message {
  private:
    . . .
  public:

      Message(const Message& other);    // copy constructor
};
```

The copy constructor has a single argument—a reference to an object of the same class (i.e., the Message class in this case) that is not changed (i.e., it is declared const). The input argument (other) is declared const because the copy constructor does not need to change the argument to initialize the new object.

The code for the Message class's copy constructor is:

```
Message::Message(const Message& other) {
        message = copystring(other.message); }
```

This constructor copies the character string that is defined by the other object. In this case, when each object is destructed only its own copy of the character string will be deleted. No memory leaks are created and no dangling pointers occur.

 Exercises

1. Add a copy constructor to the Shape class. Test your code with a simple main program.

2. Add a copy constructor to the Location class. Test your code with a simple main program.

3. Add a copy constructor to the PolyShape class. Test your code with a simple main program.

4. Examine the StopWatch class implementation. Is the default copy constructor sufficient to allow copies of StopWatch objects to be made safely or is a copy constructor needed?

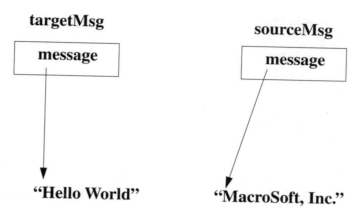

Figure 4–10   Before Assignment Statement

4.10 Assignment Operator

A class can define its own assignment operator, which defines what actions occur when a value is assigned to an object. A class-specific assignment operator is needed because, similar to a copy constructor, special actions may need to be taken to insure that the object behaves in a reasonable way when objects of the same class are assigned to one another. By default, object assignment is bitwise: a bit-by-bit copy is done from the source object (the one on the right-hand side of the assignment operator) to the target object (the one on the left-hand side of the assignment operator).

The Message class illustrates the need for a class-specific assignment operator. The following example shows two Message objects, one of which is assigned to the other:

```
Message targetMsg("Hello World");
Message sourceMsg("MacroSoft, Inc.");

...

targetMsg = sourceMsg;              // assignment
```

Before the assignment statement is executed, the structure of the objects is as shown in Fig. 4–10.

Fig. 4–11 shows the situation after the default (bitwise) assignment operation is completed.

There are two obvious, and serious, problems created by the default assignment. First, a memory leak has been created because the original targetMsg

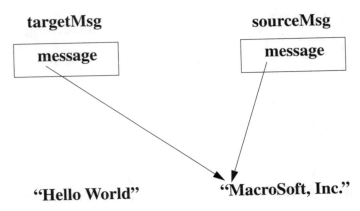

Figure 4–11   After Assignment Statement

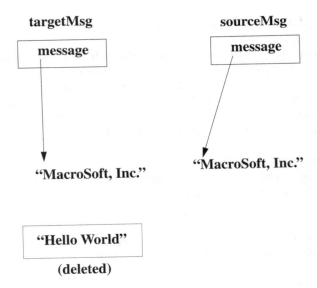

Figure 4–12   Desired Result of Assignment

string is no longer accessible but has not been returned to the memory management system. Second, both objects (targetMsg and sourceMsg) point to the same character string. Because they point to the same string, the destruction of one of the Message objects causes the other Message object to point to memory with undefined contents.

Fig. 4–12 shows what is desired by the assignment operator.

In this situation, the original targetMsg string ("Hello World") has been deallocated and the targetMsg now points to a copy of the original sourceMsg string ("MacroSoft, Inc.").

The Message class shown below includes a class-specific assignment operator:

```
class Message {
  private:
     char* message;
     ...
  public:
     ...
     void operator=(const Message& source);
     ...
};

void Message::operator=(const Message& source) {
   delete message;                    // deallocate previous string
     message = copystring(source.message); // copy new string
}
```

The name of the assignment operator is "operator=". The "operator" part is mandatory and signifies that a class-specific definition is being given for a standard C++ operator. Which standard C++ operator is being given a class-specific meaning is determined by the symbol(s) that follow immediately after the "operator" keyword.

 Exercises

1. Unsafe Address Class: The Address class represents a postal-system address defined by two character strings denoting the street address, and the city and state, and an integer zip code. All three items are required by the constructor. For example:

    ```
    Address office("123 Main St.", "Blacksburg, VA", 24061);
    Address home  ("456 Cozy Dr.", "Blacksburg, VA", 24061);
    ```

    The Address class has a method SameZip that returns 0 or 1 indicating whether the address object executing the method has the same zip code as the Address object passed as a parameter by copy. For example:

    ```
    int same = office.SameZip(home);
    ```

    Implement an unsafe version of the Address class that has neither a copy constructor nor an assignment operator. Write a main program that uses this class and show how using the unsafe class can result in run-time errors, unexpected behavior, and/or memory leaks.

2. **Safe Address Class:** Implement a safe version of the Address class. This version must be designed so that Address objects may be copied, assigned, and destructed safely and without memory leaks.

3. Add an assignment operator to the Shape class. Test your code with a simple main program.

4. Add an assignment operator to the Location class. Test your code with a simple main program.

4.11 Other Class Features

Five additional features of a class are:

- inline methods: an efficient way to implement very small methods
- this pointer:a way for an object to refer to itself
- private methods: utility methods that are useful in implementing a class, but are not intended to be part of the class's public interface
- static class variables: data that is shared among all objects of a given class
- friend classes: allow special access to the private part of a class for performance or access-control reasons

Each of these features is illustrated with an example. The examples are variations of the Rectangle class or the PolyShape class introduced in Sections 4.5 and 4.7, respectively.

Inline Methods

The PolyShape class is an example of a class possessing several very small methods. Each of the Up, Down, Right, and Left methods are exactly one line of code and, in each case, the one line of code simply increments one of the private data elements of the class. For a PolyShape object, p, an invocation of

```
p.Up(10)
```

results in the compiler generating assembly language code of the form

```
save registers on the stack
establish new call frame
push argument(s) on the stack
call p.Up
remove call frame
restore saved registers
```

As can be seen, there is overhead involved in setting up the execution environment to perform the method and to restore the execution environment after the method has been executed. For small methods, this overhead may be disproportionate to the execution time of the method itself. For the four methods in the PolyShape class, the execution time of the single instruction may be a single instruction cycle. The call instruction leads to the execution that is "out of line" because it changes the program counter to jump to a new piece of code.

When the efficiency of small methods is a concern inline functions may be used to allow the compiler to generate more efficient code than would normally be the case. For an inline method the call

```
p.Up(10)
```

would result in the compiler generating the following code:

```
p.currentY = p.currentY - 10;
```

This code is generated "in line" with the other code of the caller. The overhead of a method invocation is entirely removed. But because this efficiency comes at some price (as will be seen later) the decision to use inline functions should be made carefully.

Code Sample 4–27 shows the redefinition of the PolyShape class with the Up, Down, Right, and Left methods represented as inline methods. Notice that the code for each of the four methods has been included immediately after the definition of each method in the class definition (in the header file). This placement of the code is a suggestion to the compiler to generate inline code for all invocations of these methods. Notice that the other methods of the class are not inline methods.

Because the code for the inline methods is given in the header file, it must not appear in the code file.

Inline methods do not violate the encapsulation properties of the class, for programmers using a class with inline methods are still prohibited from direct access to the private data of a PolyShape object. However, as an optimization for inline methods, the compiler can generate the machine-level code as efficiently as if the programmer were able to do this. Thus, inline methods improve the execution time efficiency of code without sacrificing the encapsulation properties of the class.

Inline methods are a mixed blessing and thus should be used carefully because:

- The presence of the code in the header file conveys information about how the class is implemented and this violates the spirit, though not the letter, of the law of encapsulation. Programmers may attempt to make their own code as efficient as possible by clever programming tricks that exploit the implementation information revealed by the inline methods. However, if the code of the class changes—and, hence, the code of the inline methods

Code Sample 4–27   *PolyShape Class with Inline Methods*

```
class PolyShape
{
private:
    LocationNode *head;
    LocationNode *tail;
    int currentX, currentY;
    int length;

public:
    PolyShape(int x, int y);
    void Up    (int n){currentY = currentY - n;};
    void Down  (int n){currentY = currentY + n;};
    void Left  (int n){currentX = currentX - n;};
    void Right (int n){currentX = currentX + n;};
    void Mark();
    void Draw(Canvas& canvas);
    ~PolyShape();
};
```

also changes—the code with the tricks may be worse than a straightforward use of the class.

- If the code of an inline method changes, all code that uses this method must also be recompiled. This is in contrast to a regular (not inline) method. If the code of a regular method in a class is changed, only the code for that class needs to be recompiled. Thus, inline methods cause more work at compile time in exchange for some efficiency gain at run-time. It is important to know whether this trade-off is worthwhile before using inline methods.

- If an inline method is made into a regular method or a regular method is inlined, all code that uses this method must be recompiled, even if the method's code is unchanged. This recompilation is necessary because the code generated for the user of the method is different depending on whether or not the method is inline.

- There is a performance penalty to be paid for inappropriate use of inlined methods. One of the advantages of using a method call, as opposed to inline code, is that the method's code is not duplicated. If a method that has many lines of code is inlined and is called from many places in the system, then the code for that method is duplicated at every place where a call to the method occurs. This causes the size of the code of the system to grow. The proper use of inline methods should evaluate the possible reduc-

Code Sample 4–28 *Using the PolyShape Class*

```
PolyShape quad(20,20);
...

quad.Right(100);
quad.Down(50);
quad.Mark();
quad.Left(20);
quad.Mark();
quad.Down(30);
quad.Left(50);
quad.Mark();
quad.Draw(canvas);
```

tion in execution time gained by the inlining against the possible increase in the size of the code. Even though memories are large, increases in code size can affect the behavior of hardware code caches and system paging performance.

Finally, it must be kept in mind that an inline method is only a suggestion to a compiler. In some cases the compiler may refuse to inline methods that it considers too complicated to inline correctly or easily.

The "this" Pointer

In some cases, an object may need to invoke a method of another object in order to pass itself as an argument of the method or, in the example to be considered here, an object may want to return itself as the result of one of its own methods. The question is, how is an object able to refer to itself? The PolyShape class will be used to illustrate why an object may be designed to return itself as the result of a method. Code Sample 4–28 shows a typical use of the PolyShape class to draw a polygonal shape. Notice that sequences of statements are needed to perform each operation one at a time.

Instead of using sequences of statements, it might be desirable to provide an interface such that related operations can be strung together. An example of this has already been seen in the case of the stream I/O operators that can be performed one after the other in a single statement. This clearly makes the use of these operators more natural and readable. The PolyShape class can be redesigned to allow the code in Code Sample 4–28 to be written as shown in Code Sample 4–29.

Although expressions such as "quad.Left(20).Mark()" may seem strange at first, they are no more unusual than arithmetic expressions like "a + b − c". In

Code Sample 4–29   *Revising the PolyShape Class to Allow a Sequence of Method Calls*

```
PolyShape quad(20,20);
...

quad.Right(100).Down(50).Mark();
quad.Left(20).Mark();
quad.Down(30).Left(50).Mark();
quad.Draw(canvas);
```

each case the subexpression yields a result (an object) that is the subject of the next operation to be performed.

The existing definition of the PolyShape class will not allow its methods to be applied in sequence in one expression. The methods Up, Down, Right, and Left all return "void" as a result. Thus, an expression like

```
quad.Left(20).Mark();
```

cannot be done because the result of "quad.Left(20)" would be void and the subsequent expression would be an illegal "void.Mark()".

What is needed is a way for each of the operations Up, Down, Left, and Right to return as a result the same object on which they themselves operated. This involves changes in both the definition and implementation of the PolyShape class. These changes are shown in Code Sample 4–30.

The methods being changed return a result of type PolyShape&. The intent of the change would be defeated if the return type were simply PolyShape because this would indicate return by-copy. If the result were returned by copy, each operation in a sequence would operate on a different copy of the object. This is contrary to the intent of applying all operations in a sequence to the same object.

The methods of an object may refer to a predefined, special variable named "this," which is a pointer to the object itself. This special variable is understood by the compiler to be correctly typed for the current object. This means that in a method of a PolyShape class the type of "this" is taken to be "PolyShape*" (i.e., a pointer to a PolyShape object). In a method of a Rectangle class the type of "this" is taken to be "Rectangle*" (i.e., a pointer to a Rectangle object). Note that the "this" variable is predefined; it should not (and indeed cannot) be declared in the program.

The role of the "this" pointer is seen in the code for the revised Up method. After changing the state variables of the object, the code must be able to indicate that the return value is the same PolyShape object as that which the current method is operating upon. The "this" pointer can be used for this purpose. Since

Code Sample 4–30 *Using the "this" Pointer in the PolyShape Class*

```
class PolyShape
{
private:
    // same as before

public:
    ...
    PolyShape& Up    (int n);
    PolyShape& Down  (int n);
    PolyShape& Left  (int n);
    PolyShape& Right (int n);
    PolyShape& Mark  ();

};

// a portion of the implementation

PolyShape& PolyShape::Up(int n)
{ currentY = currentY - n;
  return *this;
}
```

the return type is an object, not a pointer to an object, the return value is "*this" (i.e., the object to which "this" points) and not "this" (a pointer to an object).

Private Methods

It is not uncommon that two or more methods in the public interface of a class contain repeated code. Typical examples of repeated code are methods that use the same subalgorithm to compute an intermediate value or that use the same code to perform error checking. The Rectangle class is an example of repeated code. As shown in Code Sample 4–31, the Rectangle constructor and the various move methods both perform the same manipulations of the four aggregated Location objects.

To remove repeated code it is necessary to define a new method (member function of the class) that can be called by the methods in the public interface without the new method itself becoming part of the public interface.

The abbreviated revised definition of the Rectangle class shown in Code Sample 4–32 contains a private method named AdjustCorners(). This method assumes that the upperLeft Location has been set to its correct value. Using the upperLeft and the area, AdjustCorners sets the positions the other corners of the Rectangle to their correct Locations.

Code Sample 4–31   *Repeated Code in the Rectangle Class*

```
Rectangle::Rectangle(Location corner, Shape shape)
{ area = shape;
  upperLeft  = corner;
  upperRight = Location(upperLeft.Xcoord() + area.Width(),
                        upperLeft.Ycoord());
  lowerLeft  = Location(upperLeft.Xcoord() ,
                        upperLeft.Ycoord() + area.Height());
  lowerRight = Location(upperLeft.Xcoord() + area.Width(),
                        upperLeft.Ycoord() + area.Height());
}

void Rectangle::MoveUp(int deltaY)
{ upperLeft  = Location(upperLeft.Xcoord(),
                        upperLeft.Ycoord() + deltaY);
  upperRight = Location(upperLeft.Xcoord() + area.Width(),
                        upperLeft.Ycoord());
  lowerLeft  = Location(upperLeft.Xcoord() ,
                        upperLeft.Ycoord() + area.Height());
  lowerRight = Location(upperLeft.Xcoord() + area.Width(),
                        upperLeft.Ycoord() + area.Height());
}

// ... MoveDown, MoveLeft, MoveRight similar to MoveUp
```

Code Sample 4–32   *Private Method Defined in the Rectangle Class*

```
class Rectangle
{
  private:
    Location upperLeft;
    // other Locations...
    Shape    area;

    void AdjustCorners(); // private method

  public:
    Rectangle (Location corner, Shape shape);
    void MoveUp   (int deltaY);
    // ... other Move methods
    void Draw(Canvas& canvas);
    void Clear(Canvas& canvas);
    ~Rectangle();
};
```

Code Sample 4–33 *Implementation of Revised Rectangle Class*

```
void Rectangle::AdjustCorners()
{ upperRight = Location(upperLeft.Xcoord() + area.Width(),
                        upperLeft.Ycoord());
  lowerLeft  = Location(upperLeft.Xcoord() ,
                        upperLeft.Ycoord() + area.Height());
  lowerRight = Location(upperLeft.Xcoord() + area.Width(),
                        upperLeft.Ycoord() + area.Height());
}


Rectangle::Rectangle(Location corner, Shape shape)
{ area = shape;
  upperLeft  = corner;
  AdjustCorners();  // call private method
}

void Rectangle::MoveUp(int deltaY)
{ upperLeft  = Location(upperLeft.Xcoord(),
                        upperLeft.Ycoord() + deltaY);
  AdjustCorners();  // call private method
}

// ... MoveDown, MoveLeft, MoveRight similar to MoveUp
```

Since the private method is declared in the private part of the Rectangle class, it can be accessed (i.e., invoked) by any of the methods in the Rectangle class and only from methods in the Rectangle class. The implementation of the AdjustCorners private method and the revised MoveUp method are shown in Code Sample 4–33.

In this revised code for the Rectangle class notice that the AdjustCorners method is like every other method in the class in that AdjustCorners can access the private data of the Rectangle class, and in the code file its fully qualified name is Rectangle::AdjustCorners.

The only difference between AdjustCorners and the other methods is that AdjustCorners is not visible outside of the class. Thus, the following code:

```
Rectangle rect(Location(50,50), Shape(20,20));
...
rect.AdjustCorners();
```

would be in error because it attempts to access a private part, in this case a private method, of the Rectangle class. An appropriate error message would be generated for this code by the compiler.

Code Sample 4–34 *Static Data Declared in the Rectangle Class*

```
class Rectangle
{
  private:
      Location upperLeft;
      Location upperRight;
      Location lowerLeft;
      Location lowerRight;
      Shape    area;

      static Color rectangleColor; // class variable

  public:
      Rectangle (Location corner, Shape shape);
      void setColor(Color newColor);
      //.. other methods as before
      ~Rectangle();
};
```

From within the Rectangle class the AdjustCorners method can be invoked in either of two ways:

- Simply as `AdjustCorners()` as shown above
- By using the this pointer as `this->AdjustCorners()`

In the first way the object to which the method is applied is the current object. The this pointer is assumed implicitly. In the second way the this pointer is used to explicitly indicating the current object. Both ways are correct and result in the same invocation.

Static Class Variables

Static data is way of creating data elements shared among all objects of a given class. The role of this kind of data is more clearly reflected in the names "class data" or "class-wide data," which are sometimes used to describe what C++ calls static data. Static data can be used whenever the attribute of an abstraction should apply to each and every instance of that abstraction.

To illustrate the use of static data, the Rectangle class is extended with a color attribute so that all Rectangles are always drawn with the same color. This revised definition of the Rectangle class is shown in Code Sample 4–34; note its new private data member that defines the color of the Rectangle. Because this data member is declared as static, the value of this data member is shared by all objects of the Rectangle class. Also added to the class is a method to set the color to a new value.

The class-wide effect of a static variable is illustrated by the following code. Suppose that the static variable rectangleColor has been initialized so that all Rectangles are initially drawn in a red color. The first time that the two Rectangles are drawn they will appear in red. Once the color is changed to blue, then all Rectangles drawn after that will be drawn in blue. Notice that the color is changed using the setColor method for rect2. However, this changes the color not just for that Rectangle object, but for all Rectangle objects. Thus, when the two Rectangles are drawn again after the change in color, both of the Rectangles will be drawn in blue.

```
Rectangle  rect1(...);       // constructor details not shown
Rectangle  rect2(...);
Canvas     canvas(...);
Color      blue(0, 200,0);  //a shade of blue
...
rect1.Draw(canvas);          // will be drawn in red
rect2.Draw(canvas);          // will be drawn in red
...
rect2.setColor(blue);        // change color
...
rect2.Draw(canvas);          // will be drawn in blue
rect1.Draw(canvas);          // will be drawn in blue
```

Because a static class variable is shared among all objects of a given class, its value cannot be initialized by the constructor for that class. If this were done, then every time a new object of the class is created, the value of the static class variable would be set back to its initial value. Instead, a means is needed to initialize the static class variable one time regardless of how objects of the class are created or when these objects are created. To guarantee that the static class variable is initialized only once, the initialization code is placed with the code (the implementation) of the class. For the Rectangle class, the initialization is shown in Code Sample 4–35.

Notice that the fully qualified name (Rectangle::rectangleColor) must be used in naming the variable to be initialized. Also notice that the setColor method uses the simple name (rectangleColor) of this variable.

Friend Classes

In limited, special cases, there is a need to establish a special relationship between two classes for efficiency or security reasons by making one class a "friend" of another. If class B declares that class A is a friend class, then the methods of class A are allowed to access the private section of class B. The friend declaration must be made in the class whose private section is being accessed (i.e., a class can grant access to its private section). The friend relationship is asymmetric: class A is a

Code Sample 4–35 *Initializing Static Class Variables*

```
Color Rectangle::rectangleColor = Color(200,0,0); //a shade of red

void Rectangle::AdjustCorners()
{ //...as before
}
Rectangle::Rectangle(Location corner, Shape shape)
{ // ... as before
}

void Rectangle::setColor(Color color)
{ rectangleColor = color; // change for all Rectangle objects
}

// all other methods as before
```

friend of class B does not imply that class B is a friend of class A. The friend relationship is not transitive: if class A is a friend of class B and class B is a friend of class C, class A is not automatically a friend of class C. A friend relationship between two classes devolves upon the objects of these classes: if class B declares that class A is a friend class then all objects of class A can access the private data of any object of class B that the class A object knows about.

Clearly the notion of a friend relationship must be used with great restraint because it weakens the encapsulation of the class granting the friendship, for its usual safeguards and privacy that accompany encapsulation are lessened. However, the friend relation establishes only a selective weakening of encapsulation and, if used modestly, can serve useful purposes. Used to an extreme, the friend relation becomes dangerous and corrupts a good design.

Two examples of good uses of the friend relation follow. The first example involves a manager class that requires special access to the encapsulated data of a PolyShape class. In this example, efficiency motivates using the friend relationship. The second example shows how to use the friend relation to insure that Rectangle objects can only be created in certain ways. In this example, access control is the motivation for using the friend relationship.

The first example of using the friend relation involves an application in which a number of Rectangle objects exist within a space that is represented by an object of a Space class. In different applications, the Space could model physical objects moving within a two dimensional scene, windows and other icons on a computer screen, the placement of electronic components on a board, and many others. A critical operation typically associated with such a Space class is an intersection test, that is, to determine if any two objects in the space overlap. Computing the intersection relies on knowledge of the vertices and/or edges of each of the shapes within the space. The intersection test can be time consuming if there are many objects in the space so there might be some concern for making this test as efficient as possible. Given the definition of the Rectangle class, there is no way for the Space class to access the set of Location objects that are part of the private data of a Rectangle object. One alternative is to add an accessor method to the Rectangle class that would return one or all of the Location objects of a PolyShape object. This approach is sometimes objectionable because it exposes the internal data of the Rectangle class to all other classes, not just to the Space class. A second alternative uses the friend relationship: the Rectangle object declares that the Space class is a friend class. This relationship allows the Space class to access the private data (the Location information) inside of the Rectangle class. The outline of the code that establishes the friend relationship between the Rectangle class and the Space class is shown in Code Sample 4–36.

The friend declaration is placed in the class granting the access (in this case the Rectangle class). The effect of the friend declaration can be seen in the skeleton code shown for the AnyInteresections() method, in which the private data (upperLeft, lowerRight) of the Rectangle objects are directly accessed via pointers to the two Rectangle objects. In the absence of the friend declaration, these direct accesses would be detected by the compiler as illegal.

The second example uses the friend relationship to obtain enhanced access control. Consider an application that is using Rectangles, all of which are required to be of the same Shape. Such a restriction comes from the problem domain in the form of requirements like all tiles are the same shape, all windows in this building are the same shape, or all memory chips on this layout are the same shape. To enforce the requirement of identical Shape we might consider creating a RectangleFactory class that constructs and returns Rectangle objects. The RectangleFactory is constructed with a Shape object that it will use during its lifetime. All Rectangle objects produced by a given RectangleFactory will have the same Shape. Recall that the Rectangle class does not provide a method for the Shape to be changed. Therefore, exclusive use of the RectangleFactory to create Rectangle objects enforces the application requirement.

The RectangleFactory may be used to produce Rectangle objects as follows:

```
RectangleFactory squareFactory(Shape(50,50));
Canvas canvas(...);
...
Rectangle *rect1, *rect2;
...
rect1 = squareFactory(Location(100,150));
rect2 = squareFactory(Location(200,150));
...
rect1->Draw(canvas);
rect2->Draw(canvas);
```

In this code, a RectangleFactory object is constructed so that all Rectangle objects that it produces will have a square shape that is 50 × 50. Two Rectangle objects are produced using the squareFactory. The objects produced by the

Code Sample 4–36   *Using Friend Classes for Efficiency*

```
class Rectangle
{
  private:
    Location upperLeft;
    Location upperRight;
    Location lowerLeft;
    Location lowerRight;
    Shape    area;

    friend class Space;   // allow the Space class
                          // access to the private data

  public:
    Rectangle (Location corner, Shape shape);
    //.. other methods as before
    ~Rectangle();
};

class Space
{
  private:
    // some data structure to maintain a
    // set of Rectangle objects

  public:
    Space();
    int AnyIntersections();   // determine if there are
                              // any intersections
    // ...other methods
};

// in implementation of Space class

int Space::AnyIntersections()
{ Rectangle *rect1;
  Rectangle *rect2;
  // use data structure to locate two Rectangle objects
  // rect1 and rect2

    if (... rect1->upperLeft.Xcoord() ...
            rect2->lowerRight.Ycoord() ... )
  //...
}
```

Code Sample 4–37 *The Rectangle Factory Class*

```
class RectangleFactory
{
  private:
    Shape commonShape;

  public:
    RectangleFactory(Shape shape);
    Rectangle& New(Location loc);
    ~Rectangle();
};

RectangleFactory::RectangleFactory(Shape shape)
{ commonShape = shape;
}

Rectangle* RectangleFactory::New(Location loc)
{ return new Rectangle(loc,commonShape);
}

RectangleFactory::~RectangleFactory(){}
```

squareFactory are normal Rectangle objects as shown by the way rect1 and rect2 can be manipulated using the standard Rectangle interface.

The RectangleFactory design, however, cannot truly enforce the requirement that all Rectangles have the same shape; only those Rectangles that the factory produces will have this property. There is nothing in the design of the RectangleFactory that would prevent a programmer from bypassing the RectangleFactory and directly instantiating a Rectangle object.

The friend relationship can be used to endow the RectangleFactory with the ability to truly enforce its design requirement, by modifying the Rectangle class as shown in Code Sample 4–38. Two changes are made in the Rectangle class. First, the RectangleFactory is declared as a friend of the Rectangle class. As before, this allows the RectangleFactory to access the private section of the Rectangle class. Second, the Rectangle class's constructor is moved to the private section of the Rectangle class. These two changes have the desired effect because any code that attempts to construct a Rectangle object must have access to the private section of the Rectangle class, for that is where the constructor resides. However, only the Rectangle class itself and the RectangleFactory class have access to the private section of the Rectangle class. Thus, any attempt to construct a Rectangle object outside of these two classes will be detected by the compiler as an error. Notice that pointers to Rectangles (Rectangle*) can still be created outside of these two classes because the pointer is not a Rectangle object.

Code Sample 4–38 *Using the Friend Relationship to Enforce Access Control*

```
class Rectangle
{
  private:
    // data as before

    friend class RectangleFactory;
    Rectangle(Location loc, Shape shape);

  public:
    // other methods as before
};
```

In this example, access to the constructor for a class was restricted to the named friend class. However, the same technique may be used to restrict other operations on a class-by-class basis.

Producing an Object-Oriented System

5.1 Overview of the Production Process

Producing a reliable, executable system from the files containing the classes' implementation is a process that involves three key steps:

1. rebuilding the executable system from the current implementation,

2. testing the system by executing it under varying conditions to reveal errors in the system, and

3. debugging the current implementation by locating and correcting the mistakes made in the system's implementation or design that led to these errors.

These three steps are, of course, iterative: correcting a programming mistake leads to rebuilding a new executable that is further tested and debugged. Ideally, the correction can be accomplished by a small, localized change in a single class. A weak class design or a weak system design, however, can create situations in which extensive changes in many classes, or a major redesign of the entire system, is needed to correct an error. Careful attention to class and system design during the earlier phases of the development process is the best way to minimize backtracking to the design phase when testing and debugging.

Developers must be proficient users of tools that automate the mechanical aspects of the production process. Tools that automate the rebuilding task allow developers to operate more efficiently and more reliably. The tools relieve the developer of the burden of managing a large amount of straightforward, detailed information about the steps needed to rebuild the system and he or she is thus able to operate more efficiently: less attention need be given to the mundane rebuilding task and more effort can be devoted to the critical tasks of design and implementation. The developer is also made more reliable, because the tools are more adept at retaining all of the detailed information about how to rebuild the system. Fewer mistakes, therefore, occur in the mechanical aspects of rebuilding the system. Debugging tools yield information about the system during execution without the need for any preprogramming. These tools make it easier for the developer to examine the state of the executing system and control the system's execution during the debugging task. The developer does not need to insert, and later remove, code to obtain this information and control.

The material presented in this chapter focuses on the production tasks of rebuilding and debugging and excludes other equally important topics that are simply beyond the current emphasis on object-oriented programming. The testing process, for example, is important in developing realistic systems: a more advanced course in software engineering should present techniques for generating test cases and test scenarios, criteria for measuring how completely the system has been tested, and models for estimating the system's reliability. Other important tools that help in the rebuilding process but are beyond the scope of this chapter include: code control tools which are critical for integrating coherently the work of several developers producing parts of the same system, generating a consistent version of the system, and retaining a history of the changes made to a system during development so that previous versions of the system can be recovered.

5.2 General Concepts of Rebuilding a System

The Problem

Correctly and efficiently (re)building the executable version of a system from its individual source files can be a complicated task. In well-organized object-oriented programs, the implementation consists of many interrelated files. Usually each class will be represented by a code file (e.g., one with a ".cc", ".cpp", ".cxx", or similar suffix) and a header file (e.g., one with a ".h" suffix). During development and maintenance of the system it quickly becomes very difficult to remember what parts of the system must be recompiled when a given class has been changed, what compiler options (e.g., optimization level, search paths) are needed to compile a given class, into what, if any, library should the compiled object file be inserted, and what libraries and options are needed when the object files are linked together.

The difficulty of this task is not always evident unless one has had experience with programming and managing the code for a system whose size exceeds that of typical introductory programming classes. The small-scale systems developed for such classes can be handled by a simple, brute-force strategy—recompiling everything all of the time. While this is workable for very small systems, it is horribly inefficient and often unusable for realistically sized systems. Even the modest-sized projects utilized in this book begin to tax the limitations of the brute-force approach.

To manage the rebuilding task it is necessary to understand the concept of dependencies among code units and to understand the steps that are involved in compiling and linking the system together. The compiling and linking steps are driven by the dependencies and changes made to the code units. Understanding these concepts and steps is basic to incremental development and the operation of tools that automate the mechanical steps of the rebuilding task.

Dependencies

The difficulty of (re)building an executable version of a system stems from the many dependencies that exist among the units (files) that make up the system. The notion of one file being dependent on another file can be defined as follows:

Dependent: File A is dependent on file B if it is possible that file A can be invalidated by a change in file B.

Thus, whenever file B changes, file A must be regenerated to insure its own validity. Exactly how file A is regenerated depends on its nature. Table 5–1 describes three basic kinds of dependencies and the tools that are used to regenerate the dependent file.

Table 5–1 Examples of Dependencies

Dependent File	Depends on	Tool to Regenerate
object file	source files (code and header files)	compiler
library	object files	librarian or archiver
executable	object files and libraries	linker

In addition to these, there are other kinds of dependencies, such as a grammar file that might be used to automatically generate a parser for reading the system's input. When the grammar file changes, the parser must be regenerated.

There are two kinds of dependencies among the files that make up an object-oriented system. In the first, the header file for class X may depend on the header file of class Y (X.h --> Y.h), and in the second, the code file for class X may depend on the header file of class Y (X.cc --> Y.h). Notice that code files do not depend on other code files.

The FileChooser class below illustrates these two kinds of dependencies. The definition of the FileChooser class (in FileChooser.h) uses the class File as a return type of the AskUser() method. Thus, the FileChooser.h class must include File.h as FileChooser.h depends on File.h (FileChooser.h --> File.h).

```
class FileChooser  {
private:
        //...
public:

        FileChooser(char* path, char* filter);
                              //search at path with filter
        FileChooser(char* path);    //search at path, no filter
        FileChooser();              //search at CWD, no filter
    File AskUser();                 //get file via dialog
        ~FileChooser();             //clean up
    };
```

The implementation of the FileChooser class (in FileChooser.cc) depends, of course, on FileChooser.h. Further dependencies are found in the implementation of the class's methods. The implementation of the AskUser() method is:

```
File FileChooser::AskUser() {
    Directory directory(thePath, theFilter);
    Selector selector(thePath);

    char* nextName = directory.First();
    while (nextName) {
        selector.Add(nextName);
        nextName = directory.Next();
    }

    char* fileChosen = selector.AskUser();
    return File(fileChosen);
}
```

The AskUser method uses a Directory object and a Selector object. Thus, the FileChooser.cc file depends on the Directory.h file and the Selector.h file. A summary of these dependencies is:

```
        FileChooser.h  --> File.h
        FileChooser.cc --> FileChooser.h Directory.h Selector.h
```

A final dependency is that the object file (denoted by the .o suffix) created by compiling a code file (denoted by the .cc suffix) depends on that code file. Thus,

```
        FileChooser.o --> FileChooser.cc
```

Finally, the dependencies are transitive and cumulative, so that, in total:

```
FileChooser.o --> FileChooser.cc FileChooser.h Directory.h
                  Selector.h File.h
```

This list of dependencies reflects, for example, that if Directory.h changes (i.e., the Directory class interface changes) then the FileChooser class should be recompiled to insure that it conforms properly to these changes.

Compiling and Linking

To use an automated rebuilding tool it is necessary to know:

- what steps occur in compiling and linking a system together,
- how dependencies control the compiling and linking,
- the role of search paths in locating information needed by the compiler and linker, and
- the use of flags, options, and variables to communicate parameters to the compiler and linker.

Each of these elements is presented below.

Steps in Compiling and Linking

An overview of the steps involved in compiling and linking the executable system is shown in Fig. 5–1. This overview identifies the relationships among the various tools and file types that are part of the process. The relationships are indicated by arrowed lines, which indicate what type of file is input to (or output by) each tool.

The first step in rebuilding the system is to compile all necessary source-code files into their corresponding object files. The source-code files contain the code written by the developer in the higher-level programming language (in our case ++). The compiler translates this source code into equivalent code in the instruction set of the processor on which the program will execute. The higher-level programming language is defined to be independent of the operating system and processor. While the source-code files are processor-independent, many source-code files are dependent on a particular operating system because they use services provided only by a specific one. The source code can be compiled without change on any machine with the required operating system but with different processors. Object files are processor-dependent because their compiler-generated contents are meaningful only to a single type of processor. The combination of the operating systems and processor type is referred to as the *platform*. Some source code is platform-independent, meaning that it can be compiled and executed on "any" platform. Examples of platform independent code are

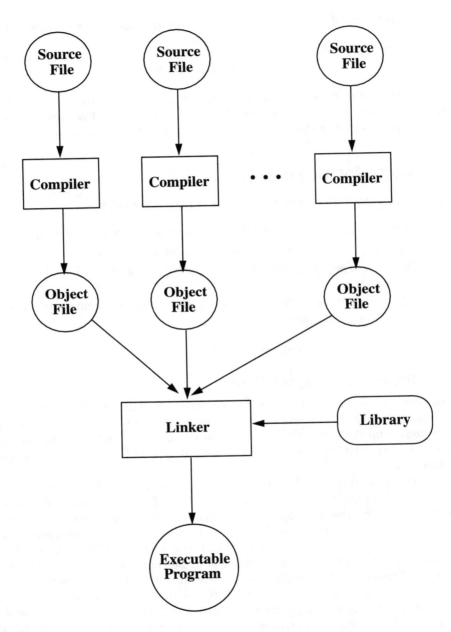

Figure 5–1

graphical packages or communication packages that operate on both Unix and Windows95 systems for any processor type.

Compiling the systems consists of one or more *independent* compilation steps. Independent in this sense means that each execution of the compiler is unrelated to any past or future executions of the compiler: no information generated by the compiler in compiling one source file is used in compiling another source file. This independence means that the source-code files may be compiled in any order. Keep in mind, however, that within each compilation the defined-before-use ordering applies—the compiler must see the definition of a class before objects of that class can be created or manipulated.

The second step in rebuilding the system is to link all necessary object files into a single executable file, which the linker accomplishes by weaving together the independently compiled object files into a single, integrated system. In linking the system together, the two most common errors are two elements with the same name and missing required elements. Duplicate names arise when developers use the same name for two different purposes; a missing element may be caused by inaccurate dependency information, leading to a failure to compile a necessary part of the system.

The single most important act of the linker is to connect the code generated for the invocation of a method (in one compilation step) with the code generated for the implementation of that method (in a second compilation step). For example, the invocation whose source code form is

```
MyClass example;
....
example.MyMethod(arg0,...,argn-1,argn);
```

might get compiled into object code of the form

```
push argn               // put arguments on stack
push argn-1
...
push arg0
call MyClass_MyMethod   // execute code of method
```

where the symbol "MyClass_MyMethod" is a compiler-generated *unresolved external reference*. When the call instruction is executed, however, the processor needs to know where the code for MyMethod can be found. The linker supplies this information (termed "resolving the external reference") by using entry-point definitions generated by other compilation steps. When the MyClass class is compiled, in an independent compilation step, the source code of the form

```
MyClass::MyMethod(arg0,...,argn-1, argn)
{...}
```

might get compiled into object code of the form

```
MyClass_MyMethod: entry
    ...
```

```
instructions generated for the
source statements of the method
...
```

where the "entry" directive indicates the entry point (the location of the beginning) of the method MyMethod. When the object file containing the invocation (and the unresolved external reference) and the object file containing the entry point are presented to the linker, the linker is able to use their combined information to resolve the external reference by replacing the unresolved external reference in the call instruction with the location of the entry point for the method's code.

The linker typically is supplied with one or more libraries. A library is simply a collection of object files that have been placed together for convenience in a single file; it also may be called an archive. Commercially available software usually comes packaged in one or more libraries, and different operating systems provide utilities that developers use to build a library from a collection of the object files they have created. The linker will usually first use all of the non-library object files to resolve external references and then use the libraries to resolve any remaining external references.

Each of the compiling and linking steps can produce error messages. The compiler, for example, will report errors in the syntax of the code written by the developer; the linker will report errors if duplicate entry point names are found during linking or if unresolved external references remain after all object files and libraries have been searched. It is important to be able to distinguish between these two types of error messages, because the developer must usually take different actions depending on which type of error occurs. It is also important to be able to distinguish between error messages generated during the rebuilding of the system from the error messages generated during execution.

How Dependencies Control Compiling and Linking

The developer's automated rebuilding tool uses the dependency information to drive the compiling and linking process. The overall effect of this tool is shown as a high-level, inefficient scheme in Code Sample 5-1, where all changed source files are recompiled along with any source files that depend on them. Once the recompilations are completed, the linker builds a new executable file. The real tool would, of course, use a more sophisticated and efficient strategy to achieve this same effect.

The automated rebuilding tool can detect changes in a file by comparing time information associated with each file, for the file system maintains the time when a file was created (creation time) and the time when the file was last written to (last modification time). A change is deemed to have occurred in the source file "source" if

```
executable.CreationTime < source.LastModificationTime
```

Code Sample 5–1 *Using Dependencies to Control Recompilation*

```
for all A in SourceFiles
   {   if (A has changed)
       {   recompile A;
           for all B in SourceFiles
           {   if B depends on A
               {   then recompile B
               }
           }
       }
   }
   link object files;
```

where "executable" is the executable file. This test implies that any source file that has been modified since the creation of the executable must be recompiled.

Search Paths

The automated rebuilding tool must be informed by the developer of the *search paths* used by both the compiler and the linker to locate needed files. A search path is simply an ordered list of directories. The compiler (actually the preprocessor of the compiler) has an *include file search path* that gives the names of directories to search when it is attempting to find an include file. The linker has a *library search path* that gives the names of directories to search when it is attempting to find a library or archive file. These search paths are specified separately, because they include files and the library files are typically stored in different places in the file system, and in ways that are entirely dependent on the tool.

Flags, Options, and Variables

By setting flags, choosing options, and defining variables, the developer can communicate parameter information to the compiler and linker. These parameters control the behavior of the compiler and linker, and what code is generated and linked.

Flags and options are parameters that affect the behavior of the compiler and linker. Options are predefined choices governing compiler and linker behavior that are either selected (turned on) or not selected (turned off) by the developer. For example, a compiler typically has an option to select the level of warnings and error messages that it produces. One setting of this option causes only the most extreme error messages to be produced and all other suppressed, while another causes all errors and severe warnings to be produced but other warnings to be suppressed. The linker may have an option that indicates whether the linker does or does not treat duplicate definitions as an error. Flags are parameters that communicate a value other than a selection among pre-defined choices. For example, the compiler typically has a flag that allows the developer to explicitly state the name of the object file to be produced rather than the default name that the compiler would use. A linker flag is the name of a library file that should be searched in resolving external references. The nature and syntax of flags and options is compiler- and system-dependent.

By defining variables the developer can control what is called *conditional compilation,* which means that some detailed code may be included or excluded in the compilation depending on the setting of a preprocessor variable. Two common cases of conditional compilation are monitoring code and platform-dependent code. Monitoring code is programmed code inserted in the system during development for testing or performance analysis later. This monitoring code is included in the compilation so that at debugging and tuning it is part of the executable test system. After debugging and tuning, the monitoring code is excluded from the compilation so that the released executable production system does not have the space and time overhead required by the monitoring code. To build a system that runs on multiple platforms it is often necessary to have two or more different versions of some detailed code, each unique to its particular platform, or platform-dependent. For example, a network-communications service or a window-management action might be used in slightly different ways on a Windows95 system than it is on a Unix system. Through conditional compilation, the correct version of the detail code for a particular platform would not be included.

Conditional compilation is achieved by defining and testing preprocessor variables. The preprocessor has a list of variables that during compilation are either defined or undefined. Tests on these variables may be inserted in the source code that cause the preprocessor to include (pass on to the compiler) a section of source code or exclude (not pass on to the compiler) a section of source code. An outline of an example of conditional compilation is shown in Code Sample 5–2, where two sections of code are surrounded by preprocessor directives. Each `#ifdef` directive tests whether the named variables (_WINDOWS_95_ and _UNIX_ in the example) are currently defined. If the variable is defined, then the subsequent lines of source code (up to the matching `#endif`) are included in the source stream produced by the preprocessor. If the variable is not defined, then the subsequent lines of source code (up to the matching `#endif`) are excluded from the source stream.

The variables tested by the preprocessor can be defined in one of two ways. The first is to use a header file containing one or more #define directives and including it before any use of the variables in conditional compilation tests. Code Sample 5–3 shows an example of header file containing a variable definition and the testing of this variable in another file.

The second way to define a preprocessor variable is as a compiler flag. The syntax and procedure for defining the preprocessor variables as compiler flags is

Code Sample 5–2 *Conditional Compilation*

```
#ifdef _WINDOWS_95_

... code to include for a Windows95 platform

#endif

#ifdef _UNIX_

...code to include for a Unix platform

#endif
```

Code Sample 5–3 *Defining and Using Variables for Conditional Compilation*

```
// This is the file Platform.h        #include "Platform.h"

#ifndef _PLATFORM_H                    ...
#define _PLATFORM_H
                                       #ifdef _WIN_95_
                                       ... code for Windows95 plat-
...                                    form
                                       #endif
#define _WIN_95_
   // use W'95 platform                #ifdef _UNIX_
                                       ...code for Unix platform
...                                    #endif
#endif
```

dependent on the compiler. The source code that tests the preprocessor variable is independent of how the preprocessor variable is defined.

Incremental Development

Software development projects of any size are always implemented in a progressive and incremental manner. It is never the case that all of the code is written before any of it is tested, evaluated, and possibly modified to remove errors or to change parts of the overall design. The many small, progressive tasks that define the incremental strategy for a given system are usually planned in advance.

Each step in the incremental development is carefully selected so that it is both testable and minimal. The ability to test each step is necessary to ensure that it is implemented correctly and that it operates correctly with the code already present. There is little point in adding a small bit of code so incomplete that there is no way to test it to determine these properties. At the same time, a step represents the smallest, testable incremental addition. If a step is too large (i.e., introduces too much new functionality and code), it becomes difficult to test it as completely as would be advisable.

Some experience is usually required to gain proficiency in identifying a good set of incremental steps. However, once learned, the ability to develop systems in testable, minimal steps will yield numerous advantages.

Incremental development is critical to developing software for the following reasons:

- **Easier testing/debugging**: at each step there is less new code introduced, lessening the number of possible bugs that and the interactions of the new code with the code already in the system. Since less code is introduced, it is easier to discover where mistakes have been made—there are simply fewer places to look. Minimizing the interactions between new and old code is important, because problems with the code from previous steps may only be revealed by later steps. While this detracts somewhat from the ideal of progressive development because backtracking may be needed, it is still enormously better than the alternative method of dealing with all of the code (and all of the bugs and interactions) in one huge, and usually unsuccessful, step.

- **Better risk control**: a project may present unusual requirements or involve system services not previously used by members of the development team. In this case, there is a certain amount of risk involved in those parts of the system. By identifying those parts of the system, the team can decide where best to tackle the high-risk parts. At times it may be better to get some of the well-understood parts working and in place first; other times the team might decide to master the high-risk parts first to be certain that unknown difficulties in these parts will not arise late in the project, when changes to large parts of the already developed code might have to be made to accommodate the components that involve the high-risk parts.

- **Better team organization**: team members have a better understanding of how their work relates to the work of other team members when incremental, collaborative steps are taken. In some cases, there may be several independent steps that can be taken, allowing the team members to work in parallel. As team members have different skills and interests, it is more likely that a given team member can be assigned tasks for which that team member is particularly skilled.

- **Concrete measurability**: the set of completed steps (often termed "milestones") can be shown to project managers as concrete evidence of progress. It is far better to have completed half of the steps and be able to demonstrate a partially functional system than to have half of the code written but not have this code integrated or visibly working.

- **Psychological benefits**: team members have a better mental attitude toward the project resulting from the satisfaction that comes with the completion of individual steps or tasks. These small intermediate rewards help to sustain the energy and enthusiasm of the team. A genuine sense of progress and direction results from the incremental approach.

The importance and utility of incremental development is reflected in the broad spectrum of technical, managerial, and organizational effects that flow from its use.

As an example of incremental development, consider a part of graphical editing system. Similar to many common drawing tools, the graphical editing system allows the user to draw, resize, move, and group together a number of basic shapes such as rectangles, circles, and lines. The user may select a color for each shape from a palette of available colors. One incremental development plan for this system is shown in Table 5–2.

The steps shown in Table 5–2 are only one of many good incremental development plans. Notice that each step focuses on adding to the system a specific capability that can be observed and tested. Also notice that new capabilities may be added to a prototype developed in an earlier step and that the prototypes from two steps may be combined.

Tools

Two broad categories of tools are toolkits and integrated development environments (IDEs). There are a wide range of tools in either category that are available from commercial vendors or from pubic-domain sources.

The toolkit approach presupposes that the user has available a number of different tools from different vendors for the same task. The user selects among these tools weighing such factors as the individual's preferences, previous experience and familiarity with the tools, cost of each tool, and availability of the tools on a given platform. The user selects one tool for each task that best suits the user's requirements. For example, in a standard programming environment the user might need an editor for composing and revising the source text, a compiler and a system for automating the rebuilding process, and a debugger.

The developer might choose to use the editor with which he or she is most familiar and productive, a commercially available compiler and rebuilding tool that produces good error messages and efficient code, and a public-domain debugger that has some novel and needed features not yet included in a production debugger. The advantages of the toolkit approach are:

Table 5–2 An Incremental Development Plan

1. draw a single rectangle at a fixed location with a fixed color; no moving, resizing or grouping is allowed.

2. draw a single rectangle at a user-selected location with a fixed color; no moving, resizing or grouping is allowed.

3. draw a single instance of each basic shape at user-selected locations each with a fixed color; no moving, resizing or grouping is allowed.

4. draw a single rectangle at a fixed location with a user-selected color; no moving, resizing or grouping is allowed.

5. draw a single rectangle at a user-selected location with a user-selected color; no moving, resizing or grouping is allowed.

6. (combine steps 3 and 5) draw a single instance of each basic shape at user-selected locations each with a user-selected color; no moving, resizing or grouping is allowed.

7. draw any number of each basic shape at user-selected locations each with a user-selected color; no moving, resizing or grouping is allowed.

8. draw a single rectangle at a fixed location with a fixed color; the rectangle can be moved by the user; no resizing or grouping is allowed.

9. draw a single rectangle at a fixed location with a fixed color; the rectangle can be moved and resized by the user; no grouping is allowed.

10. (combine steps 7 and 9) draw any number of each basic shape at user-selected locations each with a user-selected color; each shape can be moved and resized by the user; no grouping is allowed.

11. draw any number of each basic shape at user-selected locations each with a user-selected color; each shape can be moved and resized by the user; basic shapes may be grouped together (but a group may not be grouped with another basic shape or with other groups).

12. draw any number of each basic shape at user-selected locations each with a user-selected color; each shape can be moved and resized by the user; basic shapes may be grouped together, a group may be grouped with one or more other basic shapes (but a group may not be grouped with other groups).

13. draw any number of each basic shape at user-selected locations each with a user-selected color; each shape can be moved, resized, and grouped by the user.

- New tools can be added as new tasks become part of the development process,
- New and more effective tools can replace older, less effective ones without requiring any other tools to change,
- The user's expertise with common tools (e.g., editors) can be leveraged to avoid unnecessary retraining and exploit the user's already-developed skills.

The disadvantages of the toolkit approach are:

- The user interfaces of the toolkit as a whole may be inconsistent and difficult to use. Different tools may have different metaphors and conventions that cause the developer to make mistakes and become frustrated as he or she moves among the different tools.
- Information loss among the tools is more likely. Because the tools were developed without any awareness of one another, they are not able to communicate among themselves. Any such communication must be done by the developer, often at the expense of productivity. For example, when the user is debugging a file and finds a line of code that needs to be changed, the editor is not aware of which file should be edited (although the debugger knows which file it is working on it cannot communicate this information to the editor). Similarly, once the editor has changed a source file, the editor has no way of communicating this information to the rebuilding tool.

Toolkit users may feel that they bear too much of the burden of tool evaluation and tool integration and that more of this responsibility should be assumed by the tool developers. However, the tool developers and vendors may rightly claim that their interest is in producing a single tool that is the best of its kind, leaving them no time for the task of integration with other tools, that there is little or no economic incentive to integrate with other tools, especially if there are a large number of other tools with which the integration may be done.

The integrated development environment (IDE) approach envisions a single, comprehensive system-development facility within which all of the tasks related to the programming, rebuilding, and debugging of a system are conducted. In this approach the user chooses among IDEs, not among individual tools, because the IDE is a single, indivisible utility package. The advantages of the IDE approach are:

- The user interfaces of the IDE are usually consistent and easier to use because the IDE was developed as a single utility and usually has the same metaphors and conventions across all of its functions.
- Information loss among the pieces of the environment is minimized. Since the IDE is an integrated set of services, it is possible to build in

communication among its components that facilitates user activities. Thus, the debugger can communicate the file being debugged to the editor which can, in turn, inform the rebuilding tool of any changes made, all without any overt user effort.

The corresponding disadvantages of the IDE approach are:

- The IDE is a closed environment in that it is usually difficult or impossible for the average user to extend the capability of the environment by including a new tool or feature. In some cases this may cause a considerable dilemma for the user. Suppose that a newly available IDE contains one or a small number of very useful features that are not available with the IDE currently being used—it may be extremely difficult to judge the benefits of the features in the new IDE against the loss of familiarity and productivity with the existing IDE.
- The user's existing skill in using a tool is completely lost if that tool is not part of the IDE. For example, a user may have to learn a new editor in order to use a particular IDE. The years of experience, fluency, and productivity that the user has with the existing editor is lost in using an IDE that has a different editor. It is not a question of one editor being better than the other, for the two editors may have equivalent capability. It is a question of the time it takes a user to become equally productive with the new tool.

Users of IDEs may feel that they are held captive to a given IDE because of the high cost change to a different IDE entails. Also, the value that a given user or community of users attaches to a particular capability may differ considerably from the value the IDE developer assigns it.

In the following sections, two different tools are described in conjunction with the study of rebuilding software written in C++: the GNU public-domain toolset and Microsoft's Visual C++ IDE. Each of these has a dedicated user community, is a good representative of its approach, and is a worthy object of study.

5.3 Unix/GNU Toolkit

The two basic tools for rebuilding a system written in C++ are the g++ compiler and the make utility. The compiler, and its associated preprocessor, performs compiling and linking tasks depending on how it is used. The make utility uses a structured file of dependency information created by the developer and rebuilds the system according to this information. One of the basic steps of the make utility is, of course, to use the C++ compiler, in our case g++, to recompile source code files.

The g++ Compiler

The general syntax for invoking the g++ compiler is

```
g++ {Flags} {Paths} -o {Executable} {SourceName(s)} {LibraryName(s)}
```

The bracketed terms represent places in the command where optional arguments to the compiler may be given. The brackets are not included in an actual command line; they are used here only to identify the parts of the command line.

{SourceName(S)} is a list of one or more code files to be compiled. The -o {Executable} option allows the name of the compiled executable file output by the compiler to be specified. The default name of this file is "a.out".

The {Flags} in the command-line represents the setting of various compiler options. Typical compiler flags are:

```
-g       generate information for the debugger
-O       (upper case letter O) turn on code optimization
-w       turn off all warning messages
-Wall    turn on all warning messages
-c       produce only an object file; don't link.
```

The complete list of compiler options is extensive.

A program often uses existing routines and classes. Examples of these include system routines (e.g., open a file), windowing-system routines (e.g., pop up a menu), general-purpose classes (e.g., a class for string manipulation), or other collections of application specific classes (e.g., for graphics).

To use existing routines and classes the compiler must know where to find the include files that define the functions and classes being used and where to find the precompiled libraries of object files. The compiler (actually the preprocessor cpp) has a standard set of directories in the file system where it looks to find include files that are named by the #include directives. The compiler also has a standard set of directories in the file system where it looks to find libraries of precompiled object files that contain the code for the functions and classes defined in the include files. It is often necessary to direct the compiler to look in additional directories for include files or libraries. This information is given in the {PATHS} part of the general command shown above. Each additional directory to search is specified by a path name prefixed by either "-I" (for a directory containing include files) or "-L" (for a directory containing libraries). For example:

```
-I/usr/local/include -I../../include -L/usr/local/lib -L/home/cs2704/lib
```

specifies two additional include-file paths and two additional library-file paths. The include-file path -I/usr/local/include specifies an absolute path name (one starting at the root of the file system), while the include file path -I../../include specifies a path relative to the current working directory. Both of the library search paths are absolute, although relative names may also be used when appropriate.

There are two rules of good usage for organizing and naming the search paths for include files and libraries. First, directories containing include files and libraries should be named "include" and "lib", respectively. This is a common and well-understood convention. Second, the -I paths on the command line should be grouped together and appear before all of the -L paths. This is common practice.

The compiler must also be told which non-standard libraries to search. The file name for a library has a standard form:

```
lib{something}.a
```

where the .a suffix stands for the term *archive* and the "lib" prefix is required. The "{something}" gives the discriminating name for the library. Some common libraries are:

```
libm.a          math library
libc.a          c language library
libg++.a        g++ library
libXm.a         X-based motif library
```

A library to search is given to the compiler in the abbreviated form

```
-l{something}
```

For example, to search the standard g++ class library, the term -lg++ would be used. Note that the required prefix (lib) and required suffix (.a) need not, and indeed cannot, be given.

The make Utility

The *make* utility is a powerful tool for managing the creation and maintenance of systems and libraries. The actions of the make utility are controlled by a "makefile" that describes the dependencies among parts of the system, and the rules needed to rebuild parts of the system. Using the information in the makefile and the creation/modification times recorded in the file system for each file, make uses the dependency information to determine which parts of the system need to be rebuilt and, using the rule information, can dictate how to rebuild those parts.

Rules

A basic element in a makefile is a rule. The general format of a rule is:

```
{target}:       {dependency list}
          {tab} {command list}
```

The {target} names an object file or a complete system that make will build or a utility function to be performed by make. The target must be followed by the required colon character (:). The {dependency list} is a list of other elements on which the given target depends. The {command list} is a list of commands to be performed when the {target} is being built or performed by make. The {tab} is a required character that must begin the line containing the command list.

Both the dependency list and the command list must be a single line. Either list, however, may be quite long. The standard technique for making the list readable, while still ensuring that the make utility will view it as a single line is to employ a backslash ("\") character immediately preceding the carriage return that ends the current line and begins a new line. The carriage return character will cause a second line when displayed on the screen or printed but, when read by the make utility, these two characters will appear as a blank. Examples of this will be seen below.

The first kind of targets are those that name system components that make will build. A common target of this form names an object file to be built by compiling one or more code files. For example, a rule to build the FileChooser.o object file might appear as:

```
FileChooser.o:  FileChooser.cc, FileChooser.h, Directory.h, \{cr}
                Selector.h, File.h {cr}
        {tab}   g++ {...} -o FileChooser.o FileChooser.cc {...}
```

In this example, the target is named FileChooser.o. Since the list of dependencies is long, the backslash character is used to break the single logical "line" into two physical lines. The {tab} notation indicates that a tab character must begin the line containing the command. In this case, a command to compile FileChooser.cc using the g++ compiler is shown in abbreviated form. The notation {...} shows where additional parts of the command would appear.

The second type of target names a complete system or library to be built by make. For example, a target such as

```
Program:  FileChooser.o Directory.o Frame.o {...}
          g++ {...} -o Program *.o {...}
```

describes how to build an executable program named Program by having g++ link all of the object files in the current directory. Note that g++ can be used to compile code files as well as link object files. The target Program can be referred to in the invocation of make as

```
make Program
```

which will cause the make utility to find and perform the actions required by a rule whose target is named Program in a file named makefile. Alternatively, if Program is the first or only target in the makefile, then the same actions will occur simply by using the command make with no arguments.

The third type of target names a utility function performed by the makefile. A common target of this form is the "clean" target that cleans up after the make utility by removing intermediate files produced during the running of make but not needed for longer-term use. A typical example is

```
clean:
        rm *.o core ./tmp/*
```

which deletes all object files in the current directory, a core file that might have been produced when a test program crashed, and all files in a subdirectory named tmp.

Variables

A makefile may contain variables whose value may be referred to more than once in the makefile. For example, the makefile may need to give the list of include files on each of a series of compile commands or it may have to give the long list of all of the object files in two or more places in the makefile. To avoid this repetition, a variable is defined once and used in the makefile wherever its value is needed.

Variables are similar to simple macros; the value of a variable is a simple string that is inserted verbatim wherever the value of the variable is referenced.

By convention, variables are given suggestive names that are written in capital letters, such as OBJECTS, OBJDIR, TMPFILE. The value of a variable is a string of any length that is assigned to a variable using an equals sign (=) operator. For example:

```
CC= g++
COMPLIBS= -lgen -ldl -lsocket -lnsl -lg++
CCFLAGS= -Wall -O
INCLUDEPATH= -I/usr/include/X11
LIBPATH= -L/usr/lib/X11

OBJECTS=    Base.o          BasicFrame.o   Button.o           \
            Counter.o       Date.o         Directory.o        \
            File.o          FileQuery.o    FileNavigator.o    \
            FileChooser.o   Frame.o        Location.o         \
            Message.o       Selector.o     Shape.o            \
            TextBox.o       Timer.o        Program.o
```

This example defines several make variables: OBJECTS is a list of .o files written over several lines using the \{cr} technique; CC defines what the C++ compiler is called on this system—variables like this one are often defined to aid in porting the software among different platforms that may use different compilers; COMPLIBS is a list of libraries to include when an executable program is built; CCFLAGS defines options to the g++ compiler indicating that all warning messages should be displayed (-Wall) and that is should optimize the compiled code (-O); INCLUDEPATH is a compiler option specifying where to look for header files (in this case header for the X windows system); LIBPATH specifies where to look in the file system to find the X windows system library.

The value of a variable is obtained by enclosing the variable name in parentheses preceded by a dollar sign, as in $(OBJECTS) or $(CC). Several examples of using the values of variables are these:

```
LDLIBS = -lwx_motif -lXm -lXt -lX11 -lm $(COMPLIBS)
PATHS = $(INCLUDEPATH) $(LIBPATH)

Program.o:  Program.cc
        $(CC) -c $(CCFLAGS) -o $@ Program.cc

all:    $(OBJDIR) $(OBJECTS)
        $(CC) $(CCFLAGS) $(PATHS) -o Program $(OBJECTS) $(LDLIBS)
```

The first two examples show how one variable can be used in defining the value of another variable. In each case, the value of one variable is simply concatenated with the other characters around it to form the value of the variable being defined. The third example shows a rule where the command list uses several variables: the name of the compiler to use (CC) and the flags to be passed to the compiler (CCFLGS). The symbol $@ is a built-in make variable that refers to the target's name without any suffix—in this case $@ would be "Program" because Program.o is the target and the .o suffix is removed to define the current value of $@. The final example illustrates that variables can be used in both the command list and the dependency list. In all three parts of this example, the target "all" depends on everything that is named in the values of OBJDIR and OBJECTS.

Other References

Other material on the make utility may be found by following these links:

Make Tutorial

http://actor.cs.vt.edu/~kafura/cs2704/Book/Chapter5/make.tutorial.txt

The GNU Make Manual

http://www.cygnus.com/pubs/gnupro/5_GNPro_Utilities/e_GNU_Make/
make.html

5.4 The Visual C++ IDE

Visual C++ is an integrated programming environment (IDE) within which the developer can edit, rebuild, and debug an object-oriented program written in

C++. As with other IDEs, the developer does not need to leave the environment in order to perform any of these construction tasks, and all of the construction tasks are performed using the same user interface. Only the simplest usage and the most basic commands of Visual C++ are described here; more sophisticated uses and the full range of commands and options are detailed in the on-line help site and in numerous books specifically about Visual C++.

The User Interface

The user interface of Visual C++ consists of four primary areas:

- **the control area**: this area contains a collection of buttons and pull-down menus. With these controls, the developer is able to select options that define the appearance and operation of the environment and to execute commands.
- **the editing area**: this area displays for viewing and editing the source files that compose the system being developed. Each file is represented in its own subwindow, which can be independently moved, resized, mini-mized (or docked at the edge of the editing area), maximized (to take up the entire editing area), or closed.
- **the viewing area**: this area presents different views of the elements that form the system being developed. Two common views are the file view and the class view. The contents of files selected from these views are shown in the editing area.
- **the output area**: this is a scrollable subwindow that contains messages from the current command being executed in the environment. The format of this area may change depending on the command. Two common uses for the output area to show error messages generated by the compiler and to communicate information between the debugger and the developer.

These areas may be hidden, resized, or repositioned according to the user's preferences and the operation being performed. For example, during a long editing session the viewing and output areas may be hidden or minimized to allow more room to display the files being edited.

The Project Workspace

The central organizing concept of Visual C++ is the project workspace, which automates the mechanical aspects of rebuilding and debugging systems. The project workspace automatically detects and records the dependencies among source-code files, and its environment facilitates debugging by providing a high-level (symbolic) set of debugging operations. Each project workspace has a name assigned by the developer upon its creation. As with other names, the project workspace name should be indicative of the program (system) meaning; in the simplest case, each program (system) that the developer constructs is represented by a separate project workspace. The contents of a project workspace is stored in a subdirectory on disk. The subdirectory and the project workspace have the same name. The location in the file system where the subdirectory is stored is chosen by the user when the workspace is created.

To create a new project workspace, simply follow the steps shown in Table 5–3. This sequence of steps creates an empty project workspace.

Table 5–3 Creating a Project Workspace

---

1. Choose "New" from the File pull-down menu.
2. Choose "Project Workspace" from the list presented in the dialog box; then click OK.
3. In the New Project Workspace dialog box there are three items to specify:
    a. the Type of the project workspace; for simple command line programs choose "Console Application" and for the other programs used in this book choose "Application"
    b. the Name of the project workspace, and
    c. the Location of the subdirectory where the files of the project workspace will be stored. A browse button allows the developer to navigate in the file system to find an appropriate location for this subdirectory.

The *File* pull-down menu also contains other commonly used commands for manipulating the project workspace. The most frequently used commands are:

- *Save, Save All*: saves the current contents of one or all files in the project workspace to the subdirectory

- *Close Workspace*: close the current project workspace (typically used before exiting from Visual C++)

- *Open Workspace*: opens a previously created, saved, and closed project workspace

These commands are sufficient for use with simple project workspaces.

A workspace is stored in a file that has the suffix .mdp. When using the *Open Workspace* command, use the file-browser dialogue to locate the file whose name is that of the desired project workspace and whose suffix is .mdp.

Adding Classes to a Project Workspace

Classes can be added to a project workspace by creating the source-code files and inserting them into the project workspace. The source code for classes that exist prior to the creation of the project workspace (e.g., classes being reused from prior projects) can be directly inserted into the project workspace, while new classes must first be created and then inserted into the project workspace.

The view area presents the user with a class view and a file view of the contents of the project workspace. The class view shows the names of all of the classes in the project workspace. When the user clicks on a class name, the file containing the definition of the class is opened and presented in the editing area. The file view shows the names of all of the implementation files in the project workspace. When the user clicks on a file name, that file is opened and presented in the editing area. When following the common practice of putting each class definition in a separate header file and the entire implementation of that class in a separate file, the class view is a means of accessing the header files and the file view a means of accessing the implementation files.

The steps for creating new source-code files are listed in Table 5–4. When a new text file is first created, it is given a default name by the project workspace. A good practice is to immediately use the *Save As* command in the *File* menu to give the file a unique, proper name. The files that are shown in the editing area can be edited using the simple built-in editor commands that are listed in the *Edit* menu. Keyboard shortcuts are also available for these editing commands. Periodically the *Save* command should be used to save the current contents of the file to disk. If the user has modified several open files, the *Save All* command is a convenient way to ensure that all of these changes are committed to disk.

Table 5–4 Creating Source Code Files

> **1.** Choose *New* from the *File* pull-down menu.
>
> **2.** Choose *Text File* from the list presented in the dialog box; then click *OK.*
>
> **3.** Use the *Save As* command from the *File* pull-down menu to give the file a meaningful name.
>
> **4.** Create the new source code in the new text window that appears in the editing area. The source code can be created in this file using the built-in editor features.
>
> **5.** Periodically use the *Save* command from the *File* pull-down menu to save the contents of the file.

Inserting a source-code file in the project workspace charges the project workspace with the responsibility of determining the dependencies associated with the inserted files and recompiling the file (if it is an implementation file) as needed. The user does not need to take any overt action to analyze the dependencies; simply inserting the files into the project workspace is sufficient. Files can be inserted into the project workspace using the steps shown in Table 5–5.

Table 5–5 Inserting Files into the Project Workspace

1. Under the *Insert* menu, select the command *"Files into Project."*
2. From the file selection dialog box that is presented, choose the files to be inserted into the project; several files can be inserted at once.
3. Click the *Add* button on the dialog box.

It is important to remember that source-code files created within the Visual C++ IDE are not automatically inserted in the project workspace; each such file must be explicitly inserted using the above procedure.

Rebuilding the System

The *Build* pull-down menu contains three frequently used commands for building and running the executable program created from the files in the project workspace. The *Compile* command compiles the single file that has the focus (contains the cursor) in the editing area. This command is useful in the early stages of developing a class or when the code for the class has been heavily modified. Compiling such a class by itself allows the developer to correct any syntax mistakes or other problems for that class before attempting to rebuild the entire system. The Build command is used to rebuild an executable system using the current contents of the source files in the project workspace. When the system has been rebuilt successfully, the Execute command can be used to run the new system.

Table 5–6 Frequently Used Commands to Rebuild the System

• *Compile*: compile the current file (the one that has the focus in the editing area).
• *Build*: create an executable file using the files in the project workspace, recompiling only those files deemed necessary by the dependencies understood by the project workspace.
• *Execute*: run the executable file.

The project workspace assists the developer in locating lines of code where syntax errors have been detected by the compiler. Compilation errors generated by either the *Compile* or the *Build* commands are shown in the output area. When the user clicks on one of these the corresponding file is displayed in the viewing area and the cursor is positioned at the line where the error occurred. The complete error message is shown in the status line immediately below the output area.

Two other commands in the *Build* menu, *Build All* and *Update All Dependencies*, are useful when the developer wants to be certain that a consistent version of the system has been built. The *Build All* command forces a complete recompilation of the system, ignoring all existing object files. All implementation files are recompiled using the current contents of the source-code files in the project workspace. The *Update All Dependencies* command prompts the project workspace to insure that its list of dependencies is up to date. These two commands help the developer to eliminate the problems caused by an inconsistent version of the system accidentally being built.

Table 5–7 Other Useful Commands in the Build Menu

• *Build All*: recompile all files, disregarding any dependency and change information.
• *Update All Dependencies*: rescan all files and reconstruct the dependency information to ensure that the project workspace has valid dependency information.

Specifying Paths, Symbols, and Libraries

Visual C++ provides a mechanism for specifying search paths and defining options that affect the rebuilding of the system. Search paths are defined using the Tools menu and other options are specified using the Build menu.

Paths in the file system to be searched for include files or libraries are specified by using the *Options* command in the *Tools* menu. When the Options command is selected, a tabbed dialogue box appears; select the *Directories* tab. The Directories entry has a selection box labelled "Show directories for," two of whose selections are "Include files" and "library files," which correspond to paths in the file system to search for include files and libraries, respectively. The main part of the Directories entry displays the current set of paths for the current selection. Current paths may be deleted or new paths may be added to the set. When the sets of paths have been set correctly, press the *OK* button.

The *Settings* selection in the *Build* menu is used to set other options, including symbols and libraries. The Setting selection produces a tabbed dialogue box. The two tabs of interest here are labelled C/C++ and Link. Clicking on the C/C++ tab reveals an area that contains a writeable text area labelled

"Preprocessor definitions:". Any preprocessor symbol that is to be treated as defined can be added to the comma-separated list of symbols. Selecting the Link tab reveals an area that contains a writeable text area labelled "Object/library modules:" to which can be added any libraries that should be used in linking the executable file.

5.5 Concepts of Program Debugging

Errors, Faults and Failures

Debugging is difficult because its primary focus is correcting the thinking of the developer and is only secondarily concerned with correcting the program. Setting aside problems that are due to simple mechanical transcription mistakes (e.g., the developer mistakenly typed "+" instead of "-"), a problem revealed by testing a system began in the mind of the developer. The developer may have formed an inaccurate mental model of the systems's goals and constraints, conceived of an algorithm that is incomplete or incorrect, misunderstood a programming language feature (e.g., inheritance), or misused a library component. The term *error* is often defined to mean these invalid models, incorrect concepts, and misunderstandings that stem from the mind of the developer. During system development the developer's errors become manifest in the system's code. Such code is said to contain one or more *faults*. When the code containing a fault is executed, the system enters an unintended state and eventually the system experiences a *failure*, which is an observable departure of the system from its intended behavior. The failure is the outward manifestation of the problem created by the fault(s). Harmless failures are those that affect the appearance of the system, as when the output may not be formatted correctly or a button has the wrong label. A more severe failure produces incorrect results but allows the continued execution of the system, and the most severe failures cause the system to terminate immediately and abnormally with possible loss of data or corruption of other resources.

The steps in debugging a system are outlined in Fig. 5–2. First, the failure of the system is observed during a test. The term test in this sense is very broad, including an informal execution of the system by the developer during development, a formal test conducted under controlled conditions by an independent team of testers, and production use by the end user. Second, the fault(s) in the code are located. During this step other tests of the system are usually conducted to recreate the failure so as to isolate and identify the offending code. Third, the errors on the part of the developer are discovered. This step involves questioning the models and concepts employed by the developer in creating the faulty code. Fourth, once the misunderstandings are identified, a correct model or concept can be formed. The developer may reexamine the system specification, other

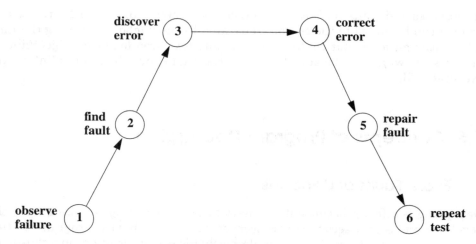

Figure 5–2   Steps in Debugging a System

documentation, or consult with other team members to construct a correct model or concept. Fifth, the fault(s) in the code are repaired by adding to, removing from, and/or modifying the system's code. The repairs made in this step may be very localized if the error was a mistake about details, or they may require widespread changes if the error was a fundamental mistake. Sixth, the repaired system is retested to ensure that the system does not fail as previously observed. This step also helps to check that the repaired code did not itself introduce any new faults into the system.

The code containing a fault and the code that is executing at the time of the failure may not be the same and may have different spatial and temporal relationships. Various spatial and temporal relationships between these two segments of code are shown in Fig. 5–3. The term spatial as used here refers to the relationship between the classes containing the two segments of code. The spatial relationships shown in Fig. 5–3 are based on whether the two segments are in the same class, in different but related classes, or in unrelated classes. Classes are related through inheritance or because objects of these classes form associations or aggregations. The term temporal as used here refers to the points in time when the two segments of code are executed. Significant temporal relationships that are shown in Fig. 5–3 are whether the two segments are both executed within a single method invocation, not within the same method invocation but within the same sequence of method invocations, or in different method invocation sequences. A method invocation sequence is an ordered list of method names such that at a given point in time during the execution each method in the sequence, except the last, has invoked the next method in the sequence and the invocation has not yet returned; the last method in the sequence is the method being executed at the given point in time.

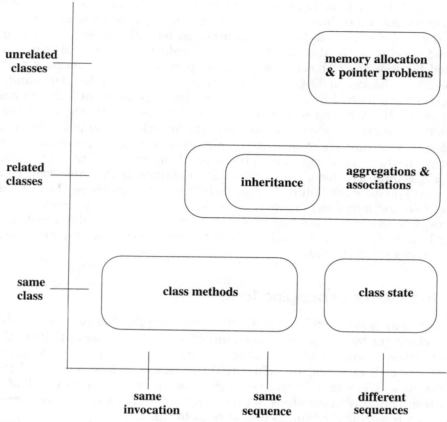

Figure 5-3   Common Debugging Situations

Commonly occurring debugging problems can be identified by their spatial and temporal characteristics. Though by no means an exhaustive list, Fig. 5–3 shows five distinct and commonly occurring situations. First, the most limited and most easily fixed cases are those in which the two segments of code are in the same class and in either the same invocation or the same invocation sequence. Often the problem is a small mistake in the detailed coding of the class's methods. Second, a slightly more difficult case is one where the two segments in the same class are executed in different execution sequences. Because different execution sequences are involved, a typical problem is the way in which the two segments are using the state information of the object of which they are both a part. This state information is the most immediate thing that ties together the two segments of code. Third, the two segments of code may lie in different classes that are related through inheritance and are executed in the same invocation sequence. These problems are often due to misunderstandings or misuse of inherited methods, unintentionally overriding a base-class virtual method so that other base class methods no longer work correctly, or conflicts over the use of protected data that is accessed by both the base class and the derived class. Fourth, the two segments of code may lie in different classes related because their objects are parts of aggregations or associations. These problems are harder to diagnose because they involve multiple classes and, possibly, different method invocation sequences; they are frequently due to misunderstanding the behavior or responsibilities of a class. Fifth, the most difficult problems to locate and correct are those that theoretically "cannot happen." This category of problems are those that occur between unrelated classes and at unrelated points in time. Furthermore, these problems often are not deterministic, that is, the failure happens under different conditions, or the same conditions do not always produce the failure. In sequential programs, problems of this kind are most often attributed to improper use of pointers or related memory allocation effects (e.g., using an object after it has been deleted). Similar problems can occur in programs that use multiple independent threads of execution that are not correctly synchronized.

The Role of Debugging Tools

Debugging tools are useful for efficiently completing the first two steps in debugging—observing failure and locating faults. These two steps essentially deal with reporting the occurrence of interesting or unusual events, providing snapshots of the system as it executes, and allowing the developer to interrogate and control the system's execution. Effective debugging tools provide support for all of these activities. The subsequent steps in debugging—identifying the errors, correcting them, and repairing the faults—cannot be automated.

The developer can employ one of two strategies in observing failures. The developer can simply run the system and wait for it to fail, which is often the first strategy employed because the developer may have no reason to anticipate if or when a failure will occur. The second strategy is to set *watch* conditions, conditions that are tested to determine if the system is in a valid state. When an invalid state is detected, the system is halted with an informative message. This second strategy is often used when the developer is attempting to recreate a previously observed failure or if the developer is wary of a particular part of the system being tested, perhaps because it is new, complex, or not well understood. The *watch* conditions may stop the system short of the actual failure, but at a point closer to the true fault. The *watch* conditions may be dynamically inserted in the system using a debugging tool or they may be preprogrammed by the developer. Inserting watch conditions dynamically depends on the details of the debugging tool. A common technique for preprogramming watch conditions in C++ is via the *assert* macro, an example of which is shown in Code Sample 5–4. In Code Sample 5–4, a method receives three input arguments: an array (a[]), the length of the array (size), and an index into the array (i). In this example, the assert is

Code Sample 5–4 *Using the Assert Macro*

```
#include <assert.h>

Result Class::Method(int a[], int size, int i)
{...
   assert(i >= 0 && i < size && a[i] > 0);
   ...
}
```

used to watch for violations of the condition: "i is a valid subscript and the value of a[i] is greater than zero." The assert macro takes a single, though arbitrarily complex, condition, which is tested each time the assert is executed. If the condition evaluates to true (non-zero), no action is taken. If the condition evaluates to false (zero) then the system is halted and a message is displayed that states the condition along with the name of the source-code file and the number of the line within this file that contains the assert.

To accomplish the second step in debugging, locating the faults in the code, it is necessary to accumulate three different kinds of information about the system's execution at the point of failure: the state of objects in the system, the current execution sequence, and previous execution sequences. The state of each object in the system indicates what information that object currently contains and what other objects it knows about. Collectively, the entire system state is represented by the union of the states of all of the objects in the system. The current execution sequence shows the sequence of events that immediately preceded the failure. Knowing this sequence gives an indication of the processing actions that were being attempted at the point of failure. In simple cases, knowing the state of key objects and the current execution sequence is sufficient to locate the fault. In more complicated cases, where the execution of the code with the fault and the execution of the code that causes the failure are more distant in time from each other, an execution history that extends further back in time is needed.

The Debugging Environment

Understanding key components of the system's execution environment—the *heap* and the *run-time stack*—is helpful in becoming a proficient user of debugging tools and more adept at locating faults in the code. The space for dynamically created objects is allocated from a memory area referred to as the system's heap. The heap memory allocated for an object contains the object's data and possibly some other information generated by the compiler for run-time purposes. The object's *this* pointer points to the beginning of the object's memory area in

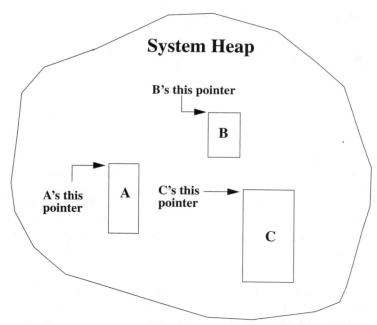

Figure 5–4   The System Heap

the heap. For three objects identified as A, B, and C, Fig. 5–4 shows the memory allocated for the objects and their respective *this* pointers.

The run-time stack provides the memory space for all automatically allocated objects, including local variables (named objects declared within a method and anonymous objects) and parameters. The high-level view shown in Fig. 5–5 illustrates the contents of the run-time stack for an invocation sequence in which a method in object A, invokes a method in object B, that, in turn, invokes a method in object C. A *stack frame* (also known as an *activation record*) is pushed onto the stack each time an invocation is made. When the current invocation returns, its stack frame is popped from the run-time stack and control is returned to the method invocation corresponding to the new top of the run-time stack. Conceptually, each stack frame has two parts containing the parameters passed to the invoked method and the local variables.

The organization of the execution environment helps to explain some of the difficulty of debugging and the limitations of debugging tools:

- To examine the state of a dynamically created object, a pointer or reference to the object is needed. Since the dynamically created object resides in the memory allocated by the heap, there is no way to access such objects except via a pointer or reference.

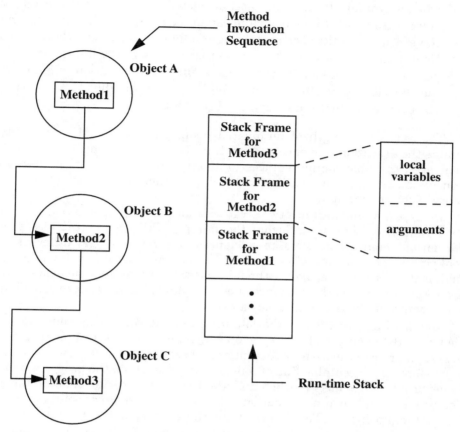

Figure 5–5 The Run-Time Stack

- It is easy to access information about the current execution sequence. because such information is contained on the run-time stack and easily available to the debugging tools. Typically, debugging tools provide commands for moving among the various stack frames in the run-time stack. By using these commands to view stack frames that are deeper in the stack, the developer is able to trace the current execution sequence backward in time to determine exactly how the computation was performed.

- It is not easy to obtain information about previous execution sequences. The run-time environment has certain irreversible actions that make it impossible to recover information about some aspects of the past history of the computation. First, when a method returns its stack frame, and all the information that it contains, it is lost and cannot be recovered. Second, when a dynamically created object is deleted, the memory occupied by that object is returned to the heap and cannot be recovered. This implies that if the execution of the code containing the fault(s) is sufficiently removed in time from the execution of the code that results in the failure, the debugger tools may not be able to provide sufficient information to identify the faulty code, because by the time the failure occurs, the stack frames and objects used in that code may have been lost.

The evident strength of automated debugging tools is their capacity to examine the execution sequence and existing objects at the time of the failure. In some cases, this information suffices to identify the fault. In other cases more extensive means must be used to gather information about past events in the history of the computation.

Breakpoints and *logs* are two strategies for gaining information about execution sequences that occur before the failure. While both strategies provide information about prior execution sequences, they do so in very different ways. Breakpoints are a means of controlling the forward execution of the program starting at a point in time before the failure occurs. Logs are a means of examining a record to unravel the sequence of events that led to the failure. Breakpoints do not require preprogramming, but logs do.

Breakpoints are used in the following manner: using the commands provided by a debugging tool, the developer dynamically inserts breakpoints into the system prior to the system's execution. A breakpoint can be inserted immediately before any executable line of code. During execution, the program will halt whenever a breakpoint is reached and allow the developer to examine the state of objects and the current execution sequence, set new breakpoints or remove existing breakpoints, and control the forward execution of the system.

The developer controls the forward execution of the system using commands provided by the debugging tool. These commands allow the developer to execute a single line of code, a fixed number of lines, or all code until the next breakpoint or failure before halting. When the line of code being executed is an invocation the user has additional options to trace the invocation on a line-by-line basis, execute the invocation as a single instruction, and, after tracing an invocation, run until the invocation returns. These commands allow the user to control the forward execution of the system and to examine the state of the system at any point in time. The difficulty of using the breakpoint approach is that the user must have a means by which to set the breakpoint so that the execution will be halted before, but still near, the point of failure. In some cases it is difficult or impossible to set a convenient breakpoint: the developer may know that the failure occurs in a given method, but if that method is executed thousands of times before the failure occurs, setting a breakpoint at the beginning of the method's code is of little use.

A log is a preprogrammed means to gain information about the past history of the execution. In this approach, the developer builds into the code output statements that write selected information to a log file. Recorded in the log file is information about the sequence of events occurring during the system's execution. The preprogrammed output statements typically write to the log file entries to record when a method has begun and/or completed execution, the values of parameters or other objects at the time an invocation occurs and/or completes, and relevant information at other points in the execution. The advantage of the log approach is that it makes available a complete history, at least as much as the developer is willing to preprogram, in a stable form. The developer may use this log to reconstruct a sequence of events that led to the failure or compare the logs of different tests to determine at what point the execution resulting in a failure diverges from a normal execution. The difficulty of the log approach is that it requires the expense of preprogramming and the developer to have a reasonable idea in advance of what information to capture, and, even then, the log file for an execution may be so large that critical information needed by the developer is lost in a mass of extraneous log entries.

Debugging Strategies

Developers must have a strategy when employing debugging tools; the debugging tools must be used in a deliberate, calculated way that enhances the probability of most rapidly identifying the fault(s) in the system. As with all tools, possessing a powerful debugging tool is not a guarantee of efficiency or effectiveness in debugging. The developer must know and put into practice strategies that guide the debugging tool's use.

It may be useful to think of debugging strategies in terms of a game metaphor: the player's (developer's) objective is to navigate a robot (the system state) through a terrain that the player has created. Adding to the terrain creates hidden opponents (faults). The opponents can convincingly lie to the robot, such as by making it think that the way ahead is clear when in fact it is the edge of a cliff. A large unexplored terrain will usually contain many opponents and many hiding places. Two opponents may sometimes collaborate to conceal each other's presence or to create together a harmful effect that neither one is capable of producing by itself (perhaps one opponent distracts the robot while the other pushes it into a hole). The opponents are devious and may set a time-delay bomb and then run away, causing the robot to crash when the opponent is far gone. The player is allowed to search the terrain (use the debugger) and replay the game under different conditions so as to reveal the presence of an opponent. While this metaphor is inaccurate in some respects, it does suggest some obvious strategies that the player might use: create a terrain that is easier to examine for possible opponents; do not give the opponents many places to hide; isolate a part of the terrain and search it for opponents; follow the trail backward from the site of a crashed robot looking for clues about the opponents and their hiding places; set traps to catch opponents. Such strategies have counterparts in debugging real systems.

Debugging strategies are either proactive or reactive. Proactive strategies are practices that the developer can use in designing and building the system so as to limit the introduction of faults. Reactive strategies are practices that the developer can use in locating faults that, despite the best use of proactive strategies, have been introduced into the system. The debugging strategies considered here are shown in Table 5–8.

Table 5–8 Debugging Strategies

Proactive	Reactive
Incremental development Scope restriction	Fault isolation Deductive reasoning Trap setting Model testing

Incremental development is the first proactive debugging strategy. While it may seem strange, this development practice is one of the most effective strategies for creating a debugged system, because it follows two of the strategies suggested by the game metaphor: it creates a "terrain" that is easier to examine for possible "opponents," and does not give the "opponents" many places to hide. The first step in incremental development creates the smallest system possible, one that incorporates the least amount of code, to achieve its goal. This gives faults in the program the fewest places to hide and makes the program easier to examine, simply because there are fewer places to look. Each step in development adds but a small increment of code. Thus, each debugging step is simpler than it would be if a large body of undebugged code were added in a single step.

The second proactive debugging strategy is to build systems that use *scope restriction* through encapsulation, information hiding, aggregation, and other design techniques to limit the visibility and accessibility of system components. This design approach creates systems that are more easily debugged because it follows the game strategy of "creating a terrain" that is easier to examine for possible "opponents." Encapsulation and other scope-restricting techniques are the equivalent of building protective walls in the terrain to trap opponents either inside or outside its bounds. Thus trapped, the opponents are easier to find.

The first reactive debugging strategy is *fault isolation*: in which the system is made smaller by removing (commenting out) or disabling (turning off options) the suspected part of the system. The smaller system is then tested again using the same conditions that produced the failure. If the failure still occurs, then the removed or disabled part of the system is known not to contain the fault, and the strategy is repeated by removing or disabling additional parts of the system until the fault becomes isolated. At some point the failure will not occur. When the failure does not occur the removed or disabled code contains the fault. The most likely site for the fault is in the last code that was removed or disabled. More extensive and detailed debugging of this suspected code can now be done with the debugger. This strategy follows the game metaphor notions of "not giving the opponents many places to hide" and "isolating a part of the terrain to search it for opponents." Notice that the debugging tools did not come into play until after the strategy had yielded a small area to examine.

The second reactive debugging strategy is *deductive reasoning*. Debugging is like detective work: starting at the point of failure, or the scene of the crime, the system state contains clues from which deductions can be made about how the failure occurred. Possible causes for the observed system state can be tested, which either reveals the fault or produces additional clues for further deduction and tests. Unlike real detectives, the developer has the advantage of using the debugging tools to replay the system's execution and examine in detail possible causes. Notice that the use of the debugging tool is, though important, secondary—the use of the tool is guided by the strategy that determines what to look for and where to look for it. Sharp deductive reasoning is better than a powerful debugging tool.

Trap setting is the third reactive debugging strategy. Cases difficult to debug are those in which the developer knows in what way the system state has been damaged but can not gather much evidence about how or when the damage occurred. For example, the system may fail because a state variable has an incorrect value, but such a value can be the result of many actions in the system. Frequently, the execution of the code that causes the failure is found in a different execution sequence from the one that executed the faulty code. A starting point for debugging can be found by setting a trap to identify when and where the system state was damaged. Two ways of setting a trap are to use the debugging tool to set a watch condition or to use assert macros. Both of these techniques allow the developer to be notified when the damage to the system state occurs. With this starting point, other strategies can be used to locate the fault.

Model testing, the fourth reactive debugging strategy, comes into play in those situations where the system being debugged is too complex to apply the other strategies. If the developer has an idea of what components are involved in the failure, a scaled-down model of the system can be built and tested. The model must be able to exhibit the same failure as the real system. If such a model can be constructed, locating the fault in the simpler model can also reveal the fault in the more complex, real system. Although this may sound difficult, it is often easy to construct the model for testing. For example, in a graphical editor system, if there is a problem with the resizing of polygons, then a special test program that creates a single hard-coded polygon can be built and tested.

The following list provides some other hints, information, and suggestions about debugging:

- **Find the fault that caused the failure**. The system may contain several faults: simply finding some fault does not mean that this fault caused the observed failure. While the discovered fault should be corrected, debugging should continue in search of the fault that caused the observed failure. Retesting the system after correcting the fault will easily reveal if the right fault has been found. It is also a good idea to be able to explain how the fault caused the failure. Without such an explanation either the wrong fault has been found or the developer may not know how to correct the fault.

- **A fault may remain undiscovered for some time**. If the testing is not thorough, it is possible for a fault to remain dormant through many steps in the incremental development of the system. When the failure does occur, the obvious places to look—in the most recently added code—are not the right places. This does not mean that incremental development and fault isolation should be abandoned; it does mean that the developer needs to be aware of the possibility of a long-dormant fault.

- **Do not replace one fault with another**. Faults are introduced by errors in the mind of the developer. The developer must be sure that misconceptions causing particular faults has been corrected before attempting to correct the fault in the code, or else the original fault may well be replaced by a new, though different, fault.

- **Avoid hopeful corrections**. Developers may sometimes change code hoping that the change will remedy the failure even if there is little or no evidence that the original code contains a fault. This practice has little chance of succeeding. The developer must be disciplined enough to reject an ill-conceived and unjustified change. The surest way to avoid hopeful corrections is to insist on an explanation for how the fault produced the failure. Absent such an explanation, there is no reason to believe that the change will have the desired effect. At best, the change will mask the real fault, in which case an even more difficult debugging task is left for later—discovering and removing the masking code and then finding the underlying fault.

- **Avoid frustration**. Debugging can easily lead to unproductive frustration, especially when the writer of the code is also the person doing the debugging. Frustration results when the developer cannot find the problems of his or her own making. Adopting a game playing attitude may help: envision the faults as opponents in the game metaphor.

- **Get help**. Because faults result from developers' errors, a developer may not be able to see past the misconception that lies at the heart of the problem. It may be useful to involve a mind that does not share the misconception. Another team member may be useful in this role. Sometimes it is enough simply to try to explain the failure to someone else: the mere act of articulating one's thinking can force the misconception out into the open.

Even with these strategies and hints, the developer must realize that there is no shortcut in the difficult work of debugging—patient determination, consistent application of effective strategies, and knowledgeable use of debugging tools provide the only real path to success.

Debugging Tools

In the next sections, two debugging tools will be considered. The toolkit approach is represented by *gdb,* the GNU debugger, and its variants such as *xxgdb.* (Other Unix toolkit debuggers are also available in the public domain.) The IDE approach is illustrated by the debugger embedded in the Visual C++ environment. Other integrated development environments similar to Visual C++ include a debugger as part of the standard set of integrated capabilities.

5.6 A Unix Debugger

Presented in this section is information on how to use a source-code debugging system, **gdb** (the **G**nu **DeB**ugger), and **xxgdb**, a graphical user-interface to the gdb debugger under the X Window System. Through the graphical user interface provided by xxgdb, the developer is provided with a simple-to-use environment for debugging programs. The interface provides simple mechanisms for controlling program execution through breakpoints, examining and traversing the call stack, and displaying values of variables and objects. All of these operations are done at the source-code level.

Gdb has many commands, more than are covered here. For more information about *gdb* consult *Debugging with GDB*, a reference manual for the *gdb* debugger.

To use *xxgdb* the program must be compiled with the g++ compiler using the "-g" compiler flag set. For example, the command:

```
g++ -g -o prog prog.cc
```

compiles the file prog.cc. The -g flag causes the compiler to insert information into the executable file (named "prog") that *gdb* and *xxgdb* require in order to work.

Starting *xxgdb*

To start the *xxgdb* simple enter its name ("xxgdb") on the command line. Fig. 5–6 shows the graphical display that will be presented.

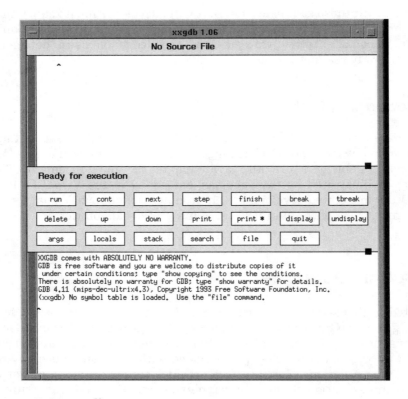

Figure 5–6   xxgdb

From top to bottom, the *xxgdb* display consists of the following subwindows:

File Window: Display the full pathname of the file displayed in the source window, and the line number of the caret.

Source Window: Shows the contents of the source file that is being debugged. The name of this file is given in the file window. In the initial window, the source window is empty except for a single caret symbol (^). During a debugging session, the relevant source code will appear in this subwindow; this source window will scroll during the execution of the program so that the current line being executed is always visible.

Message Window: This window provides information-feedback messages from the debugger relating to the execution status of the program and error messages generated by xxgdb.

The message window in the initial xxgdb display shown in Fig. 5–6 says "Ready for execution," which is the initial state of gdb. Other status information will appear in this place throughout a session.

Command Window: In the middle of the screen, the command window contains a set of twenty buttons for commonly used debugging commands; each button is labeled with the name of a command. To execute the command, simply click the left mouse button on the corresponding button in the command window. The meaning of each command is explained below.

Dialogue/Display Window: This window is an area for displaying output from the program or from gdb. Alternatively, any gdb command can be entered in this window. The dialogue/display window initially contains the gdb disclaimer message, which begins with the words "GDB comes with … "

The relative sizes of the source, command, and the dialogue/display windows can be adjusted by dragging the grip (a small square near the right edge of the horizontal border) with the left mouse button down. During a debugging session it may be convenient to resize these windows to allow the most useful information to be seen more easily.

Selecting, Searching, and Quitting

The first category of commands are those that control the overall operation of the debugging session. The command window contains three buttons for beginning a debugging session, quitting *xxgdb*, and searching through the source code of the program being debugged. These buttons are:

file: Presents a directory navigator that allows the user to select a text file to be displayed, an executable file to debug, or a core file to debug. In the navigation display, directory entries are marked with a trailing slash (/) and executables with a trailing asterisk (*). Filenames beginning with a dot (.) or ending with a tilde (~) are not listed in the menu.

quit: Terminates the execution of xxgdb and the program that is being debugged.

search: Initiates a search dialogue allowing the user to search for a given string within the file displayed in the source window. The search may go forward or backwards from the current location (indicated by the caret symbol in the source window). The carriage return is used to initiate a search and draw down the search panel.

It is important to remember that the file you select for debugging must be an executable file that has been compiled with g++ by using the "-g" compiler option.

When an executable file is selected, *xxgdb* loads the executable file in preparation for debugging and it displays the source text of the file in the source window.

Setting Breakpoints

The second set of commands deal with breakpoints—designated points within the program where the program will halt and return control to the debugger, allowing the user to examine the state of the program at that point. Breakpoints are typically placed at strategic locations in the program at which the user believes the most relevant and revealing information can be obtained about the program's bug.

It is common during debugging that new breakpoints will be added and existing breakpoints deleted. As the user gains more insight into the program's execution, the places at which the most useful information can be obtained changes. New breakpoints may be added at any time that the debugger is in control (i.e., the program is halted at a breakpoint). Removing or deleting a breakpoint means that the breakpoint is removed from the program and the program will no longer halt its execution at that point.

Breakpoints can be set and deleted using the following buttons in the command window:

break: Insert a new breakpoint into the program. The caret symbol in the source window indicates where the breakpoint will be placed. If the caret is not at the desired breakpoint location, simply move the caret to the beginning of the source line and click on the break button. A stop sign will appear next to the source line.

tbreak: Adds a special kind of breakpoint that is used only once, which means that the program's execution will halt when the flow of control next reaches this breakpoint and then the breakpoint will automatically be deleted. This command is useful for setting breakpoints that are only needed temporarily.

delete: Removes an existing breakpoint. The breakpoint that is deleted is indicated by the current placement of the caret in

> the source window. The breakpoint on the current source line is the one removed.

Note that is not necessary to delete a breakpoint to proceed past it. Gdb automatically ignores breakpoints on the first instruction to be executed when you continue execution without changing the execution address.

Controlling the Program's Execution

The third set of commands are those that allow the user to control the program's execution at a finer level than is efficient with breakpoints. Typically, these commands allow the user to control the line-by-line execution of the program once a breakpoint has been reached. The relevant commands are:

run: Starts the program's execution immediately after it has been loaded.

cont: Short for "continue," this command resumes the program's execution after the program has halted at a breakpoint. The program will halt when it reaches a breakpoint, completes normally, or experiences a run-time error that would normally abort the program.

next: Executes one complete source statement. If the source line contains one or more method invocations, these methods are executed to completion without halting. The program will be halted when the complete source statement has completed.

step: Similar to the next command, step differs in how method invocations are treated. If the source statement contains a method invocation, the program is halted at the first line in the invoked method.

finish: This command allows the program to resume execution and halt again when the current method invocation is competed. This command is typically used sometime after a step command has begun executing a method.

A typical debugging technique combines the use of breakpoints and the step/next commands to control program execution. A breakpoint is used to establish course-execution control. When halted at a breakpoint, the subsequent code is traced using the finer-grain step/next commands. As this code is being traced, the commands discussed below are used to examine the state of the system.

Examining the Execution History

The fourth set of commands allows the user to examine the state of the system being debugged. The user is to review the history of method invocations (the run-time stack) that ended in the current point of execution and the arguments and local variables of the current method, or any other method in the current history. Variables that are simple types as well as objects of user-defined classes may be checked.

Each stack frame is assigned a simple integer number by the debugger. The current frame (the frame corresponding to the method that is currently execut-ing) is number 0 (zero). The frame corresponding to the method that invoked the current method is number 1, and so on. These numbers have no significance to the program; they are simply used to allow the developer to refer to a particular frame in the run-time stack. This number is used on several commands.

Most commands for examining the stack and other data in the program operate on whichever stack frame is selected at the moment. In particular, when-ever gdb is asked for the value of a variable in the program, the value is that of the variable in the selected stack frame. There are special gdb commands to select a frame.

The commands related to the run-time stack are:

stack: Displays a succinct representation of the sequence of method invocations that are on the run-time stack.

up: Changes the frame being examined to one level higher on the run-time stack.

down: Changes the frame being examined to one level lower on the run-time stack.

args: Shows the arguments of the method corresponding to the cur-rently selected stack frame.

locals: Shows the local variables of the method corresponding to the currently selected stack frame.

For the up and down commands, it is important to remember that "up" in the run-time stack advances away from the method currently being executed, backward in time, toward the outermost frame, to higher frame numbers, to frames that have existed longer. Conversely, "down" advances toward the method currently being executed, forward in time, toward the innermost frame, to lower frame numbers, to frames that were created more recently.

Examining Variables

The fifth set of commands allow the value of variables and objects to be examined. Often these values give the best evidence of the effects of the program's bug. With xxgdb, both the value of built-in types (int, float, char, char*, and so on) and the values of objects of user-defined classes can be viewed with equal ease.

The value of a variable or object can be viewed by identifying the variable or object and using one of the following command buttons:

print: Displays the value of a selected variable or object

print*: Displays the value of the variable or object that is pointed to by the selected variable.

display: Displays the value of a selected variable in the display window, updating its value every time execution stops.

undisplay: Stops displaying the value of the selected variable in the display window. If the selected variable is a constant, it refers to the display number associated with an expression in the display window.

The value of a variable may be examined in one of several ways. In the simplest case, the variable is not a pointer and its name is visible in the source window. When this happens, simply highlight the name of the variable in the source window and press the print button. The value will appear in the dialogue/display window. If the variable is a pointer to an object, highlight the name of the pointer variable and use the print* command button. The value will, as before, appear in the dialogue/Ddsplay window. If the name of the variable is not currently visible in the source window you can type its name in the dialogue/display area, highlight the name in the dialogue/display area, and use the "print" or "print*" command buttons as before.

5.7 The Visual C++ Debugger

The Visual C++ development environment contains a powerful debugger that allows the developer to monitor and control the program's execution as well as inspect the program's state. Described here are the basic commands needed for many simple debugging situations.

To use the debugger, it is important that a debug version of the program be built. The debug version contains information and special code that allows the debugger to examine and control the program during execution. The default configuration for the environment is to build both a debug version, containing the extra information and code, and a release version, which does not. The current configuration is shown in a small selection box above the view area. The debug configuration is named `Win32 Debug`. If the debug version is not currently selected, use the selection box controls to select it as the current configuration. The debug version can be disabled or enabled using the Configurations dialog box under the `Build` menu.

Starting and Stopping the Debugger

Three commands control the overall starting and stopping of the debugger. They are listed in Table 5–9. The `Go` command is used to begin the execution of the program under the debugger. When the execution under the debugger begins, the arrangement of the areas in the Visual C++ window and the contents of some menus changes to the debugger format, which is explained below. Typically, the developer has set some initial breakpoints, so that after the `Go` command, the program runs until a breakpoint is reached (whose condition is true if it is a conditional breakpoint), the end of the program is reached, or the program abnormally terminates due to a failure. The `Go` command is also used to resume execution after a breakpoint. The debugging session is ended using the `Stop Debugging` command. This command immediately terminates the program and the debugger, returning the window arrangement and the menu contents to that of the original configuration for building and editing the system. The developer may realize that the program has executed past a point that he or she wanted to examine. Since there is no general way to undo the program's execution, the `Restart` command can be used to begin the execution of the program again without leaving the debugger environment.

Table 5–9 Starting and Stopping the Debugger

• `Go`: begin or resume the execution of the program.
• `Stop Debugging`: terminate the program at the current point of execution in a normal fashion
• `Restart`: begin the execution of the program from the initial state

The Debugger Display

When the program is being executed under the debugger, the format of the Visual C++ display is changed to show three horizontal areas: the view area, the edit area, and the debugging-information area. This format of the Visual C++ display is designed to make the debugging information more prominent and easily accessible. The view area and the edit area have the same contents and purpose as previously described in Section 5.4.

During debugging, the edit area is managed by the debugger which uses it to display the file containing the current line of code. This aids the developer in seeing the code as it is executed. An arrow is drawn in the left margin to point to the line of code being executed. The position of the cursor in the edit area also has significance for some of the debugger commands: by placing the cursor at a particular line or at a particular variable, the developer is able to focus the debugger on that item. Using the cursor in this way makes it convenient for the developer to specify a line of code at which a breakpoint is to be set or indicate a variable whose value should be displayed.

The debugging-information area typically has two side-by-side windows: on the left is displayed information about the current execution context and, on the right, the state of variables that are being watched. The current execution context contains a scrollable list that shows the current invocation sequence. By selecting different entries in this list, the developer is able to examine the current sequence of method invocations and determine the variables currently being used by each of these methods. Variables of interest can be added to the watched area and their current values will be displayed and updated as the execution progresses.

The current execution-context window has three tabs at the bottom that allow the developer to select what information about the selected method invocation is displayed. The Auto tab displays the value of variables that are close to the line of code being executed by the method. The Locals tab displays all of the local variables of the method being executed. Finally, the *this* tab displays the current state of the object in which the method is executing.

Setting Breakpoints

A breakpoint is a debugging annotation added to a line of executable code that makes the program stop immediately before executing that line of code and turns control over to the debugger. When the program is stopped at a breakpoint, the debugger commands can be used to examine and change the values of variables and objects, set new breakpoints or remove existing breakpoints, and control the subsequent execution of the program. It is often necessary to eliminate a breakpoint once it has done its job and the developer no longer wants the program to stop at the breakpoint. This is called deleting the breakpoint. A breakpoint that has been deleted no longer exists; it is forgotten.

Breakpoints may be set in two different ways; both begin by placing the edit area's cursor in the line of code where the breakpoint is to be added. When this is done, one way of adding a breakpoint is to follow the steps shown in Table 5–10 using the *Edit* menu. The Breakpoints dialogue box shows the list of breakpoints that are currently set. An alternative method of setting a breakpoint is to use the breakpoint button, whose icon is a hand held up in a "stop" gesture. This button is located immediately above the editing area. To set a breakpoint in this way, position the cursor as before in the edit area and then click the breakpoint button.

Table 5–10 Setting a Breakpoint

1. In the edit area, place the cursor at the line where the breakpoint is to be set.
2. Select `Breakpoints` from the `Edit` menu.
3. In the Location tabbed area, click on the arrow at the right of the `Break at` box. Select the line number shown there.
4. Click OK to complete the command.

A breakpoint is visually represented in the source-code file by a small colored dot appearing in the left margin of the file next to the line of code. This visual cue makes it easy to see where breakpoints have been set.

Breakpoints can be removed in either of two ways. One way is to use the list of current breakpoints shown in the bottom part of the `Breakpoints` dialogue box. Next to this list is a `Remove` button. To remove a breakpoint, simply select the breakpoint from the list and press the Remove button. A second way to remove a breakpoint is to position the edit cursor in a line containing a breakpoint (the colored-circle visual cue indicates which lines have breakpoints) and click the breakpoint button (the upheld hand icon). Once a breakpoint has been removed, it no longer has any effect on the program's execution.

A conditional breakpoint is a breakpoint that will stop the program's execution only when a given boolean condition is true. The condition can be attached to the breakpoint when the breakpoint is created or it can be attached to an already existing breakpoint. To attach the condition when creating the breakpoint, create the breakpoint using the `Breakpoints` dialogue. After the breakpoint has been entered in the `Break at` box, press the `Condition` button. To attach the condition to an existing breakpoint, select the breakpoint from the list of breakpoints at the bottom of the `Breakpoints` dialogue box and then press the `Condition` button. Pressing the `Condition` button causes a `Breakpoint Condition` dialogue box to appear. Near the top of this box is an editable line where an arbitrary boolean condition can be placed. This boolean condition is written in the same syntax as normal C++ conditions (e.g., x == 10 && y < z). The condition will be part of the breakpoint information shown in the breakpoint list in the `Breakpoints` dialogue box. Also, when a conditional breakpoint is reached in the execution, a pop-up dialogue box will appear showing the condition.

Controlling the Program's Execution

The program being debugged can be run and, when breakpoints are encountered, its future execution can be controlled via a set of commands. The commands are available either by menu selections or by buttons. Alternatively, when a debug version terminates abnormally, the developer is given the choice of terminating the program or entering the debugger at the point where the program failed. This latter method of entering the debugger is commonly used when a particular failure occurs for the first time. The commands to control the program's execution are listed in Table 5–11.

Table 5–11 Commands for Controlling the Program's Execution

- `Step Into`: execute the next line of code and stop again whenever control reaches a different line of code
- `Step Over`: execute the next line of code (and any method calls made by it) and stop again
- `Step Out`: complete the execution of the current method and stop again when control returns to the invoking code
- `Run to Cursor`: resume execution and stop at the line containing the cursor

There are four commands for controlling the execution of the program when the program is halted (typically via a breakpoint) in the debugger: the three variations of the `Step` command and the `Run to cursor` command. These commands are shown in Table 5–11. Each of these four commands is similar in that they resume the execution of the program and specify a "nearby" stopping point; they differ in how the stopping point is defined. The `Step In` command begins executing the current line of code and stops again when a different source line has been reached. If the code is a sequence of simple statements (without method calls or branches) then the `Step In` command has the effect of executing one line after another. The developer can execute the `Step In` command repeatedly to reach a desired point in the execution. If the line of code being executed has a method call, then the execution will stop at the first line of code in the invoked method. It is this case that gives meaning to the `In` part of the command's name. The `Step Over` command is similar to `Step In`, except that with it the debugger does not step into method calls. With the `Step Over` command, the debugger will execute until control reaches another line of code in the current method. The `Step Over` command is useful when the focus of debugging is on the current method and not the methods that it uses. It is also useful in stepping over system calls and library method (e.g., stream I/O methods or windowing-system methods). The `Step Out` command completes the execution of the current method and stops again when control has returned to the invoking method. This command is useful when a method has been stepped into and the developer wants to quickly finish the invoked method and continue debugging at the point of the invocation. Finally, the `Run to Cursor` command allows the user to directly specify how far the execution should proceed. The developer places the cursor at a line of code to specify where the execution should stop again. The developer must be careful that the specified line will actually be executed and not branched around.

The commands for controlling the program's execution can be selected in any of three ways. First, all of the commands are contained in pulldown menus. The Go command is part of the Build menu under the Debug option, and all of the commands are available under the Debug menu in the debugger display. Second, a debugger toolbar contains buttons with icon labels for each of the commands. If this toolbar is not visible in the debugger display, it can be made so by selecting the Toolbars option in the View menu and clicking on the Debug choice. Third, there are keyboard shortcuts for each of the commands: Go, (F5); Stop Debugging, (Alt+F5); Restart, (Shift+F5); Step Into, (F8); Step Over, (F10); Step Out, (Shift+F7); and Run to Cursor, (F7).

Examining the Current Execution Sequence

When the program has stopped at a breakpoint or because it experienced a failure, it is often useful to review the sequence of method invocations that have led to the current point of execution and to examine the arguments and local variables of the current method. Information of this sort is obtained by looking at the "call stack."

Each time your program invokes a method, the information about where in your program the invocation was made from is saved in a block of data called a stack frame. The frame also contains the arguments of the call and the local variables of the function that was called. All the stack frames are allocated in a region of memory called the run-time stack. When your program stops, the Visual C++ debugger has commands for examining the stack that allow you to see all of this information. The debugger automatically selects the stack frame for the currently executing method and describes it briefly.

The current sequence of method invocations can be examined via the scrollable Context list in the debugging information area (the left-most part of the debugging information area). The scrollable list is organized in a stack-like fashion: the current method being executed is at the top of this list, the method that invoked the current method is the next item in the list, and so on. By selecting different entries in this list, the developer can view the information about each method comprising the current execution sequence. For the currently selected method, the developer can view the most recently used data items (Auto tab), all of the local data of the method (Local tab), and the current values of all of the data of the object performing the method (this tab).

Examining Variables

There are three ways to review the values of variables and objects. Each way of displaying this information has its own best use depending on how much context is associated with the information, over what time span is the information useful to the developer, and how much manipulation the developer must perform to obtain the information.

The first means of displaying the value of variables and objects is by holding the cursor stationary anywhere in the name of a variable or object in the edit area, which prompts the debugger to display adjacent to the cursor the current value of the variable or object. This technique is the simplest and easiest way to examine the value of variables and objects. However, the information is transitory in that when the cursor moves, the information disappears.

The second means of displaying the value of variables and objects applies to any variable or object included in the current execution sequence. Information about these variables and objects can be obtained by using the context portion (the left region) of the debugging-information area. The variables and objects that are part of the selected context are displayed in this area. It is useful to examine variables and objects by this method to gain a deeper understanding of the sequence of events underlying the current invocation sequence. The variables in this display are organized by the methods or objects of which they are a part and are ordered in time (the most recent invocation at the top of the Context selection list). The information in this display also changes over time as the execution sequence changes.

Watching the variable or object provides a third means to review their values. The value of such variables and objects is displayed in the watch part (the right part) of the debugging-information area. To create a watched variable, use the QuickWatch dialogue box, accessible from either the Debug menu or from the debug toolbar. In the QuickWatch dialogue box, the name of the variable or object to be watch is entered in the Expression field. The Current value portion of the dialogue box displays the current value of the named variable or object. To maintain a continuing watch on the variable or object, click the AddWatch button. The value of the watched variable is then continuously displayed in the watch area. Watching a variable or object is useful when its value is frequently needed during a particular debugging operation. Having the value in the watch area makes the value conveniently accessible at all times.

Inheritance

6.1 Introduction to Inheritance

*G*eneralization captures the common or shared aspects of abstractions. It is not unusual to find such generalizations in everyday experience—for example, the statement "all computer workstations have a monitor" expresses a generalization about computer workstations, and identifies a common attribute among the various abstractions for a computer workstation. Similarly, the statement "all telephones can make connections through the telephone switching system" expresses a similarity in behavior: all abstractions of telephones will possess a behavior that allows them to make connections.

When a group of abstractions in an application domain share similar features, the classes representing these abstractions may also be similar. This is natural because a class is intended to reflect the attributes and behavior of a class. Thus, similarities in the abstractions will result in similarities among the classes representing them. However, nothing that has been seen so far allows a group of classes to express any similarities that they might share.

Inheritance expresses sharing among classes. Classes may share a common implementation (code and/or data), a common interface, or both. When inheritance is used to create interface sharing, each class sharing the common interface must implement the methods described in the shared interface, although these classes may have other methods in addition to those in the shared interface. The classes sharing a common interface can, and usually do, implement differently the methods in the shared interface. When inheritance is used to create implementation sharing, each of the sharing classes builds on the shared implementation to define its own operations.

Inheritance extends the class concept to distinguish between a base class which defines the shared interface and implementation, and a derived class that inherits the shared elements from the base class. Equivalent terminology used in other object-oriented languages is superclass and subclass to refer to base and derived classes, respectively.

Inheritance is the most critical aspect of object oriented programming because it has implications in several important dimensions. Three of these dimensions are:

- **programming**: expressing the similarities among a related set of classes in a single base class makes unnecessary the repetition of code in each of the derived classes. Not only does this create an immediate savings for the classes at hand, but it also establishes a foundation on which future derived classes can be built more efficiently.

- **design**: in the largest sense, software design is a form of knowledge engineering, because it attempts to represent in software a model of the real world. A good designer does more than organize software structures; he or she tries to reflect in the software the existence and organization of abstractions in the problem domain. Thus, if there are similarities among the abstractions, there should be a corresponding way to represent these similarities in the software. The more direct and explicit the software can be in representing these similarities, the better a model it will be of the application domain.

- **software engineering**: software has a long lifetime and undergoes many changes and extensions during its existence. Therefore, important qualities of software are the degrees to which it is flexible—can be modified to add new features, and extensible—can accommodate the creation of new elements not originally anticipated.

Learning how to exploit the power of inheritance is the hallmark of a successful object-oriented programming.

6.2 Using Inheritance to Share Implementation

Using inheritance to share implementation is illustrated by example in this section, where two classes sharing an implementation is described. First, the complete implementation of each class is shown, assuming that each was developed as an independent class. Then, a base class that captures those aspects of the implementation comment to the two classes is defined. Finally, the original classes are then reimplemented using inheritance. Objects of the two new derived classes will have the same interface and behavior as objects of the original classes.

Code Sample 6–1 *The Number Class*

```
class Number {
  private:
    int value;
    TextBox* textBox;
  public:
      Number(int initValue = 0);   // start at initValue
    void ShowIn (TextBox& tbox);   // place to display value
    void Show();                   // display current value
    void Next();                   // increment
    void Reset();                  // get new value from user
    int  Value();                  // reply current value
        ~Number();                 //
};
```

The definition of the Number class is given in Code Sample 6–1. This class captures the abstraction of an integer value that can be incremented by one, without limit. Objects of this class can be used to count the occurrence of some event. The constructor specifies the starting value for a Number object, zero by default. The Next() operation increments the value of the Number object by one. The current value of the Number is returned by the Value() accessor method. The Number class also provides a facility to display its current value to the user in a TextBox as a character string. The ShowIn method creates an association with a TextBox where the Number's value should be displayed. The Show() method triggers the actual displaying of the current value in the TextBox. Finally, the Reset() method allows the user to provide a new value for the Number. This method assigns a new value to the Number by converting to an integer the character string read from the TextBox.

The Cycler class is similar to the Number class, except that the integer value maintained by the Cycler is constrained to a range determined by the base of the Cycler. The base value is specified when the Cycler object is constructed. The value of a Cycler object must always be in the range from 0 to base-1. Cycler objects are useful for counting events that are numbered cyclically, like seconds in a minute (0-59) or hours in a day (0-23). Like a Number, the Cycler also contains methods for creating an association with a TextBox that will display its current value in the TextBox and for obtaining a new value from the user. The definition of the Cycler class is shown in Code Sample 6–2.

The similarities in the Number and Cycler classes are evident in their definitions, and include both the data that each maintains and the code for some of their methods. Specifically, the similarities are:

Code Sample 6–2   *The Cycler Class*

```
class Cycler {
  private:
    int value;
    int base;
    TextBox* textBox;
  public:
        Cycler(int b = 10);          // modulo base b
    void ShowIn (TextBox& tbox);      // place to display value
    void Show();                      // display current value
    void Next();                      // increment
    void Reset();                     // get new value from user
    int  Value();                     // reply current value
        ~Cycler();                    // clean up
};
```

```
        Data:
                value      : an internal integer value
                TextBox*   : a pointer to a TextBox
        Code:
        ShowIn: provide a TextBox where value is displayed
          Show: display the current value in the TextBox
        Reset: use the TextBox to get new value from user
        Value: returns the current internal value
```

Notice that the Next method is *not* similar: its implementation distinguishes the classes from each other. Notice also that the constructors and destructors are not the same. Because the constructor and destructor each take the class name, it is not possible that they be shared among classes with different names.

Identifying the similarities among classes is a process of generalization resulting in a new class. The new class is referred to as the base class (also sometimes called the superclass or the parent class). The classes over which the generalization is made are referred to as the derived classes (or subclasses or child classes). The base class is named so as to reflect its role as a generalization. In the example, the generalization is formed over classes that have a numeric property (Numbers and Cyclers have numeric values) and a property of being displayable to the user. Thus, one name for the generalized (base) class is DisplayableNumber; other names such as InteractiveNumber, GUIValue, and VisualNumeric are possible.

The classes over which the generalization is formed are viewed as specializations. Each of these classes contains distinctive properties (data and/or methods) that are beyond the similar properties captured in the base class. These distinctive properties also differentiate a class from other classes that are

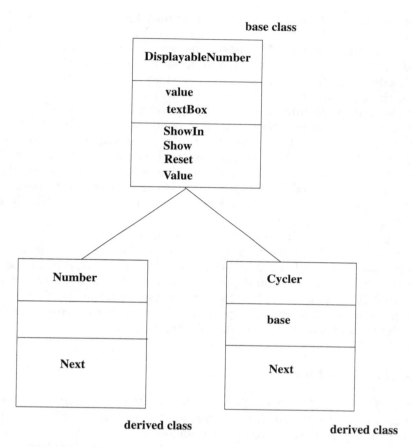

Figure 6–1   Generalization-Specialization Hierarchy

specializations of the same generalization. Thus, both Number and Cycler are specializations of DisplayableNumber, each is a particular kind of Displayable-Number. The specializing property in this example is the Next() method. The Next() method is not part of the generalization because it has a different meaning in the two classes.

A generalization-specialization hierarchy is used to organize the generalized class and its specializations. The generalization-specialization hierarchy for the example is shown in Fig. 6–1. The class for a generalization is placed above the classes of its specializations. Each class in the hierarchy is represented by a class diagram with three sections: the top section gives the name of the class, the middle section gives the data of the class, and the bottom section gives the methods of the class. A line is drawn between a generalization (in this case DisplayableNumber) and its specializations (Number and Cycler).

Inheritance is the object-oriented programming form of a generalization-specialization hierarchy. The term inheritance is used because each derived class inherits from the base class the base class's code and data and need not be repeated in the definition of the derived class. For example, since the Number class inherits from the DisplayableNumber class, the Number class implicitly has all of the data and methods of the DisplayableNumber class. The only elements defined in the Number class are the specializing features that make it distinctive. In this case only a Next() method is added by the Number class. This method is distinctive in the sense that the generalization does not contain a Next() method and the Next() methods of the other specializations of DisplayableNumber are different from the Number class's Next() method. Similarly, the Cycler class inherits all of the data and methods of the DisplayableNumber class and adds to that inherited data a new data element, the base of the Cycler, and an additional method, New().

The programming advantage of inheritance is that the definition and implementation fixed in the base class does not have to be repeated in the derived classes. Clearly, this reduces the amount of coding that has to be done to add a new derived class. Perhaps more importantly, because the base class may have existed for a long period of time its implementation is, therefore, more likely to have been tested and debugged. In this way inheritance aids in the more efficient development of more reliable software systems.

Object Structure

The structure of an object instantiated from a derived class may be thought of as a series of layers—each layer corresponds to one level in the inheritance hierarchy. For example, the structure of a Cycler object is shown in Fig. 6–2. Cycler objects have two layers, one corresponding to its base class, DisplayableNumber, and one layer corresponding to its derived class, Cycler. Each layer adds the data and methods defined by the corresponding class definition. Thus, the object possesses the union of all of the methods and data of all of the classes from which it directly or indirectly inherits.

The layered object structure helps to explain why a derived class object is able to respond to methods that are defined and implemented in the base class. An example of this is shown in the following code:

```
Cycler octal(8);
...
TextBox tbox(...);
...

octal.ShowIn(tbox);            // apply base class method
octal.Next();                  // apply derived class method
octal.Show();                  // apply base class method
```

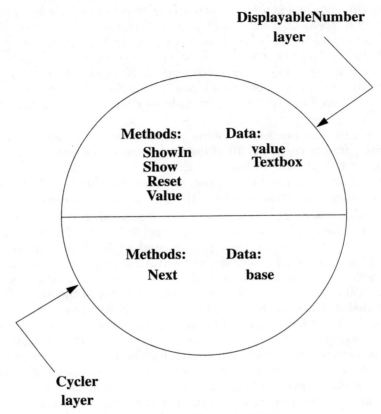

Figure 6–2 Logical Structure of a Cycler Object

As seen in this code, a Cycler object is able to perform those methods defined in the derived class (i.e., Next) as well as those defined in the base class (i.e., ShowIn and Show).

Multiple Levels of Inheritance

A derived class can itself be a base class whose implementation may be shared by classes derived from it. In this manner, inheritance extends over several, and perhaps many, levels. The example using DisplayableNumber and Cycler had only two levels, but more extensive use of inheritance to share implementations is possible and even common.

To illustrate multiple levels of inheritance, consider a JumpCounter that can be incremented by one or by an arbitrary amount. Such an object might be used to show the current length of a file where the length of the file may be changed by appending a single character (increment by one) or by appending an entire string (increment by the length of the string). Alternatively, the Jump-Counter may represent the current page number in a document. In some cases the user turns the pages one at a time. In this case the JumpCounter should be able to increment its value by one each time its Next method is called. In other cases, the user may jump ahead many pages, by following a link or reference. In this case the JumpCounter should be able to change by an arbitrary integer amount.

The inheritance needed to define a JumpCounter is shown in Fig. 6–3. Because the Number class has all of the functionality necessary to implement a JumpCounter except the ability to increase the internal value by a given amount, the JumpCounter class is derived from the Number class. Recall that the Number class is itself derived from the DisplayableNumber class.

Notice that the JumpCounter overloads a method that is defined in a class from which it inherits. The Next() method is defined in the Number class and the JumpCounter defines an overloading of the method, Next(int). In general, many overloadings are possible, either defined within a single class or accumulated across several levels of inheritance. An overloading that is introduced in a derived class should maintain the conceptual similarity of the use of the name of the overloaded method. In the case of the JumpCounter, the two variants of the Next method have conceptual similarity; the two methods provide alternative ways of increasing the value of the Number. By contrast, the conceptual similarity would be violated by introducing an overloading of the Next method that had the meaning "this is the amount by which the next increment should increase the value." Such an overloading weakens the meaning of Next by confusing whether it applies to the current operation or to a future operation.

The essential point is that a JumpCounter object responds to all methods of its immediate class (JumpCounter) as well as to all of the methods of its ancestor classes (Number and DisplayableNumber). This is illustrated by the following code:

```
JumpCounter    fileLength;
TextBox        lengthDisplay(Location(100,100), Shape(50,20));
...
fileLength.ShowIn(lengthDisplay);
                        // uses method in DisplayableNumber
fileLength.Show(lengthDisplay);
                        // uses method in DisplayableNumber
...
fileLength.Next();      // add 1 using method in Number
...
fileLength.Next(50);
                        // add 50 using method in JumpCounter
...
fileLength.Reset();     // uses method in DisplayableNumber
```

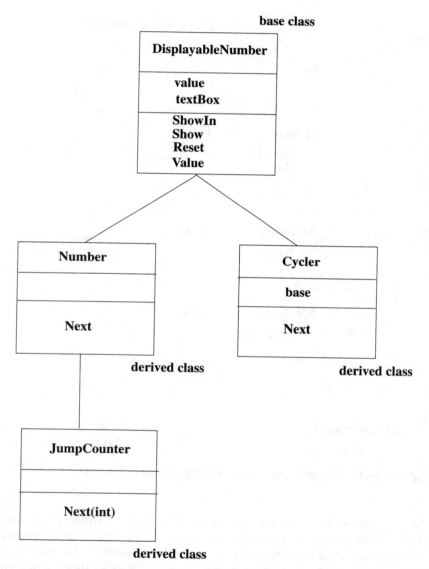

Figure 6–3 Multiple Levels of Inheritance

The layered nature of the object structure again helps to explain the behavior of the JumpCounter object in this code. As shown in Fig. 6–4, a JumpCounter object has three layers, one for the derived class, JumpCounter, a second for the base class of JumpCounter, Number, and the third for the base class of Number, namely DisplayableNumber.

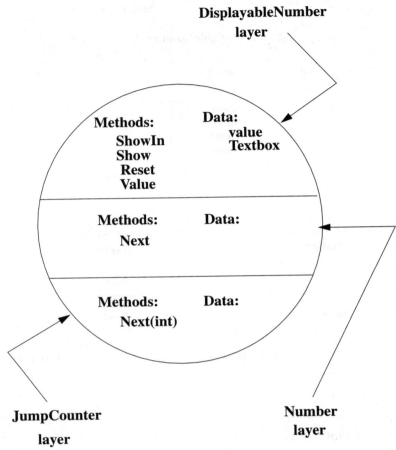

Figure 6–4   Object Structure of a JumpCounter Object

In general an inheritance diagram may form a deep and/or broad tree structure. Each node in the tree denotes a class that inherits from its parent (base class) and also serves as a base class for its descendents. The exercises below, when completed, will build an inheritance graph that looks like the one shown in Fig. 6–5.

Designing a new derived class by inheritance commonly makes the introduction of a new variation or extension of an existing class easier than would be reimplementing the class entirely from scratch.

It will become clearer as more is learned that designing the "right" inheritance structure is both important and difficult. Much of the effort in object-oriented programming is invested in the search for good inheritance structures.

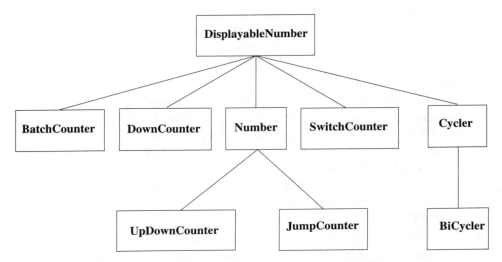

Figure 6–5   An Inheritance Hierarchy of Displayable Numbers

 **Exercises**

1. The class DownCounter maintains an integer counter whose nonnegative value, given initially by a constructor argument, is decremented by one on each call to its Next operation until the value reaches zero. Upon reaching zero, subsequent calls on Next will have no effect; the value remains at zero. The value of a DownCounter object can be displayed in a TextBox. Using an inheritance diagram, show how the DownCounter class is defined by inheritance from Displayable-Number.

2. The class UpDownCounter maintains an integer counter whose nonnegative value, given initially by a constructor argument, is incremented by one on each call to its Next operation. The UpDownCounter class also has a Previous method that decrements the counter's value by one. The counter's value cannot be decremented lower than its initial value. The value of a UpDownCounter object can be displayed in a TextBox. Using an inheritance diagram, show how the UpDown-Counter class is defined by inheritance from Number.

3. The class BiCycler is to be defined that maintains an integer counter that is incremented modulo the base given by the constructor. The BiCycler class also has a Previous method that decrements the

counter's value by one. When the internal value is zero, the Previous operation sets the internal value to the largest possible value (i.e., base-1). Using an inheritance diagram, show how the BiCycler class is defined by inheritance from Cycler.

4. The class SwitchCounter maintains an integer counter that is incremented or decremented by the Next method depending on the current direction of the SwitchCounter. Initially the SwitchCounter is directed up. When up, the value is incremented by one when Next is called. When in the "down" direction the value is decremented by 1 when Next is called. The Switch method changes the direction to the opposite of its current setting. Using an inheritance diagram, show how the SwitchCounter class is defined by inheritance from Displayable-Number.

5. The class BatchCounter maintains an integer counter that is incremented by one only when the Next operation has been called n times. The value of n is given as a constructor argument. This class counts batches of Next operations. It may be used, for example, to increment a one-minute counter only after its Next method has been called sixty times by a one-second Clock. Using an inheritance diagram, show how the BatchCounter class is defined by inheritance from Displayable-Number.

6.3 Inheriting Operations and Data

In C++, the relationship between a base and derived classes is represented syntactically as follows:

```
class DisplayableNumber {...};                       // base class
class Number : public DisplayableNumber {...};
                                                     // derived class
class Cycler  : public DisplayableNumber {...};
                                                     // derived class
```

The additional syntax ": public DisplayableNumber" is used in the definition of each derived class to name the base class from which the derived class inherits.

The keyword public in this context means that all of the public methods defined in the base class (DisplayableNumber) become part of the public interface of the derived class (Number, Cycler). These inherited methods represent the code sharing that is achieved by inheritance. Alternatives to the use of the public form of inheritance are described later in this chapter.

Code Sample 6–3 *Syntax of Inheritance*

```
class DisplayableNumber {
   public:
      DisplayableNumber(int init = 0);
                                    // initial value zero by default
      void ShowIn(TextBox& p);
      void Show();
      void Reset();
      int  Value();
      ~DisplayableNumber();
};

class Number : public DisplayableNumber {
   public:
      Number(int init = 0);
      void Next();
      ~Number();
};

class Cycler : public DisplayableNumber {
   public:
      Cycler(int b, int init = 0);
      void Next();
      ~Cycler();
};
```

The public interface of the classes DisplayableNumber, Number, and Cycler are shown in Code Sample 6–3. The same basic class structure is used to define both a base and a derived class. Both base and derived classes have constructors and destructors: the only difference between a base and a derived class is their roles in the inheritance relationship that relates them to each other.

Notice that the base class DisplayableNumber forms a complete class—it defines an unchanging integer that can be displayed in a TextBox. In some limited cases this may be all that is needed. For example, a portion of an interactive testing system may need to display a final score to the user as follows:

```
TextBox scoreBox(Location(100,100), Shape(75, 50));
int score;

        // interact with user; determine final score

DisplayableNumber finalScore(score);
finalScore.ShowIn(scoreBox);
finalScore.Show();
```

The classes derived from DisplayableNumber introduce the ability to change the number dynamically. Each new derived class embodies a different way to change the value.

The critical point is that, through inheritance, Number and Cycler objects have not only those methods defined in the Number and Cycler classes, but also those methods inherited from the public interface of the base class, Displayable-Number. For example:

```
Number count(10);       // initially 10
Cycler  binary(2);      // base 2

TextBox display(Location(10,10), Shape(50,50));
TextBox onoff  (Location(20,20), Shape(50,50));

count.ShowIn(display);
binary.ShowIn(onoff);

count.Next();           // increment by 1
binary.Next();          // increment by 1 modulo 2

count.Show();           // display updated value
binary.Show();          // display updated value

int c = count.Value();  // get value of Number object
int b = binary.Value(); // get value of Cycler object
```

As this example illustrates, the Number and Cycler objects can respond both to the methods defined in their immediate classes (Next) and to the inherited methods (ShowIn, Show, Reset and Value) that are defined in the base class DisplayableNumber.

The Protected Section

Data can also be placed in the base class. In the example above, the value and textBox variables are common to both the Number and Cycler classes. This data should be promoted to the base class. The variable textBox is used only in the methods ShowIn, Show, and Reset, all of which are in the base class (Display-ableNumber). Thus, the textBox variable can be placed in the private data area of the base class. The variable value, however, is needed in both the base class, where it is used by the Show and Reset methods, and in the derived class, where it is used in the Next method.

Data to be shared among the base and derived classes is placed in a new region, the protected section, in the base class. Data placed in this new section is accessible to the base class and to the derived classes. Similar to the private: and public: sections, the new section is introduced by the protected: keyword. The

Code Sample 6–4 *Example of the Protected Section*

```
class DisplayableNumber {
   private:
      TextBox* textBox;                    // place to display value

   protected: // the following are accessible in derived classes
      int       value;                     // internal counter

   public:
            DisplayableNumber(int init);   // initial value
      void ShowIn(TextBox& p);
      void Show();
      void Reset();
      int  Value();                        // reply current value
         ~DisplayableNumber();
   };
```

class definition, including the data private and protected data, for the DisplayableNumber base class is shown in Code Sample 6–4.

The protected section is needed because neither the private nor public sections are adequate places to put the shared data. If the shared data is placed in the private section of the base class, it is inaccessible to the derived classes. This is, of course, contrary to what is needed. If the shared data is placed in the public section of the base class, then although it is accessible to the derived classes, it is also accessible as public data in the interface of the derived class, which means that the data looses its encapsulation and is exposed to the user of the objects created from the derived class. This is also contrary to what is required.

The protected section contains data (and operations) that are accessible to the base class, and derived class, but inaccessible everywhere else. In other words, protected data (and operations) are not part of the public interface of either the base class or the derived classes.

Even though the protected data is not part of the public interface, many designers argue that the data should remain in the private section and accessor methods should be placed in the protected section. This way, the data remains the private concern of the class in which it is declared and can still be accessed by the derived classes. Using this approach the DisplayableNumber class would be written as show in Code Sample 6–5.

Because the accessor methods are in the protected section, they are not part of the public interface of the base or any derived class. The accessor methods are, however, visible to the derived classes. Thus, the Number's Next method would be written as follows:

```
void Number::Next() { setValue( getValue() + 1); }
```

Code Sample 6–5   *Using Protected Accessor Methods*

```
class DisplayableNumber {
   private:
      TextBox* textBox;           // place to display value
      int       value;            // internal counter

   protected:                     // the following accessor methods
                                  // are visible in derived classes


      void setValue(int v);       // sets "value"
      int  getValue();            // gets "value"


   public:
         // ... as before
   };
```

This example also illustrates why some developers argue against the accessor method approach: as shown here, two method invocations are necessary to simply increment the value of the Number by one. This overhead may be disproportionate to the additional encapsulation gained by the accessor-method approach.

Constructors

The constructors for derived classes, like those for the Number and Cycler classes, must be related to the constructors of their base classes, like DisplayableNumber. The constructor for the Number class has an integer argument that should be used to initialize the Number's internal value. However, the DisplayableNumber class also has a constructor for that purpose. In this case, the Number's constructor argument should simply be passed on to the DisplayableNumber's constructor. The C++ syntax for this is:

```
Number::Number(int init) : DisplayableNumber(init) { }
```

The additional syntax ": DisplayableNumber(init)" means that the derived class constructor argument (init) is used as the base class constructor argument. In this case, no other initialization is done in the derived class (the body of the Number's constructor has no code).

The Cycler class illustrates a different relationship between the constructors of the derived and base classes. The first integer value for the Cycler's

Code Sample 6–6 *Order of Constructor Execution*

```
class DisplayableNumber
{ private: int value;
  public: DisplayableNumber(int init);
};

class Cycler : public DisplayableNumber
{ private: int base;
  public: Cycler(int init, int b = 10);
};

DisplayableNumber::DisplayableNumber(int init)
{ cout << "DisplayableNumber Constructor " << init << endl; }

Cycler::Cycler(int b, int init) : DisplayableNumber(init)
{base = b; cout << "Cycler Constructor " << b << endl; }

void main()
{ Cycler cycler(8, 20);}
```

constructor is the base of the Cycler and the second integer value is the initial value of the Cycler. This is reflected in the Cycler's constructor as follows:

```
Cycler::Cycler(int b, int init) : DisplayableNumber(init)
{ base = b; }
```

In this case some of the derived class's constructor arguments are used to construct the base class while others are used to initialize the data in the derived class itself.

The constructors of the base and derived classes are executed in a prescribed order: the base class is constructed first, then the class immediately derived from the base class, etc. The order in which the constructors are executed is illustrated by the code shown in Code Sample 6–6. This code uses trivialized classes that have the same inheritance relationships and the same constructors as the real classes for which they are named. The output from the main program clearly shows that the base class constructor is the first one to be executed, followed by the constructor of its derived class.

The output from this program is

```
DisplayableNumber Constructor 20
Cycler Constructor 8
```

which clearly shows that the DisplayableNumber base class constructor is executed before the constructor of the derived Cycler class. It also confirms that the second argument of the Cycler's constructor (20) has been passed from the Cycler constructor to the DisplayableNumber constructor.

The execution of the constructors guarantees a derived class that the base class layers have been properly initialized before the derived class constructor is executed. This is useful in those cases where derived classes use the data or methods of the base class to perform their own initialization.

In summary, the constructor arguments are distributed from the bottom up (i.e., proceeding from the most derived class to the base class) and then the constructors are executed top down (i.e., proceeding from the base class to the most derived class).

A Complete Derived Class

Having declared the protected data in the base class, the code for the derived classes is:

```
class Number : public DisplayableNumber {
public:
  Number(int init = 0);
  void Next();
 ~Number();
};

class Cycler : public DisplayableNumber {
private:
  int base;
public:
  Cycler(int b, int init = 0);
  void Next();
 ~Cycler();
};
```

and the code for the methods of these classes is:

```
Number::Number(int init) : DisplayableNumber(init) { }
void Number::Next() { value = value + 1; }
Number::~Number() {}

Cycler::Cycler(int b, int init) : DisplayableNumber(init)
  { base = b; }
void Cycler::Next() { value = (value + 1)%base; }
Cycler::~Cycler() {}
```

Exercises

1. Implement and test the DisplayableNumber base class, the Number derived class, and the Cycler derived class.

2. Implement and test the DownCounter class. Your test program should show a DownCounter object's value in a TextBox and have a button labeled Next which, when pressed, causes the object's Next operation to be executed.

3. Implement and test the UpDownCounter class. Your test program should show an UpDownCounter object's value in a TextBox and have buttons labelled Next and Previous which, when pressed, cause the object's Next and Previous operations, respectively, to be executed.

4. Implement and test the BiCyler class. Your test program should show a BiCyler object's value in a TextBox and have buttons labelled Next and Previous which, when pressed, cause the object's Next and Previous operations, respectively, to be executed.

5. Implement and test the SwitchCounter class. Your test program should show a SwitchCounter object's value in a TextBox and have buttons labeled Next and Switch which, when pressed, cause the object's Next and Switch operations, respectively, to be executed.

6. Implement and test the BatchCounter class. Your test program should show a BatchCounter object's value in a TextBox and have a button labelled Next which, when pressed, causes the object's Next operation to be executed.

6.4 Replacing Inherited Methods

A derived class is capable of redefining, by overriding, an inherited method, replacing the inherited method with one that is specifically designed for the derived class. Because they are suited to its behavior, the derived class may want to inherit many of the base class's methods. What is considered in this section is how to selectively replace an inappropriate base class method with one appropriate to the derived class. The invocation of a method that has been replaced will result in the replacing method being invoked rather than the replaced method. The replacement is transparent to the code performing the invocation because the replacing method has the same signature (the same name and same arguments) as the method it replaces.

The substitution achieved by replacement is often referred to as the receiving object "doing the right thing." The receiving object is aware of its internal structure and, in response to an invocation, selects an appropriate method for execution. The invoker of the method is, and is best, unaware of how the receiving object determines which of its methods to execute. Of course, the receiving object is restricted to executing a method that matches the signature (name and ordered list of argument types) of the invocation.

An Example

The RestartCounter class is an example of a class in which method replacement is needed. A RestartCounter object is just like a Number object, except that the Reset method always sets the internal value back to an initial value that is given when the RestartCounter is constructed. The RestartCounter does not use the TextBox to obtain the value to which it is reset.

Fig. 6–6 is the inheritance diagram for the RestartCounter class. This diagram implies that a RestartCounter object has the following methods:

- ShowIn, Show, Value (from DisplayableNumber),
- Next (from Number), and
- Reset (from RestartCounter).

The Reset method defined in DisplayableNumber has been overridden by the Reset method defined in RestartCounter.

Notice the difference between overloading and overriding. Overloaded methods have the same name but different argument lists (signatures). Overridden methods have the same name and the same arguments (signatures). In the JumpCounter class the Next method is overloaded because the two methods JumpCounter::Next(int) and Number::Next() have different signatures. Thus, a JumpCounter object has both of the Next methods. However, a RestartCounter object has only one Reset method—the one defined in the RestartCounter class (RestartCounter::Reset()).

The definition of the RestartCounter class and its code is

```
class RestartCounter : public Number {
 private:
   int original;
 public:
        RestartCounter(int init=0);
  void Reset();                    // overrides inherited method
        ~RestartCounter(();
};

RestartCounter::RestartCounter(int init) : Number(init) {
        original = init; }
```

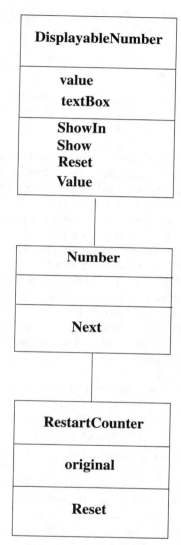

Figure 6–6 Inheritance Diagram for RestartCounter Class

```
void RestartCounter::Reset() { value = original; }

RestartCounter::~RestartCounter() {}
```

To emphasize again the role of inheritance, the following code illustrates that a RestartCounter object includes all of the (non-overridden) methods of its ancestors (Number and DisplayableNumber):

```
TextBox display(Location(100,100), Shape(50,50));
RestartCounter restart(7);
restart.Next();                 // from Number
restart.ShowIn(display);        // from DisplayableNumber
restart.Show();                 // from DisplayableNumber
restart.Reset();                // from RestartCounter (overrides
                                //    DisplayableNumber::Reset()
```

Method Lookup

When an invocation is received by an object with a layered structure (i.e., an object whose structure is defined through inheritance) a method lookup occurs to determine which method in the layered object to execute in response to the invocation. This method lookup is performed by the receiving object transparently to the invoker. The method lookup described below should be viewed only as a conceptual aid, for in C++ such a lookup does not actually take place at run-time. However, the method lookup described is conceptually correct and gives an intuitive way to understand the notion of overriding.

Method lookup is a bottom-up search; it always begins in the level corresponding to the most-derived class. For a JumpCounter object, the method lookup begins in the JumpCounter layer; for a Number object, the method lookup begins in the Number layer. If a method matching the invocation is found, it is selected for execution and the method lookup is complete. If a matching method is not found, the method lookup continues the search by moving to the layer immediately above the current layer.

The layered structure for a RestartCounter object illustrates overriding and method lookup. As shown in Fig. 6–7, a RestartCounter object has three layers: RestartCounter, Number, and DisplayableNumber. The figure shows the invocation of the methods Next(), Restart(), and Show().

The invocation of Reset is simple because a matching method is immediately discovered in the first layer (RestartCounter). Thus, the invocation of Reset() on a RestartCounter object is bound to RestartCounter::Reset. This illustrates the effect of overriding because the method lookup will always find the Reset in the RestartCounter layer as opposed to the Reset method in the DisplayableNumber level. The invocation of Next is bound to the method Number::Next because the method lookup:

- begins at the RestartCounter layer but did not find a matching method, and
- continues at the next higher layer (i.e., the Number layer), where the lookup finds the matching method Number::Next

Finally, the method lookup for the invocation Show() is:

- unsuccessful at the RestartCounter layer,
- unsuccessful at the Number layer, and
- successful at the DisplayableNumber layer.

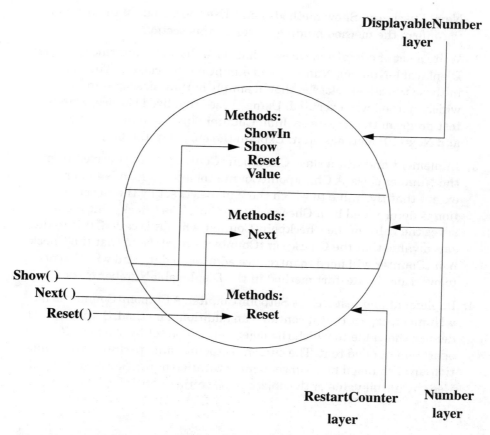

Figure 6–7 Method Lookup in a RestartCounter Object

Thus, the invocation of Show on a RestartCounter object is bound to DisplayableNumber::Show.

 Exercises

1. Write a set of trivialized classes that have the same interfaces as the DisplayableNumber, Number, and RestartCounter classes. The methods in these trivialized classes should simply output messages indicating which method was executed. Using these trivialized classes, write a test program that creates a RestartCounter object and invokes the

Next, Reset, and Show methods on it. Use the output of the program to confirm the method bindings given in this section.

2. Write a set of trivialized classes that have the same interfaces as the DisplayableNumber, Number, and JumpCounter classes. The methods in these trivialized classes should simply output messages indicating which method was executed. Using these trivialized classes, write a test program that creates a JumpCounter object and invokes the Next and Next(10) methods on it. Explain the output of the program.

3. Implement and test a class CheckpointCounter that is derived from the Number class. A CheckpointCounter object is like a Number, except that the value to which the Number is set by the Reset operation is determined by a Checkpoint method. The Checkpoint method saves the value of the CheckpointCounter when it is called. It is to this saved value that the CheckpointCounter is reset. Note that the CheckpointCounter will need to introduce additional data and will also need to override the Restart method in the DisplayableNumber class.

4. Implement and test a class SetpointCounter. A SetpointCounter is like a Number, expect that it contains an additional method, Setpoint, that defines the value to which the object should be set by the next Reset operation applied to it. The current setpoint value performs this function until changed by a subsequent invocation of the Setpoint method. Use the initial value of the object as its initial setpoint.

6.5 Extending Inherited Methods

Extending an inherited method is a variation of replacing a method. The distinguishing features of extending an inherited method is that the extending method in the derived class overrides the inherited method (i.e., the extending method has the same signature as the inherited method), and invokes the inherited method to perform part of its work.

Because the overriding method itself uses the method that it overrides, it appears to extend the inherited method by adding new actions to the method's execution.

An example of extending an inherited method occurs in the Cycler class. As the class was defined earlier, it inherits a Reset method from the DisplayableNumber class. However, this inherited method allows any number to be entered by the user—possibly one outside the range of the Cycler. If this occurred, the program could access this erroneous value, via the Value method. To prevent this problem from occurring, a safer (more restricted) Reset method is needed in the

Code Sample 6–7 *Extending an Inherited Method in the Cycler Class*

```
class Cycler : public DisplayableNumber
{
   private:
     int base;
   public:
     Cycler(int b, int init = 0);
     void Next();
     void Reset();      // overrides and extends the Reset
                        // method inherited from DisplayableNumber
   ~Cycler();
};


void Cycler::Reset()
{
                                   // no preprocessing
  DisplayableNumber::Reset();  // invoke overridden method
  value = value % base;        // postprocessing
}
```

Cycler class. To override and extend the inherited Reset method, the Cycler class would be redefined as shown in Code Sample 6–7.

In this method, the overridden base class method is itself invoked. To distinguish between the two Reset methods, the syntax "DisplayableNumber::Reset" is used in the Cycler's Reset method to indicate the Reset method in the base class (DisplayableNumber). Without this additional syntax to specify the base class name, it would be assumed that the Cycler's Reset method was making a recursive call on itself, when that is clearly not what is desired here.

Fig. 6–8, using the Cycler class as an example, depicts the sequence of events that occurs when an extended method is executed. In step 1, an invocation of the Reset method occurs. Because the derived class method overrides the inherited method, this invocation will result in the execution of the derived class method (Cycler::Reset). In step 2, the derived class method invokes the inherited method (DisplayableNumber::Reset). When the base class method returns, in step 3, it returns to the Cycler::Reset method. Finally, in step 4, the derived class method returns, completing the invocation. Because the control begins and ends in the derived class method, the derived class method can perform any necessary preprocessing actions before invoking the base class method (after step 1 and before step 2) and can perform any necessary postprocessing actions before returning (between steps 3 and 4).

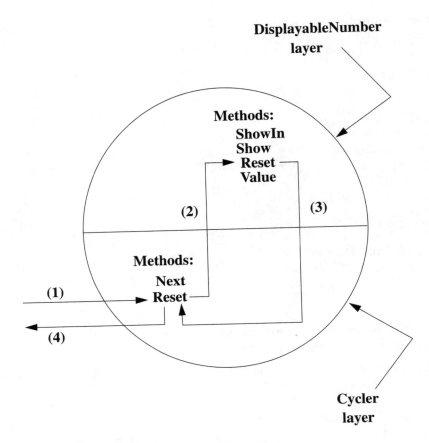

Figure 6–8 Extending an Inherited Method

 Exercises

1. Implement and test a class AutoCounter. An AutoCounter object is like a Number object except that the Next method in the AutoCounter object does both the incrementing of the value and the update of the TextBox display. Use the technique described in this section to override and extend the Number class's Next method in the AutoCounter class.

2. Reimplement and test the BatchCounter class. In this case, Batch-Counter inherits from the Number class. However, the BatchCounter class now overrides and extends the Number class's Next method.

3. Implement and test a MonotonicCounter class derived from the Number class. A MonotonicCounter is like a Number except that the value to which it reverts by a Reset operation can never be smaller than its value prior to the Reset operation. In other words, the value given by the user is ignored if it is less than the current value of the Monotonic-Counter.

4. Reimplement and test the BatchCounter class. In this case, the Batch-Counter class has, as a private data member, a Cycler object. The Cycler object is used to keep track of the number of Next operations that have been done in the current batch of Next operations.

6.6 Hiding Inherited Methods

The Problem

It is occasionally, though rarely, necessary to prevent a base class method from appearing in the public interface of a derived class. This must happen, however, if the inherited method is inappropriate to objects of the derived class and when the action taken by the inherited method is in conflict with the specialization introduced by the derived class. The two examples explored below illustrate this situation, and three ways of hiding inherited methods are discussed.

Hiding inherited methods is a controversial technique. Some argue that it is a violation of the "is-a" principle that underlies inheritance. The standard for judging the appropriateness of inheritance is whether the derived class "is a" kind of the base class. Strictly interpreted, a hidden method is an exception to the "is-a" rule: the derived class is a kind of the base class, but it cannot perform this action defined in the base class. This argument is clearly correct if the hiding is too extensive because, with sufficient hiding two very dissimilar abstractions can be related through inheritance. For example, if the class Dog defines the properties "bark," "fetch," and "eat food" then a class Cat can be derived from Dog by hiding "bark" and "fetch" and adding "purr" and "sleep." In this case, the inheritance does not reflect a meaningful relationship in the underlying abstractions. Others argue, however, that hiding is acceptable if used judiciously in limited circumstances. In their view, some specializations are, in fact, defined by a limitation on a more generalized notion. For example, a Window class would define many operations (show, hide, move, resize, change color, and iconify, among others) all of which save the resize operation are needed to define a Fixed-SizedWindow abstraction. In this case, hiding the single operation seems acceptable.

Code Sample 6–8 *Inheriting an Inappropriate Method*

```
class Rectangle
{ //...
  public:
    Rectangle(Shape shape);
    void SetLocation(Location loc);
    void SetShape(Shape shape);
    void Draw();
    void Clear();
    void Rotate();
};

class Square : public Rectangle
{
  // inherits SetShape method
};
```

The first example of inheriting an inappropriate method involves the Rectangle class shown in Code Sample 6–8. The Rectangle defines a number of methods that are useful in defining a Square class. However, if class Square is derived from the Rectangle class, it will inherit the SetShape method, which is not an appropriate method for the Square class because it would allow a Square object (by definition, with equal height and width) to be set to an arbitrary Shape. There is no guarantee that the argument passed to the SetShape method would object the restrictions of the derived Square class.

The second example of inheriting an inappropriate method is in the DisplayableNumber hierarchy. Suppose that a new ProgramControlledCounter class is to be developed whose objects behave just like objects of the Number class, except that the value of ProgramControlledCounter objects can only be changed by the program and not by the user. Because of the conceptual and implementation similarity between the ProgramControlledCounter class and the Number class, the ProgramControlledCounter class should be derived from the Number class. However, the Number class inherits from the DisplayableNumber base class a Reset method that allows the user to change the value of the Number object. To define a safe ProgramControlledCounter class it is necessary to remove the Reset method from its public interface. The relevant portions of the inheritance structure are given in Code Sample 6–9.

Solutions

There are three means of dealing with an inappropriate inherited method: the developer can define a harmless overriding method, use private/protected

Code Sample 6–9 *ProgramControlledCounter Class*

```
class DisplayableNumber
{
  public:
    void Reset(); // allow user to change value
};

class Number : public DisplayableNumber
{
  //...
};

class ProgramControlledCounter : public Number
{
  // inherits the Reset method
};
```

inheritance, or revise the class hierarchy. Each of these approaches has its own advantages and drawbacks that will be seen by applying them to the examples given above.

Solution One: Overriding the Method

A simple way to deal with an inappropriate method is to retain the method in the public interface but remove its unwanted effect by overriding it and replacing it with a derived class method that either does nothing or takes a benign action. The relevant parts of the code for the Square class using this approach is shown in Code Sample 6–10. This overriding SetShape method guarantees that if the SetShape method is applied to a Square object, the dimensions of the Square are unaffected. In effect, the invocation is silently ignored.

Alternatively, the SetShape method could be redefined in the Square class to take the dimensions of the Shape object passed as the argument for the new size of the Square. The code for this alternative is

```
void Square::SetShape(Shape shape)
{ Rectangle::SetShape(Shape(shape.Width(),shape.Width()));
}
```

where only the width of the Shape parameter is used.

The drawback of the do-nothing and benign overriding methods is that they potentially convey misleading information about the class to programmers using the class. It is not unreasonable that a programmer would expect a method to have some effect, especially when the method involved (like SetShape) is known to have effects on objects of all other classes. Another drawback of this approach

Code Sample 6–10   *Overriding the Inappropriate Method in the Square Class*

```
class Square : public Rectangle
{
  public:
    Square(int side);            //constructor sets the Shape
    void SetShape(Shape shape); //override inherited method
};

// in the implementation

Square::Square(int side) : Rectangle(Shape(side,side)) {}
void Square::SetShape(Shape shape) {} // do nothing
```

is finding a reasonable interpretation in the face of type casting. If an object of the Square class is type cast to a Rectangle, the SetShape method applied to the type cast object will be the Rectangle class SetShape method. Is this reasonable? From one point of view it is, because a type cast was performed to view the Square as a Rectangle and to treat it as such. From another point of view, though, it is unreasonable, because the object is actually a Square and its state should not be altered to a form that is not valid. This difficulty can be overcome by changing the base class to make the SetShape method virtual. However, this involves changing the base class and does not resolve the basic issue of the inappropriate method.

Solution Two: Protected/Private Inheritance

The second solution uses protected/private inheritance. Thus far, derived classes always used the keyword public in front of the base class name, as in

```
class Square : public Rectangle {...}
```

This use of the public keyword implies that all public methods in the base class become public methods in the derived class. Changing the public keyword to protected (private) means that the public methods of the base class become protected (private) methods in the derived class. By using protected or private inheritance, inappropriate base class methods can be excluded from the public interface of the derived class. The Square class is defined in Code Sample 6–11 using private inheritance.

An obvious disadvantage of using private/protected inheritance is that the base class methods that are appropriate for the derived class are also hidden along with the inappropriate methods. In the case of the Square class, this seems disproportionate because only one of the inherited methods is unwanted, while all of the others are useful methods in the public interface of the Square class.

Code Sample 6–11 *Using Private Inheritance in the Square Class*

```
class Square : private Rectangle
{
  // ...
};
```

Code Sample 6–12 *Selectively Revealing Hidden Inherited Methods*

```
class Rectangle
{ //...
  public:
    Rectangle(Shape shape);
    void SetLocation(Location loc);
    void SetShape(Shape shape);
    void Draw();
    void Clear();
    void Rotate();
};

class Square : private Rectangle
{
  public:
        Square(int side);
    void SetSide(int side);
        Rectangle::SetLocation;
        Rectangle::Draw;
        Rectangle::Clear;
        Rectangle::Rotate;
        ~Square();
};

// implementation file
Square::Square (int side) : Rectangle(Shape(side,side)) {}

void Square::SetSide(int side)
{ SetShape(Shape(side,side));
}

Square::~Square() {}  //no actions necessary
```

It is possible, however, to name those method hidden by private/protected inheritance that should be visible in the public interface of the derived class. The syntax required to reveal those methods hidden by private/protected inheritance is shown in Code Sample 6–12. In this code the Shape class inherits privately

Code Sample 6–13 *Altering the Inheritance Hierarchy*

```
class Quadrilateral
{ //...
  public:
    Quadrelateral(Shape shape);
    void SetLocation(Location loc);
    void SetShape(Shape shape);
    void Draw();
    void Clear();
    void Rotate();
};

class Rectangle : public Quadrilateral
{
  public:
    Rectangle(Shape shape);
    void SetShape(Shape shape);
    ~Rectangle();
};

class Square : public Quadrilateral
{
  public:
    Square(int side);
    void SetSide(int side);
    ~Square();
};
```

from the Rectangle class, thereby hiding all inherited methods. However, the public interface of the Square class declares the fully qualified names of those inherited methods that should be revealed in the public interface of the Square class. Notice that only the fully qualified name of the method is given; no return type or argument list is needed.

The Square class defines five public methods in addition to the constructor and destructor, only one if which, the SetSide method, is newly defined in the Square class. The other four public methods of the Square class are obtained by private inheritance and then explicitly named in the public interface of the Square class. These four methods are: SetLocation, Draw, Clear, and Rotate. Notice that the implementation of the Square class needs only to provide the code for the methods added in this class (the constructor, the destructor, and the SetSide method).

Solution Three: Revise the Inheritance Hierarchy

In some cases changes in the class hierarchy can eliminate cases where an inappropriate method is inherited. In both of the examples, Square and ProgramControlledCounter, the inappropriate method was one that allowed the object to be changed in a manner that conflicted with the meaning of the derived class. The nature of this change can be used to divide the class hierarchy into two parts—those classes for which the change is appropriate and those classes for which the change is not appropriate. To reflect this division it may be necessary to introduce a new base class that contains the methods needed by both of the sets of classes.

The problem with the Square and Rectangle classes can be resolved by factoring the common methods into a new base class, Quadrilateral, and establishing two derived classes, Rectangle and Square. Each of the derived classes introduces methods that allow their dimensions to be altered as appropriate for their class.

In this revised class hierarchy, no inappropriate methods are inherited. The Rectangle class inherits all of the methods of the Quadrilateral class and adds a method that allows both dimensions of a Rectangle object to be changed. Similarly, the Square class inherits all of the methods of the Quadrilateral class and adds a method that allows only a change in dimensions that will affect both dimensions simultaneously.

 Exercises

1. Define the outline of a revised class hierarchy that deals with the inappropriate method inherited by the ProgramControlledCounter class.

2. Show how private/protected inheritance could be used to resolve the problem of the inappropriate method inherited by the ProgramControlledCounter class.

3. Under what circumstances would you use private inheritance rather than protected inheritance? Why?

6.7 Type Casting

Concept

Type casting is the act of viewing an object of a derived class as an object of its base class. For example, a Number object may be viewed as an object of the class

Number or as an object of the class DisplayableNumber. Viewing an object of a derived class in this way is sensible because the derived class (e.g., Number) object has all of the properties (code and data) of the base class (e.g., Displayable-Number) object. Because any operation that can be applied to a base class object can also be applied to a derived class object, it is safe to use an object of the derived class where an object of the base class is expected.

Type casting is the foundation for a powerful form of polymorphism. In the sense that it is used here, polymorphism refers to the ability to manipulate in a uniform manner objects that are of different classes. A base class defines the uniform set of methods that can be applied to any objects of the base class and, more importantly, an objects of any of its derived classes. The term type casting describes this technique because the exact "type" (i.e., class) of an object is "cast" away in favor of a more generic type (the base class of the object).

Through polymorphism it is possible to create flexible and extensible software structures. A software structure that is defined only in terms of the properties of a base class can, without change, accommodate any object of a derived class by type casting the derived class object to its base class type. In this sense, the software structure is very flexible as it can be applied to a wide class of specific objects. The NumberPanel defined below exemplifies this kind of flexibility. The NumberPanel is a manager for objects that are derived from Displayable-Number; it treats the objects that it manages as DisplayableNumbers only, unaware of their exact derived class type. Thus, it is possible for a NumberPanel to manage any collection of Number, Cyclers, BiCyclers, etc. objects. The NumberPanel also illustrates why polymorphic structures are extensible: since they can be applied to any class derived from the base class, the derived class need not even be known at the time the polymorphic structure is designed and implemented. Thus, the NumberPanel can manage objects whose classes did not exist at the time the NumberPanel was built. Extensibility means that a software system can be extended by adding new derived classes whose objects can be manipulated by other, existing parts of the system.

Type casting does not change the object—it only changes what parts of the object are visible through that type case. For example, a single Number object might be viewed as shown in Figure 6–9. When viewed as a DisplayableNumber object, the single object reveals only the base class portion of its structure, but when viewed as a Number object, all of the object's structure is revealed.

Syntax

There are two different forms for expressing the type cast in C++ and each form has two variations depending on whether the type cast results in a reference to an object or a pointer to an object. The difference is only one of syntax; all of these forms and variations achieve the same overall effect. Which form to use depends on stylistic consideration. Which variation (whether to use an object or a

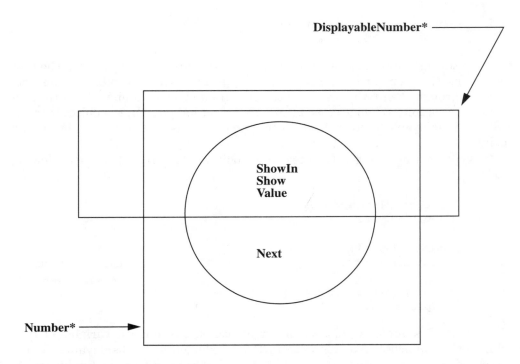

Figure 6–9 Type Casting

pointer to an object) is sometimes dictated by circumstances. The two different forms of type casting are

```
(BaseClassName) derivedClassObject
```

and

```
BaseClassName (derivedClassObject)
```

In the following example, only the first form will be used.

Type casting using a pointer to an object is illustrated in the following code:

```
TextBox display(Location(100,100), Shape(75, 50));
Number* Number = new Number(100);
DisplayableNumber* number;

Number->Next();

number = (DisplayableNumber*) Number;  // type cast
```

```
number->ShowIn(display);
number->Show();
```

In this example, a Number object is accessed through two pointers: the first is of type Number* and the second is of type DisplayableNumber*. When accessed through the first pointer, the object is treated as a Number object (having a Next operation). When accessed through the second pointer, the object is treated as a DisplayableNumber object. The type cast is used to initialize the second pointer.

Type casting using references to an object is illustrated in the following code:

```
TextBox display(Location(100,100), Shape(75, 50));
Number number(100);

number.Next();
DisplayableNumber& displayable = (DisplayableNumber&) Number;
                                              // type cast
displayable.ShowIn(display);
displayable.Show();
```

In this example, a Number object is accessed through a variable of type Number (Number) and a reference to DisplayableNumber (displayable). When accessed through the number variable, the object is treated as a Number object because that is the type of the variable. Thus, the Next() operation defined in the Number class can be applied to the object using the variable number. In other words, the variable number gives a Number class view of the object, a view that contains the Next method. When the same object is accessed via the variable displayable, it is treated as DisplayableNumber because that is the variable's type. Thus, the ShowIn and Show methods can be applied to the object identified by the variable displayable because these operations are defined in the Displayable-Number class. Also notice that since object and references are used, the dot operator(.) is used to apply a method.

Methods can only be invoked when they are in the view defined by the type (or class) of the variable used to access the object. Examples of errors are:

```
DisplayableNumber* numberPtr;
Number *count1 = new Number(100);
Number  count2(200);

numberPtr = (DisplayableNumber*)count1;
DisplayableNumber& numberRef = (DisplayableNumber)count2

numberPtr->Next();                         // error

numberRef.Next();                          // error
```

Code Sample 6–14   *Type Casting to Create a Polymorphic Structure*

```
class NumberPanel
{
   private:
      DisplayableNumber *number[3];         // for simplicity
      int last;
      Frame *frame;
   public:
         NumberPanel();
      void Add( DisplayableNumber* num );   // add num to panel
      void ShowIn( Frame& fr);
                           // frame in which to show all objects
      void Show();          // Show all objects in the panel
};
```

Both of these accesses are in error because each attempts to use an operation that is not defined for the DisplayableNumber portion of the object. The object certainly has a Next method, but the view that is taken of that object (as a DisplayableNumber) does not reveal that aspect of it.

An Example

In this example, type casting is used to create a polymorphic NumberPanel class. The NumberPanel manages a collection of three objects of the Displayable-Number class or any of its subclasses, while the NumberPanel class hides the existence of the TextBoxes used to display the objects and thus simplifies the management of several DisplayableNumber objects. Also, the NumberPanel defines a Show operation that will be applied to each of the objects it manages. The definition of the NumberPanel is shown in Code Sample 6–14. For simplicity, the NumberPanel can only manage up to three objects.

The NumberPanel interface defines a method to Add another Displayable-Number to the NumberPanel and to display its value in a given Frame when required by the Show method. The ShowIn method specifies the Frame where the NumberPanel is displayed. Notice that the DisplayableNumber added to a NumberPanel does not provide a TextBox in which its value is displayed—a Text-Box is automatically supplied by the NumberPanel. The code for the Number-Panel is shown in Code Sample 6–15.

The interesting aspect of the NumberPanel is that it is not restricted to a particular kind of DisplayableNumber. This means that it is not necessary to build several classes such as CounterPanel, CyclerPanel, or SwitchCounter-Panel. The NumberPanel works for any single subclass of DisplayableNumber, or for any combinations of subclasses: a NumberPanel may contain two Number

Code Sample 6–15 *Implementation of the NumberPanel Class*

```
NumberPanel::NumberPanel()
{  last = -1;
   frame = (Frame*)0;
}


void NumberPanel::Add( DisplayableNumber* num)
{   if ( last < 2 )
    {
      number[++last] = num;
      TextBox* tbox = new TextBox();
      num->ShowIn(*tbox);
      if (frame ) frame->Display(*tbox);
    }
}


void NumberPanel::ShowIn( Frame& fr)
{ frame = &fr;}

void NumberPanel::Show()
{   if (last > -1 )
      for(int i = 0; i <= last; i++)
         number[i]->Show();
}


NumberPanel::~NumberPanel() {}
```

objects and one Cycler object, or one Number object, one Cycler object and one SwitchCounter object, for example. The NumberPanel can provide this level of generality because it is built to depend only on the methods defined in the DisplayableNumber class.

The following code shows the NumberPanel's flexibility:

```
Frame       display(Location(100,100), Shape(200,200));
NumberPanel panel;
Number      number(100);
Cycler      octal(8);
JumpCounter length(0);

panel.ShowIn(display);

// add different kinds of counters to the panel

panel.Add((DisplayableNumber*)&number);
panel.Add((DisplayableNumber*)&cycler);
```

```
panel.Add((DisplayableNumber*)&octal);

// manipulate individual counter objects
number.Next();
octal.Next();
length.Next(50);

// display all of the new values

panel.Show();
```

In this code, the NumberPanel is managing three different kinds of DisplayableNumbers (a Number, a Cycler, and a JumpCounter). The type cast used in calling the NumberPanel::Add method, however, allows the NumberPanel object to treat them all as objects of their common base class (DisplayableNumber). This is possible because the NumberPanel uses only the methods defined in the base class.

Implicit and Explicit Type Casting

Type casting may be explicit or implicit. When explicit, the program contains code that directs the exact type casting that is done, as in

```
Number *number;
DisplayableNumber *displayable = (DisplayableNumber*)number;
```

This is explicit type casting because the program code clearly states the casting from a derived type to a base type. Implicit type casting occurs when objects of different types are assigned or copied without an explicit type cast. For example, the assignment

```
Number *number;
DisplayableNumber *displayable = counter;
```

is an implicit type cast.

Type casting commonly occurs in parameter passing. The formal parameter type is declared using the base type, while the type of the actual argument value is declared using a derived class. For example, the NumberPanel class has a method declared as

```
NumberPanel::Add(DisplayableNumber * dn);
```

This method might be called with either explicit or implicit type casting.

The NumberPanel::Add method is called with an explicit type cast in the following example:

```
NumberPanel panel;
Number *n = new Number(100);
panel.Add((DisplayableNumber*)n);
```

In this case, the formal parameter type is DisplayableNumber*, while the actual argument is of type Number*. On the call to the Add method, the actual argument is type cast to agree with the type of the formal parameter.

The following example uses an implicit type cast to invoke the Number-Panel::Add method:

```
NumberPanel panel;
Number *c = new Number(100);
panel.Add(c);
```

In this case, the Number* object is provided as an argument to a method defined to accept a DisplayableNumber* as its parameter. The example illustrates implicit type casting in that the program does not directly specify the type cast, but merely implies that one should be performed.

It is strongly recommended that implicit type casting be avoided so that the programmer's intent is clearly expressed in the code. The explicit type cast conveys visibly that the programmer was aware of the casting and deliberately chose to enact the cast. In the absence of an explicit type cast, other programmers (testers, maintainers, various members of the development team) cannot be certain about the programmer's intent. Is the absence of a type cast merely an oversight? or a mistake? Compilers will commonly issue warning messages when implicit type casts are performed.

Safety

The safety of implicit or explicit type casting is determined by whether the casting widens or narrows the type of the object. A type cast is said to widen the type of an object when a derived class object is type cast to a base class object. The term widen is used because the object type resulting from the cast applies to a wider collection of classes than the original type (class). For example, the type DisplayableNumber is a wider type than the type Number. A type cast is said to narrow the type of an object when a base class is type cast to a derived class object. Narrow reflects that the type cast describes the object to a more limited class of objects. For example, type casting a DisplayableNumber object to a Cycler object makes the type of the object more determined.

A type cast that widens the type of an object is always safe, but a type cast the narrows the type of an object is dangerous. Widening an object's type is always safe because the object, through inheritance, has all of the method of the wider type. For example, the type cast that widens a Number object to a DisplayableNumber type is safe because a Number object has all of the methods of the DisplayableNumber class. However, if a DisplayableNumber object is type cast to a class derived from DisplayableNumber, there can be no guarantee provided by the compiler that the operations on the resulting object are safe. Consider the following example:

```
DisplayableNumber *DNptr;
Number number = new Number(100);
Cycler *cycler;

DNptr = (DisplayableNumber*)number;      // safe; it widens
cycler = (Cycler*)DNptr;                 // error

cycler->Next();                          // who knows what this will do!
```

The first type cast is safe; it widens the type of the number object from a Number class object to a DisplyableNumber object. The second type cast is unsafe and, in this example, is erroneous, because the narrowing type cast from DisplayableNumber to Cycler, while legal to the compiler, results in the variable cycler pointing to a Number object and not a Cycler object. The danger of this type of type casting becomes clearer in the last line when the Next method is applied to the object. Because the compiler believes (through the type casting explicitly insisted upon by the programmer) that the object is a Cycler object, the Cycler::Next method will be applied to an object that is actually a Number object. In the code for the Cycler::Next method, a reference is made to the base value of the object. However, the object in this case is a Number object and does not possess a base value. Clearly this situation is incorrect but, unfortunately, results in no compile-time warnings or errors.

 ## Exercises

1. Implement and test a NumberPanel class as described in this section.

2. Implement and test a program that uses a NumberPanel to manage two Number objects and a Cycler object.

3. Implement and test a program that uses a NumberPanel to manage an UpDownCounter object, a BiCycler object, and a SwitchCounter object.

4. Implement and test a class BiDisplay that allows a single DisplayableNumber object to be displayed in two different Frames simultaneously. The BiDisplay's Show() method connects the DisplayableNumber to a TextBox in one Frame and then uses Show to display the value there. The BiDisplay then repeats these actions for a TextBox in the other Frame.

5. Implement and test a class Summation that displays in a TextBox the total of all of the values of the DisplayableNumber objects that have been Added to the Summation object. The class should be able to handle up to five DisplayableNumber objects.

6. Extend the NumberPanel class to include a Reset method that resets each of its constituent DisplayableNumbers objects.

7. Implement and test a class SplitDisplay that manages a single DisplayableNumber or one of its derived classes. The SplitDisplay creates two TextBoxes for the DisplayableNumber, both displayed in the same Frame. The Frame is passed as an argument of the SplitDisplay's ShowIn method. One of the two TextBoxes is always used to show the current value of the DisplayableNumber. The other TextBox is used only for the user to enter a new value during a Reset operation.

6.8 Interface Sharing

Interface sharing is the definition of methods in a base class that are guaranteed to be available in all derived classes, even if these methods are not implemented in the base class. Not requiring that the methods be implemented in the base class distinguishes interface sharing from type casting. Methods that are guaranteed to be present in all derived classes define a shared interface in the sense that all objects of derived classes can be manipulated through this common interface, even if the user of the object is not aware of the object's exact type. Methods defined in the base class, of course, are part of this shared interface. However, a guarantee can be given in a base class even when the method is implemented only in the derived classes. In this way, interface sharing is similar to type casting, but it is more powerful because it allows derived class methods to be used in addition to base class methods.

A revised version of the Clock class, the relevant code of which is in Code Sample 6–16, is an example of a class in which interface sharing is needed. From the point of view of a Clock object, the Number and Cycler classes must be treated as two distinct classes. Despite the code sharing in the Number and Cycler classes, their types are not similar enough for them to be treated interchangeably or uniformly by the Clock class, which implies that the Clock class must have distinct data members and overloaded methods to interact with both Number and Cycler objects.

Not only are the Number and Cycler classes distinct types, but all of the many subclasses of DisplayableNumber are distinct. To deal with all of these subclasses, the Clock class would need numerous pointer variables, numerous overloaded ConnectTo methods, and repeated code in the Notify method, as shown in Code Sample 6–17.

Code Sample 6–16 *Revised Clock Class*

```
class Clock {
 private:
    Number*   number;        // Connect(ed)To a Number
    Cycler*   cycler;        // Connect(ed)To a Cycler
    ...
 public:
    ...
    ConnectTo(Number& cnt);
    ConnectTo(Cycler& cnt);
    ...
};

void Clock::ConnectTo(Number& cnt) { number = &cnt;);
void Clock::ConnectTo(Cycler& cnt) { cycler = &cnt;);
void Clock::Notify() { if (number) number->Next(); else
                       if (cycler) cycler->Next();    }
```

When designing a real system, such a situation is not tolerable for three reasons. First of all, it leads to fragile software, because whenever a new subclass of DisplayableNumber is introduced, the Clock class must also be modified. Second, the code is large: the amount of code written and the amount of compiled object code grows as the number of subclasses increases. And third, the code is inefficient: the long if-then-else structure in the Notify method increases the execution time of the method as the number of subclasses increases.

For building more efficient and flexible systems, another technique must be used. The specific problem is that the Clock class uses a method (Next) defined in the various derived classes (Number, Cycler, etc.) but not defined in their base class (DisplayableNumber). As was seen with the NumberPanel, it is possible through type casting for the Clock class to use any of the methods defined in the base class even though the actual object is a Number or Cycler. Type casting will not suffice, however, when the method to be called is not in the class to which the actual object is cast. For example, type casting a Number object to a Displayable-Number yields an interface that does not include the Next method.

Virtual Methods

The shared interface is defined by declaring one or more methods to be "virtual" or "pure virtual." For a virtual method, the base class provides a default definition of the method. In some cases, the default definition may be a do-nothing or null method—one that takes no actions. A pure virtual method is one in which the base class does not provide a default method definition. In this case, the

Code Sample 6–17   *Repetitive Code in the Clock Class*

```
class Clock {
 private:
     Number*       number;        // Connect(ed)To a Counter
     Cycler*       cycler;        // Connect(ed)To a Cycler
     BiCycler*     biCycler;      // Connect(ed)To a BiCycler
     UpCounter*    upCounter;     // Connect(ed)To a UpCounter
     DownCounter*     downCounter;
                            // Connect(ed)To a DownCounter
     BatchCounter*    batchCounter;
                            // Connect(ed)To a BatchCounter
     JumpCounter*     jumpCounter;
                            // Connect(ed)To a JumpCounter
     SwitchCounter*  switchCounter;
                            // Connect(ed)To a SwitchCounter
     ...
 public:
     ...
     ConnectTo(Number&         cnt);
     ConnectTq(Cycler&         cnt);
     ConnectTo(BiCycler&       cnt);
     ConnectTo(UpCounter&      cnt);
     ConnectTo(DownCounter&    cnt);
     ConnectTo(BatchCounter&   cnt);
     ConnectTo(JumpCounter&    cnt);
     ConnectTo(SwitchCounter&  cnt);
     ...
};

void Clock::ConnectTo(Number&    cnt)  { counter  = &cnt;};
void Clock::ConnectTo(Cycler&    cnt)  { cycler   = &cnt;};
void Clock::ConnectTo(BiCycler& cnt)   { biCycler = &cnt;};
void Clock::ConnectTo(UpCounter& cnt)  { upCounter = &cnt;};

... // rest of ConnectTo methods for other subclasses

void Clock::Notify() { if (number)      number->Next();
                else
                    if (cycler)     cycler->Next();
                else
                    if (biCycler)  biCycler->Next();
                else
                    if (upCounter) upCounter->Next();
                ... // similar tests for other subclasses
                 }
```

Code Sample 6–18 *Declaring a Virtual Method*

```
class DisplayableNumber {
   private:
      ...
   public:
      ...
      virtual void Next();                    // virtual Next method
      ...
};

// in implementation file

void DisplayableNumber::Next() {}            // null default definition
```

responsibility for providing the required method implementation is passed to the derived class.

A virtual method in a base class allows an overriding derived class method to be called even if the caller is only aware of the base class type. In our example, the DisplayableNumber class would define a virtual Next method with an empty (null, do-nothing) implementation. Each derived class would then override the virtual method with the real method—the real method would provide the implementation that is appropriate for the derived class. A Clock object would then be able to call the Next method of a DisplayableNumber derived class object even if (and especially if) the exact type of the called object is unknown by the Clock object.

The DisplayableNumber class with a virtual Next method would be declared as shown in Code Sample 6–18. The Number class, and all other subclasses of DisplayableNumber, remain unchanged. Each of these subclasses contains an overriding Next method. Note that the virtual keyword only appears in the definition of the class (i.e., when the method is defined in the .h file) and not in the implementation (i.e., where the code for the method is given).

The Clock class can now be redeclared to take advantage of the shared interface. The important part of this redefinition is shown in Code Sample 6–19, where it should be noted that only a single base class pointer is needed, the argument passed to ConnectTo can be either a pointer or a reference to a DisplayableNumber object, and the Notify method invokes the Next method uniformly for all types of DisplayableNumber objects. This solves the three problems noted above, because as the number of subclasses of DisplayableNumber increases, the Clock

Code Sample 6–19 *Redefining the Clock Class*

```
class Clock
{
    private:
       DisplayableNumber *number;    // only know about base class

    public:

       void ConnectTo(DisplayableNumber* dn);
       void Connectto(DisplayableNumber& dn);
       void Notify();

};

// in implementation file

void Clock::ConnectTo (DisplayableNumber* dn) { number = dn; }
void Clock::ConnectTo (DisplayableNumber& dn) { number = &dn; }

void Clock::Notify()
{  number->Next();         // invokes derived class method
   number->Show();         // invokes  base class method
}
```

class remains unchanged; the repetitive source and object code is eliminated; and the execution time of the Notify method is constant.

The revised Clock and DisplayableNumber classes may be used as follows:

```
    Clock     oneMinute(60*1000),
              oneSecond(1000);
    Number    minutes(0);
    Cycler    seconds(60);

    oneMinute.ConnectTo( (DisplayableNumber&) minutes);
    oneSecond.ConnectTo( (DisplayableNumber&) seconds);

    oneMinute.Start();
    oneSecond.Start();
```

In this instance two different derived class objects are passed as arguments to the ConnectTo method. In one case, the object is a Number object, and in the other, the object is a Cycler object. However, because of the shared interface defined by the virtual Next method, the Clock class is able to handle uniformly all objects derived from the DisplayableNumber class. Alternatively, the same effect can be accomplished using pointers as the following code shows:

```
Clock    oneMinute60*1000),
           oneSecond(1000);
Number   *minutes  = new Number(0);
Cycler   *seconds  = new Cycler(60);

oneMinute.ConnectTo( (DisplayableNumber*) minutes);
oneSecond.ConnectTo( (DisplayableNumber*) seconds);

oneMinute.Start();
oneSecond.Start();
```

In this code the Number and Cycler objects are passed by pointer.

Pure Virtual Methods

In some cases, a default implementation cannot reasonably be given in a base class. It is, perhaps, questionable whether it is a good design decision to provide an empty Next method in the DisplayableNumber class, because providing a class with a Next method suggests that something will happen to advance the state of the object when the method is invoked. The fact that nothing happens may reasonably be viewed as counterintuitive or misleading. In other cases, it is clear that no reasonable default implementation can be given for a method. Consider, for example, the design of a base class that generalizes the concept of a geometric shape. While it is desirable to be able to require that each particular shape (Rectangle, Circle, etc.) be able to draw themselves via a Draw method or report their screen area by an Area method, there is clearly no default implementation of either of these methods that passes any reasonable standard.

A pure virtual method declares a method that must be implemented in a derived class because no implementation of the virtual method is given in the base class. A pure virtual method is used when the dynamic binding of a virtual method is desired, but no default implementation is given in the base class. A pure virtual method is a virtual method because the derived class method is used when the pure virtual method is invoked.

The syntax for declaring a pure virtual method is shown in the following redefinition of the DisplayableNumber class. To avoid confusion this new class is called an AbstractDisplayableNumber.

```
class AbstractDisplayableNumber {
...
public:
    virtual void Next() = 0;        // pure virtual method
...
};
```

The additional syntax "= 0" is used to denote a pure virtual method. The intuition behind this syntax is somewhat strained—it may simply have to be committed to memory.

A class containing one or more pure virtual methods is referred to as an abstract base class. The word abstract is used to suggest that the class can describe a wide range of possible objects, depending on how the pure virtual methods are implemented by the derived classes. In contrast, the term concrete class is sometimes used to refer to a class that does not have pure virtual methods or has given implementations for all such methods. This class is concrete because it denotes a fixed, specific type of object. It is not possible to create objects of abstract classes. For example, the following code would not be allowed:

```
AbstractDisplayableNumber adn(100);     // not allowed
```

This restriction enforces the guarantee that a pure virtual method will be implemented by a derived class. If a derived class does not implement all of the pure virtual methods that it inherits, then it is also considered an abstract class. Thus, objects with unimplemented pure virtual methods cannot be created. This restriction is reasonable because an abstract base class is incomplete, it does not provide the implementation of its pure virtual methods.

It is possible, and often done, to have *pointers* to abstract base classes. Such pointers are needed in order to be able to refer to a derived class object without knowing its exact type, as in the following code where a class is derived from AbstractDisplayableNumber:

```
class ConcreteCounter : public AbstractDisplayableNumber {
  ...
};
void ConcreteCounter::Next() { ...some implementation ... }
```

The next examples illustrate what can and cannot be done with abstract classes and pointers to abstract classes.

```
AbstractDisplayableNumber *adn; // ok - pointer to abstract class
ConcreteCounter          *cc;   // ok - pointer to concrete class

AbstractDisplayableNumber n(100);     // no - class is abstract
ConcreteCounter c(100);        // ok - instance of concrete class

cc = &c;                              // ok - types are the same
adn = &c;                             // ok
```

The last line of code above ("adn = &c;") is meaningful because it allows a concrete object (i.e., an object of a concrete class) to be manipulated only by knowing its abstract base class.

Manipulating an object of a concrete class through a pointer to its abstract base class is both useful and safe. It is useful because it allows very flexible systems to be invented; the system can manipulate a wide variety of concrete objects knowing only their general (abstract class) properties. It is also safe to manipulate objects in this way because the pure virtual methods are guaranteed to be implemented in the concrete object—that is what makes them concrete. For example, the usage

```
AbstractDisplayableNumber *adn;
ConcreteCounter c(100);

adn = &c;

adn->Next();
```

is always safe because the Next method is guaranteed to be implemented in whatever concrete object is pointed to by the pointer adn.

Polymorphism

The term polymorphism is used to describe how objects of different classes can be manipulated uniformly. Through polymorphic techniques it is possible to write code (such as the Clock class above) that manipulates many different forms (subclasses of DisplayableNumber) of objects in a uniform and consistent manner without regard for their individual differences. The flexibility and generality of polymorphic structures is one of the significant advantages of object-oriented programming. Learning how to recognize opportunities to exploit this possibility takes practice.

The strategy for developing a polymorphic structure begins with identifying the common methods across a group of similar but not identical types of objects. A class hierarchy is then defined in which the common methods are placed in a base class, while the remaining methods are organized into classes derived from this base class. The interface of the base class defines the shared interface through which an object of any of the particular subclasses may be manipulated. It is important to remember that while methods of the shared interface must be **declared** in the base class, they may be left abstract with the subclasses assuming the responsibility for providing the **definition** (code) for the abstract methods.

The general class structure for polymorphism is shown in Fig. 6–10. The base class contains one or more virtual functions (vm1, vm2, vm3) that represent the shared interface through which the objects of the derived classes may be manipulated. The virtual functions may be given default implementations in the base class, or they may be defined as pure virtual functions. These virtual functions are defined, or overridden if necessary in the derived classes. If the base class methods are pure virtual ones, then the methods must be defined in derived classes from which objects are to be instantiated. If the base class methods are virtual, but not pure virtual, then the methods may be overridden in the

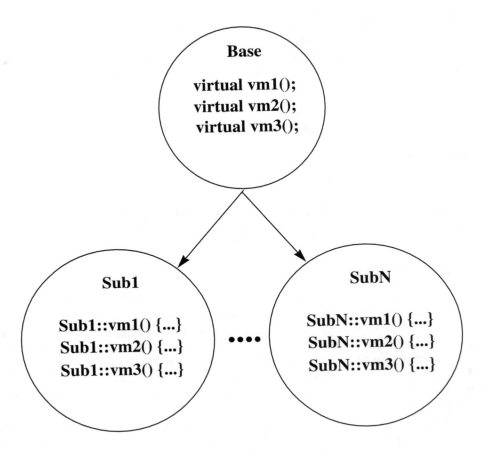

Figure 6–10   Class Structure for Polymorphism

derived classes. Objects can be instantiated from the derived class even if the virtual methods are not overridden.

Several examples of polymorphism will be given. To stress the importance and generality of this concept, the examples are taken from class hierarchies that are implemented in different object-oriented programming languages. Only the high-level structure of the classes is presented so that the important point is not obscured by the differences in syntax among the various languages.

One example of polymorphism can be found in the Abstract Windowing Toolkit (AWT) class hierarchy. This class hierarchy is part of the Java run-time environment and the classes are written in Java. A portion of the AWT class hierarchy is shown in Fig. 6–11. The *Component* class is the base class for numerous derived classes, only some of which are shown in Fig. 6–11. This base

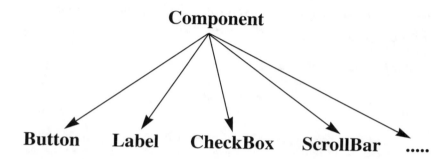

Figure 6–11 The Component Class Hierarchy

class represents the shared interface of a range of different entities that can appear in a user interface built with Java and the AWT.

The Component class includes a method *inside(int, int)* that determines if the point defined by the two integer input parameters lies inside the given component. This method is useful, for example, in determining if the user has just clicked on a button—it can check if the current coordinates of the mouse are inside a button when a click event occurs. Exactly how a component checks for inside will depend on its nature and geometry. Nonetheless, it is meaningful to inquire of any component whether the coordinates are inside of that component.

Using the polymorphism enabled by the Component class, the essential pieces of a simple ComponentManager are shown in Code Sample 6–20 (rendered in C++). The critical element of this ComponentManager is its ability to manipulate any of the subclasses of Component. When the *inside* method of the ComponentManager is invoked, it in turn queries the Component objects that it knows about in search of one that contains the coordinates (x,y). If such a Component is found, then a pointer to that Component is returned. Otherwise, a null value is returned indicating that the point does not lie inside of the Components managed by the ComponentManager.

Static and Dynamic Binding

The term dynamic binding describes the mechanics of virtual functions. "Binding" refers to the act of selecting which body of code will be executed in response to a function invocation. In languages like C, the binding is done completely at compile-time, even if overloaded methods are involved. Binding done at compile-time is also called "static binding," static in the sense that once set, it does not change. However, with virtual methods, the binding cannot be done completely at compile-time because the actual body of code to execute when a virtual function is called depends on the actual class of the object, something that is not

Code Sample 6–20   *Use of Polymorphism: Component Example*

```
class ComponentManager {
  private:
    Component *member[10];
    int          number;
    ...
  public:

    ComponentManager() : number(0) {}
    void Enroll(Component *cmp) { member[number++] = cmp; }
    Component* inside(int x, int y) {
          for(int next = 0;   next<number; next++)
            if (member[next]->inside(x,y) )
                return member[next];
          return NULL;
    }
    ...
};
```

known at compile-time. To see the need for binding at run-time, consider the Clock class defined above, a portion of this is repeated here:

```
class Clock {
private:
        DisplayableNumber *number;
                                // only know about base class
public:

        void Notify();
};

void Clock::Notify() {
        number->Next();        // invokes derived class method
        ...
}
```

The binding for the invocation of the Next method in the Notify method cannot be done at compile-time because the compiler does not know the actual class of the object being pointed to by the pointer variable number. In fact, there is no single binding that will suffice as different Clock objects may be bound to different subclasses of DisplayableNumber. What the compiler does instead is to build an efficient way of performing the binding at run-time.

Exercises

1. Define and implement a TextDisplay base class that captures the common properties of the TextBox and Message classes. The intent of this base class is to exploit polymorphism so that other classes can manipulate an object of type TextDisplay without being aware of, or dependent upon, knowledge of the exact class of the object.

2. Using the TextDisplay class, define and implement a class Flex-Counter by revising the Number class. A FlexCounter can be connected to either a TextBox or a Message object. Be sure to exploit the polymorphic properties of the TextDisplay class.

3. Using the TextDisplay class, define and implement a class Flex-DisplayableNumber by revising the DisplayableNumber class. A FlexDisplayableNumber is defined so that its method ShowIn can accept either a TextBox object or a Message object as a parameter.

4. Illustrate the flexibility properties gained through inheritance by finding the number of associations that can be built using the Clock class (as revised in this section), the TextDisplay, and the FlexDisplayable-Number.

5. Define and implement a revised Button class named VirtualButton to serve as a base class for wide range of specific types of buttons. Include in the VirtualButton class a virtual method "void OnPush()" which defines an action that the button object should perform when its corresponding button on the screen is pushed. The default behavior for this method is to do nothing. A do-nothing button would be used as follows:

```
VirtualButton vButton("Test", Location(20,20), Shape(60,20));
  Frame window("ButtonTest", Location(100,100), Shape(200,200));
   Panel panel(window, Location(20,20), Shape(100,50));
   //...

   void OnPush(char* buttonName)
   { if vButton.isEqual(buttonName) vButton.OnPush();
   }
```

6. Define and implement a revised Button class named AbstractButton that functions like a VirtualButton except that the OnPush method is declared to be a pure virtual method.

7. Define and implement a class StartButton that is derived from Virtu-alButton. A StartButton object can be connected to a Clock object in an association. The OnPush method of the StartButton should call the Clock::Start method.

8. Define and implement a class StopButton that is derived from Virtual-Button. A StopButton object can be connected to a Clock object in an association. The OnPush method of the StopButton should call the Clock::Stop method.

6.9 Refactoring of Base Classes

Developing a derived class may lead to a redesign or a refactoring of the base class which is done so that the derived class can be accommodated without sacrificing the integrity of the base class itself. In general, the interface between the base class and its derived classes is as important, and requires as much effort to develop and maintain, as the interface between an object and the object's clients. The example given in this section illustrates a situation in which base class redesign is needed to accommodate a new derived class.

Refactoring a base class is often required to preserve the base class's information-hiding properties of the base class. Information hiding is a software engineering principle stating that knowledge of design decisions (the information) should have the narrowest possible dissemination (the hiding). This principle helps to insure the independence of different parts of the system. Furthermore, information hiding promotes easier maintenance and adaptation of software, because a change in a design decision does not have a widespread impact if information about that design decision has been circumscribed. However, if many, or seemingly unrelated, parts of the system are conditioned on knowledge of that design decision, then a change in the design decision may render invalid these other parts of the system.

As an example, the DisplayableNumber class must be refactored to accommodate an OctalNumber class because the Show method is inappropriate for the new class. An OctalNumber object is just like a Number object, except that the OctalNumber object's value is displayed using octal-number notation and not as a decimal value. For example, an OctalNumber object with the decimal value 23 would be displayed in its octal representation as 27. While most of the methods in the Number and DisplayableNumber classes are exactly those needed to implement an OctalNumber, the Show method is inappropriate because it displays values in a decimal notation.

Simply overriding the Show method in the OctalNumber class leads to a loss of information hiding. A first approach to modifying the Show method is to provide an overriding Show method: the inherited Show method must be replaced (overridden) by a Show method that displays the value in octal notation. However, overriding the Show method leads to a dilemma regarding the sharing of data between the base and derived classes. The Show method uses the TextBox variable to display the DisplayableNumber's current value. To override the Show method in a derived class, the TextBox variable must be placed in the protected region of the base class. This change, while workable, significantly enlarges the scope (i.e., weakens the protection) of the TextBox variable, as the base class no longer completely encapsulates the existence of the TextBox variable. Therefore, both the base class and its derived classes are dependent on the following design decisions:

- The DisplayableNumber's value is displayed in a TextBox,
- The TextBox is accessed via a pointer,
- The name of the pointer is textBox, and
- The TextBox has a SetText method.

If any of these design decisions change, then both the base class and all of its derived subclasses are vulnerable to change. Notice how serious a problem this is: a derived class (OctalNumber) may need to be changed because of a change in a class (TextBox).

The cause of the problem is that the Show method performs two related, but separable, actions, which are formatting the character string to be displayed, and displaying the string in the TextBox. The design dilemma is easily resolved by recognizing that the OctalNumber class only needs to override the first action, and only the second action requires knowledge of the TextBox class and the TextBox variable. A new virtual method, char* Format(), is added to the base class to perform the first action. The revised Show() method will use the Format method.

Separating the two actions of the Show method leads to the revised definition and implementation of the DisplayableNumber class shown in Code Sample 6–21. Notice that the Format method is a virtual method, meaning that an overriding of this method by a derived class will be used in preference for the default (decimal formatting) given in the DisplayableNumber class.

Note, however, this refactoring of the base class is incomplete because the Reset method has not been accounted for. When Reset is called, it is expected to produce a new value for the DisplayableNumber by parsing the string obtained from the TextBox. However, this parsing is done assuming that the string represents a decimal value. Once again, this is inappropriate for the OctalNumber class because the string "77" parsed as a decimal value is clearly different from this same string parsed as an octal value.

In the Reset method there are found again two separable actions: obtaining from the user the string that represents the new value, and parsing this string to determine the new value. Following the principle of information hiding, the first

Code Sample 6–21   *Refactoring the DisplayableNumber Class*

```
class DisplayableNumber
{
    private:
      TextBox* textBox;

    protected:
      int value;
      virtual char* Format();              // produce string to display

    public:
      DisplayableNumber(int initValue = 0);
      void ShowIn(TextBox& p);
      void Show();
      void Reset();
      ~DisplayableNumber();

};

char* DisplayableNumber::Format()
{   char* asString = new char[10];
    ostrstream format(asString);
    format << value;                        // use decimal formatting
    return asString;
}

void DisplayableNumber::Show()
{
    if (textBox) textBox->SetText(Format());
}
```

of these actions will remain the private concern of the base class. The second action will be established as a virtual method in the protected section of the base class. The additional changes needed in the DisplayableNumber are shown in Code Sample 6–22.

Using this approach, implementing the OctalNumber class becomes straightforward, the code for which is shown in Code Sample 6–23. Since Octal-Number inherits from Number, the only method that the OctalNumber must implement is the Format method. The Format method is declared in the protected section of the OctalNumber class so that it does not become a part of the public interface of this class.

Code Sample 6–22 *Additional Refactoring of the Base Class*

```
class DisplayableNumber
{
    private:
      TextBox* textBox;

    protected:
      int value;
      virtual char* Format();        // produce string to display
      virtual int Parse(char* input);
                                     // convert user input to value

    public:
      // ... as before
};

int DisplayableNumber::Parse(char* input)
{  int decimalValue;
   istrstream format(input);
   format >> decimalValue;                  // use decimal formatting
   return decimalValue;
}

void DisplayableNumber::Reset()
{
   if (textBox) value = Parse(textBox->GetText());
}
```

Exercises

1. Implement and test the refactored DisplayableNumber and Octal-Number classes described in this section.

2. Implement and test a class HexNumber that is like a Number except that it displays itself in hexadecimal notation. Develop this class as a subclass of Number using the refactored DisplayableNumber class.

3. Implement and test a PageNumber class that is like a Number except that it displays itself with the string "Page" preceding the decimal value of the number. Develop this class as a subclass of Number using the refactored DisplayableNumber class.

4. Implement and test a DollarNumber class that is like a Number except that it displays itself with the character $ preceding the

Code Sample 6–23 *Defining the Octal Number Class*

```
class OctalNumber : public Number
{ protected:
     char* Format();
     int   Parse(char* input)

  public:
    OctalNumber(int init);
    ~OctalNumber();
};

// in the implementation file

OctalNumber::OctalNumber (int init) : Number(init)
{
}

char* OctalNumber::Format()
{ char* asString = new char[10];
  ostrstream format(asString);
  format << oct << value; // format value as octal
  return asString;
}

int OctalNumber::Parse(char* input)
{ int octalValue;
  istream is(input);
  is.flags(ios::oct);
  is >> octalValue;
  return octalValue;
}

OctalNumber::~OctalNumber() {}
```

decimal value of the counter. Develop this class as a subclass of Number using the refactored DisplayableNumber class.

6.10 Multiple Inheritance

Multiple inheritance occurs when a derived class inherits from more than one base class. Previous examples used only single inheritance, where each derived class inherited from exactly one base class. Multiple inheritance has an intuitive

Code Sample 6–24 *Creating a NamedNumber Using Multiple Inheritance*

```
class NamedNumber : public Number, public Named
{
  public:
    NamedNumber(int initialValue, char* name);
    ~NamedNumber();
};

// implementation

NamedNumber::NamedNumber(int intialValue, char* name)
  : Number(initialValue), Named(name) {}
```

appeal because it allows the behavior of several base classes to be combined in a direct and seemingly obvious way. However, multiple inheritance is not supported in all object-oriented languages. Java, for example, does not provide multiple inheritance. The controversy surrounding multiple inheritance stems from the subtle problems that can arise when it is used, such as the question of what the behavior of a derived class should be if it inherits identical methods (i.e., methods with the same signature) from more than one of its base classes that have different code?

In this section, two situations are described where multiple inheritance is useful and straightforward: combining orthogonal (independent) base classes, and combining an abstract interface with a concrete implementation. The former facilitates improved reuse by allowing combinations of existing base classes, while the latter creates additional flexibility and enhances polymorphism.

Combining Orthogonal Base Classes

If two base classes have no overlapping methods or data they are said to be independent of, or orthogonal to, each other. Orthogonal in this sense means that the two classes operate in different dimensions and do not interfere with each other in any way. Such classes may be inherited by the same derived class with no difficulty.

Classes can be found or deliberately constructed to represent properties that are, or are likely to be, orthogonal to other classes. Such classes can then be easily inherited together with other classes to combine their properties. The term "mixin classes" is sometimes used to describe these classes, because it is convenient to mix in their properties with other classes. An example of a mixin class is the Named class shown in Code Sample 6–25, which represents the property that an entity has a character string "name." A Named object must be

Code Sample 6–25   *A Simple Mixin Class*

```
class Named
{
  private:
    char* name;
  public:
         Named(char* originalName);
    int   IsNamed(char* possibleName);
    char* GetName();
    void  SetName(char* newName);
         ~Named();
};
```

constructed with a name, its name can be queried (GetName), changed (Set-Name), and tested against another name (IsNamed).

Objects that are required to have a name can acquire this property by inheriting from the Named class in addition to any other class from which it might inherit. For example, to create a NamedNumber—an entity that has all of the capability of a Number and, in addition, has a character string name, can be easily defined using multiple inheritance as shown in Code Sample 6–24.

Notice that the NamedNumber inherits publicly from both the Number class and the Named class. Also notice that the constructor of the NamedNumber must pass the appropriate constructor arguments to both of its base classes. Since the NamedNumber has no private data of its own, the body of its own constructor has no code.

The combined behavior of the NamedBehavior class can be seen in the following example code, which declares and operates on a NamedNumber.

```
NamedNumber time(0, "Elapsed Time");
...
time.Next();                    // method inherited from Number class
if (time.IsNamed("Elapsed Time") )...
                                // method inherited from Named class
...
cout << time.GetName() << " is " << time.Value() << endl;
```

In this code, the NamedNumber object responds to methods that it inherits from the Number base class (Next, Value) as well as methods that it inherits from the Named base class (IsNamed, GetName).

The Named class may be used in many contexts. Other entities possessing names are Frames, Canvases, and Buttons. Rather than including their name property independently in each of these classes, the developer can have each class use multiple inheritance to acquire it from the Named class. In addition to being a more efficient programming effort, because of reuse, the Named class

Code Sample 6–26   *The Clock Class Revisited*

```
class Clock
{
    private:
        DisplayableNumber *number; // only know about base class

    public:

        void ConnectTo(DisplayableNumber* dn);
        void Connectto(DisplayableNumber& dn);
        void Notify();
};


// in implementation file

void Clock::ConnectTo (DisplayableNumber* dn) { number = dn; }
void Clock::ConnectTo (DisplayableNumber& dn) { number = &dn; }

void Clock::Notify() { number->Next();
    // invokes derived class method
                        number->Show();
                            // invokes base class method }
```

provides a single, uniform set of methods. Thus, it is easier to remember that the name of an object can be accessed via a method GetName and not getName in the Frame class and NameIs in the Button class.

Combining Interfaces and Implementations

Multiple inheritance can be used to enhance separation. Separation is one of the most basic principles of good software engineering and object-oriented design, and may be observed in the structure of a class, where the interface of the class is separated from its implementation. It is also at work in polymorphism because the accessing class is separated from knowledge of the exact type of the object being manipulated; the separation in this case is achieved by the base class. While a base class used in a polymorphic way does provide a degree of separation, the accessing class is still restricted to using only classes derived from this specific base class.

The limits on separation achieved by a base class can be seen in the Clock class, the definition of which is reviewed in Code Sample 6–26. Objects of this class can form an association with any object derived from DisplayableNumber. Through polymorphism, the Clock object does not have to be aware of—is

Code Sample 6–27 *The Animation Class*

```
class Animation
{
  public:
    Animation(...);
    ...
    void Next();        // generate the next image in the
                        // animation sequence; make this the
                        // current image to be shown

    void Show();        // present the current image
    ...
};
```

separated from the knowledge of—the exact type of the object with which it forms the association.

While the Clock class is useful, its reuse potential is limited by its dependence on the DisplayableNumber base class, which prevents use of the Clock in associations with objects requiring the services of a Clock object but which themselves are not DisplayableNumbers. An example of such a class is an Animation class: an Animation object has a series of images that it will display, and to achieve the animations effect, the images must be displayed a given rate. Driving the animation via a Clock object is the obvious answer; at the end of each time interval the Clock requests that the animation show its next image. (The outline of the Animation class is shown in Code Sample 6–27.) However, the Clock object cannot form an association with an Animation object, only with DisplayableNumber objects. It is clearly inappropriate to derive Animation from DisplayableNumber. Another alternative is to form a new Clock class, AnimationClock, that inherits from Clock and can form an association with an Animation object. This approach, though, has the drawback that the AnimationClock inherits unwanted data and operations (i.e., those that refer to a DisplayableNumber).

The increased separation that can be achieved via multiple inheritance is made clear by a close examination of the Clock class. The Clock class depends on very little: it only uses a Next and a Show method. These two methods are defined in the subclasses of DisplayableNumber, but they are also methods present in the interface of the Animation class. What is needed is a technique for generalizing the common properties of the DisplayableNumber and the Animation class. Inheritance is a technique based on generalization, and since multiple base classes are involved, multiple inheritance is a possible solution to the problem.

The desired separation is achieved by combining, through multiple inheritance, a pure abstract base class with a class that provides the concrete implementation of the abstract methods. Recall that the term abstract class refers to a base class that has at least one pure virtual method. A pure abstract class is one

Code Sample 6–28 *Pure Abstract Base Class*

```
class Sequenced        // pure abstract class
{
  public:
    void Next() = 0;
                    // compute the next element in the sequence
    void Show() = 0;
                    // present the current element in the sequence
};
```

in which all of the methods in the class are pure virtual methods. The pure abstract base class needed in the Clock example is shown in Code Sample 6–28.

The Sequenced class captures the similarity between the DisplayableNumber classes and the Animation class. The pure virtual methods allow these similarities to be defined without requiring any implementation being defined in the Sequenced class itself. The responsibility to implement the pure virtual methods is assumed by the classes derived from the Sequenced class.

The Clock class can now be redefined as shown in Code Sample 6–29 to depend on the Sequenced class and not on the DisplayableNumber class. This change improves the reusability of the Clock class because it allows a Clock object to form an association with a wider group of objects, any object that inherits from Sequenced. This change also improves the clarity of the Clock class because it expresses more directly and simply the expectation that a Clock object has of the object with which it forms an association.

The Sequenced class may be combined with the DisplayableNumber hierarchy in one of three ways:

- DisplayableNumber could inherit from Sequenced using single inheritance, an approach that would make it possible to treat any subclass of DisplayableNumber as a Sequenced entity. This approach is simple and has the broadest impact on the DisplayableNumber hierarchy.

- Individual subclasses of DisplayableNumber could inherit from both DisplayableNumber and Sequenced using multiple inheritance. This approach allows selected members of the hierarchy to be treated as Sequenced entities, possibly expressing the intention that only certain DisplayableNumbers will be used in association with a Clock.

- New classes that inherit from both a subclass of DisplayableNumber and Sequenced using multiple inheritance could be defined, which allows the increased reuse and flexibility of the Sequenced class to be exploited without changing any of the existing code. This approach is necessary when the existing code is in a library and cannot be changed.

Code Sample 6–29 *Revised Clock Class*

```
class Clock
{
    private:
        Sequenced *sequence; // only know about base class

    public:

        void ConnectTo(Sequenced* dn);
        void Connectto(Sequenced& dn);
        void Notify();};

// in implementation file

void Clock::ConnectTo (Sequenced* sq) { sequence = sq; }
void Clock::ConnectTo (Sequenced& sq) { sequence = &sq; }

void Clock::Notify() { sequence->Next();
                       sequence->Show(); }
```

Code Sample 6–30 *Multiple Inheritance Using the Sequenced Class*

```
class TimedNumber : public Number, public Sequenced
{
    public:
        TimedNumber(int initialValue);
};

class TimedAnimation : public Animation, public Sequenced

{
    public:
        AnimationSequence(...);
};
```

Similarly, the Animation class can inherit directly from the Sequenced class using single inheritance, or a new class can be defined using multiple inheritance.

The approach of defining new classes using multiple inheritance is illustrated in Code Sample 6–30 defining the TimedNumber and the Timed-Animation classes. The TimedNumber class and the TimedAnimmation class are named to reflect the intention of using them in association with the revised Clock class.

A critical aspect of the definition of the TimedNumber and TimedAnimation classes is the way in which they satisfy the responsibility imposed by the Sequenced class. The pure virtual methods in the Sequenced class impose on their derived classes the responsibility to implement a Next and a Show method. The TimedNumber satisfies this responsibility by inheritance from the Number class. The same is true for the TimedAnimation class.

Associations of a Clock with a TimedNumber object and a TimedAnimation object may now be created. The associations are created by the following code:

```
Clock slowTimer("Slow", 1000);
Clock fastTimer("Fast", 50);
...
TimedNumber count(0);
TimedAnimation *movie = new TimedAnimation(...);
...
slowTimer.ConnectTo( (Sequenced&)count );
fastTimer.ConnectTo( (Sequenced*)movie );
```

The essential element in this code is the ability to type cast TimedNumber and TimedAnimation objects as objects of type Sequenced. This type cast is valid because TimedNumber and TimedAnimation inherit from the Sequenced class.

Finally, the introduction of the Sequenced class allows the Clock class to be used in association with other classes that might be defined in the future. For example, a Sampler class that periodically reports the status of some resource, like how much a file has been transferred over a network or how much of a document remains to be printed might be defined. Through multiple inheritance and the Sequenced class, no changes need to be made to the Clock class in order for a Sampler object to be driven by a Clock object.

 Exercises

1. Define and implement a Linked mixin class that defines the property of a singly linked list. Define and implement a simplified Number class for testing. Using multiple inheritance, define, implement, and test a LinkedNumber class that combines the abilities of your Number and Linked classes.

2. Examine the other methods in the DisplayableNumber class and determine which, if any, of them would also be reasonable methods in the Animation class. Revise the definition of the Sequenced class and the Animation class accordingly.

3. Both a mixin class, like Named, and a class like Sequenced use multiple inheritance. What is the essential difference between these two uses of multiple inheritance?

Templates

7.1 Introduction to Templates

A number of common programming situations require the same class structure to be applied to different data types. Examples of such situations are the following:

queue class

- a queue of characters entered by a user
- a queue of mouse events that have occurred and are waiting to be handled

list class

- a list of windows that currently appear on the screen
- a list of menu items in a menu

set class

- a set of one or more buttons
- a set of currently available pens or colors

In each case the same basic algorithms and supporting data structures are needed. What varies among uses of the class is the type of data being manipulated.

A good mechanism for dealing with these situations should avoid repetitive programming and preserve the type safety normally expected of a well-designed class. Avoiding repetitive code means that it should not be necessary to implement MouseEventQueue and CharacterQueue as distinct classes when the

Code Sample 7–1 *Queue Template Class*

```
template <class QueueItem> class Queue {

    private:

        QueueItem buffer[100];
        int head, tail, count;

    public:
                    Queue();
        void        Insert(QueueItem item);
        QueueItem   Remove();
                    ~Queue();

    };
```

only difference between them is the type of data contained in their queues. Preserving the type safety means that we do not want to avoid the repetitive code by writing an overly general (type-dumb) class. For example, it is possible to implement a single Queue class that manipulates "void*" types, but this design is overly general because it allows anything to be put into the queue (e.g., Mouse-Events in a CharacterQueue).

A template is a parameterized class whose parameter denotes the varying type of data. The syntax in C++ to introduce a template for the queue class is as follows:

```
template < class QueueItem > class Queue { ... }
```

Enclosed in the angle brackets after the keyword template is the template parameter. In this example the template parameter, QueueItem, is a class. For a Queue, QueueItem is intended to denote the type of the items that the Queue will hold. The template parameter may be used in the parameterized class (Queue) in one or more of the following ways: to define the argument type of a method in the parameterized class, to define the type returned by a method in the parameterized class, or to define the type of local data that is defined in the parameterized class. These uses of the template parameter are shown in the expansion of the Queue class shown in Code Sample 7–1.

In the code for the Queue template class shown in Code Sample 7–1, QueueItem is first used to define the type of the buffer array, which is used to hold the elements currently in the queue. The parameter of the Insert method is defined as a QueueItem, matching the declaration of the buffer array where the input value will be stored. Finally, the result returned by the Remove method is also of type QueueItem, since this is the type of data extracted from the buffer array.

A parameterized type (template) can be used to create a new class by instantiating the template with an appropriate parameter. The template may be

Code Sample 7–2 *Syntax for Implementing the Methods of a Template Class*

```
template<class QueueItem>
    Queue<QueueItem>::Queue()
                                        { ... }

template<class QueueItem> void
    void Queue<QueueItem>::Insert(QueueItem item)
                                        { ... }

template<class QueueItem> QueueItem
    Queue<QueueItem>::Remove()
                                        { ... }

template<class QueueItem> int
    int Queue<QueueItem>::Size()
                                        { ... }

template<class QueueItem>
    Queue<QueueItem>::~Queue()
                                        { ... }
```

used to create a new class in two ways. The first way directly creates an object as shown here:

```
    Queue<int> intQueue;              // a queue of integers object
```

In this case, the object intQueue is defined as an instance of the parameterized typed Queue where the parameter is taken as an int type. The second way uses the typedef to define a type (class) name:

```
    typedef Queue<int> IntegerQueue;
                                // a class for a queue of integers
    IntegerQueue intQueue;
```

In either case an object that acts like a queue of integers is created, and can be manipulated in the usual ways. For example, the queue of integers can be tested as follows:

```
        intQueue.Insert(100);          // add 100
        intQueue.Insert(200);          // add 200
        int x = intQueue.Remove();     // remove 100
        intQueue.Insert(300);          // queue now has (200,300)
        int x = intQueue.Size();       // size is 2
```

Notice that there is no difference in the way the intQueue object is accessed. An object created from an instantiated template is indistinguishable from an object created from a non-parameterized class.

To complete the implementation of a template class, each of its methods must be defined. The syntax for a template method must carry a preamble that associates it with the template and with the template's parameters. This leads to the (somewhat wordy) syntax shown in Code Sample 7–2.

Code Sample 7–3   *A Complete Template Class*

```
template <class QueueItem> class Queue {
  private:
      QueueItem buffer[100];
      int head, tail, count;
   public:
                  Queue();
      void        Insert(QueueItem item);
      QueueItem Remove();
      int         Size();
                  ~Queue();
  };

  template <class QueueItem>
     Queue<QueueItem>::Queue() : count(0), head(0), tail(0) {}

  template <class QueueItem>
     void Queue<QueueItem>::Insert(QueueItem item) {
            assert(count <100);
            buffer[tail] = item;
            tail = (tail + 1)% 100;
            count++;
     }

  template <class QueueItem>
     QueueItem Queue<QueueItem>::Remove() {
            assert(count > 0);
            int val = head;
            head = (head + 1)%100;
            count--;
            return buffer[val];
     }

  template <class QueueItem>
     int Queue<QueueItem>::Size() { return count; }

  template <class QueueItem>
     Queue<QueueItem>::~Queue() {}
```

Each method definition is preceded by a template specification (template<
class QueueItem>). In addition, the class name contains the template syntax
(Queue<QueueItem>::). Note that in the case of the Remove method, the return
type comes after the initial template specification and before the class name.

The complete code for the parameterized Queue class is shown in Code
Sample 7–3.

Templates also differ from non-parameterized classes in where the method definitions are placed. In non-parameterized classes, the method definitions are put in a code (.cc or .C of .cpp) file. However, for a parameterized class the method definitions are placed in the header (.h) file itself. This is necessary so that when the compiler is asked to elaborate a template (e.g, by seeing a declaration of the form Queue<int>), it need only examine the header file (that has been referenced in a #include statement) to find all of the information that it needs to fully understand how to elaborate the template and generate the code for the required class.

 Exercises

1. Write a program that creates and manipulates two queues of type Queue<int>. Declare one of the queues directly as a Queue<int> and declare the other queue using a typedef.

2. Use the code developed in exercise one to determine if you can assign a queue to a queue. Does this do what you expect? Explain.

3. Write a program that creates and manipulates two queues of type Queue<Location>. Declare one of the queues directly as a Queue<Location> and declare the other queue using a typedef.

4. Compile the following two declarations. Which one has a syntax error?

   ```
   Queue<Queue<int>>
   Queue <Queue <int> >
   ```

5. Draw a picture showing what structure is defined by the declaration in exercise four.

6. Write a test program that declares and manipulates the queue structure defined in exercise four.

7. Named Collection: Implement and write a program to test a template class that maintains a collection of up to 100 elements, each of which has an associated name. The type of the elements is defined by the template parameter while the name is always a string (a char*). The following example illustrates how the template could be used:

   ```
   NamedCollection<int> collection;
   ...
   collection.Add("first", 10);
                       // associate 10 with the name "first"
   collection.Add("next", 20);
                       // associate 20 with the name "next"
   ...
   ```

```
if (collection.Contains("next"))
  { int val = collection.ValueOf("next");
     ...
  }
```

You may assume that duplicate names do not occur.

8. Shown below is the code for an IntArray class. Create a template version of this class and write a program to test your template.

```
class IntArray {
private:
   int array[100];
public:
        Array();
   int& At(int i);
        ~Array();
};

IntArray::IntArray() {};
int& IntArray::At(int i)
        {assert(0<i && i < 100);
         return array[i];
        }  IntArray::~IntArray() {}
```

9. Using your Array template, write a test program to create and manipulate a two dimensional integer array as follows: typedef Array< Array<int> > Matrix. How do you access elements in this two dimensional array?

10. Write a test program that declares and manipulates an array of queues.

11. Write a test program that declares and manipulates a queue of arrays.

7.2 Template Parameters

A template class makes assumptions about the operations that the template itself may safely apply to objects of the class defined by the template parameter. Because C++ does not provide a means to explicitly state these assumptions, the assumptions are implicit and must be conveyed by the documentation of the template class or inferred by examining the code of the template class. As the assumptions may be subtly imposed, a good template designer will ensure that the documentation for a template explicitly lists all of the requirements that must be met by the template parameter.

The Queue template class makes three assumptions about the QueueItem template parameter.

The first assumption made by the Queue template is in the declaration of the array of QueueItems:

```
template <class QueueItem> class Queue {
private:
    QueueItem buffer[100];
...
};
```

This declaration assumes that QueueItem has a default constructor (i.e., a constructor that takes no arguments). A default constructor is needed in order to declare an array of a given type. Classes like Location, Shape, and Frame that have default constructors can be used to elaborate the Queue template. However, an error message will result from:

```
Queue<Message>   QueueOfMessages;
Queue<Clock>     QueueOfClocks;
```

because these classes do not have default constructors.

The second assumption made by the Queue template is the assignment of QueueItems:

```
template <class QueueItem>
    void Queue<QueueItem>::Insert(QueueItem item) {
        ...
        buffer[tail] = item;
        ...
    }
```

This assignment statement assumes that the QueueItem class has an appropriately defined assignment operator. All classes have a default assignment operator—a bit-wise copy. In simple classes, this is an appropriate assignment operator. For example, in the case of Queue<int> and Queue<Location>, the default assignment operator is appropriate. However, the default assignment operator may not be appropriate for a class that contains pointers as private data. For example, the Message class and the Clock class each contain pointers as private data.

The third assumption the Queue template makes is in the way QueueItems are returned by the Remove method:

```
template <class QueueItem>
    QueueItem Queue<QueueItem>::Remove() {
        ...
        return buffer[val];
    }
```

Code Sample 7–4 *The Displayable Template*

```
template <class T> class Displayable {
    private:
      T*          displayed;
      TextBox* textBox;
    public:
      Displayable(TextBox* tbox);
                                    // textbox to show in
      void ShowThis(T* d);          // what to show
      void Show();                  // show current value
      void Reset();                 // reset displayed from textBox
      ~Displayable();
};
```

This code returns a copy of the object in the internal buffer. This code assumes that an appropriate copy constructor is defined for the class being substituted for QueueItem.

Other templates make more demanding assumptions about the class or type used to elaborate the template. Consider this template declaration for a Displayable template as shown in Code Sample 7–4.

This template is designed to point to a TextBox in which a current value will be displayed and from which a new value can be read. The template also contains a pointer ("displayed") to an object of the template's parameter type. To achieve its intent, the template must make assumptions about how the value can be obtained from the displayed object and how a new value can be given to the displayed object. Since the type of the displayed object is now known (its type is the template's parameter), the template code must make assumptions about (impose constraints on) the type that is used to elaborate the template. The code for the Displayable template is shown in Code Sample 7–5.

The implementation of the Displayable template assumes that the instantiating type has two methods:

- char *ToString() : returns a character string representation of the value of the object, and

- void FromString(char*) : derives a new value for the object from a character string representation.

Any type satisfying these two assumptions may be used to elaborate the Displayable template. No type or class lacking either of these methods can be used to elaborate the template; for example, it is not possible to have Displayable<int>, Displayable<char*>, or Displayable<Counter> for all of these lack the required methods ToString and FromString.

Code Sample 7–5 *Implementation of the Displayable Template*

```
template <class T>
    Displayable<T>::Displayable(TextBox *tbox)
        {textBox = tbox;   displayed = (T*)0;}

  template <class T>
    Displayable<T>::ShowThis(T* d) { displayed = d; }

  template <class T>
    Displayable<T>::Show() { textBox->SetText
    (displayed->ToString()); }

  template <class T>
    Displayable<T>::Reset() { displayed->FromString
    (textBox->GetText()); }

  template <class T>
    Displayable<T>::~Displayable(){}
```

Exercises

1. Write a class named Integer that holds a value of type int. This class should have the ToString and FromString methods defined for it. Write a test program that uses this class to elaborate the Displayable template and display an integer in the TextBox.

2. Write a class named Real that holds a value of type float. This class should have the ToString and FromString methods defined for it. Write a test program that uses this class to elaborate the Displayable template and display a float value in the TextBox.

7.3 Variable and Constant Template Parameters

Template parameters may be variables or constant values, including a constant class name. When a variable is used as a template parameter, a value for the variable must be supplied when the template is elaborated. A template may also have both a class parameter and a variable parameter. A constant template parameter is used to define special-case templates, which are often used in conjunction with a general template to define a special variant of the general

Code Sample 7–6 · *Queue Template Class with a Variable Parameter*

```
template <class QueueItem, int size> class Queue {
   private:
      QueueItem buffer[size];
      int head, tail, count;
   public:
                    Queue();
      void          Insert(QueueItem item);
      QueueItem Remove();
      int           Size();
                    ~Queue();
};
```

template. A special variant is often needed because there are a few cases in which the assumptions made by the general template are not appropriate and an alternative template is needed. Both of these kinds of template parameters are described in this section.

Variables as Template Parameters

A variable as a template parameter is shown in the redefinition of the Queue template shown in Code Sample 7–6. Notice that the template has two parameters: QueueItem defines the type of the elements maintained by the queue, and size defines the maximum number of elements that can be in the queue at any one time.

Both template parameters are used in the declaration of the buffer array

```
QueueItem buffer[size];
```

where QueueItem defines the base type of the array and size defines the length of the array. The size template parameter is used in the code for the template, as shown in Code Sample 7–7. Notice that the full list of template arguments must be given at numerous places in the definition.

Notice that the size parameter is used whenever the array length is needed. Thus, instead of head=(head+1)%100; being used to adjust the index of the head of the queue, the code uses the template variable size to refer to the length of the buffer, as in head = (head + 1) % size;.

Queues of various types and size may be declared and used as follows:

```
Queue<int,100>         smallIntegerQueue;
Queue<int, 1000>       largeIntegerQueue;
Queue<float, 100>      smallRealQueue;
Queue<float, 1000>     largeRealQueue;
```

Code Sample 7–7 *Implementation of the Revised Template Class*

```
template <class QueueItem, int size>
   Queue<QueueItem,size>::Queue() : count(0), head(0), tail(0) {}

   template <class QueueItem, int size>
      void Queue<QueueItem, size>::Insert(QueueItem item) {
            assert(count <size);
            buffer[tail] = item;
            tail = (tail + 1)% size;
            count++;
   }

   template <class QueueItem, size>
      QueueItem Queue<QueueItem, size>::Remove() {
            assert(count > 0);
            int val = head;
            head = (head + 1)%size;
            count--;
            return buffer[val];
   }

template <class QueueItem, int size>
   int Queue<QueueItem, size>::Size() { return count; }

template <class QueueItem, int size>
   Queue<QueueItem, size>::~Queue() {}
```

```
smallIntegerQueue.Add(10);
largeIntegerQueue.Add(20);
smallRealQueue.Add(1.4159);
largeRealQueue.Add(0.123);
```

The type of an object created via a template depends on all of the template's parameters. It was previously seen that instantiating the template different types created objects of different types. Thus, using the previous declaration of the queue template:

```
Queue<int>   intQueue1;
Queue<int>   intQueue2;
Queue<float> realQueue;
```

created objects of two different types. As usual, objects of the same type can be assigned to each other while objects of different types cannot. This is illustrated by the following code:

```
        intQueue1 = intQueue2;         // OK, queues of the same type
        intQueue1 = realQueue;
                                // ERROR - queues of incompatible type
        realQueue = intQueue2;
                                // ERROR - queues of incompatible type
```

The type compatibility of objects created by templates with multiple parameters is similar: two template elaborations are the same if and only if they are elaborated with the same parameters. This means that any class parameters must be the same and any variable parameters must have the same value. Here, these rules are illustrated using the modified (two parameter) Queue template:

```
        Queue<int,    100>   largeIntegerQueue1;
        Queue<int,    100>   largeIntegerQueue2;
        Queue<int,     10>   smallIntegerQueue;
        Queue<float, 100>    largeRealQueue;

        largeIntegerQueue1 = largeIntegerQueue2;
                        // OK, queues of the same type

        largeIntegerQueue1 = largeRealQueue;
                        // ERROR - queues of incompatible type

        largeIntegerQueue1 = smallIntegerQueue;
                        // ERROR - queues of incompatible type
```

The first assignment is between compatible types—both the QueueItem type (int) and the size value (100) are the same. However, the second two assignments are in error. The first error occurs because the QueueItem parameters do not agree (int vs. float) although the size parameter is the same (100). The second error occurs because the size parameter is different (100 vs. 10), although the QueueItem parameter is the same.

Special-Case Templates

There may be certain classes that cannot be used to elaborate a general template because the class does not satisfy the assumptions made by the template about the class given as its parameter. It was seen earlier that the Displayable template made assumptions about its parameterizing class. A portion of the definition of the Displayable template is repeated in Code Sample 7–8 for reference.

The important thing is that the Displayable template assumes that the instantiating class has methods ToString and FromString that convert between

Code Sample 7–8 *Displayable Template Repeated*

```
template <class T> class Displayable {
    private:
       T*        displayed;
       TextBox* textBox;
    public:
       Displayable(TextBox* tbox);// testbox to show in
       void ShowThis(T* d);        // what to show
       void Show();                // show current value
       void Reset();               // reset displayed from textBox
       ~Displayable();
    };


...

template <class T>
   Displayable<T>::Show() { textBox->SetText
   (displayed->ToString()); }

template <class T>
   Displayable<T>::Reset() { displayed->FromString
   (textBox->GetText()); }
```

the class's internal representation of its value and an external string representation.

Certain obvious uses of the Displayable template will not work because the instantiating class (or type) does not have the methods required by the template. For example:

```
Displayable<int>      intDisplay;
Displayable<float>    realDisplay;
Displayable<Location> locationDisplay;
```

will not work because none of these built-in types has the methods required by the Displayable template. While it might be possible to add the required methods to the Location class, it is not possible to do this for the built-in types int and float.

A "special case" version of the Displayable template can be defined for ints as shown in Code Sample 7–9. Notice that the template parameter is a fixed (or constant) type: namely the built-in type int. This template provides the special-case definitions of the ToString and FromString methods that are needed by the template but which are lacking in the int type.

Code Sample 7–9 *Special-Case Displayable Template*

```
class Displayable<int> {
    private:
      int*       displayed;
      TextBox* textBox;
      char* ToString(int v);
      int   FromString(char* text);
    public:
      Displayable(TextBox* tbox);
                                  // textbox to show in
      void ShowThis(int* d);      // what to show
      void Show();                // show current value
      void Reset();               // reset displayed from textBox
      ~Displayable();
};


char* Displayable<int>::ToString(int v) {
    char* buf = new char[10];
    ostrstream format(buf);
    format << v;
    return buf;
}

int Displayable<int>::FromString(char* text) {
    istrstream(text) format;
    int value;
    format >> value;
    return value; }

Displayable<int>::Displayable(TextBox *tbox)
    {textBox = tbox;   displayed = (int*)0;}

void Displayable<int>::ShowThis(int* d) { displayed = d; }

void Displayable<int>::Show()
    { textBox->SetText(ToString(*displayed)); }

void Displayable<int>::Reset()
    { *displayed = FromString(textBox->GetText()); }

Displayable<int>::~Displayable(){}
```

Code Sample 7–10 *Partial Definition of the List Template*

```
template <class BaseType> class List {
   private:
      ...
   public:

             List();
   void      First();    // set current element to first element
   void      Next();     // advance to next list element
   int       Done();     // is there a "current" element?
   BaseType& Current();  // reply current value
   void      Insert(BaseType val);
                         // insert after current element
   void      Delete();   // delete current element
   ~List();
};
```

Exercises

1. Extend the IntArray template developed in Exercise 8 in Section 7.1 to include a template argument defining the length of the array.

2. Define and implement a special-case template for Displayable<float>.

3. Write a program that instantiates three IntArray objects, two of the same size and one of a different size. Show that you can assign and retrieve values at different array positions in each object.

4. Using the three objects created above, try assigning each one to the other two. Which assignments are valid (will compile) and which produce error messages?

7.4 Templates with Related Parameters

Two or more templates may be designed to be used together. It is frequently the case for such templates that they share a common parameter. That is, in order for the templates to cooperate as intended, it is necessary that they manipulate a common type that is defined by one of their template parameters.

A singly linked list will be used to illustrate two related templates. One of the template classes in the example is the template for the list itself, whose partial definition is given in Code Sample 7–10. In this definition, the type of the data maintained in the list is given by the template parameter BaseType.

The list is intended to be used as follows:

```
List<int> list;            // create a list of integers

list.Insert(100);          // add six elements to the list
list.Insert(200);
list.Insert(300);
list.Insert(400);
list.Insert(500);
list.Insert(600);

list.First();                        // start at first element
while(!list.Done()) {                // iterate through the list
    cout << list.Current() << endl;
                                     // print current element
    list.Next();                     // move to next element
}

list.First();              //
list.Next();               //   move to third element...
list.Next();               //
list.Delete();             //   ...and delete it

list.First();
list.Next();               // for second element...
list.Current() = 999;      // ...change its value
```

The List template provides for a list of arbitrary length. The methods of the List template allow elements to be inserted and deleted from the list. Iteration through the list is provided by the method First, Next, Current, and Done. Since the Current method returns a reference, it is possible to assign a new value directly to an element in the list without having to delete the existing element and insert a newly created element.

A design issue for this template class is how to maintain the structure of the list. A general list implementation usually uses a linked-list technique, where each element in the list maintains a pointer to the next element in the list. However, the int type does not come equipped with a pointer that can be used for this purpose.

To maintain the structure of the list, another template related to the List template is defined. This second template will provide the needed pointer and will also be placed where the value of the list element is stored. In essence, this second template is creating the abstraction of an entity in a linked list that maintains a value of the same type as that defined for the list itself. Since an element in a linked list structure is sometimes referred to as a "node" in the list, the template class is defined as shown in Code Sample 7–11.

The fact that the Node template and the List template use the same name (BaseType) to refer to their template argument does not guarantee that the same type will be used to elaborate both templates. Only the pattern of usage will

Code Sample 7–11 *The Node Template*

```
template <class BaseType> class Node {
      private:
         BaseType            value;
                   // value contained in this node in the list
         Node<BaseType> *next;
                   // next element in the list
      public:


                             Node(BaseType base);
         BaseType&           Value();
         void                ConnectTo(Node<BaseType>* nxt);
         Node<BaseType>* Next();
                             ~Node();
      };
```

guarantee this effect. The code for the List template shown in Code Sample 7–12 illustrates how the two templates are related.

Notice that the Node template maintains a private data member of Base-Type; this is the value that will be held by the Node when it is in the linked list. The next pointer is the link to the next element in the linked list. The type of the next pointer, Node<BaseType>, correctly indicates that a Node of a given Base-Type points to another Node of that same BaseType.

Two of the methods of the Node template provide ways to manipulate the value portion of the Node and two others provide ways to deal with the linked-list portion of the Node. The constructor and Value methods allow the Node's value to be initialized, read and updated. The ConnectTo and Next methods allow a Node to be linked to another Node and for this link to be followed.

The code for the Node template is straightforward, as shown in Code Sample 7–12.

The relatedness of the List and Node templates is achieved in the data and code of the List class. The private data of the List class is shown in Code Sample 7–13.

The List class maintains three pointers, each of type Node<BaseType>* where BaseType is the parameter of the List class itself. Thus, the type used to elaborate the List template is also used to elaborate the Node template. The relatedness comes because of the relationship between the two templates defined in the List template. The three pointers indicate the first element in the list (head), the current element in a traversal of the list (current), and the element immediately preceding the current element (previous).

The most interesting methods of the List template are those for inserting and deleting an element. The Insert method is given a value of the BaseType

Code Sample 7-12 *Implementation of the Node Template*

```
template <class BaseType>
Node<BaseType>::Node(BaseType base) :value(base), next(0) {}

template <class BaseType>
BaseType& Node<BaseType>::Value(){return value;}

template <class BaseType>
void Node<BaseType>::ConnectTo(Node<BaseType>* nxt)
     {next = nxt; }

template <class BaseType>
Node<BaseType>* Node<BaseType>::Next() {return next; }

template <class BaseType>
Node<BaseType>::~Node(){}
```

Code Sample 7-13 *Relationship Between the List and Node Templates*

```
template <class BaseType> class List {

   private:
      Node<BaseType> *head;
                      // beginning of list

      Node<BaseType> *current;
                      // current element in traversal

      Node<BaseType> *previous;
                      // previous element; needed for deletion

   public:

   ... // shown above

};
```

that is to be added into the list. The method first creates a new Node<BaseType> object to hold the value (and supply the pointer needed to build the linked list), and this new object (newNode) is then added as the first element of the list, if the list is empty, or added immediately after the current element. An assert is used to insure that the program will abort if there is no "current" element. The implementation of the Insert and Delete methods is given in Code Sample 7–14.

Code Sample 7-14 *Implementation of the Insert and Delete Methods*

```
template <class BaseType>
   void List<BaseType>::Insert(BaseType val) {
      Node<BaseType> *newNode = new Node<BaseType>(val);
      if (!head) {
         head = current = newNode;
         return; }
      assert(current);
      newNode->ConnectTo(current->Next());
      current->ConnectTo(newNode);
      current = newNode;
   }

   template <class BaseType>
   void List<BaseType>::Delete() {
      assert(current);
      Node<BaseType> *temp = current;
      if(current == head) {
         head = head->Next();
         current = head;
         delete temp;
         return;
      }
      assert(previous);
      current = current->Next();
      previous->ConnectTo(current);
      delete temp;
   }
```

The Delete method removes the current element from the list and disposes of it. Two assert calls are used to ensure that the current and previous pointers are not null. As with the Insert method, the Next and ConnectTo methods of the Node class are used to maintain the current structure of the list.

 Exercises

1. Write the destructor for the List template. Be sure that memory leaks are avoided.

2. Complete the implementation of the List template and test your implementation for a variety of classes.

3. Revise the List template by adding a method that allows a new element to be appended to the end of the list.

4. Revise the List template by adding a method that allows a new element to be prepended to the front of the list.

5. Design and implement a DoubleLinkedList template. Test your implementation for a variety of classes.

7.5 Templates and Inheritance

Templates may be used in many combinations with inheritance. It is possible to combine inheritance and templates because a template class is a class, albeit one with a parameter. Combining these language features allows the parameterization ability of templates to be used in conjunction with the specializing abilities of inheritance. Four combinations of templates and inheritance are presented in this section:

- a template class that inherits from another template class,
- a non-template class that inherits from a template class,
- a template class that inherits from a non-template class, and
- a template class that uses multiple inheritance.

Each of these combinations will be illustrated by an example showing how the two features are combined and what advantages are possibly gained by using them together.

Inheritance Between Template Classes

In this case, both the base and derived classes are templates. In the usual way, inheritance is used to extend the base-class template through the addition of new methods and/or data in the derived-class template. A common situation in this case is that the template parameter of the derived class is also used as the template parameter of the base class.

An extension of the queue template defined in Section 7.1 will be used to illustrate this combination of templates and inheritance. A common extension of the queue data structure is the addition of a method allowing the first element in the queue to be returned without being removed from the queue. Such a queue, an InspectableQueue, has all of the methods of a basic queue. It is desirable, therefore, to use inheritance so that the InspectableQueue need not repeat the definition of methods already given in the Queue template class. Also, like the Queue template, the InspectableQueue will be defined as a template so that it

Code Sample 7–15 *Using Inheritance Between Templates*

```
template <class QueueItem> class Queue
{
   private:

      QueueItem buffer[100];
      int head, tail, count;

   public:
                Queue();
      void      Insert(QueueItem item);
      QueueItem Remove();
                ~Queue();
};

template <class QueueItem> class InspectableQueue
         : public Queue<QueueItem>
{
   public:
                InspectableQueue();
      QueueItem Inspect();
                    // return without removing the first element
                ~InspectableQueue();
};
```

can be reused for many different classes. The definition of the InspectableQueue template is shown in Code Sample 7–15.

The InspectableQueue template can be elaborated and objects of the elaborated template can be declared as shown in the following code:

```
InspectableQueue<Location> locations;
Location loc1(...);
Location loc2(...);
...
locations.Insert(loc1);                 // base class method
locations.Insert(loc2);                 // base class method
...
Location front    = locations.Remove(); // base class method
Location newFront = locations.Inspect();// derived class method
...
```

When the declaration InspectableQueue<Location> is elaborated, the compiler must also take into account the inheritance between this template class and the template Queue class. The declaration of the InspectableQueue template states that the template parameter given to the InspectableQueue template,

Location in this example, should also be used in elaborating the base class. In other words, the inheritance hierarchy implied by the code above is equivalent to:

```
InspectableQueue<Location> : public Queue<Location> {...}
                                        // suggestive syntax only
```

This code is not correct C++ syntax but it conveys the spirit of how derived-class template can relate to its base-class template.

Inheritance from a Template Class

A non-template derived class can inherit from a template base class if the template's parameter is fixed by the nature and definition of the derived class. In this case the template parameter is determined by the designer of the derived class. A programmer using the derived class need not be aware that a template is used in the definition of the derived class. In the normal sense of inheritance, the public methods of the template class will be public methods in the derived class. Thus, the programmer using the derived class can use both the derived- and base-class methods to manipulate a derived-class object. To the programmer using the derived class, the types involved in the inherited operations reflect the template parameter decided upon by the designer of the derived class.

A variation of the Polygon class illustrates a non-template class that inherits from a template class. A polygon shape is defined by a list of points. The list is of unknown length and may change during its lifetime, with new points being added or existing points being removed. A Polygon object should also know how to draw itself on a canvas by drawing a sequence of lines connecting each pair of adjacent points. Thus, the Polygon class is a combination of two capabilities: the capability to maintain a list of points and the capability to draw itself. Instead of implementing all of the methods to maintain a list, the list capability is inherited from the List template where the List template is elaborated with the Location class. The Polygon derived class adds to these inherited methods the capability to draw itself. The design of the Polygon class is shown in Code Sample 7–16. The List template interface is repeated in this sample for reference.

The template parameter is fixed by the Polygon class because the Polygon can only be a List of Locations. The Polygon class is itself not a template, because all of the types in the Polygon class are fixed.

The Polygon class can be used as shown in the following code example. Notice that the Polygon object can be manipulated using both the methods inherited from the template base class (e.g, Insert) and the methods defined in the Polygon class itself (e.g., Draw). This code example also illustrates that to the programmer using the Polygon class, the presence of a template class is not evident.

Code Sample 7-16 *Polygon Class Inherits from the List Template*

```
template <class BaseType> class List {
   private:
      ...
   public:

               List();
   void        First();    // set current element to first element
   void        Next();     // advance to next list element
   int         Done();     // is there a current element?
   BaseType&   Current();  // reply current value
   void        Insert(BaseType val);
                           // insert after current element
   void        Delete();   // delete current element
   ~List();
};


class Polygon : public List<Location>
                           // Polygon "is-a" list of Locations
{
   public:
      Polygon();
      void Draw(Canvas& canvas);
                           // draw itself in a canvas
};
```

```
Polygon poly;
...
poly.Insert(Location(20,20));     // inherited from template
poly.Insert(Location(30,30));     // inherited from template
// insert other locations
poly.Draw(canvas);                // derived class method
```

This code reveals an important part of the Polygon class's design. The Insert method applied to a Polygon requires a Location object as its parameter. The class of the Insert method's argument is determined by the parameter of the List template. Since the Polygon class inherits from List<Location>, the Insert method's argument is required to be a Location object.

Inheritance by a Template Class

In this case, the derived class is a template class, but the base class is a non-template class. Under these circumstances, the template parameter only has meaning to the derived class, not to the base class. As with all other uses of public

Code Sample 7–17   *The Sequenced Interface and the Clock Class*

```
class SequencedInterface
{
   public:
        virtual void Show() = 0;
        virtual void Next() = 0;
};

class Clock
{
private:
        SequencedInerface *sequenced;
public:
        Clock() {}
        void ConnectTo(SequencedInterface& sq) { sequenced = &sq;}
        void ConnectTo(SequencedInterface* sq) { sequenced =  sq;}
        void Notify() { sequenced->Next();
                        sequenced->Show(); }
};
```

inheritance, though, the derived class does present in its public interface all of the methods inherited from the base class, plus any other methods added by the derived class.

Illustrating this case is a template that binds an interface, defined by the methods of an abstract base class, and the class whose methods implement the interface. The example revisits the Clock class presented in section 6.10. The Clock class depends only on two methods in the objects to which it was connected: a Next method and a Show method. Instead of binding the Clock class to a specific class hierarchy, such as the class hierarchy whose base class is DisplayableNumber, it is more useful to allow a Clock object to be connected to any other object that has these two methods. In Section 6.10, multiple inheritance was used to combine an abstract base class whose pure virtual methods defined the interface and another class that provided the implementation of the methods required by the abstract base class. That same problem is solved here using templates. The abstract base class and the Clock class defined in terms of this abstract base class are shown in Code Sample 7–17.

This template uses an object whose class is given by the template's parameter to satisfy the requirements of the abstract base class from which the template inherits. The object is given to the template as a constructor argument, and a reference to this object is retained as part of the template's private data. In Code Sample 7–18, the private data seqItem in the template refers to this object. When the template is asked to perform its Show method, it simply forwards this request to the seqItem object; the same occurs for the Next method. If

Code Sample 7–18 *Defining the ImplementsSequenced Template by Inheritance from a Non-Template Class*

```
template class <SequencedImplementation> class Sequenced
                                  : public SequencedInterface
{
   private:
        SequencedImplementation& seqItem;
   public:
        Sequenced(SequencedImplementation& item) : seqItem(item)
{}
        void Next() { seqItem.Next();}
        void Show() { seqItem.Show();}
};
```

the class used to elaborate the template does not define a Show or a Next method, the compiler will issue error messages to this effect. Thus, at run-time, the program is guaranteed that the seqItem object does provide the needed Show and Next methods.

The template can be used as shown in the following code. Here a Clock and a Counter object are created with the intention of connecting the Clock object to the Counter object. However, the Clock's ConnectTo method requires that the object to which the Clock will be connected is a derived class of Sequenced-Interface. The Counter class, however, inherits from DisplayableNumber and not from SequencedInterface. By elaborating the ImplementsSequenced template with the Counter class, an indirect relationship is established between the Counter class and the SequencedInterface class through the programming in the Sequenced template. This indirect relationship is established in two steps: first the Sequenced template is elaborated with the Counter class, and then an object of this elaborated template class (timedCounter) is constructed with an object of the Counter class (time). These two steps are shown in the single line of code that creates the timedCounter object:

```
Clock timer;
Counter time(0);
...
Sequenced <Counter> timedCounter(time);
...
timer.ConnectTo( (SequencedInterface&)timedCounter );
..
timer.Notify();  // invokes Next and Show in time object
```

The critical part of the code above is where the timedCounter id type cast to a SequencedInterface object, which is possible because the timedCounter object is an instance of the class Sequenced<Counter>, whose base class is Sequenced-

Interface. Thus, the derived class object is properly type cast to an object of its base class. This allows the Clock class only to be aware of the fact that the object to which it is connected satisfies the interface defined in the SequencedInterface abstract base class.

The Sequenced template can be elaborated with any class that provides a Show and a Next method. The example was given earlier of an Animation class (Section 6.10) that had both of these methods. An Animation object could also be connected to a Clock object, as shown below.

```
Clock timer;
Animation movie(...);
...
Sequenced <Animation> timedAnimation(movie);
...
timer.ConnectTo( (SequencedInterface&)timedAnimation );
..
timer.Notify();   // invokes Next and Show in movie object
```

This code demonstrates the template's value: it can be used to allow objects of any class possessing a Show and a Next method to be type cast safely to a SequencedInterface type, regardless of whether the object's class inherits from the SequencedInterface base class. The type casting is safe because when the template is elaborated the compiler will confirm that the class being used to elaborate the template has the required Show and Next methods. The type casting fulfills its role by allowing the Clock class to remain unaware of the exact class of the objects to which it is connected.

Templates and Multiple Inheritance

Multiple inheritance is used in a variation of the technique in which a template binds an interface defined by an abstract base class to an implementation provided by an arbitrary class. The technique used in the ImplementsSequenced template creates this binding by inheriting from the abstract base class and holding a reference to the implementing class. One drawback of this design is that only the methods defined in the interface are available through the template; it might be necessary that all of the methods of the implementing class be accessible through the template. This requirement can be met by using multiple inheritance.

Code Sample 7–19 shows both the Sequenced template, which uses single inheritance, and the SequencedObject template, which uses multiple inheritance. The Sequenced template uses single inheritance and association to bind the implementation and the interface. The associated object, seqItem, contains the real implementation of the Next and Show methods, while the SequencedObject template uses multiple inheritance. As with the Sequenced template, the SequencedObject template inherits from the abstract base class SequencedInterface. In addition, the

Code Sample 7–19 *Templates Using Multiple Inheritance*

```
template class <SequencedImplementation> class Sequenced
                                   : public SequencedInterface
{
    private:
        SequencedImplementation& seqItem;
    public:
        Sequenced(SequencedImplementation& item) : seqItem(item)
{}
        void Next() { seqItem.Next();}
        void Show() { seqItem.Show();}
};


template class <SequencedImplementation> class SequencedObject
        : public SequencedImplementation,
          public SequencedInterface
{
    public:
        SequencedObject(SequencedImplementation& item)
                        : SequencedImplementation(item) {}
        void Next() { SequencedImplementation::Next();}
        void Show() { SequencedImplementation::Show();}
};
```

SequencedObject also inherits the implementation of its methods from Sequenced-
Implementation. Notice that SequencedImplementation is the template parameter!
Both templates require the same constructor argument; an object of the class
defined by SequencedImplementation. The Sequenced template maintains an asso-
ciation with this object, and the SequencedObject template uses it to initialize its
SequencedImplementation layer. Similarly, the forwarding methods in the
Sequenced template forward their invocations to the seqItem object, but the
SequencedObject forwards its invocations to the methods in its own base class.

From the perspective of the programmer using the Sequenced and
SequencedObject templates, they are extremely similar. The code necessary to
elaborate the template and construct an object is, except for the difference in the
template names, identical. This similarity is illustrated in Code Sample 7–20,
which shows an object being constructed using both templates.

However, there is one major difference between the Sequenced and
SequencedObject templates. Because the Sequenced template used single inheritance, objects of the Sequenced template can only be type cast to Sequenced-
Interface. In other words, the SequencedImplementation class can only be
viewed as a SequencedInterface object. In contrast, the SequencedObject
template inherits from both SequencedImplementation and SequencedInterface,

Code Sample 7–20   *Using the Sequenced and SequencedObject Templates*

```
Clock timer;
Counter time(0);
...
Sequenced <Counter> timedCounter(time);
...
timer.ConnectTo(
        (SequencedInterface&)timedCounter );
...
timer.Notify();
```

```
Clock timer;
Counter time(0);
...
SequencedObject <Counter> timedCounter(time);
...
timer.ConnectTo(
        (SequencedInterface&)timedCounter );
...
timer.Notify();
```

which allows SequencedObject objects to be type cast to either a SequencedInterface object or a SequencedImplementation. This flexibility provides the programmer with the ability to type cast a template object as if the object satisfies the SequencedInterface, which it does through inheritance, and to type cast the same template object to the SequencedImplementation class, which is legitimate because the template also inherits from SequencedImplementation.

 ## Exercises

1. Design and implement an AppendableList template that inherits from the List template. Your AppendableList template should introduce a method that allows a new element to be appended to the end of the list.

2. Design and implement a PrependableList template that inherits from the List template. Your PrependableList template should introduce a method that allows a new element to be inserted at the front of the list.

3. Design and implement a template named ActionButton that can be used to create a Button that, upon being pushed, performs an action. The ActionButton template takes a single template argument, OnPushAction. The ActionButton template inherits from the non-template class, Button. The template constructor takes an object of the class OnPushAction. The ActionButton template maintains an association with this object of the OnPushAction class, and adds a single method, void OnPush(), that it forwards to the object with which it is associated.

4. Design and implement a Named template that can be used to add the property of character-string name to the class that is the template's parameter. Your template should allow a NamedCounter object to be created and manipulated as illustrated below:

```
Counter count(0);
Named<Counter> namedCounter(count, "Seconds");
. . .
if (namedCounter.IsNamed("Seconds")) . . .
char* name = namedCounter.GetName();
namedCounter.Next();
. . .
Counter& ctr = (Counter&)namedCounter;
```

5. The Named property was added to a class earlier by multiple inheritance and by templates in the exercise above. What are the differences between these two approaches?

6. Write a test case to verify that an object of the class Sequenced-Object<Counter> can be type cast to a Counter object while an object of the class Sequenced<Counter> cannot be type cast to a Counter object.

Operator Overloading

8.1 Introduction to Operator Overloading

Operator overloading is the ability to define a new meaning for an existing (built-in) operator. The list of operators includes mathematical operators (+, -, *, etc.), relational operators (<, >, ==, etc.), logical operators (&&, | |, !, etc.), access operators ([], ->), the assignment operator (=), stream I/O operators (<<, >>), type conversion operators, and several others. While all of these operators have predefined and unchangeable meanings for the built-in types, each operator can be given a specific interpretation for individual user-defined classes or combinations of user-defined classes. C++ is particularly generous in the flexibility it offers to programmers in extending these built-in operators; not all object-oriented languages allow this.

There are a number of reasons why a class designer may decide to provide extensions to one or more of the built-in operators:

natural, suggestive usage: The most natural way to convey the intended meaning of an operation may be through the predefined operators. For example, in defining a class to represent complex or rational numbers, the best way to represent adding two complex numbers or adding two rational numbers is by giving a new (extended) meaning to the plus operator (+) rather than invent a member function with a suggestive name ("addTo").

semantic integrity: In order to copy the objects being pointed to, classes that have pointers to objects frequently need a specialized assignment operator. The failure to properly handle assignments can lead to either memory leaks or run-time errors.

uniformity with base types: Templates often impose requirements on their arguments that can only be met by both built-in types and user-defined types when the user-defined types provide overloaded operations. For example, a

Code Sample 8–1   *Safe Array with Operator Overloading*

```
class Array
{
  private:
      int array[20];
  public:
        Array(int init = 0);
    int& operator[](int i);    // overloaded subscript operator
        ~Array();
};
```

Set template may require that its instantiating type have an equality operator (==) in order to implement the test for membership in the Set.

In many cases, the use of overloaded operators serves some or all of these purposes simultaneously.

8.2 Overloading Basic Operators

A simple example to introduce operator overloading is a safe array of integers. The array is to be safe in the sense that the subscripting operation will ensure that the subscript is within bounds. If the subscript is out of bounds, the program will terminate. The declaration of the safe array is defined as shown in Code Sample 8–1.

In this case, the subscripting operator, referred to as "operator[]," is defined to take a single integer input argument. The subscripting operator returns a reference to the subscripted element of the array after checking that such an element exists in the array. This class is intended to be used as follows:

```
Array array;

array[0] = 1;
array[1] = 1;
for (int i = 2; i < 20; i++)
                        // compute first twenty Fibonacci numbers
    array[i] = array[i-1] + array[i-2];
```

The compiler, upon encountering the expression "array[0]," will check to see if the class of array (in this case Array) contains a class-specific definition for the [] operator. Because the Array class contains such an overloaded operator method, the compiler will arrange for code to be generated that is the equivalent of

```
array.operator[](0)
```

Code Sample 8–2 *Implementing an Overloaded Operator*

```
int& Array::operator[](int i)
{
    assert(0 <= i && i < 20);
    return array[i];
}
```

which matches the definition of the method given in the Array class. Similarly, the statement

```
array[i] = array[i-1] + array[i-2];
```

would be treated as:

```
array.operator[](i) = array.operator[](i-1) + array.operator[](i-2);
```

Since the overloaded subscript operator returns a reference (specifically an int&), it is legitimate to have the subscript operator appear in an expression on the left-hand side of the assignment operator.

Notice that aside from its declaration, the Array object looks and feels like a built-in array type. This similarity is also suggested by the following code which shows Arrays and built-in arrays being intermixed:

```
Array safe;
int    regular[20];

// define contents of arrays safe and unsafe

regular[10] = safe[10];
safe[11]    = regular[11];
safe[0]     = safe[0] + regular[0]
```

The built-in array type and the Array act the same, except that the Array will cause a clean and informative error message when a subscript out-of-bounds problem arises, while the built-in array will silently permit the erroneous access and the resulting corruption of data lying adjacent to the built-in array in memory.

The operator[] method would be implemented as shown in Code Sample 8–2. Again, notice that there is nothing special about the operator[] method, except that its name must be exactly as written in Code Sample 8–2 to communicate to the compiler that this method is, in fact, to be treated as an overloading of the built-in [] operator for objects of the Array class.

Two safe arrays may be added or subtracted by overloading the addition (+) operator and the subtraction (–) operators. The interface of the Array class would then be changed as shown in Code Sample 8–3.

Code Sample 8–3   *Overloading Other Operators in the Safe Array*

```
class Array
{  private:
       int array[20];
   public:
           Array(int v=0);
     int&  operator[](int i);          // subscript   operator
     Array operator+(Array& other);    // addition    operator
     Array operator-(Array& other);    // subtraction operator
           ~Array();
};
```

Notice that the addition and subtraction operators return a reference to an Array object that holds the result of their operations. The two Array objects being added are not changed: instead a new Array object is created and returned by reference.

The Array addition operator allows the following usages:

```
Array a,b;          // initialized to 0
Array one(1);       // initialized to 1

// give values to arrays a and b

Array c = a + b;
Array d = a - b + one;
```

The first of these two assignment statements produces an array, each of whose elements is the sum of the corresponding elements in the two arrays a and b. The second assignment shows that the overloaded addition and subtraction operators for the Array class may be used in more complicated expressions.

The compiler will, upon encountering the expression a + b determine if there is a class-specific overloading of the addition operator. Since a and b are objects of the Array class, and this class contains an operator+ method with matching argument types, the compiler will generate code that is the equivalent of

```
a.operator+(b)
```

where the object on the left-hand side of the addition in the expression "a +"b (a) plays the role of the called object and the object on the right hand side (b) plays the role of the argument value. Similarly, the statement

```
d = a - b + one
```

will be compiled into code that is equivalent to

```
Array& anonymous = a.operator-(b);
d = anonymous.operator+(one);
```

Code Sample 8–4 *Implementing the Array Addition Operator Overloadings*

```
Array Array::operator+(Array& other)
{   Array result;

    for(int i=0; i<20; i++)
      result[i] = array[i] + other[i];

    return result;
}


Array Array::operator-(Array& other)
{   Array result;

    for(int i=0; i<20; i++)
      result[i] = array[i] - other[i];

    return result;


}
```

where "anonymous" is used to refer to the object created dynamically by the subtraction operator.

The use of the default assignment operator in the Array class is sufficient. The default assignment operator simply performs a bit-level copy from the source to the target object. In this case, assignments such as

```
Array f, g;
// assign values to g
f = g;
```

will work as intended: the data in Array g will be copied to the data in Array f.

The implementation of the Array addition and subtraction operators is as illustrated in Code Sample 8–4. Each operation allocates a new Array object that it will return by copy as its result. Notice that the assignment statement in each method uses a combination of built-in and overloaded subscripting operators. The term array[i] uses the built-in meaning for subscripting because "array" is an array of the base type int. The terms other[i] and result[i] use the meaning of subscripting defined in the Array class, because each of them are objects of the Array class.

A member function that redefines an operator can itself be overloaded. The terminology for this can be confusing because the term operator overloading refers to methods that redefine the built-in operators while the term overloading

Code Sample 8–5   *Overloading the + Operator in the Array Class*

```
class Array
{  private:
      int array[20];
   public:
      ...
      Array operator+(Array& other);     // addition operator
      Array operator+(int increment);    // add increment to all
      ...
};


// in implementation

Array Array::operator+(int increment)
{ Array result;

   for(int i = 0; i< 20; i++)
      result[i] = array[i] + increment;

   return result;

}
```

refers to methods that have the same name but different signatures. To illustrate this difference, another + operator will be defined for the Array class. This new + operator will allow a value to be added to each element of the Array; its partial class definition and implementation is shown in Code Sample 8–5.

Using both of the overloaded addition operators together allows the following code to be written:

```
Array one(1);           // all elements are 1
Array two = one + 1;    // add 1 to each element
  Array three = one + two;
                     // pairwise addition of Arrays one and two
```

The first assignment statement uses the overloading of the + operator that has an int as its argument. This line is equivalent to the code

```
Array two = one.operator+(1);
```

The second assignment statement uses the overloading of the plus operator that has an Array object as its argument. This line is equivalent to the code

```
Array three = one.operator+(two);
```

Of course, other overloadings of the addition operator can be added as required by the needs of the application.

 Exercises

1. Array Multiplication Operator:Extend the Array class to include an operator that allows each element of the array to be multiplied by a given constant. For example:

```
Array  a;
Array& b = a*6;   // multiply each element by 6
```

2. Extend the Array class to include a test for an equality operator that returns 1 if all elements of the two Array objects are the same, and 0 otherwise. For example:

```
Array  a;
Array  b;

// give values to a and b

if ( a == b) {// uses equality operator
              // code for when they are equal
            }
```

3. Extend the Array class to include a test for inequality by overloading the predefined operator "!=".

4. Extend the Array class to include a test for "<" between two Array objects. One Array object is "<" another if each element of the first Array object is strictly less than the corresponding element of the second Array object.

5. Extend the Array class to include another overloading of its equality operator. This additional overloading would be used to test whether each element in the array is equal to a given integer value. An example of the use of this operator is:

```
Array a;

//...give values to a

if (a == 0)
{ // all elements of a are zero
}
```

6. Define a class Association that maintains an association between up to 100 pairs of integer values. The first element of each pair is the subscript and the second element is the value. Association class should be usable as illustrated in this code:

```
Association pairs;
pairs[10] = 20;       // record the pair (10, 20)
pairs[1000] = 0;      // record the pair (1000, 0)
...
int p = pairs[10];    // returns 20
int q = pairs[1];     // returns 0 if no pair
```

7. Define another class Association that maintains an association between up to 100 (string, integer) pairs. The character string element of each pair is the subscript and the integer element is the value. Association class should be usable as in this code:

```
Association pairs;
pairs["oranges"] = 20;        // record the pair ("oranges", 20)
pairs["apples"] = 0;          // record the pair ("apples", 0)
...      int p = pairs["oranges"];   // returns 20
int q = pairs["pears"];
                    // returns 0 if no pair with this string
```

8.3 Operator Overloading and Non-Member Functions

There are two situations under which operator overloading must be done by functions that are not members of a specific class. The first is when the class to which the member function should be added is not available for modification. This frequently occurs with classes that are in standard class libraries; an example is the stream input-output (I/O) library. The second instance is when type conversion of the arguments involved in the operation is desired. The first case is considered in this section and the second in the next section.

To allow operator overloading by non-member functions, the rules used by the compiler involve two steps. If an expression of the form "x op y" is encountered, the compiler will check:

- is there a member function in the class of object x of the form "operator op(Y)" where Y is the class of object y, and, if not,

- is there a non-member function of the form "operator op(X,Y)" where X is the class of object x and Y is the class of object y.

The rules are applied in this order. An overloaded operator will be used if either of them is satisfied.

When operator overloading is achieved using non-member function, there are two cases to be considered: the overloaded operator uses only the public interface of the class(es) involved in the overloading, or it requires access to the private data of the class(es). If the former, the non-member function is written simply as a normal function. If the latter case, a special "friend" designation is used to grant access to private data, access which otherwise would be denied because the function is not a member of the class whose private data is being accessed.

Non-Member Functions Without Special Access

Overloading of the stream I/O operators for the Array class illustrates the use of non-member function to overload an operator when the class in which the operator is defined is unavailable for modification. Without operator overloading, the usual way to print the contents of an Array object is as follows:

```
Array a;

// give values to a

cout << "[ ";
for(int i = 0; i< 19; i++)
    cout << a[i] << ", ";
cout << a[19] << " ]";
```

This prints out a comma-separated list of numbers enclosed in brackets, and is tedious code to write each time. It can, however, be placed in the Array class as a print method. Code Sample 8–6 shows the definition of the Array class and the implementation of the print method.

This approach to displaying the array may be improved upon by noting that the stream I/O operators (<<, >>) can be overloaded. If such an overloading could be accomplished, then it would be possible to write:

```
Array array;

// give values to array

cout << array;
```

But, overloading the stream I/O operators presents an apparent problem because it seems to require that the operator overloading occur in the library class that implements stream I/O. Changing the library classes may be impossible, because the source code is not available, or at least troublesome, due to the need to understand the classes that implement the stream I/O functionality.

Code Sample 8-6 *Input-Output (I/O) Using a Standard Method of a*
Class

```
class Array
{
    private:
      int array[20];
    public:
            Array();
      int&   operator[](int i);           // subscript    operator
      Array& operator+(Array& other);     // addition      operator
      Array& operator-(Array& other);     // subtraction operator
      void   Print();
            ~Array();
};

// in implementation

 void Array::Print()
{
      cout << "[ ";
      for(int i = 0; i < 19; i++)
          cout << array[i] << ", ";
      cout << array[19] << " ]";
}
```

Code Sample 8-7 *Defining a Stream I/O Function*

```
ostream& operator<< (ostream& os , Array& a)
{
    os << "[ ";
    for(int i = 0; i < 19; i++)
        os << a[i] << ", ";
    os << a[19] << " ]";
}
```

C++ allows operators to be overloaded by functions that are not members of a class. To provide the overloading of the stream I/O operators, the I/O functionality could be implemented as shown in Code Sample 8-7.

The class ostream in this example is the actual type of the predefined library variable cout (similarly cin is implemented by the class istream). Upon examining the statement

```
cout << array;
```

where array is an object of the class Array, the compiler will check to see if there is an overloaded operator of the form "operator<<(Array)" in the ostream class (which it will not find) and then will check for a non-member overloaded operator of the form "operator<<(ostream&, Array)" (which it will find).

Since the overloaded stream output operator is defined in terms of an ostream object, it applies not only to cout but to other objects that inherit from the ostream class. The ofstream class, for file output, inherits from the ostream class. Thus, the overloading above allows

```
ofstream outFile("array.data");

Array array;

// give values to array

outFile << a;
```

Similarly, writing to "string streams" is also possible.

Non-Member Function with Friend Access

Non-member functions may be given special access to the private or protected data of a class in instances where they need information about the class that is not accessible through the public interface of the class, or efficiency considerations make it necessary for the non-member function to bypass the public interface and be given direct access to the class's encapsulated data.

It should be stressed that granting special access to private data should be used sparingly. Unnecessary use of this feature undermines the value of encapsulated data and weakens the structure of the system.

Special access is required, for example, when efficient binary level I/O is added to the Array class given above. What is desired is a way to write the contents of the Array into a file in binary, not ASCII (text) form. This approach to I/O is faster and is more compact: it is faster because one write operation is done to write the entire array, and more compact because an integer, say 5,210,500, is stored in four bytes (32 bits) in the binary form file but requires at least eight byes in ASCII. However, to perform the binary-level I/O operation, it is necessary to know the address of the array to be written, but it is undesirable to add a method in the Array class to return the base address of its encapsulated array, as this would allow any code to manipulate the encapsulated array. A better design in this situation is to allow the non-member function that implements the stream I/O to have special access. This allows the overloading function, and only the overloading function, to have access to the base address of the encapsulated array.

Code Sample 8–8 *Declaring a "friend" Stream I/O Operator*

```
class Array {
    private:
        int array[20];
    public:
    ...
        friend ofstream& operator<< (ofstream& ofs, Array& a);
    ...
};
```

The binary form of stream I/O should look and behave as the other forms of stream I/O overloading. Thus, binary form of the stream I/O should be usable as follows:

```
ofstream binaryFile("array.bin");

Array a;

//... give values to a

binaryFile << a;                 // output array in binary form
binaryFile.close();
```

To make this work, an overloading of the stream I/O operators may be written that operates on files (ofstream, ifstream). For output, the following non-member functions is needed:

```
ofstream& operator<< (ofstream& ofs, Array& a)
{
    ofs.write((char*)(a.array), 20*sizeof(int));
    return ofs;
};
```

As can be seen, this non-member function requires access to the private data of the Array class. To allow this access to be granted, it is necessary to give the non-member function special permission. This is accomplished via a class declaring another function (or class) as its "friend." For the non-member function considered here, the Array class would be modified as shown in Code Sample 8–8. The friend declaration grants the access to the private data that is required.

Notice also that two overloadings of the stream I/O operators have been defined—one for ostream& objects (like cout) and one for ofstream& objects (like the binaryFile above). These overloadings perform ASCII output for streams that are typically viewed by users and binary I/O on files.

Exercises

1. Implement and test an overloaded stream output operator for the Number class that does not use friend access.

2. Implement and test an overloaded stream output operator for the Message class that does not use friend access.

3. Implement and test an overloaded stream output operator for the Number class that uses friend access.

4. Implement and test an overloaded stream output operator for the Message class that uses friend access.

5. Implement and test an overloaded stream output operator for the Association class, creating an association between pairs of ints defined in the exercises accompanying Section 8.2.

6. Implement and test an overloaded stream output operator for the Association class, creating an association between a char* and an int defined in the exercises accompanying Section 8.2.

8.4 Type Conversion Operators

Type conversion is the act of producing a representation of some value of a target type from a representation of some value of a source type. Type conversion from int to long, and from int to float are among the familiar base (built in) types conversions. These type conversions are meaningful because the source value has a natural, useful projection in the universe of values defined by the target type. For example, the integer 2 has a natural conversion to the floating point value 2.0.

Type conversion is needed to resolve mismatched types in assignments and expressions, or when passing parameters. The existence of type conversions makes it possible to use one type when a different type may be expected, the type conversion bridging the difference between them.

Type conversions may be either implicit or explicit, as shown in the following examples using built in types:

```
int i;
float f;

f = i;          // implicit conversion

f = (float)i;   // explicit conversion

f = float(i);   // explicit conversion
```

With implicit type conversion, the compiler is given the responsibility for determining that a conversion is required and how to perform the conversion. With explicit type conversion, the programmer assumes this responsibility. Notice that there are two different, but equivalent, syntaxes for explicit conversion.

Type conversions involving user-defined classes are also meaningful. The following examples illustrate conversion between a user defined class and a built-in type and conversion between two user defined types.

The first example, illustrating type conversion between a user-defined class and a built-in type, uses the class Counter introduced in chapter 6, on inheritance. Objects of this class can be incremented by a Next operation and displayed in the user interface by associating the Counter with a TextBox. The internal integer value of a Counter can be extracted by the Value method so that a Counter object can be used in contexts where an integer values is expected:

```
Counter count(0);

// manipulate count

if ( count.Value() > 0) ...

if ( count.Value() == 100) ...

cout << count.Value();
```

This syntax, however, is awkward and unnatural.

Because a Counter object can be viewed as an integer value that has added capabilities (i.e., the ability to be displayed in the user interface), it is sensible to expect that a Counter object could be used in the following, more direct, ways:

```
Counter count(0);

// manipulate count

if ( count > 0) ...

if ( count == 100) ...

cout << count;
```

In this code, the expectation is that a Counter object can be treated as a simple integer. One way to achieve this effect is to add to the Counter class overloaded operators for such functions as comparisons, arithmetic, and/or stream I/O. A simpler alternative is to use type conversion.

A type-conversion operator is added to the user-defined Counter class as in Code Sample 8–9, where the operator overloading defines a type-conversion operator that can be used to produce an int type from a Counter object. This

Code Sample 8–9 *Defining a Type Conversion Operator*

```
class Counter
{
  ...
 public:
    ...
    operator int();
    ...
};
```

Code Sample 8–10 *Constructors as Type Conversion Mechanisms*

```
class Counter : public DisplayableNumber
{
  ...
  public:
     Counter(int i);
     ...
};
```

operator will be used whenever an implicit or explicit conversion of a Counter object to an int is required.

Notice that constructors also play a role in type conversion. The constructor for a Counter object is defined in the Counter class as shown in Code Sample 8–10. This constructor can be viewed as a way of converting an int value to a Counter object. In general, a class's constructor that takes a single argument of a type other than that class itself serves as a type converted from the argument type to the class.

 Exercises

1. Revise the Message class to allow correct type conversion from a char* to a Message and from a Message to a char*.

2. Revise the Number class to allow correct type conversion from a Number to an int and from an int to a Number.

3. Revise the Number and Counter classes to allow correct type conversion from a Number to a Counter and a Counter to a Number.

4. Revise the Shape class to allow a Shape object to be type converted correctly to both an int and a float where the int and float values represent the area of the rectangle described by the Shape object.

8.5 Type Conversion and Operator Overloading

Type conversions are often provided to lessen the duplication that frequently occurs when overloading operators. A typical example of this duplication is encountered in defining binary, commutative operators (such as + and *). Suppose that an overloaded set of arithmetic operators is needed in class X so that an int may be added to an object of class X. This requires two operator overloadings: one for the case of "X + int" and one for the case of "int + X." To eliminate this duplication, a type conversion is defined that converts an int to an X and provides a single overloading for the case "X + X." Thus, both "int + X" and "X + int" become the single case "X + X."

A set of classes for manipulating colors will be used in this section to illustrate type conversion and operator overloading. Colors generated by a computer are a combination of three primary colors (red, blue, and green). Each of these colors has an intensity value associated with it. The range of intensity values determines how many different colors may be produced. If we assume that the intensities are in the range 0-63, then the color aqua is generated by using no red and intensities of 50 for both green and blue. The color purple is obtained from aqua by adding red at intensity 63 and increasing the blue intensity by 13.

Operator overloading makes it possible to program with colors in the most natural way. The phrase "add red at intensity nine to aqua" suggests using operator overloading to create a set of arithmetic operators that could be used as follows:

```
Color aqua(Red(0), Green(50), Blue(50));

Color darkRed = Red(63);
Color purple  = darkRed + aqua + Blue(13);
Color peach   = purple - Blue(13) - Green(3);

Color test1 = darkRed + peach;
Color test2 = peach + darkRed;

cout << aqua    << endl;
cout << purple  << endl;
cout << peach   << endl;
cout << darkRed << endl;
```

This usage reads naturally and the stream output generated is a readable description of the color. For example, outputting the color aqua results in:

```
(red:0, green:50, blue:50)
```

Code Sample 8–11 *Base Class for the Primary Colors*

```
class PrimaryColor
{  protected:
     int intensity;
   public:
     PrimaryColor(int i) : intensity(i) {}
     PrimaryColor(const PrimaryColor& c)
                                 { intensity = c.intensity; }
     friend ostream& operator<<(ostream& os,
            const PrimaryColor& pc);
};


ostream& operator<<(ostream& os, const PrimaryColor& pc)
{ os << pc.intensity;
  return os;
}
```

Defining classes for the primary colors is straightforward. Because each of these colors has a common structure they can be defined via inheritance from the base class that is shown in Code Sample 8–11.

The base class, PrimaryColor, defines a single data value representing the color's intensity value. In addition to the two constructors, a stream output operator is defined as a non-member friend function. The friend permission is used in the stream output operator to access the intensity data in the protected region of the PrimaryColor object. The first constructor of the PrimaryColor class can be viewed as a way to construct a PrimaryColor object using an int value or as a type conversion operator that converts an int value into a PrimaryColor object.

The individual classes Red, Green, and Blue can be derived from Primary-Color; Code Sample 8–12 presents the Red class in detail; the Green and Blue classes are similar. Operator overloadings for the addition and subtraction operators are given for each of the Red, Green, and Blue classes. The overloadings allow the normal arithmetic operators to be used to add and subtract colors in the same way that integer values are added and subtracted. For example, the code:

```
Red lightRed(20);
Red darkerRed(100);
Red darkestRed = lightRed + darkerRed;
Red lessRed = darkestRed - Red(30);
```

shows how Red objects can be declared and manipulated using these overloaded operators.

In addition to providing greater readability, the introduction of the simple classes for Red, Green, and Blue also helps to avoid certain errors that would

Code Sample 8–12   *Definition of the Red, Green, and Blue Classes*

```
class Red : public PrimaryColor
{
  public:
    Red(int i) : PrimaryColor(i) {}
    Red operator+(const Red& r) {return Red
                                   (intensity + r.intensity; }
    Red operator-(const Red& r) {return Red
                                   (intensity - r.intensity; }
};

class Green : public PrimaryColor
{
  // similar to Red class
};

class Blue : public PrimaryColor
{
  // similar to Red class
};
```

occur were only basic int types used instead. For example, if a programmer unintentionally wrote the following code using only integer values:

```
int color = 10; // meant to be red
int shade = 20; // meant to be red
int hue = 20;   // meant to be green
...
int shade = color + hue;
```

the addition of a red integer and a green integer cannot be detected by a mistake by the compiler although it represents a programming mistake. The compiler is unable to help because the only type involved is the single type int. However, by introducing the Red, Green, and Blue classes this code becomes:

```
Red   color(10);  // meant to be red
Red   shade(20);  // meant to be red
Green hue(20);    // meant to be green
...
shade = color + hue;  // compile-time error
```

and the compiler is able to detect the unintended mixing of the two color values because of the extra types introduced by the Red, Green, and Blue classes.

The more general Color class can now be defined in terms of the three PrimaryColor classes. Each object of the Color class has encapsulated values that

Code Sample 8–13 *Type Conversions for the Color Class*

```
class Color
{
   private:
       Red    red;
       Green green;
       Blue  blue;

   public:
       Color(Red r, Green g, Blue b)
                   : red(r), green(g), blue(b) {}

       friend ostream& operator<< (ostream& os, const Color& color);

       friend Color    operator+ (Red    r, Color c);
       friend Color    operator+ (Green g, Color c);
       friend Color    operator+ (Blue   v, Color c);
       friend Color    operator+ (Color c, Red    r);
       friend Color    operator+ (Color c, Green g);
       friend Color    operator+ (Color c, Blue   b);

       friend Color    operator- (Red    r, Color c);
       friend Color    operator- (Green g, Color c);
       friend Color    operator- (Blue   v, Color c);
       friend Color    operator- (Color c, Red    r);
       friend Color    operator- (Color c, Green g);
       friend Color    operator- (Color c, Blue   b);

};
```

represent that color's combination of red, green, and blue intensities. Ignoring the possibility of type conversions, a first attempt at defining the operator overloading for the Color class is shown in Code Sample 8–13.

These cases are necessary to account for all the combinations of primary colors, whether the Color is the right- or left-hand operand, and whether the operation is addition or subtraction.

A cleaner solution can be obtained by using type conversion to elevate a PrimaryColor object to a Color object before applying the overloaded addition or subtraction operator, which leads to the class defined in Code Sample 8–14. In this class, the three constructors with a single argument play the role of type conversion operators because they produce an object of one class, a Color object, from an object of a different class, Red, Green, or Blue.

Code Sample 8–14 *Defining the Color Class Using Type Conversions*

```
class Color
{
  private:
    Red    red;
    Green  green;
    Blue   blue;

  public:
    Color(Red r, Green g, Blue b)
                    : red(r), green(g), blue(b) {}

    Color(const Red&    r) : red(r), green(0), blue(0) {}
                                     //convert Red to Color

    Color(const Green& g) : red(0), green(g), blue(0) {}
                                     //convert Green to Color

    Color(const Blue&  b) : red(0), green(0), blue(b) {}
                                     //convert Blue to Color

    friend ostream& operator<< (ostream& os, const Color& color);

    friend Color   operator+ (const Color& c1, const Color& c2);
    friend Color   operator- (const Color& c1, const Color& c2);
};
```

The compiler utilizes the type conversion implicitly when it encounters an expression involving objects that are not of the same class. For example, in the code

```
Color hue(Red(50), Green(50), Blue(50);
Color shade = Red(10) + hue;
```

the expression "Red(10) + hue" involves an operation between an object of the Red class and an object of the Color class. No operator overloading is immediately recognized for this case. However, there is available the overloaded addition operator in the Color class that provides a way of adding together two objects of that class. Furthermore, there is a type conversion that defines how to convert the Red object to a Color object. Thus, the last statement above would be interpreted as if the programmer had written

```
Color shade = Color(Red(10)) + hue;
```

For clarity, the programmer may prefer to write the code with the explicit type conversion operator. However, the compiler will supply the type conversion implicitly if such is required.

In summary, the use of type conversion operators, overloaded operators, and implicit type conversion by the compiler allows a compact set of operator overloadings to be written that provide for flexible ways of operating on value of different classes.

 Exercises

1. Include in the definition of the PrimaryColor class a type conversion operator that converts a PrimaryColor to an int. Rewrite the stream output operator so that it is no longer a friend function of the Primary-Color class.

2. Include in the definition of the PrimaryColor class a type conversion operator that converts a PrimaryColor to an int. Experiment with the effect this has on expressions that involve mixing objects of the Red, Green, and Blue classes, such as Red(10) + Green(5).

3. Construct a different design for the color classes in which the Red, Green, and Blue classes define type conversion operators that convert objects of their classes to Color objects. For example, the type conversion applied to the object Red(10) would yield the object Color(Red(10), Green(0), Blue(0)). You will need to redefine parts of the Color class to make this design work. Are there differences between this design and the one above?

4. Use the concepts of operator overloading and type conversions to define a Fraction class that could be used as follows:

```
Fraction f(3,2); // represents 3/2 = 1.5
Fraction g(5,3); // represents 5/3

...

Fraction h = f + 1;
Fraction i = 1 + f;
Fraction j = h - 1 + i;
```

Introduction to Design

9.1 Introduction to Object-Oriented Design

*T*he ability to *design* an object-oriented system is simultaneously the most important skill for a software developer to possess and the most elusive to learn. Design skill is important because a system's design determines to what extent the system realizes most of the crucial software-engineering principles such as separation, encapsulation, information hiding and key design goals such as abstraction and generalization. The skill of good object-oriented design is elusive because, like all design activities, it cannot be reduced to a mechanical process. Good designers bring to their task both native ability that emerges as insight and inspiration, and experience gained through practicing the art of object-oriented design on numerous software projects. While insight, inspiration, and experience cannot be articulated, the heuristic rules and guidelines that characterize a good design may be elicited for study.

The best way to develop design skill is to design systems using the techniques, representations, and patterns that have been developed by and are used by experienced designers. Design techniques are collections of strategies, questions, approaches, and rules that help to generate and shape ideas that lead to a good design. In this chapter, techniques are described for designing an individual class by analyzing a system's specification, a class-inheritance hierarchy from a collection of individual classes, and an extensible-object structure to cope with complex logic.

Design representations are graphical, semi-formal notations and diagrams that effectively communicate the critical aspects of a design structure. These representations are useful in that they externalize a designer's ideas so that they can be subject to analysis, evaluation, and comparison with alternative designs, act as a blueprint for those implementing the design, and document the final design for those performing later maintenance and extension. Design representations are described in this chapter for classes and class hierarchies, object structures, and object interactions.

Students of object-oriented design should study the artifacts (designs) produced by good designers in much the same way that art students study the great masters, architecture students study famous structures and buildings, and writing students study the classics in literature. For students of object-oriented design, the notion of a design pattern has recently emerged and allows great (or at least commonly needed and fundamental) designs to be studied.

Although these three elements of design—techniques, representations, and patterns—are described independently, their practical use must be integrated. Also, the material presented here is only a small part of what is known about object-oriented design: there are numerous design techniques, different representations, and a growing catalog of patterns.

9.2 Class Design

The ability to design a class is fundamental to developing good object oriented systems because the class is the basic programming unit—classes define individual abstractions, abstractions related through inheritance, and generalized abstractions in class templates. A good designer is one who can generate ideas for possible classes from a problem description and shape these ideas into a concrete class.

Knowledge of good class design is represented in the form of heuristic rules for discovering a class design and guidelines for evaluating a class design. The heuristics rules suggest things to look for in a specification that might indicate where a class could be defined. These rules have arisen from the accumulated experience of designers. However, designers must remember that heuristic rules do not guarantee a successful design, they may not apply in all cases, and they indicate only a starting point for further work. The guidelines are qualitative measures for evaluating a design. They can be viewed as a checklist of features that should be possessed by a good design. The designer must make an assessment of whether the class does or does not possess each feature. Because the measures are qualitative, good judgement on the part of the designer is important in applying such measures.

The heuristic rules and qualitative measures are used together in an iterative manner. It is not uncommon that a rule can suggest the beginning of a good class design—the rule triggers some thought in the mind of the designer which, though it usually lacks the detail of a complete class design, yields as it is develops the qualitative measures that can be applied to assess the emerging design. The measures can also help in making decisions about which design of several alternatives is most appropriate. The measures may suggest continuing with the design, backtracking and considering other alternatives, or even eliminating the idea from further consideration.

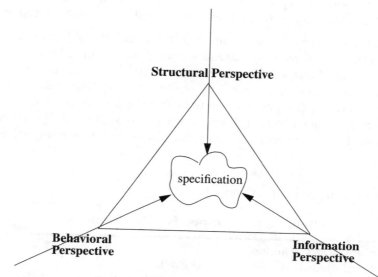

Figure 9-1   Three Perspectives

Discovering Class Design

Ideas for classes can be generated by considering the system specification from different perspectives. As shown in Fig. 9-1, three different perspectives are described and illustrated:

- behavioral perspective, emphasizing the actions of a system;
- structural perspective, emphasizing relationships among components; and
- information perspective, emphasizing the role of information and its manipulation.

Each perspective inspires ideas for possible classes by suggesting general categories of entities to look for in the specification, posing certain kinds of questions that might be asked about the system, and focusing on a particular dimension of the overall system to concentrate the designer's thinking. The combination of these three perspectives is a large category of commonly encountered classes.

Behavioral Perspective

The behavioral perspective centers on the actions that a system takes. The analysis of actions is a natural starting point because systems are often described in terms of what the system does. In a similar sense, software is developed to accomplish some end and is purchased because of what it can do. Terms such as "accomplish" and "do" illustrate the fundamental role of a system's activity.

The purpose of identifying an action is to reveal the object that performs the action. In the object oriented view of software an action is performed by the method(s) of some object(s). Simple actions might be performed by a single object. More complex actions might require the collaboration of several objects. In each case, however, the actions emanate from a performing cast of objects. Natural questions to ask about each action are given in Table 9–1; their answers begin to reveal the components and organization of the underlying object structure.

Table 9–1 Behavioral Perspective Questions

Behavioral Perspective Questions
What object initiates the action?
What objects collaborate in performing the action?
What objects are altered by the performance of the action?
What objects are interrogated during the action?

The study of a system's actions often leads to objects that fall into well-known general categories. General categories of objects that are often associated with actions are actor, reactor, agent, and transformer.

An **actor** has a specific purpose, mission, agenda, goal, outcome, or plan. It knows what result at least a part of the system is meant to achieve, and it is equipped with the programming to drive the system toward this result. An actor object may embody knowledge about and enforce the sequencing of activities that must occur; contain strategies for evaluating and selecting among different ways to achieve the result; and have ways of coping with exceptional conditions by recovery, backtracing, or graceful termination.

A **reactor** responds to events which are characterized by the fact that they are asynchronous and cannot be scheduled in advance, such as in an interactive drawing programing, where the user may be allowed to select a shape on the screen by clicking a mouse button at any time. Events may originate from a variety of sources, three categories of which are:

- **internal events:** events generated by other objects within the system itself. For example, a timer object may generate an event that signals the end of a prescribed time interval. The reactor object must determine what should occur at this time and initiate the corresponding action. A specific situation is an animation sequence in which the reactor must arrange for the next step in the animation to occur.

- **external events:** events originating in another system. A toolkit, for instance, may have several interacting programs that share data. When one of the programs updates the data, the other programs must react accordingly. A specific case of this is a spreadsheet program that creates the data for a table appearing in a document-formatting program. When the spreadsheet recomputes new values for the table, the formatting system must update its document in response.
- **interface events:** events initiated by the user through mouse movements (dragging, clicking), keyboard actions (pressing or releasing keys), or interactive user-interface components (buttons, sliders). The system may contain different reactor objects for these different types of user events.

Regardless of the event's source, the reactor object must determine the appropriate reaction and at least initiate the response. Some reactor objects maintain a state or history of past events, and their reaction to the current event is conditioned by this history. For example, a mouse-event reactor that needs to distinguish between a single click and a double click needs to keep track of information about the recent past. Other reactor objects are stateless and always have the same reaction. For example, a "center text" button always reacts in exactly the same way, whatever the data.

In the third category of objects associated with actions is an **agent** which is an intermediary that assists other objects in some way. The purpose of the agent is twofold: first, to relieve the other objects of the responsibility for performing the service that the agent provides; second, to conceal or hide the details of how the agent performs its service. Agent objects promote reuse because they can be used in any system where their service is needed. Agent object improve the reliability and flexibility of a system through information hiding because no other part of the system is aware of how the agent's service is implemented. An agent may play one of several roles:

- **Messenger**: this type of agent provides a data-delivery service through which one part of the system can relay information to other parts of the system. Like postal systems and package delivery companies, the messenger relieves the sender of the responsibility of locating the recipient, arranging for the transportation, tracking the progress of the item, and arranging the delivery. Distributed mail systems, for example, depend on message agents.
- **Server**: this type of agent is essential to the client-server model; common use of servers is as producers or consumers of data. The server relieves its clients of the burden of knowing where and how the data is stored. Servers may obtain the data from local tables, disk files, network connections to

remote databases, or generate the data via simulation. In all cases, the client is protected from the details of how the server performs its task.

- **Finder**: this type of agent locates particular data or other objects. For example, the messenger agent may employ the services of a finder agent to locate a recipient, or the server agent may use one to locate a particular record in a database. The finder contains knowledge of how and where to search for the desired entity and how to recognize the sought for entity when it is discovered.

- **Communicator**: this type of agent engages in dialogue with the user. A variety of user-interface devices may be used by the communicator to provide its service; for example, a communicator interacting with the user to obtain the name of a file where data is to be found or placed might conduct a simple fill-in-the-box dialog, allowing the user to select a file from a list of filenames that the communicator found in a particular directory, or allowing the user to navigate through the file system seeking the desired file.

Many other kinds of agents exist. These four are meant only to suggest the kinds of objects included in this category.

In the fourth and final category of objects associated with actions is a **transformer**. A transformer object alters in some way the data that passes through it. A transformer often has very little knowledge of either the producer or the consumer of the data and little understanding of the meaning of the data that it is manipulating. These limitations reflect the narrow scope of the transformer object. Two examples of transformers are:

- **Formatter**: this type of transformer changes the appearance of the data. Commonly encountered formatters are dislayers, marshallers, and encoders. A displayer object renders its data in a human readable form. Low-level displayers are similar to the stream I/O objects that change the binary (internal) representation of a value into the string representation shown to the user. A high-level displayer is a paragraph object that knows how to align the text contained in a paragraph and arrange for line breaks, hyphenation, and spacing. A marshaller object is responsible for creating a linearized representation of its data. Marshaller objects are used in file operations to pack data into blocks for more efficient use of disk operations and in remote operation systems to pack the arguments of an operation into a single buffer. An encoder object is used to change the appearance of the data, though not into a human-readable form. Encoders are used to convert data into a standard representation format so that it can be exchanged with other programs and encrypt the data for secure communication over untrusted networks.

- **Filters**: this type of transformer screens the data for certain characteristics. The filter removes from the data any item that does not meet its criteria. For example, a filter may remove all lines in a text file that do not contain a search keyword. Other filters might look for patterns in the data, or other more complex search criteria. Web search engines and library catalog searchers are large-scale examples of filters. Transformer objects are often used in a sequenced or pipelined arrangement; a filter transformer may select data from a database, pass the selected items to a displayer transformer to put it into human-readable form, and pass this data through an encrypter transformer for secure transmission.

Structural Perspective

Classes can be discovered by focusing on the relationships described or implied by a specification. A relationship defines a pattern, organization, or structure among a set of entities. Since the entities are likely candidates for classes, discovering and analyzing the relationships is a way of discovering classes. This is a productive approach because the statement of a system's functionality often involves the use of relationships to explain the intended nature of some part of the systems; words or phrases like *consists of, uses, enforces, maintains*, and *group of* all indicate relationships.

A relationship can be analyzed by asking questions that identify the classes and objects it implies, as listed in Table 9–2. The answers to these questions lead the designer from the relationship to classes of objects that are in some way involved with it.

Table 9–2 Structural Perspective Questions

Structural Perspective Questions
What objects are involved in the relationship?
What objects are necessary to sustain (implement, realize, maintain) the relationship?
What objects not in the relationship are aware of and exploit the relationship?
What objects not in the relationship are used by the related objects?

Study of a system's structure often leads to objects that fall into well-known general categories. General categories of objects that are often associated with particular structures are acquaintance, containment, and collection.

The first category of objects that can be discovered from the structural perspective is **acquaintance**. In an acquaintance structure, some objects know about one or more of the other objects. This is the simplest form of structural relationship that allows one object to interact with another. Concretely, one object would have a pointer or a reference to the object that it knows about. There are two kinds of acquaintance relationships: symmetric and asymmetric.

- **Symmetric**: an acquaintance in which the objects are mutually acquainted; they know about one another. For example, in a drawing tool, a Rectangle object and a Canvas object may know about each other. The Canvas is acquainted with the Rectangle, and other similar objects that appear on the Canvas, so that the Canvas knows how to redraw itself. The Rectangle is acquainted with the Canvas because the Rectangle object contains the detailed information on how the Rectangle should be drawn (location, shape, color, etc.) using the methods provided by the Canvas (e.g., DrawLine).

- **Asymmetric**: an acquaintance is which the known object is unaware of the knowing object. For example, in a system where a Clock object is started by the user pressing a *Start* Button, the Button object must know about the Clock object, but the Clock object need not know about the Button object.

There are certain properties that apply to both forms of acquaintance. The acquaintance may be persistent or transitory. A persistent acquaintance is one that lasts for a substantial period of time, perhaps even throughout the entire execution of the system. A transitory acquaintance lasts for only a short time, maybe just the duration of one method invocation. The acquaintance may also be direct or indirect. In a direct acquaintance, one object may immediately refer to the other. In an indirect acquaintance, some intermediary object must be accessed in order to refer to the known object.

Containment objects may be discovered from the structural perspective as well. In a containment structure the objects form a part-whole structure. Terms in the specification like *contains*, *consists of*, and *has* are indicative of a containment relationship. Two uses of the containment relationship are:

- **Collaborator**: a structure in which the whole is created by the interaction of it parts. Two different areas of a system where collaborative relationships might be sought are in the description of the application-specific entities and in the user interface. An application-specific entity description might state: "A StopWatch consists of a clock display, a Start button and a Stop button. The clock display has two hands and the numerals 1 through 12 arranged in a 12-hour clock manner." The containment relationship occurs twice in this description. First, the StopWatch is described as having three components contained within it: a clock display and two buttons. Second, the clock display is described as having two components: the hands and the numerals. In a containment relation, the containing entity is represented as a class whose aggregated objects are of classes defined by the contained entities. In the StopWatch example, the StopWatch class would aggregate objects of the ClockDisplay and Button classes. Similarly, the class ClockDisplay would aggregate objects of the ClockHands and ClockNumerals classes. Containment relationships can also be found in the description of the user-interface structure; as in "The drawing tool interface has a drawing area and three menus through which the user can control the operations of the tool." The word *has* denotes the containment relationship between a DrawingTool class and the aggregated objects it contains, namely, an object of the DrawingArea class and three objects of the Menu class.

- **Controller**: a controller object exerts substantial, and possibly total, control over its objects. An example of a controller is the Boss in the Boss-Worker model: in this model, units of work, called tasks, are presented to the Boss by client objects. The Boss delegates a task to a Worker, which performs the tasks and delivers the result to the Boss. The result then is forwarded to the client. In a controller structure, the Workers are completely concealed by the Boss and are invisible to the client. The Workers usually have no contact with each other and even may have no contact with other objects except for the Boss object. In some cases, the Workers perform identical actions and the Boss delegates the task to the next available Worker. This situation frequently arises in parallel-processing computations where each Worker may be on a separate processor, or in programs with multiple independent threads where each Worker has its own thread of control. In other cases, each Worker performs a distinct computation. For example, the Boss may play the role of a DataSource while each Worker represents a different, specific source (a LocalFile Worker, a RemoteFile Worker, a DataBase Worker, etc.).

The structural perspective may also reveal **collection** objects. In a collection structure, the individual objects maintain their external visibility. Collection is similar to containment in that both are groupings, but collection differs from containment in that collection does not totally conceal the grouped objects, whereas containment completely aggregates and hides them. The variations among collections are determined by the nature and the degree of control that is imposed on the group. Three kinds of collections are peer, iteration, and coordinator. The first two of these exert limited control on their objects. Coordinators have greater influence over their members. The three kinds of collections are:

- **Peer**: a collection in which objects are of equal status (hence the name) and are undifferentiated by the collection, which imposes no control over them. The collection exists simply to give a name to the logical structure of the objects that it contains and, perhaps, to provide resources for these objects to use. Such a form of collection is described in the statement: "The user interface has three buttons to start, stop, and reset the system." The three buttons form a logical grouping; the word *has* suggests a possible containment relation. However, the object may not be completely aggregated by the grouping, and so a peer collection might be more appropriate. Thus, a class ControlButtons might be created to represent the group. In practical terms, the ControlButtons might provide resources that are needed by the button objects in the graphical user interface system. The three button objects are peer objects within the ControlButtons group.

- **Iterator**: a collection providing some indexing (ordering, sorting) function over its objects. The grouped objects are not necessarily of the same class but they have a shared interface that allows the group to realize the indexing function. The indexing may be as simple as the order in which the objects were added to the collection (as, for example, items in a pull-down menu) or more complicated (as, for example, items in a database indexed by a key field).

- **Coordinator**: a collection designed to maintain some property or invariant condition among its objects. For example, a RadioButton collection may enforce the property that only one among all of the Button objects in the RadioButton may be in the "pushed" state at any one time. Thus, pushing one of the buttons has the side effect of unpushing any other previously pushed button. The coordinator exerts some control over the objects in the collection, but the coordinated objects maintain their visibility, and can be known and operated upon by objects outside of the collection. The collection is intended not to conceal the coordinated objects but to assist these objects in implementing a group-wide property.

Information Perspective

Classes can be discovered by examining the information content of a system and the way such information is manipulated. This point of view is useful because information processing is a significant aspect of most software systems, as reflected by terms like "information systems" and "information age" in relation to computerized systems. In some cases, information-processing capabilities are the most important services a system can offer to its users. The specifications of these systems are especially concerned with describing the information and its manipulation.

Information can be viewed as data or state. In simple terms, data is the information processed by the system and state is information used by the system to perform that processing. As an example of the difference between data and state, the specification of a document preparation system might refer to the notion of a paragraph. The user of the system defines the words that make up the paragraph—the paragraph's data. When processing this paragraph, the system may have state information such as a variable that determines if the end of paragraph has been reached. This variable determines whether the paragraph processing will continue or terminate. While the distinction between data and state information cannot always be perfectly drawn, the differences are often clear enough that it useful to make the distinction.

Table 9–3 enumerates four factors that distinguish data from state information. Data is user-centered information and is defined in terms of concepts in the application domain. In contrast, state information is primarily an artifact of the system itself: the state information may change if the system design changes, but the data usually remains unaffected by changes in the system (except, of course, if the system is changed to require different data or data in a different format). The lifetime of data exceeds the lifetime of the system's execution, while state information does not. For example, in the document-preparation system, the paragraph data exists before, during, and after the execution of the system. However, the state information indicating the end of paragraph has been reached only has meaning and existence while the program is executing. Finally, data is of direct concern to the user—who is using the system precisely because the system processes the data in some manner. However, the user is not interested in the state information that the system maintains for its own use.

Table 9–3 Distinctions Between Data and State

Factor	Data	State
Primary Focus	Application/User	Program/System
Role	processed by system	guides processing
Lifetime	exists beyond program execution	same as program's execution
Source/Visibility	user	system

When data or state information is referred to in a specification, some of the questions that can be asked about the information in order to identify classes and objects related to the information are shown in Table 9–4.

Table 9–4 Information Perspective Questions

Information Perspective Questions
What objects are needed to represent the data or state?
What objects read the data or interrogate the state
What objects write the data or update the state?

The study of a system's information often leads to objects that fall into well-known general categories. Some of the object categories of ten relevant to data are:

- **Source or sinks:** a repository of data outside of the system. A source is any entity outside of the program (system) that generates data, and a sink is any entity outside of the program (system) that receives data. An entity can be both a source and a sink; an updatable database is an example. Sources and sinks include local files and databases, remote files and databases, and servers. Objects that directly represent the sources and sinks should always be considered in the design. Reader objects and writer objects are obvious kinds of objects to consider for each source and sink, respectively.

- **Query**: the description of the data sought from a source. In the simplest case—reading sequentially from the source—the description is empty; the mere fact that the query is attempted implies what is sought by the program. For a randomly accessed source, the query may simply contain an index of the required record or block of data. In more complicated cases—highly structured databases, for example—the query may contain a wealth of information indicating how to select, combine, reduce, and reorder information in the database. The role of the query object is to provide a simply programmed interface by which this complex information can be managed most effectively.

- **Result**: the data returned by a source or directed to a sink. In the simpler cases, the result may be nothing more than a block of data. More complex cases arise when dealing with more complicated data organizations. For example, a digital library system might return as the result of a query a set of titles that satisfy the query and rank them by some relevance criteria. Here, the object that represents the result has a more intricate structure and a more sophisticated interface. Correspondingly, the program may generate a complex result that has to be transmitted to the sink in a sequence of more primitive, lower-level operations. The purpose of the result object is to provide an interface that relieves the other parts of the system of the burden of being aware of the lower-level details of how the complex data is communicated to sources or sinks.

- **Buffer**: multiple logical data items contained in one physical unit. The data is transferred from the source or to the sink in terms of the physical units of data. Buffers are often used to improve the performance of lower-level I/O operations. For example, more efficient use is made of network bandwidth and disk controllers if data is written in fewer, larger blocks. A buffer for a sink gathers the data written to it by the program and actually transmits this accumulated data as one physical unit when the buffer is sufficiently full. A buffer for a source reads the data in larger physical units and delivers this data as requested by the program. When the buffer is empty, another physical unit is obtained from the source.

- **Cache**: an object anticipating the need for data not yet requested by the program. A cache for a source might read ahead, trying to guess what data the program will request next. If the cache's guess is a good one, the program will discover that its requested data is readily available. This effect, improving the latency of lower-level I/O operations, is the principle motivation for a cache. The extent to which a cache is successful depends on how accurately it can guess the future needs of the program. In some situations, effective caching strategies are possible—for instance, a cache for a sink might retain previously written data in expectation that this data might be requested again in the near future. Another example is in a digital library system where it may be a good guess that additional data about the titles given in response to a user's query are likely to be requested in the near future.

- **Synchronizers**: enforcers of timing or sequencing constraints. Constraints are usually necessary to ensure the correct operation of a source or sink. For example, a source may only work correctly if read operations are performed sequentially (i.e., each read operation is issued only after the previous read operation has completed). More complex constraints might exist for an updatable database that imposes the restriction that write operations cannot take place while a read operation is in progress. In this case, a synchronizer object is needed to regulate the reading and writing activity.

In addition to these classes of objects, iterators and transformers, discussed earlier in this section, are also frequently relevant to the information perspective. Iterators and transformers can be discovered from the structural or behavioral perspectives, respectively.

General categories of objects that are frequently relevant to state are:

- **Recorder**: a representation of the current state of the system. All information needed to evaluate the current condition of the system is contained in recorder objects. The state information stored includes the processing options that currently apply (e.g., the current drawing color), the current mode of the system (e.g., "add" or "delete" mode), the prevailing boundary conditions ("there can be no more than 100 sides on a polygon"), and program flags (e.g., "shape currently selected"). Because the state information is of such varied character, there may be several classes each of which represents a related part of the current state of the system.

- **Scheduler**: able to prioritize a system's currently available courses of action. In sequential programs, any one of a variety of actions may possibly produce the desired answer. For example, in a maze search program, there are several alternative paths to test at each intersection. The role of the scheduler is to determine in what order these possibilities are evaluated. In concurrent programs—programs with multiple independent threads of control—the scheduler is responsible for selecting which thread to execute next from among all threads that are capable of executing. The scheduler may take a variety of application-specific details into account in making its selection.

- **Maintainer**: determine the actions to take in the current state of the system and determine the next system state. In simple systems, every action of which the system is capable can be performed at any time. In such simple systems the maintainer is trivial and perhaps not even needed. However, in more complex systems, the system's response is dependent on previous actions ("a paste can only occur after a cut or copy operation"), the current mode of the system ("in add mode a new shape is placed where the user clicks while in delete mode the shape where the user clicks is removed"), or the current recorded state ("if a shape is selected then highlight the shape"). In these more complex systems, the maintainers must be more highly structured; the correct design and implementation of the maintainers can be the most challenging issue faced by the developer. A structured design technique is available to design and implement complex maintainers.

Combining the Three Perspectives

Table 9–5 summarizes the combined categories of classes that are discussed above. Though these categories are not exhaustive and are meant only to illustrate the varied kinds of objects that can be discovered by analyzing a specification, they provide a useful foundation for beginning the analysis of a specification.

The three perspectives are meant to be used together and in combination. For example, an initial analysis of a specification may discover a data source (information perspective), and study of the data source reveals the need for a filter (behavioral perspective) to process the data from the source. Further analysis may discover that the filter has an asymmetric acquaintance (structural perspective) with a communicator (behavioral perspective). The communicator conveys its output to a buffer (information perspective) that is connected to a sink (information perspective). As illustrated by this example, an object in one perspective may lead to objects in another perspective.

Table 9–5 Combining All Three Perspectives

Behavioral	Structural	Information
• **actors**	• **acquaintances**	• **data**
• **reactors**	• symmetric	• sources/sink
• system events	• asymmetric	• queries
• external events	• **containment**	• results
• user events	• collaboration	• buffers
	• controllers	• caches
• **agents**	• **collection**	• synchronizers
• messengers	• peers	• **state**
• servers	• iterations	• recorders
• finders	• coordinators	• schedulers
• communicators		• maintainers
• **transformers**		
• formatters		
• filters		

Evaluating A Class Design

A proposed class design must be evaluated to determine whether the proposed design should be accepted, revised, or rejected. In the early stages of design many ideas for classes may be discovered. In fact, it is a good practice to generate as many ideas as can be thought of in a brainstorming and uncritical mode. The goal of this early phase is to discover possible classes. At a later stage a possible class must be analyzed to determine if it is substantial enough to be represented as a class, if it duplicates or overlaps with another class, or whether it should be refined into two or more other classes.

Five aspects of a proposed class design should be evaluated as shown in Table 9–6. All of these aspects should be considered for each class. It may also be useful to apply them in the order listed since this ordering proceeds from the highest to the lowest level of detail.

Table 9–6 Class Design Evaluation

Class Design Evaluation
Abstraction: does the class capture a useful abstraction?
Responsibilities: does the class bear a reasonable set of responsibilities?
Interface: is the interface of the class clean and simple?
Usage: is the class design consistent with how it is actually used?
Implementation: is their a reasonable implementation for the class?

The abstraction captured by the class is the first aspect of a class design to evaluate. Recall that capturing an abstraction is the most fundamental role of a class, so this is most critical. The abstraction may come from the application domain (e.g., Automobile or Employee), from the user interface (e.g., StartButton or FileChooser), or from the computation (e.g., ListManager or MenuBar). Specific tests to determine the adequacy of the abstraction are:

- **Identity**: simple and suggestive names for the class and for all of its operations can be found if a class captures an abstraction. Difficulty in finding a good name for a class or its operations is usually a sign of a weak abstraction, as are names that contain vague modifiers. For example, terms like simple or complex in a name should be questioned, particularly if they are not derived from application domain terms. If an application has some labels that contain only letters and digits and other labels that can contain any character, referring to these as "SimpleLabel" and "ComplexLabel" is not helpful. Unless there are more meaningful application terms for these labels, better names might be AlphaNumericLabel and Label. In these names the vague meaning of "simple" has been replaced by a more specific indication of the class's intent and the vague meaning of "complex" has been dealt with by simply eliminating the modifier. The same rule applies to the methods of a class.

- **Clarity**: the meaning of a class can be given in a brief, dictionary-style definition. The definition should be short (the equivalent of one or two short, declarative sentences), use precise terms, and fully convey the intent of the class. A definition of this form is difficult to write because it requires careful thought and precise use of language. However, the effort to construct this definition leads to a confirmation that the class is well defined, creates a compact reference for potential reusers of the class, and establishes a basis for the class's documentation.

- **Uniformity**: the operations defined for the class should have a uniform level of abstraction. This means that the names and arguments of the class's methods must be at a similar level of conceptualization. For example, consider the following partial class definition:

```
class ShapeManager
{...
 public:
    ...
    AddShape(Shape* s);
    RemoveShape(Shape* s);
    ReplaceShape(Shape* by, Shape* with);
    FindRectangle(Rectangle r);
    ...
};
```

In the ShapeManager class, all of the methods refer to objects of the class Shape except for the single method FindRectangle, whose name and argument refers to a lower-level concept. The uniformity of this class can be improved by eliminating the FindRectangle method or replacing it with a FindShape method that is consistent with the level of conceptualization of the other methods of the class.

Second to be evaluated are the responsibilities assigned to the class. A class's responsibilities are what it is expected to remember over time, the effects it is expected to have on other parts of the system, and the services that it is expected to provide for other objects in the system. Specific tests to determine the adequacy of a class's responsibilities are the extent to which the responsibilities are:

- **clear**: it should be easy to determine whether or not the class is charged with a specific responsibility. Any doubts about a class's responsibilities signal danger because it raises the possibility that the specifier, the implementor, and the user of the class may all have different interpretations of the class's responsibilities. This lack of common understanding can only lead to unwelcome situations.

- **limited**: the responsibilities placed upon a class should not exceed those required by the abstraction on which it is based. Adding extraneous responsibilities obscures the purpose of the class, confounds (re)users, and increases the difficulty of implementing the class.

- **coherent**: the responsibilities of a class should make sense as a whole. Coherence is lost when two distinct abstractions are represented by the same class. When this occurs, the responsibilities of the class will represent the union of the responsibilities associated with each of the two abstractions. Because the abstractions are distinct, though perhaps similar, the overall responsibilities of the class loses coherence.

- **complete**: the responsibilities given to a class must completely capture those of the corresponding abstraction. Not only does a missing responsibility weaken the class of which it should be a part, but it also disturbs the coherence of the other class(es) in which the responsibility is placed.

The interface of the class is the third aspect of a class to be evaluated. A well-designed class interface is clearly important; it is the concrete programming device by which objects of the class are manipulated. Programmers are more likely to (re)use, and to (re)use correctly, a class that has a well-designed interface. Specific aspects of a class's methods to assess are:

- **naming**: the names of the methods should clearly express the method's intended effect on the object. Methods that have different effects should be given names that are distinctly different. A class can be confusing and even hazardous to use if the names of methods with different effects are too similar. For example, consider the following class interface:

```
class ItemList
{...
   public:
      void Delete(Item item);
            // take Item's node out of list and delete Item
      void Remove(Item item);
            // take Item's node out of list but do not delete Item
      void Erase (Item item);
            // keep Item's node in list, but with no information
};
```

Each of these methods has a different effect on the List and on the parameter Item, but their names are easily confused. Many programming mistakes could easily arise if Delete is used when Remove or Erase is intended. The remedy for this situation might be deeper than a simple change of names in the interface; the entire class design might need to be reconsidered.

- **symmetry**: if a class has a pair of inverse operations, the names and effects of the corresponding methods should be clear. A typical example of symmetric operations is the pair of accessor methods for a class property X that might be named GetX and SetX to reflect their mutual relation to the property X. The interface should be reexamined if it has only one of a pair of inverse operations (e.g., a "get" method but not a "set" method). Is there a sound design decision to provide only one of the pair? If not, include the missing operation.

- **flexibility**: the methods of the class, particularly the constructor, should be overloaded to provide a variety of different uses. There are three ways in which overloading increases the flexibility of the interface. First, it allows the method to be invoked using the form of data that is most readily available at the invoking site. For example, consider the class interface

```
class ItemList
{...
  public:
     ...
     AddItem(Item item, int index);
     Item FindItem(int index);
     ...
};
```

that identifies Item objects by their position ("index") in a list. If it is known that character string data is often available at the invoking site (the index has been read as a character string), then it is reasonable to consider adding overloaded AddItem and FindItem method that allow the index to be given as a character string. Via this overloading, the class assumes the responsibility of converting the character string to an integer index.

Second, overloading allows only the necessary arguments to be supplied. The interface can be tailored to allow the invocation to assume more or less control over the details of the operation: the more parameters in an overloading, the more control is given to the invocation. For example, the class below contain several overloadings of a Draw method:

```
class DrawingArea
{...
  public:
    ...
    void Draw(Shape s);
    void Draw(Shape s, Color outline);
    void Draw(Shape s, Color outline, Color fill);
    ...
};
```

The programmer using a DrawingArea object can ignore the Color parameters if they are not relevant or if the Colors selected by the DrawingArea object itself are acceptable. However, the programmer is able, when needed, to use the overloadings that allow one or both of the Colors to be specified.

Third, overloading can be used to relieve the programmer of remembering the order of arguments. For example, the AddItem method in the ItemList class above requires both an Item and an index. An overloading could be provided so that the Item and the index could be specified in either order. Overloading should only be used, of course, when the overloaded methods all have exactly the same effect on the object.

- **convenience**: default values provide a more convenient way to use methods. The parameters of the class's methods should be arranged in an order that allows default values to be supplied wherever possible. Question whether a default can be provided for each parameter, rearranging the methods or possibly introducing a new method to allow the default to be expressed.

The fourth aspect of a class to be evaluated is its usage. An otherwise well-designed class may lack useful methods because it is often difficult for the class designer to foresee all of the important contexts in which the class may be used. By examining how the objects of the class are used in different contexts, it is possible to discover these missing operations. For example, consider the following definition and use of the Location class:

```
class Location
{ private:
     int xCoord, yCoord; // coordinates
  public:
     Location(int x, int y);
     int XCoord(); // return xCoord value
     int YCoord(); // return yCoord value
};
...
//usage
Location point(100,100);
...
point = Location(point.XCoord()+5, point.YCoord()+10);
                   // shift point
```

The code to shift the point relative to its current coordinates is possible using the existing interface of the Location class. If the Location class is commonly used in this way, the class designer should consider adding a new method to it. The revised definition and use are:

```
class Location
{ private:
     int xCoord, yCoord;                  // coordinates
  public:
     Location(int x, int y);
     int XCoord();                        // return xCoord value
     int YCoord();                        // return yCoord value
     void ShiftBy(int dx, int dy);
                   // shift point relative to current coordinates
};
...
//usage
Location point(100,100);
...
point.ShiftBy(5,10); // shift point
```

This change in the class design improves both the simplicity and readability of the code using the Location class.

The implementation of the class is the fifth and final aspect to be evaluated. The implementation is the most detailed, the most easily changed, and the least important of all of the aspects of a class. A class that represents a sound abstraction and has a well-designed interface can always be given a better implementation if the class's existing implementation is weak. The implementation can, however, point to two ways in which a class can be improved. First, an unwieldy and complex implementation may indicate that the class is not well conceived or is simply not implementable. In this case, the design of the class and its underlying abstraction must be reconsidered. Second, an overly complex implementation may also indicate that the class has been given too much responsibility. If this is the case, then either the class can be partitioned into two or more classes, or new classes can be developed that are used internally by the original class. The first strategy is visible to the users of the class while the second strategy is invisible. In either instance, new classes are developed which may help to reveal previously missing abstractions in the application domain or may simply be useful classes in the computational structure.

 Exercises

Read the description of a data visualization system in Table 9–7 and then answer the questions below.

1. Using the behavioral perspective, identify several classes for the Data Visualization System.

2. Evaluate the classes that are found in terms of their abstraction, responsibilities, and interface.

3. Using the behavioral perspective, identify several classes for the Data Visualization System.

4. Evaluate the classes that are found in terms of their abstraction, responsibilities, and interface.

5. Using the behavioral perspective, identify several classes for the Data Visualization System.

6. Evaluate the classes that are found in terms of their abstraction, responsibilities, and interface.

9.3 Class Hierarchy Design

Basic Principles

The design of a class hierarchy embodies a scheme for classifying a set of related classes according to a generalization-specialization principle. As shown in Fig. 9–2, there are three directions in the tree-structured hierarchy. Classes toward the top of the hierarchy (toward the root of the tree) are more generalized classes. The similarities among classes at one level are elevated to the classes at the next higher (more generalized) level. In the opposite direction, the classes descending from a given class are specializations of that class. Each specialization adds behavior and/or data that simultaneously makes the specialized class more specific, more capable, and less general. The specializing class is a refinement of the more general base class from which it is derived. The third direction in the

Table 9–7 Specification of a Data Visualization System

Specification of a Data Visualization System

Many applications in science and engineering disciplines generate large volumes of data that must be understood by the scientist or engineer. Because of the volume of data (megabytes of numerical data) it is difficult or impossible to easily understand the import of the data or to recognize a critical point in the data.

Develop a data visualization systems that provides a scientist or engineer with a two-dimensional graphical representation of a large set of data. Through computer graphics techniques and effective use of colors, the system allows the user to navigate within the displayed representation, to request specific details of a particular part of the data, to see the representation change over time, or to filter the data on which the representation is based.

The basic functions of the visualization systems are:

selection: the user must be able to select the file containing the data that is input to the visualization system. The user initiates the selection through a button in the user interface.

representation: the data is limited to display on a two-dimensional x-y coordinate system. The axis of this system must be drawn and some labeling of the axis must be given. The user, through the file format or through the user interface, must have some means of determining what symbol will be used to represent the data (e.g., a small filled point, an alphabetical letter, a cross-hair).

filtering: the user must be able to set the limits of the x-y coordinates that are presented in the display. For example, a user might specify that the data to be displayed must have an x coordinate between −100.0 and +100.0 while the y value must be in the range from 50.2 to 125.5. Data values outside of this range are ignored. The axis in the representation must be scaled so that the selected range extends across the entire area allocated to the representation. In other words, by selecting successively smaller ranges, the user will have the effect of "zooming" in on a part of the data.

timed display: the user must have a way of requesting that the data be displayed in a time sequence with additional data appearing at each time step. It is possible that a different file format may be required to support this option.

The user interface for the data visualization system contains a display area (a Canvas object) on which the data is displayed on a x-y axis. The user interface also contains a number of TextBoxes in which the user enters the limits of each axis for filtering the data. A number of buttons are present to control different options or initiate different functions (e.g., open a new file, begin timed display).

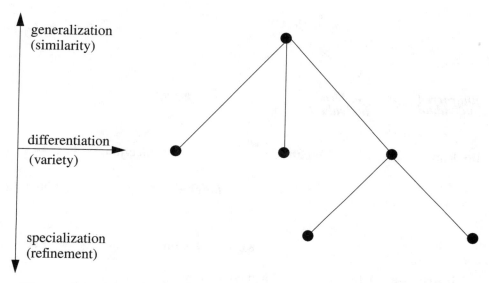

Figure 9–2 Inheritance Dimensions

hierarchy is across the classes that have the same immediate parent class. Each of these peer classes specializes the parent class in a different way, creating variety among the derived classes.

The role of the class hierarchy designer is not only to design the class hierarchy but also to create a rationalization of the class hierarchy. Rationalization in this sense means the creation of a logical, well reasoned (i.e., a rational) explanation for the organization of the hierarchy. The rationalization is concretely presented in the form of a logical condition that describes the refinement introduced by each specializing class. The logical conditions serve two purposes. First, the logical conditions identify the way in which the generalized (base) class is refined by the specialized (derived) class. Thus, the generalization-specialization direction in the class hierarchy is rationalized. Second, the difference between two peer classes can be understood by comparing their logical conditions. Through this comparison the variety (differentiation) direction in the class hierarchy is rationalized.

As an example of a rationalized class hierarchy, a small portion of Smalltalk's much more elaborate class hierarchy is shown in Fig. 9–3. In this portion of the class hierarchy, the universe of all Objects is divided into three classes: Boolean represents an object with unordered values, Magnitude represents individual objects that can be ordered with respect to each other, and Collection represents groups of objects as opposed to individual values. Individual ordered objects (i.e., the derived classes of Magnitude) are distinguished by the nature of the scale that determines how the objects are compared. The Char class has no scale; it is a simple predefined ordering

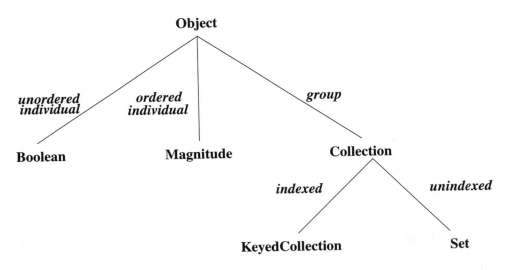

Figure 9–3   A Rationalized Class Hierarchy

of it elements. Individual objects of the Char class can be compared to each other but there is no sense of distance in the ordering. For example, the character A comes before the character B, but there is no sense that A is closer to or farther away from B than B is from C. The Number class is defined by a one-dimensional scale (such as for integers or floating-point numbers) where distance is an integral part of the nature of the values of this class. The Point class is defined by a two-dimensional scale, such as a Cartesian space or a computer screen. In contrast to ordered values are groups of objects represented by the Collection class. Two different collections are shown: Set and KeyedCollection. The rationalization for these two subclasses is that the objects of a KeyedCollection are indexed by the key value associated with each object, while the objects in a Set are unindexed. This rationalization of the class hierarchy makes it easier to understand the organization of the concepts in the hierarchy and guides where an extension should be made if new classes are added to the hierarchy.

There is a general strategy for finding a class hierarchy and its rationalization. The strategy has three steps:

1. Analyze all classes that have the same immediate parent (or, at the beginning, all classes).

2. Divide the classes into groups based on discriminating properties; all classes in a group should share the discriminating property associated with that group, which no class outside of the group has.

3. Establish a base class for each group; the discriminating properties are the rationalization of the base classes.

These three steps are repeated iteratively until all the classes have been categorized, at which point there is a rationalization for the class hierarchy. It may be that not all of the classes can be placed into groups in the second step. These other classes can be considered again in a later iteration. The Flight Control Panel example below applies this general strategy in the design of a class hierarchy.

The rationalization of a class hierarchy is an important element in object-oriented software design for several reasons. First of all, it is a test of the adequacy of the class hierarchy. An inability to define the logical conditions among classes is a sign that the class hierarchy is not well founded. Additional work or a different approach is needed to complete the rationalization.

Second, it is a way of explaining and justifying the class hierarchy. The names of the classes and the logical conditions among them create a vocabulary and a set of relationships by which the designer can articulate the design of the class hierarchy. This vocabulary also lends insight into how the designer conceives of the concepts in the application domain.

Rationalization also furnishes a concrete artifact for debate and discussion. A class hierarchy embodies a way of thinking about the concepts in the application domain; members of the development team can use it as a device to test whether their conceptualizations of the application domain entities are similar. Such a comparison is impossible without a concrete, shared, external representation such as the one provided by the class hierarchy.

Similarly, it provides a means of understanding the class hierarchy. A (re)user of the class hierarchy can use the logical conditions to learn about its structure and organization. The more logical and systematic the rationalization, the easier it will be for the (re)user to develop an understanding of the class hierarchy.

The rationalization is a handy guide for locating a desired class in the hierarchy. A (re)user needing a particular class can start at the root of the hierarchy and ask which of the logical conditions of its subclasses best describes the desired class. By iterating through this process, either a suitable class will be found or it will be clear that the class hierarchy does not contain a suitable class.

As the class hierarchy is extended, rationalization gives an indication of where further variety is possible. If the logical conditions attached to the classes derived from a given class are exhaustive, then additional variety is not possible because the existing derived classes have accounted for all possibilities. However, if this is not the case, then new subclasses can be introduced and the nature of these subclasses might be hinted at by what is left over by the existing conditions.

Designing and rationalizing the class hierarchy is an evolutionary process. Hence, the class hierarchy designer must approach the task of identifying and classifying the common properties among classes with the realization that: there may be more than one good class hierarchy, so alternatives should be explored. Exploring the design may involve backtracking to an earlier point and moving for-

Radar

Horizon/Attitude

Engine
Speed

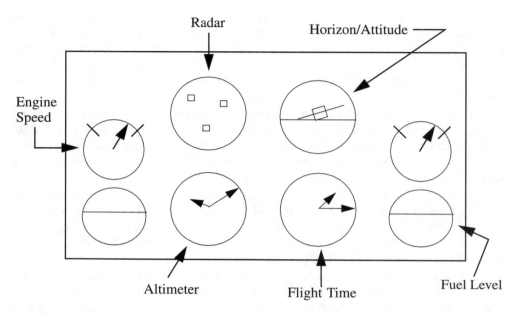

Altimeter   Flight Time   Fuel Level

Figure 9–4   The Layout of the Flight Control Panel

ward again in a new direction. Alternative designs can be compared on the basis of
the clarity of their rationalization and the possibility of further extension.

Additionally, the designer must proceed knowing that use and iteration are
necessary to refine the class hierarchy; it is unlikely that the complete hierarchy
will be seen at the start except for a hierarchy that is very small or one which is
virtually identical to an existing hierarchy. For example, the class hierarchy at
the heart of the Smalltalk system evolved over the period of many years of use
and refinement.

Creating a good class hierarchy is both a challenging and a rewarding task.

An Example of Designing a Class Hierarchy

The principles of designing a class hierarchy are illustrated through the Flight
Control Panel example described below. This panel is part of a larger flight simulator. Designing a good class hierarchy is important in this project because the
Flight Control Panel may be modified during development, expanded in later
version of the flight simulator, and components of the panel might be reused on
other projects that have some of the same instrumentation.

The Flight Control Panel consists of different types of dials, gauges, and
displays that provide the pilot with status information during the simulated
flight. The panel is organized as shown in Fig. 9–4. The simulated aircraft has

two engines and two fuel tanks. The left and right sides of the panel have a pair of instruments that show the engine speed and the fuel-tank level. The bottom center of the panel contains an altimeter and a clock. The two hands of the altimeter display the current altitude of the aircraft; one hand is calibrated in 1000-foot units and the other is calibrated in 100-foot units. The clock gives the elapsed time since takeoff in hours and minutes. The top center of the panel features a radar and a horizon/attitude display. The radar shows various icons and text representing other aircraft in the vicinity, while the horizon/attitude display's small centered icon represents the aircraft. This icon rotates about its center point to indicate the alignment of the aircraft's vertical axis to the ground. A horizontal line in this display indicates the alignment of the aircraft's horizontal axis with the ground. When the line is in the middle of the display, the aircraft is in level flight. The degree to which the line is toward the top or bottom of the display indicates how much the aircraft is descending or ascending.

An initial set of class is easy to find in this problem. Each of the different types of instruments is a candidate for the definition of a class. These classes might be named:

- Altimeter,
- Clock,
- Radar,
- FuelGauge,
- HorizonAttitude, and
- Speed.

The more difficult issue is how to organize these classes into a class hierarchy.

Several iterations of the a class hierarchy design for the Flight Control Panel are shown. Each iteration deepens the organization of the classes. The rationalization of the class hierarchy is developed at the same time as the hierarchy itself.

First Iteration

The first step in organizing the Flight Control Panel's classes is to identify any properties common to all of them. One evident property is that all of the elements are circular in shape. This property can be captured in a base class. All of the classes derived from this base class will inherit the property of being circular. There is no other evident property shared by all of the instruments. Therefore, groups of classes that share a new common property are sought. Some of the instruments convey information by a rotating hand; the classes representing these instruments are FuelGauge, Altimeter, and Clock. These three classes can be organized into a sub-hierarchy whose base class is named Dial. The rationalization for the Dial class is "rotating hand." The class hierarchy at this point in shown in Fig. 9–5.

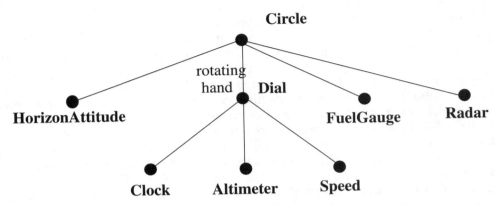

Figure 9-5 Flight Control Panel Hierarchy: First Iteration

Second Iteration

Following the general strategy, the immediate descendents of the Circle class, Radar, Dial, Speed, and HorizonAttitude, are analyzed. Notice that this set of classes is a mixture of original classes (Radar, Speed, HorizonAttitude) and a base class (Dial) created in the first iteration. A discriminating property among these four classes is that the Dial and Speed classes display a single value or condition while the Radar and HorizonAttitude classes display multiple values or conditions. Using these groups as a guide, two new base classes may be invented: Indicator, a base class for single-value instruments, and Display, a base class for multiple-value instruments. The rationalizations for the Indicator and Display classes leads to a reconsideration of the name of the Circle class: the rationalization for the Indicator class would be read as "an Indicator is a single-value Circle," but the term Circle is inappropriate in this context. A more precise statement is, "an Indicator is a single-value Instrument that is shaped like a Circle." The name Instrument is more suggestive in this context and, thus, the name of the Circle class is changed to Instrument. Fig. 9–6 shows the class hierarchy after the second iteration.

Third Iteration

In this iteration, the classes derived from Indicator and those derived from Display are considered. Of the two classes derived from Indicator, Dial and Fuel-Gauge, the rationalization "rotating hand" has already been developed for the Dial class. This leads naturally to finding the corresponding rationalization for the FuelGauge class. Instead of a rotating hand, the FuelGauge indicates its value with a horizontal line that moves up and down to show the level of the fuel in the tank. FuelGauge may therefore be described as a is as a sliding-position Indicator. In addition, neither of the two classes derived from Display, Radar and HorizonAttitude, has a rationalization. One essential difference between these

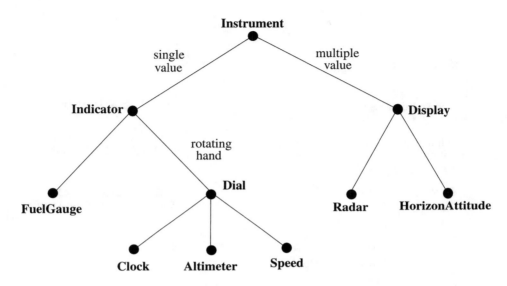

Figure 9–6 Flight Control Panel Hierarchy: Second Iteration

two classes is that the Radar has a varying, unbounded number of items that it can display, while the HorizonAttitude class works with a fixed, bounded number of items. The rationalizations "varying number" and "fixed number" can be used for these classes. To check that this makes sense, the rationalization would indicate that "a Radar is an Instrument for a varying number of multiple values" and that "a HorizonAttitude is an Instrument for a fixed number of multiple values." Since these interpretations are consistent with the understanding of these classes, the rationalization is acceptable. The class hierarchy after the third iteration is shown in Fig. 9–7.

Fourth Iteration

The fourth and final iteration reconsiders the classes derived from the Dial base class: Speed, Altimeter, and Clock. In searching for discriminating characteristics, it can be found that the Altimeter and the Clock have two rotating hands but the Speed indicator has only one. As there may be more specific kinds of indicators introduced in future versions of the system, it could be useful to make explicit this distinction. Therefore, a new base class, TwoHandDial, may be introduced as a class derived from Dial that becomes the class from which both Altimeter and Clock are derived. Clearly the rationalization for the TwoHand-Dial class would be "two hands," while the rationalization for the Speed class would be "one hand." To check that the accumulated rationalizations are sensible, the Clock class would be described as "an Instrument that displays a single value using two rotating hands" where the single value is understood to be the

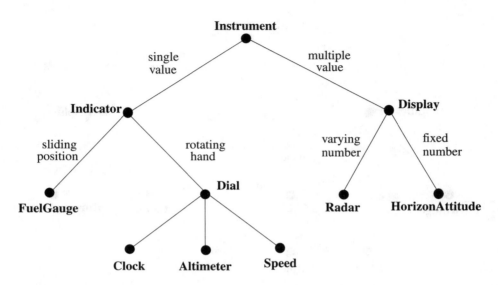

Figure 9–7 Flight Control Panel Hierarchy: Third Iteration

elapsed flight time. It is also sensible to describe the Speed class as "an Indicator that displays a single value using a single rotating hand." To complete the rationalization, the subclasses of TwoHandDial, Clock and Altimeter, should be considered. One essential difference between these two classes is that the Altimeter is bidirectional: its hands can move both clockwise and counterclockwise. The Clock, however, is unidirectional, as its hands can only move forward in the clockwise direction. If these properties are used for the rationalization of these two classes, the class hierarchy design is complete. The final class hierarchy is shown in Fig. 9–8.

 Exercises

1. Revise the fourth-iteration class hierarchy developed for the Flight Control Panel assuming that the FuelGauge was changed so that it had a single hand indicating positions between a position marked "empty" and a position marked "full."

2. Revise the fourth-iteration class hierarchy developed for the Flight Control Panel assuming that the HorizonAttitude instrument was split into two instruments, the Horizon instrument and the Attitude instrument.

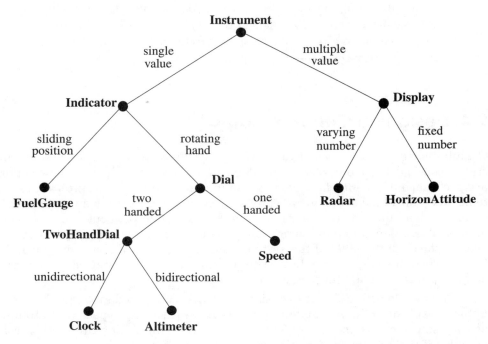

Figure 9–8 Flight Control Panel Hierarchy: Final Iteration

3. Revise the fourth-iteration class hierarchy developed for the Flight Control Panel assuming that a new instrument is added to indicate the position of the landing gear by displaying one of three text strings: "retracted," "extended," or "locked".

4. Revise the fourth-iteration class hierarchy developed for the Flight Control Panel assuming that a new kind of instrument is added to the panel, a status light for the engine temperature. The light is either green, indicating a temperature for normal operations, or red, for a temperature that is too high.

5. Revise your answer to question number 5 by adding two other kinds of status lights. One kind of status light blinks when it changes to the red state, while the other kind beeps when it changes to the red state.

6. The FuelGauge and the HorizonAttitude display are similar in that both have a movable horizontal line. Give specific advantages and disadvantages of revising the fourth-iteration class hierarchy developed for the Flight Control Panel so that the HorizonAttitude class inherits from the FuelGauge class.

7. The class hierarchy developed in this section for the Flight Control Panel was organized on the basis of the *appearance* of the instruments. Develop an alternative class hierarchy on the basis of some other characteristic of the instruments.

9.4 Designing Complex Logic

Complex logic is often needed to control programs with numerous actions and states, especially when current state determines whether, which, or how actions are performed. User-interface systems, communication protocols, interactive systems, and embedded systems typically exhibit complex logic. As an example of a state-dependent action, consider a user-interface system with cut and paste commands. The paste command should only be possible after a cut operation has been performed; the state of the system reflects whether this has happened. The logic of such systems is complicated to program due to the state dependence of actions and the usually large number of states.

Complex logic is difficult to design. In realistically sized systems, the combinatorial explosion of (state, action) pairs creates such a large space that attempts at easy solutions are usually defeated. In addition, the design difficulty is compounded if the system specification is stated in an informal manner (e.g., in natural language). It is difficult to analyze informal specification for crucial properties such as freedom from internal contradiction (consistency), absence of ambiguity (clarity), and coverage of all relevant cases (completeness).

Accordingly, complex logic is tough to capture in an object-oriented style. It may not be clear how the if-then-else, or case statement form, of the logic can be transformed into an object structure. Also, it may not be apparent how the other objects in the application relate to the states and actions of the system. If the actions are made methods of some objects, how does the object know the state of the system so that the object can decide on the proper way to deal with the action? On the other hand, turning the states into objects may not seem natural or in keeping with the object-oriented philosophy.

The processing of mouse events in a simple graphical editor will be used in this section as an example of how to design and implement complex logic in an object-oriented form. The key ideas developed by this example are how to present the processing logic in a graphical, semiformal representation, and transliterate this graphical representation into code. The real design work is accomplished in the first of these steps, for the transliteration step is straightforward. Two different transliterations are given; one is much more object-oriented than the other.

This section's example is small so that it can be presented completely. However, it should be clear that the same technique used here can be used for larger, more complex problems as well.

Table 9–8 Specification for the Graphical Editor

Specification for the Graphical Editor
The graphical editor presents the user with an initially clear drawing area and waits for the user to draw, move, and resize any of a set of predefined shapes. To draw a shape, the user left-clicks outside of any currently drawn shape and is presented with a popup menu of possible shapes to choose from. The user selects one of these shapes and then left-clicks again in the drawing area to indicate where the selected shape should be placed. The user may select an existing shape to manipulate by depressing the left mouse button inside or on the border of the shape. A selected shape is displayed with a border that is thicker than normal to reflect the fact that it is selected. To move a selected shape, the user depresses the left mouse button inside the shape and then drags the shape to its new position. To resize a shape, the user depresses the left mouse button on the border of the shape and then drags the mouse. Dragging away from the border increases the shape's size and dragging in toward the shape reduces it.

Representing Complex Logic

Given in Table 9–8 is a natural-language statement describing how mouse events should be handled in a simple graphical editor system. Only two mouse events are used: depressing the left mouse button and dragging (moving the mouse while the left mouse button remains in the depressed state). The specification details how the user creates and manipulates shapes. Clearly, this specification could be complicated further by introducing more actions (e.g., grouping shapes together, ungrouping shapes, rotating shapes, saving to a file), and employing alternative user-interface mechanisms (e.g. using a pulldown menu in addition to the popup menu to select the shape to be drawn). The technique for handling the simpler case described below can also be applied to these more complicated cases.

A state-transition diagram will be used to represent the specifications in a graphical, semiformal manner. The state-transition diagram is graphical because it is drawn using circles, arrowed lines, and textual annotations, and is semiformal because it lies between the informality of a natural-language expression, where no direct analysis can be done, and the full formality of a mathematical expression that can be subject to rigorous analysis. The state transition diagram has a prescribed form (a syntax) and there are heuristic rules that can detect certain weaknesses in the specification.

As implied by its name, a state transition diagram depicts states of the system, drawn as circles or ovals, and transitions between states, drawn as arrowed lines. Each state has a name suggestive of the system condition to which it corresponds. Possible states in the graphical editor system might be these:

- Awaiting: no shape is currently selected

- Moving: the user is dragging a shape to a new position
- Resizing: the user is changing the size of a shape
- Drawing: a new shape is being selected for drawing

Transitions are indicted by arrowed lines that connect states. The direction of the arrow shows which of the two states is the starting state and which is the ending state. The transition usually contains an annotation of a condition and a set of actions. A given transition may only be taken if the condition specified for that transition holds. The condition may use actual program variable names or operations that could clearly be computed from the information available in the starting state. The set of actions for a given transition is executed when the transition is taken.

The operation of a state transition diagram is captured in the following steps:

1. if the system is in a given state,
2. and if the condition is true of a transition directed away from that state,
3. then perform the actions associated with the transition,
4. and enter the state to which the transition is directed.

If none of the conditions for a state hold, then the system remains in the current state and no action is taken. In a properly formed diagram at most one of the conditions can be true at any one time. These steps are applied in a state until a transition is taken to another state, where the steps are applied again until another transition is taken, and so on. In a properly constructed state transition diagram, every execution of the real system corresponds to a sequence of transitions in the diagram and every sequence of transitions in the diagram corresponds to a legal execution of the real system.

The state transition diagram denotes a single initial state; the initial state for the graphical editor system is the state in which it is awaiting a user action. The initial state has a single transition directed into it to denote that it is the initial state. The action on this transition expresses initializing operations that are performed when the system begins.

A part of the graphical editor system is illustrated in the state-transition diagram shown in Fig. 9–9. This diagram focuses on two states, the initial state Awaiting and the state Moving. The initial transition into the Awaiting state shown below specifies that the drawing area is cleared when the system begins. Two other transitions and their associated annotations are also shown. The first transition, from Awaiting to Moving, is taken when a left-click occurs within a shape. This shape is referred to in the condition part of the annotation by the name "s," which is also used in the action part of the condition where s is assigned to the program variable current. When the condition is true, the action is taken and the Moving state is entered. The second transition shows a case where the starting and ending state of the transitions are the same; a moving

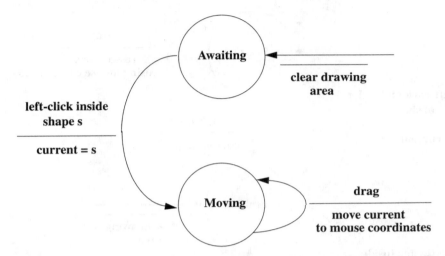

Figure 9–9 State Transition Diagram with Awaiting and Moving States

shape causes the system to remain in a state where that shape can be moved again. Notice that the annotation on a transition is written with a horizontal line separating the condition on the top from the action on the bottom.

The state transition diagram easily reveals that the written specification is incomplete. An inspection of the state transition diagram shows that the only transition from the Moving state leads back to the Moving state. This means that once the Moving state is entered, the system stays in that state forever. Clearly this is an oversight. While it would be difficult to recognize this oversight in the written specification, the graphic form directly exposes this weakness. Lacking this insight, the question of how to terminate the moving of a shape might not otherwise arise until the coding phase at which point it is more expensive and more difficult to resolve the oversight.

The written specification is amended and the resulting state transition diagram, including the Resizing state, is shown in Fig. 9–10. The written specification is amended to include the statement: "The dragging operation is terminated when the user releases the left mouse button." This same issue arises for the Resizing state and a similar statement is added to the specification: "The resizing operation is terminated when the user releases the left mouse button."

However, examination of the transition actions for the corrected specifications for the Moving and Resizing states reveals that the wording and structure of the written specification are ambiguous. The specification states that "the user may select an existing shape to manipulate" and that a selected shape highlights its border. Ambiguity arises because the word *may* is open to several interpretations. In its stronger sense may could be interpreted as must, and in its weaker

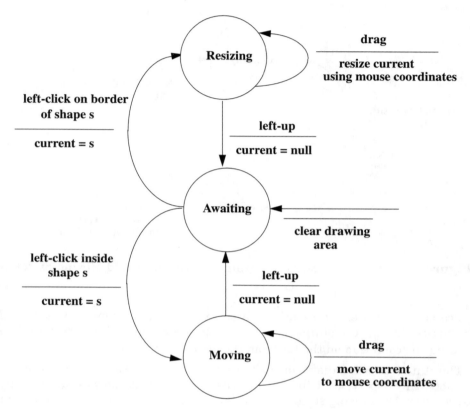

Figure 9–10   State Transition Diagram for Corrected Moving and
Resizing States

sense may could be interpreted as describing a permissible but not required act. A second source of ambiguity lies in the structure of the specification. That statement of how to "select" a shape for manipulation immediately precedes the description of the moving operation. Is the specification of selection to apply only to the moving operation? Or to the resizing operation that follows later as well? Furthermore, the term select is used in two places in the specification, once in reference to how to choose an item from the popup menu ("The user selects one of the shapes") and again in the context of identifying a shape for manipulation. Are these the same or different operations? Does the highlight apply to both cases in some way, or only to the latter case?

When ambiguities in the written specification are corrected, the state transition diagram may be revised as shown in Fig. 9–11. The diagram indicates that the stronger sense of may is used and that highlighting applies to both moving and resizing operations. The written specification will use different terms to

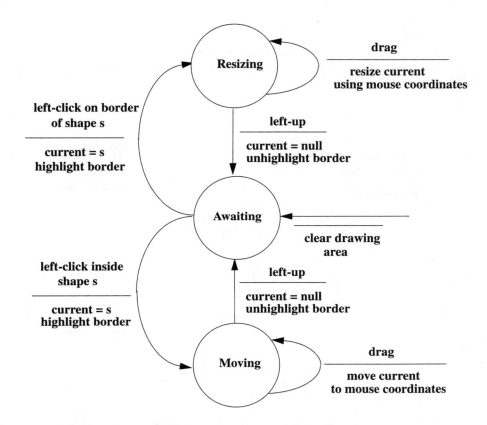

Figure 9–11   Correcting the Transitions for Highlighting Actions

describe choosing from a menu item and selecting a shape. Notice that the transitions into the Moving and Resizing states include as their actions the highlighting of the selected shape and that transitions out of these two states include the actions to unhighlight the selected shape.

The final step in the development of the state transitions diagram deals with that part of the specification for drawing a new shape. Drawing a new shape is defined in two steps: (1) choosing a new shape from a menu, and (2) placing the new shape within the drawing area. These two steps are modeled by two states named Choosing and Placing. In defining the conditions and the actions related to these two states the written specification is found to be incomplete in these two ways:

- the specification does not say how the user selects an item from the menu, and
- the specification does not say whether the menu remains visible after the selection, if the menu is automatically dismissed, or if the user must take some action to dismiss the menu.

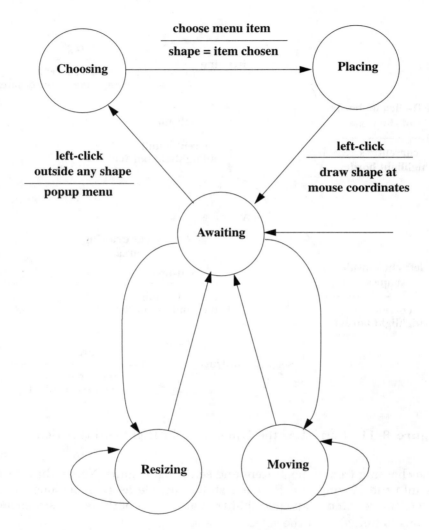

Figure 9–12   Adding the Choosing and Placing States

The written specification will be revised yet again to indicate that the user selects a menu item by a left click and that the menu should be automatically dismissed after the selections. With these changes in the specification, the Choosing and Placing states are added to the state transition diagram as depicted in Fig. 9–12. The annotations for the previous transitions are not repeated again in this figure.

Table 9-9 Revised Specification for the Graphical Editor

Revised Specification for the Graphical Editor
The graphical editor presents the user with an initially clear drawing area and waits for the user to draw, move, and resize any of a set of predefined shapes. To draw a shape, the user left-clicks outside of any currently drawn shape and is presented with a popup menu of possible shapes to choose from. The user **chooses** one of these shapes **by left-clicking on** one of the menu items. After the choice is made, the popup menu disappears. The user then left-clicks in the drawing area to indicate where the selected shape should be placed. The user **must** select an existing shape to **move or resize** by depressing the left mouse button inside or on the border of the shape. A selected shape is displayed itself with a border that is thicker than normal to reflect the fact that it is selected. To move a selected shape, the user depresses the left mouse button inside the shape and then drags the shape to its new position. **The moving operation is terminated when the user releases the left mouse button.** To resize a shape, the user depresses the left mouse button on the border of the shape and then drags the mouse. Dragging away from the border increases the shape's size and dragging in toward the shape reduces it. **The resizing** operation is terminated when the user releases the left mouse button.

The written specification, incorporating all changes thus far, is repeated in Table 9-9 with the changes in bold. Clearly, the original specification was incomplete and ambiguous in several important areas. The development of the state transition diagram served as a useful device to discover these problems and to represent the specification in more precise way. In addition, the state transition diagram, as a graphical representation, more clearly shows the structure of the system's behavior: the major conditions in which the system exists are modeled as states and the actions that drive the system among its states are modeled as transitions.

Implementing the Design

A state-transition diagram can be transformed into an object-oriented structure by representing each state by a class. The implementation of the class representing a given state is derived from the annotations of all transitions that exit from that state in the state transition diagram. The implementation includes code for:

- testing the conditions of each transition leaving the state,
- performing the actions of the transition whose condition holds, and
- returning an object that represents the state of the system after the actions have been taken.

Code Sample 9–1 *General Class for Representing System Data*

```
class SystemData
{ // system-dependent data that represents (1) the current
  // condition of the system as required to test the
  // conditions on transitions, and (2) system components
  // that are operated upon in the actions of the
  // transitions.
}:
```

Code Sample 9–2 *Base Class for Classes Representing States*

```
class State
{public:
   State& Next(SystemData& condition) = 0;
};
```

A state is represented by a class because each state has a distinct set of transitions with distinct conditions to evaluate and distinct actions to take. Note that the use of classes to represent states is counter-intuitive. Usually, it is expected that there will be multiple objects of a given class in use at one time. However, in this case, only one object of a class will exist at any one time.

Each class must have access to those parts of the system that it needs to test it conditions and perform its actions. For example, in the graphical editor system, the conditions and actions make reference to the system components current, shape, and mouse coordinates. Testing the condition "outside of any shape" implies that the class has access to a list of all of the current shapes and a means of determining whether the mouse coordinates lie outside of a shape. Finally, the action "draw shape at mouse coordinates" implies that the class has access to the drawing area. Of course, the specific components that are accessed by the states are system dependent. Thus, the structure of this system data can only be defined in the most general terms. The SystemData class shown in Code Sample 9–1 introduces a name to refer to this collection of system-dependent information.

All classes that represent states have the same interface—which is captured in an abstract base class. Code Sample 9–2 shows this shared interface. Each class has a single method, Next, which has as its parameter the collection of system data needed by any state to properly interrogate the system's condition and modify the system as required by the state's actions. Because the Next method may modify the system's condition, the SystemData is passed by reference. The value returned my the Next method is a State object representing the new state of the system.

Code Sample 9–3 *The Class for the MovingState*

```
class Moving: public State
{
  public:
    Awaiting();
    State& Next(SystemData& condition);
};

// in implementation

Moving::Moving()
{}

State& Moving::Next(SystemData& condition)
{
  if (condition.MouseEvent == DragEvent)
  { ...update SystemData for drag event
    return *this; // stay in Moving state
  }

  if (condition.MouseEvent == LeftUp)
  { ...update systemDate for button release
    return *(new Awaiting() ); // change to Awaiting state
  }

}
```

An example of a class for a specific state is coded in Code Sample 9–3. Here, the Moving state is defined as a derived subclass of the abstract base class State. This derived class implements the Next() method as required by the base class. The Moving class also provides a constructor which has no code as the Moving state maintains no state dependent information. Classes for other states may have state-dependent information and may also provide methods other than the Next method.

The implementation of the Moving class's Next method is the critical part of this class. This method tests the SystemData to determine whether a relevant event has occurred. As shown in the state-transition diagrams, the two relevant events in the Moving state are a drag event that leaves the system in the Moving state and a left-mouse-button-up event that returns the system to the Awaiting state. The Next method achieves this change of states by returning a state object for the correct state of the system. If the system remains in the Moving state, the Next method simply returns the current object (itself an object representing the Moving state). If the system should return to the Awaiting state then a new object representing that state is constructed and returned.

Table 9–10 Circle Placement System

Circle Placement System
The Circle Placement System allows a user to create, position, move, and delete fixed sized circular shapes in a drawing area. The user interface operates in the following way:

- The user can create a new circle by left-clicking outside of the boundary of any existing circle; a new circle is created whose center is at the position where the user left-clicked.
- The user can change the position of an existing circle by positioning the cursor within the boundary of the circle and dragging (i.e., moving the mouse/cursor with the left mouse button depressed). The dragging ends when the user releases the left mouse button.
- The user can delete an existing circle by positioning the cursor within the boundary of a circle and doing a shift-left click (holding down the *shift* key while clicking the left mouse button).
- The user can change the position of an existing circle by positioning the cursor within the boundary of the circle and doing an alt-left click (holding down the *alt* key while clicking the left mouse button). The circle is moved one radius to the left.
- The user can change the position of an existing circle by positioning the cursor within the boundary of the circle and doing an alt-right click (holding down the *alt* key while clicking the right mouse button). The circle is moved one radius to the right.

 Exercises

Read the description of the control logic for the Circle-Placement System given in Table 9–10 and answer the questions that follow.

1. Draw a state-transition diagram for the Circle Placement System.

2. Construct the class hierarchy for the states in the Circle Placement System.

3. Construct the data should be part of the SystemData class for this system.

4. Implement and test the Circle Placement System using the class hierarchy that represents the system states and the SystemData class developed in this section.

9.5 Design Representations

There are three specific uses for a high-level, graphical design representation. First, the representation provides a language that quickly describes an idea being considered by a single designer or a design team. Because it can be quickly drawn and easily modified, the representation aids in thinking about the design and exploring design alternatives. Second, the representation is a means of documenting a design. The design document serves as a guideline for the implementor and, later, for those who will modify and maintain the system. The graphical and high-level nature of the representation make it useful as a documentation device because through them it describes only the essential structural elements, leaving the code and other documentation to add more detailed information. Third, once represented, the design may itself be the object of reuse. Commonly occurring design solutions may be identified, documented, and collected for use in situations other than the ones in which they were initially encountered. The recent development of design patterns is a realization of this idea. One of these patterns is shown and discussed in Section 9.6.

The design representation presented here employs three kinds of diagrams:

- class diagrams which show the static relationships among classes;
- object diagrams which show the static relationships among objects;
- object interaction diagrams which show the dynamic, time-ordered interaction among objects.

The first two diagrams depict relationships that are static in the sense that they do not change over time. Object-interaction diagrams are used to illustrate sequences of interactions (method invocations) among objects. The sequence of interactions are usually those in a typical or significant scenario.

Class Diagrams

The class diagram depicts the public interface of a single class and the other classes it uses or is used by. An example of two classes as they appear in a class diagram is shown in Fig. 9–13.

Each class is shown as a divided rectangle whose topmost portion contains the name of the class. Below the name of the class, the methods of the class's public interface are given. In this example, the Shape class has three public methods (MoveTo, Draw, and Erase), while the Circle class has four methods (MoveTo, Draw, Erase, and Radius). Finally, if appropriate, the bottom portion contains key instance variables of the class. Note the distinction made between abstract classes and concrete classes. The name and methods of abstract classes are written in italics, and those of concrete classes appear in the normal font. An abstract class corresponds to a C++ class that contains one or more pure virtual

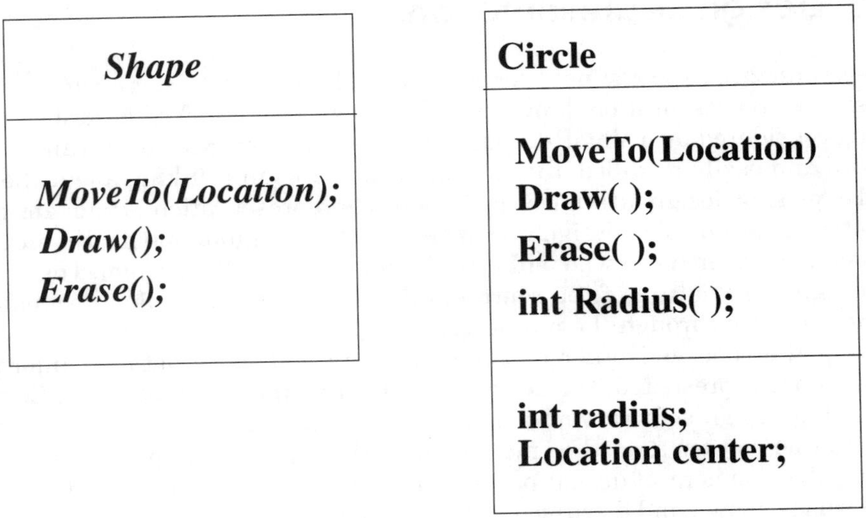

Shape
MoveTo(Location); *Draw();* *Erase();*

Circle
MoveTo(Location) Draw( ); Erase( ); int Radius( );
int radius; Location center;

Figure 9–13   Composite Pattern Example of Two Classes

methods. Recall that an abstract class defines an interface that must be completed by a derived, concrete class. There are no objects of the abstract class.

The class diagram allows four different relationship among classes to be represented. They are:

- **inheritance**,
- **association** (also called **acquaintance**),
- **aggregation** (also called **composition**), and
- **creation**.

It is important to remember that these are relationships among classes, not among objects of these classes.

The inheritance relationship is shown in the class diagram shown in Fig. 9–14, which indicates that the concrete classes Rectangle and Circle (and others, denoted by the ellipsis) are derived from the Shape class.

For simplicity, the diagram showing inheritance only gives the names of the classes; the more complete class representation showing the public interface and private instance variables would normally be given. Notice again that italics are used in the name of the Shape class to connote that it is an abstract class.

An aggregation (or composition) relation is shown by an arrow from the composing class to the composed class. For example, the Circle class has a private data member of type Location that records the center of the circle. This data member is not shared between Circle objects, and would be drawn as shown in Fig. 9–15.

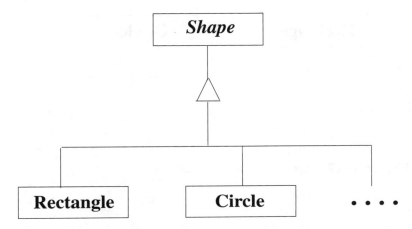

Figure 9–14 Representing Inheritance

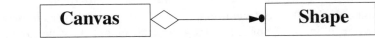

Figure 9–15 Representing Aggregation

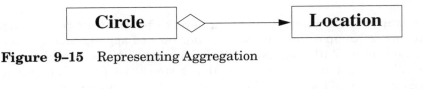

Figure 9–16 Representing a Multiple Instance

Both single-instance and multiple-instance relationships can be represented in class diagrams. The relationship between the Circle class and the Location that represented the center of the Circle is an example of a single-instance relationship, for each Circle has exactly one center. A multiple-instance relationship occurs in the Canvas class that maintains a collection of Shape currently appearing on the Canvas. As shown in Fig. 9–16, a small, filled circle at the point of the arrowhead is used to indicate a multiple-instance relationship. This relationship is read as "A Canvas contains many Shapes."

An association or acquaintance relationship is used to denote sharing among classes. For example, a Rectangle or a Circle may both use the same instance of a "Pen" class to implement their Draw and Erase methods. In this case, a simple solid line with an arrow is used to show the relationship. The example of the Rectangle, Circle and Pen classes would be drawn as shown in Fig. 9–17.

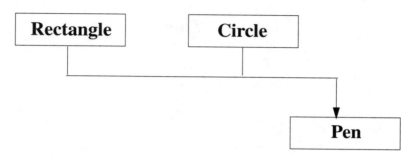

Figure 9–17   Representing Sharing

Figure 9–18   Representing a Creation Relation

It is important to understand the difference between composition (specifically, the form of composition that was earlier termed aggregation) and association (acquaintance). With composition the composed object is viewed as a part of the composing object in the same sense that a wheel is a part of an automobile. However, the driver of the automobile is not a part of the automobile although an automobile object may know about (be associated with) its driver.

The last relationship between classes is that of creation. This relationship is evident when objects of one class (the created class) may be generated as a result of the computation of another class (the creating class). For example, a Pen object in Fig. 9–17 may be created by an object of the PenPalette class. The PenPalette class may read information form a configuration file or interact with the user to determine the characteristics of the Pen object that it creates. The creation relation is shown by a dotted line in Fig. 9–18.

Occasionally, the significance of the relationship between classes is conveyed more fully by showing a key fragment of an algorithm that illustrates how the relationship is used. For example, Fig. 9–16 showed that the Canvas class has several Shapes, but this diagram did not help the reader to understand the purpose behind this relationship. A typical reason for the relationship is that when told to Draw itself, a Canvas object would direct each of the Shapes contained within it to Draw themselves. Such an explanation helps to deepen the reader's understanding of why the Canvas class has several Shapes and how it manipulates them.

An algorithm annotation can be added to a class diagram by placing the algorithm fragment in a separate box and connecting this box to a method of the appropriate class. This is illustrated in Fig. 9–19.

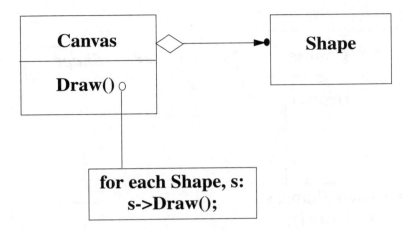

Figure 9–19   Representing a Code Fragment

Algorithm annotation must, of course, be used with restraint. Cluttering a class diagram with nonessential algorithmic details undermines the purpose of the diagram. Such unnecessary annotations add volume without aiding understanding of the class structure.

The individual relationships presented above can be collected together in a single diagram as shown in Fig. 9–20.

This class diagram shows that a Canvas has (by composition/aggregation) several Shapes each of which may be an subclass of the abstract Shape class. The Draw method of the Canvas class will call the Draw method of each composed Shape. Since Shape is an abstract class, the Draw method applied to a Shape will actually be done by some object that is a (unknown to the Canvas class) subclass of Shape. Different subclasses of Shape can share the same Pen that is produced by the PenPalette class.

Object Diagrams

Suppose that an application has a 500 x 500 pixel drawing area that is dived into three regions as follows:

- Approximately half of the drawing area, on the right side, is a single region bordered by a rectangle. The upper left hand corner of this region is at coordinates (260,0), its width is 240 pixels, and it height is 500 pixels.
- The left side of the drawing area is subdivided into two equally sized regions each of which is bordered by a rectangle. The upper left corner of the top subregion is at coordinates (0,0). The upper left corner of the

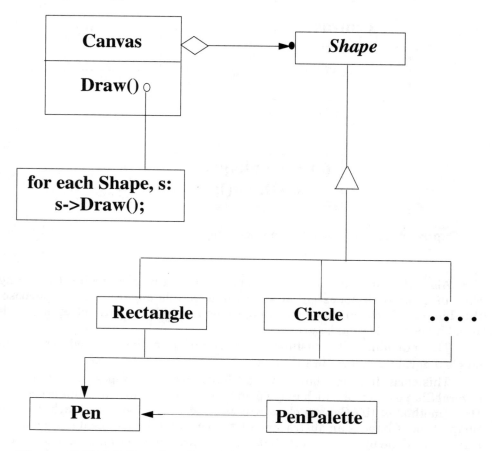

Figure 9–20   A Complete Example

bottom subregion is at coordinates (0,260). Each subregion has a width
and height of 240 pixels.

The borders should be drawn with a thickness of five pixels.

Using the classes for a drawing tool mentioned earlier, the drawing area
could be implemented by a Canvas object, each of the three drawing regions by
Rectangle objects, and the border width would be handled by associating an
appropriately initialized Pen object with the Canvas object.

However, the class diagrams for these classes does not convey some essential information about the structure of the drawing area. For example, the class
diagram does not indicate that the Shapes known by the Canvas are specifically

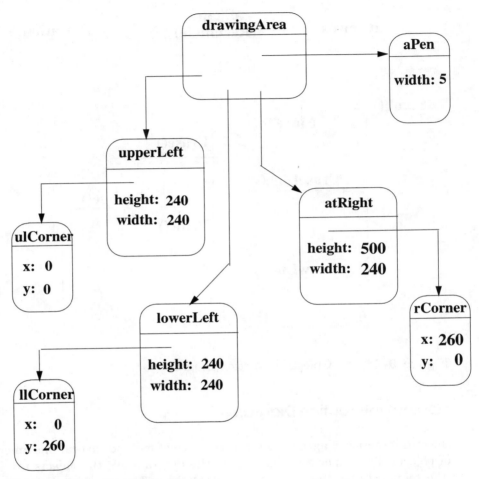

Figure 9–21 An Object Diagram

Rectangles, or that there are exactly three Rectangle objects known by the Canvas; nor does it show the location of each Rectangle object, or the value of the Pen object's width. Answers to questions such as these are provided by an object diagram.

An object diagram for the drawing areas described above is shown in Fig. 9–21. The drawingArea object is an instance of the Canvas class and has pointers to three Rectangle objects (upperLeft, lowerLeft, atRight). Each of the Rectangle objects has a composed Location object. Since the diagram depicts objects, the actual values of each Rectangle object's Location, height, and width can be shown in the diagram. Also, the width of the Pen object (aPen) used by the drawingArea object can be shown explicitly.

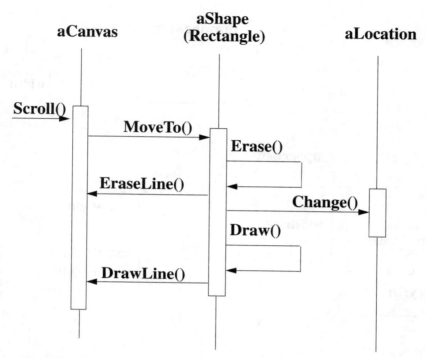

Figure 9–22   An Object Interaction Diagram

Object Interaction Diagrams

An object-interaction diagram shows a sequence of method invocations among a set of objects. The important elements of the diagram are the objects involved and the sequencing of the invocations among them. The compact, direct way in which the sequence of invocations is presented in the diagram starkly contrasts with the obscure manner in which the same relationships exist in the source code. In the source code, the sequence of interactions is dispersed, with each class's code containing one part of the sequence. The invocations are also interspersed with the other code in each class. The object-interaction diagram, however, extracts the essential information and presents it in a single, integrated, and succinct form.

An object-interaction diagram is shown in Fig. 9–22. This diagram involves three objects (aCanvas, aShape, and aLocation). Time flows from the top of the diagram to the bottom; invocations are drawn as horizontal arrows labeled by the name of the method being invoked. Objects appear as thin vertical rectangles when processing invocations; when idle, they are drawn as vertical lines.

The diagram shows the scenario (the sequence of invocations) that occurs when a Canvas object is asked to perform its "Scroll" method. In this diagram, the aCanvas object receives the Scroll method invocation to initiate the sequence. The aCanvas object uses the MoveTo method to reposition the aShape object at its new viewing position. In this example the aShape object is assumed to be an object in the Rectangle class. To reposition itself, aShape calls its own Erase (from its current location) and Draw (at its new location) methods. In between erasing and drawing, aShape changes its location by using the Change method in the aLocation object. Finally, to perform the erasing and drawing, the aShape object "calls back" to the aCanvas object, using the EraseLine and Draw-Line methods of the Canvas class.

9.6 Design Patterns

Definition and Structure of a Design Pattern

Once represented, a design may itself be reused by designers other than the original one. Individual designers have always been able to reuse their own designs or those that they had learned about informally from others. However, a broadly understood design representation makes it possible for a designer to communicate well-understood, well-tested designs to other practitioners faced with similar design problems and to students learning about object-oriented design concepts.

A reusable design must include more information than just the design diagrams. Among other things, the problem that the design is meant to address must be defined. This information is important because it allows potential reusers, faced with a particular problems, to identify available designs that are candidates for reuse. Another kind of information that is needed in a reusable design concerns the trade-offs implied by the design. Typically, designers must achieve a balance between such competing goals as efficiency, flexibility, fault tolerance, and simplicity. A single problem may give rise to several useful designs, each offering a different balance among the design factors.

A **design pattern** is a proposed format for presenting a reusable design. The structure of a design pattern is defined in the book *Design Patterns*[1] as:

> A design pattern systematically names, motivates, and explains a general design that addresses a recurring design problem in object-oriented systems. It describes the problem, the solution, when to apply the solution, and its consequences. It also gives implementation hints and examples. The solution is a general arrangement of objects and classes that solve the problem. The solution is customized and implemented to solve the problem in a particular context.

---

[1] Gamma, Helm, Johnson, and Vlissides (page 360).

The first sentence of the definition expresses the *intent* of a design pattern: to present in a consistent and coherent manner the solution to a recurring design problem. The next two sentences of the definition outline the *content* of a design pattern. The last two sentences explain the *usage* of a design pattern. The usage makes clear that a design pattern is not a program or code; it is a design that must be tailored to fit the specific requirements of a particular problem and then implemented. *Design Patterns* contains a collection of design patterns, one of which is studied in detail here.

A design pattern includes the following twelve elements:

name: Each pattern has a unique, short descriptive name. The collection of pattern names creates a specialized vocabulary that designers can use to describe and discuss design ideas.

intent: The intent is a succinct (one-to-three sentence) description of the problem addressed by the design pattern. The intent is useful in browsing design patterns and aids in recalling the purpose of a pattern when the name alone is not a sufficient reminder.

motivation: The motivation explains a typical, specific problem representative of the broad class of problems that the pattern deals with. It should be clear from the motivation that the problem is widespread and not trivial. The motivation usually includes class diagrams and/or object diagrams along with a textual description.

applicability: This element is a list of conditions that must be satisfied in order for a pattern to be usable. The conditions express goals that the designer is trying to fulfill (e.g., the ability for clients to be able to ignore the difference between compositions of objects and individual objects), complicating aspects of the problem (e.g., an application uses a large number of objects), and constraints (e.g., storage costs are slight because of the sheer quantity of objects).

structure: A description of the pattern using class diagrams and object diagrams. The class and object names are generalizations of those that appear in the specific example given in the motivation. For example, the Builder pattern motivation uses an example that has a base class named TextConverter with derived classes ASCIIConverter, TeXConverter, and TextWidgetConverter. The class diagrams in the structure section names the base class Builder and has a single representative derived class named ConcreteBuilder.

participants: Each class in the structure section is briefly described. The description is a list of each class's responsibilities and purpose in the design.

collaborations: The important relationships and interactions among the participants are described. Object-interaction diagrams may be used to illustrate complex interaction sequences.

consequences: This section explains both the positive and negative implications of using the design pattern. Positive implications might be increased flexibility, lower memory usage, easier extensibility, support for particular functionality, or simplified usage. Negative implications might be inefficient behavior in particular cases, complex class structure for certain problems, loss of guarantees of system behavior, or overly general design with attendant loss of performance or storage costs. It is important that authors of design patterns present, and readers of design patterns understand, positive as well as negative consequences. All designs achieve a compromise among many competing forces and no design can avoid have some negative consequences.

implementation: A representative implementation is shown for the classes given in the structure section. Because the structure section is generalized, so also is the implementation provided in this section. This section is meant as a high-level guide on how to represent the pattern in a given programming language.

sample code: The essential code for a typical problem (often the one presented in the motivation) is given. This code illustrates in detail how the pattern would be applied to the particular problem.

known uses: This is a list of systems, libraries, tools, or frameworks that have dealt with the design problem addressed by this design pattern. The example systems may have used a variation of the design pattern as a solution.

related patterns: Other design patterns that are thought to be useful in combination with this pattern are listed. This list provides additional guidance to designers by offering pointers to other patterns that could potentially help.

An Example of a Design Pattern

The *Composite* pattern, given in *Design Patterns*, will be used as an example of a design pattern. The **name** of the pattern is "Composite," suggesting the pattern deals with composing objects. The **intent** of the pattern is stated as follows:

> Compose objects into tree structures to represent part-whole hierarchies. Composite lets clients treat individual objects and composites of objects uniformly.

The intent expresses both the subject matter of the pattern (trees of objects related by a part-whole relation) as well as the goal of the pattern (uniformity of treatment). The **motivation** presented for this pattern describes a typical graphical drawing tool that allows users to draw a variety of predefined basic shapes (rectangles, lines, circles, rounded rectangles, polygons, etc.) and also allows shapes to be composed together. A composite shape is treated as a newly defined basic shape in that it can be composed with other basic or composite shapes. A set of operations (draw, move, resize, etc.) can be applied to any shape (basic or composite). Both a class diagram and an object diagram are used to illustrate a design solution. The class diagram is shown in Fig. 9–23.

The **applicability** section defines two conditions: (1) part-whole hierarchies are being represented, and (2) uniformity of treatment for parts and a whole is sought. The conditions mirror the basic ideas presented in the statement of the pattern's intent. The **structure** section contains the generalized class diagram shown in Fig. 9–24.

In the generalized class diagram, the specific kinds of parts are represented by a single class "Leaf," while the class named "Composite" represents a whole. The abstract base class, "Component," defines an interface that must be implemented by Leaf classes and the Composite class. The abstract base class reflects the uniform treatment of Leaf and Composite objects. Note also that the generic "Operation" method is an abstraction of some application-specific operation.

The **participants** section lists the responsibilities of each of the four classes that appear in the structure (Component, Leaf, Composite, Client). For example, the responsibilities of the Composite class are to define the behavior of "a composition of objects, to store the composed (sub)objects, and to implement the operations defined in the abstract base class."

The **collaborations** section defines how the Composite pattern's participants work together to meet their individual responsibilities and achieve the effect intended for the pattern. For instance, in this example, in the Composite pattern, the client interacts with the Leaf or Composite objects only through the abstract interface defined in the Component class. This collaboration captures a key feature of the pattern: the client is able to manipulate Components without regard for whether they are Leaf class objects or Composite class objects.

Two of the **consequences** of using the Composite pattern are that it makes it easy to add new kinds of basic components (i.e., Leaf classes)—they are simply

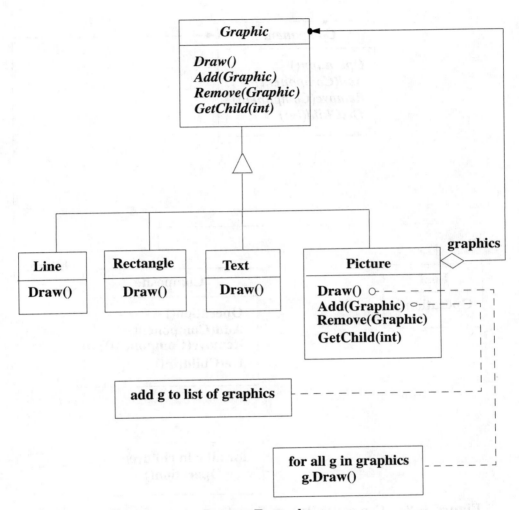

Figure 9-23 Composite Pattern Example

added as another class derived from Component—and it can make the design overly general in those cases where only certain combinations of objects have semantic meaning (for example, a document may be viewed as a Composite of paragraphs, tables, sections, etc. However, a correct document must have exactly one title and a table may not have sections within it. It is difficult to enforce these kinds of restrictions with the Composite pattern as the pattern places no limitations on the way in which a Composite can be formed. Notice again that both the strengths and the limitations of the pattern are identified.

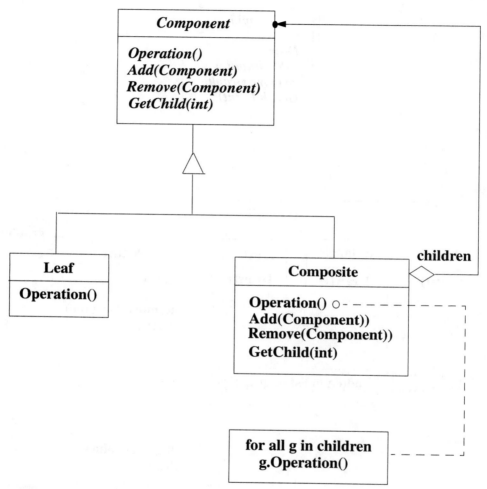

Figure 9–24   Composite Pattern Structure

The **implementation** section presents issues relevant to the detailed coding of the classes in the pattern. For example, the trade-off between safety and transparency is considered in this section of the Composite pattern. This trade-off involves where to place the methods for manipulating the children of a Composite. If these methods are placed only in the Composite class, it is safer (because attempt to apply them to Leaf components is detected as a compile-time error) but it is also less transparent (because Leaf and Composite objects cannot be treated as uniformly as might be desired). Placing the methods in the Component base class yields the opposite trade-off. A compromise strategy introduces a method *Composite* Get Composite()* in the Component base class. This method is defined in the Leaf derived class to return a *null* pointer and defined in the Composite derived class to return its *this* pointer. This strategy minimizes the loss of transparency, as all base class methods apply equally to both Leaf and Composite objects, while it retains a large measure of safety by leaving to the Client the responsibility to differentiation between objects of the two derived classes.

The **sample code** section gives C++ code for an example of a part-whole problem. This most detailed level of presentation helps to give a concrete representation of the pattern that can be compiled and used for experimentation.

The **known uses** section lists three application domains (user interface toolkits, a compiler, and financial portfolios) where the pattern has been observed.

Finally, four **related patterns** are noted, including the Iterator pattern that can be used to traverse composite structures.

Summary

A design pattern is a means of fostering reuse of design knowledge and experience rather than the reuse of a specific implementation. A design pattern falls between a general design heuristic and actual code: it is less general (more limited) than a design heuristic or guideline, which might express, for example, that a class interface should be a coherent and complete set of methods for an abstraction. While heuristics are intended to apply to the broadest range of cases, a design pattern is intended to capture in more detail a single structure or abstraction. At the same time, a design pattern is more general than an implemented class hierarchy or framework. Hierarchies and frameworks are limited in their reuse potential to a single programming language, a single (or small range) of situations, and perhaps even a single operating system or run-time environment. A design pattern, however, has none of these limitations. A design pattern is sufficiently focused to be useful, but general enough to be applicable in a range of applications.

The ultimate value of design patterns will only be realized by an organized, extensive collection of patterns that encompasses generic design problems as well as problems t specific to particular applications domains. One might imagine a collection of patterns for real-time systems, distributed/concurrent/parallel applications, and other important application areas. The collection of patterns in *Design Patterns* is an important beginning.

V

W, X, Y, Z